CW00537728

Rick and Morty

SHOW ME WHAT YOU GOT

THE GALLERY 1988 ARTWORK

Rick and Morty: Show Me What You Got

The Gallery 1988 Artwork

ISBN: 9781789092073

Published by
Titan Books
A division of Titan Publishing Group Ltd.
144 Southwark Street
London
SE1 0UP

www.titanbooks.com

First edition: November 2019

1 3 5 7 9 10 8 6 4 2

A CIP catalogue record for this title is available from the British Library.

Printed and bound in China.

Did you enjoy this book?
We love to hear from our readers. Please e-mail us at:
readerfeedback@titanemail.com or write to Reader Feedback
at the above address.

To receive advance information, news, competitions, and exclusive offers online, please sign up for the Titan newsletter on our website:
www.titanbooks.com

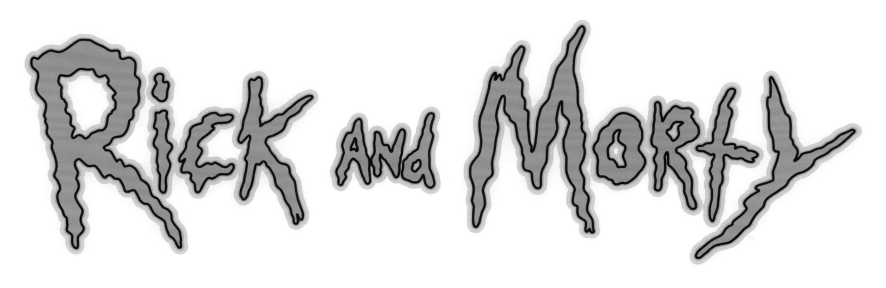

SHOW ME WHAT YOU GOT

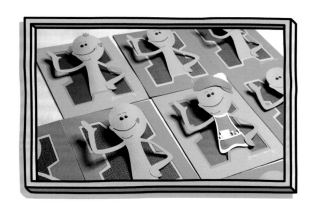

THE GALLERY 1988 ARTWORK

TITAN BOOKS

Contents

FoRewoRd

by James McDeRmott

My name is James, and I have an entire *Rick and Morty* wardrobe, which is awkward as a forty-one-year-old father of two wearing clothes intended for teenagers. This is AA for *Rick and Morty* fans waiting way too long for next season, right? Am I in the right place? Oh, OK good, the delays are out of my control, don't blame me.

It's been an honor to be the art director for such a prolific show. By the end of each season I'm struck by a strangely cathartic feeling as if I had been in my own therapy cocoon exorcising my demons the whole time. On my first week of production I designed Cronenberg Rick, Cronenberg Morty, Snuffles' mech suit, and Scary Terry. Never in my wildest imagination would I have ever believed that they would be turned into complex cosplay costumes, which look impossible to build in any realistic fashion by you guys, the fans.

When I first saw the pilot I was blown away at how good it was, considering most pilots are a work in progress, or normally not well executed. There was a clear distinction of masterful storytelling and equally outlandish art that illustrated the balance of writers and artists contributing to its purest form of concept. In a feeble attempt of excitement, I showed my wife the pilot but she didn't find it funny. That's when I knew I absolutely had to work on it and that it was going to be a hit! My wife is not the intended demographic for this show, but I love her anyway.

During the show's humble beginnings, writers would ask me "This is good, right?" Internally we were in hysterics every day but afraid we were in our own crippling bubble and not entirely sure how the public would respond to this peculiar taste of comedy. We were just passionately making something we wanted to see exist in the world, not peddling to a specific audience, and certainly never knew it was going to get the reaction it did. Three successful seasons later and Rick is still a nihilistic

sociopath, shoving alien seeds up his grandson's butt, alcoholic, burping grandpa that doesn't pay any mind to success because… what does it all mean? WUBBA LUBBA DUB DUB!!

The infinite world building is all made possible through the extraordinary efforts set forth by our amazing crew who push their boundaries to bring you the organized chaos of *Rick and Morty* art. It really takes a village. I'm truly inspired every day by the remarkable artists that share brain-melting ideas to support an uncompromising vision and timelessness to all the alien worlds and civilizations that the show dares to dream up. ONLY this world owns these devices. The show's inspiration mines from 70s sci-fi, 80s horror, and practical effects movies mixed with current day topics that are twisted sideways, and Frankensteins the idea behind the art into undeniably unique designs. A common joke around the office is if we don't destroy the worlds we build, it typically means the writers haven't finished writing the episode and decide to tear it all down and reconstruct it with a dramatic new ending. Awww yeah, that's what you get for playing god.

I love seeing the fervent enthusiasm of fan art by people that are just as excited by the show as I am, and now we own your souls! Always read the fine print. The online fan theories are sometimes so elaborate, from Evil Morty's plans to infiltrate each season, to Mr. Poopybutthole actually being a parasite, to which Morty we're actually watching from what timeline – whaaaaaat, mindfuck! – get your time travel right, dawg! FYI we really don't think about it as much as you do but it's entertaining to watch it all unfold like cats chasing lasers. Now go assimilate, ding-dongs, and look at cool art by diehard fans because the cosmic horrors of next season are taking way too long! Enjoy!

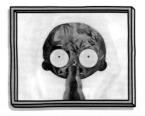

Anthony Petrie
Sometimes Science is More Art than Science
18 x 24"

What did you want to convey or represent with your art piece?

My piece is representative of all the people and creatures that Rick has to tolerate, crammed into his brain, with Morty being the centerpiece.

How did the concept come to you? How long did it take to complete?

I wanted to do something referencing science in relation to Rick and was researching phrenology charts. Aesthetically, the piece is a nod to that, but I also like that conceptually it's complete nonsense, just like the pseudoscience. It took about two weeks to complete.

What is your favorite Rick and Morty episode? Is there a specific moment that resonates with you?

My favorite Rick and Morty episode is 'Meeseeks and Destroys,' and favorite moment from an episode is How They Do It: The Plumbus, from 'Interdimensional Cable 2.'

If you could be in a single episode, which would it be?

I'm not sure, but definitely not 'Rick Potion No. 9'…

Do you have a favorite character and, if so, what do you like most about them?

Mr. Poopybutthole, for obvious reasons.

What was your process for creating this artwork? How did you prepare to create the piece?

I created the piece on the computer, using Adobe Illustrator for the base forms, and added texture in Photoshop. Preparation included watching every Rick and Morty episode.

What was your favorite part of creating the artwork?

My work is normally very detailed, so my favorite part of this piece is the amount of negative space and the simplicity of the color and texture. It was also the first time I've used fluorescent ink.

Above: (From left to right) close-ups of the final artwork plus a 3D composition of the framed piece alongside a Plumbus.

Anthony Petrie is an award-winning poster artist and designer based in Los Angeles. His portfolio includes work across a broad range of mediums and he likes creating good design for good people. Anthony has been working professionally as a commercial artist for over fifteen years, collaborating with some of the most influential brands in the world. His graphic design, illustration, and product designs can be seen everywhere, from the entertainment and broadcasting industries to sports and athletic brands.

Jackie Huang

Mr. Meeseeks

3.5 x 4.5"

Nan Lawson

Let's Get Riggity Wrecked!
Rick and Morty
8 x 10"

What did you want to convey?

I love drawing dynamic duos, and Rick and Morty are one of the most iconic duos on television. I wanted to keep it simple and focus on the two of them.

What do you appreciate most about the show?

I love the show. The thing I appreciate most is no matter how insane the plot is, the family dynamic is completely realistic and relatable.

What is your favorite *Rick and Morty* episode? Is there a specific moment from the show that resonates with you?

I am still haunted by the ending of 'Rick Potion #9,' watching as Morty buries his dead parallel universe self and takes over his life.

Do you have a favorite character and, if so, what do you like most about them?

I mean... Rick. He's unapologetically the worst person ever.

What was your favorite part of creating the artwork?

The colors!

How is your *Rick and Morty* piece similar to, or different from your other works?

I've done a lot of pop culture couples in the past. I wanted to represent this dynamic duo in the same style.

What excited you most about getting to participate in this exhibition?

I got to watch *Rick and Morty* episodes while drawing Rick and Morty.

Nan Lawson is a Los Angeles based illustrator and artist. She can create detailed portraits or simple characters that are both unmistakably in her style. She makes work for kids' literature and picture books but she is also known for her pop culture gallery work.

Bryan Brinkman
Michael and Pichael
11 x 14"

What did you want to convey or represent with your art piece?

My piece is a five layer 3D-Cel recreation of the set of *Cooking Things and Opposite News with Michael and Pichael.* Seen in 'Interdimensional Cable 2: Tempting Fate.' It conveys the shared space in which these conjoined twins are able work simultaneously on their programs.

How did the concept come to you? How long did it take to complete?

The concept behind my 3D-Cel pieces is based on my own interests and studies in animation and the history of the medium. I love to collect animation cels, and I sometimes lament that the art form has gone digital because we lose the physical connection to the art. Though as an animator, I'm very happy with the speed of digital (especially being able to undo). Creating a dimensional piece takes as much time in pre-planning as it does in execution. Usually taking about a week.

Can you talk about the storytelling power of your piece?

My piece is more of a spoiler to the joke. I just love the idea that these two shows could be built and set up in a single studio, so I wanted to convey the space and depth to show how it would function.

What do you appreciate most about *Rick and Morty*?

When I lived in LA years ago, a friend brought me to a *Channel 101* screening, and I saw some of Justin Roiland's work. I found the concept of the event and the films in it so inspiring. They were made fast and cheap, and they all exuded a passion for creation. When *Rick and Morty* came out, I felt that spirit continued. It's loose and fun in its dialogue, but deep in its ethos and storytelling.

If you could be in a single episode, which would it be?

Any post-credit scene.

What was your process for creating this artwork?

First I try to look for a scene that lends itself to depth. My creation process begins digitally. I build the scene and illustrations as layers in Photoshop. Then I print out each layer on transparency cel paper and paint it by hand to bring out the colors. This was the first 3D-Cel piece where I integrated the frame into the piece. I printed and cut out the TV screen frame for the top layer. Once all the layers are painted, I build wooden frames and separators that fit into the sides of the shadowbox and keep the layers spaced apart. I finished the piece by taping and gluing it all together.

What was your favorite part of working on the artwork?

Trying to capture the silly faces.

Why do you create art?

I grew up absorbing so much art, cartoons, comics, and films. At this point, I feel like I'm just squeezing out a mixture of all of those influences and trying to make something unique out of it.

How has the aesthetic of *Rick and Morty* informed your piece?

One of the reasons I quickly gravitated to *Rick and Morty* was that the style of the show was similar to my own illustration style. Therefore, my piece ended up being a recreation of one of my favorite moments, instead of my interpretation of the show's style.

Bryan Brinkman is an animator/artist from New York City. He currently creates graphics for *The Tonight Show Starring Jimmy Fallon* and *Saturday Night Live.* He is the lead animator at *Picture This!* in NYC, a monthly live animation and comedy show. You can find more of his work at www.bryanbrinkman.com.

Above: 1) A sketch of the composition before work began. 2) The acetate layered under the frame. 3) A close-up of the piece fully assembled. 4) A 3D composition of the separate elements coming together.

Barry Blankenship
Smooth Landing
18 x 24"

What does your piece convey?

When I think of *Rick and Morty*, I think of them exploring different worlds, and Rick is kind of a drunk so I assume they find themselves crash landed on many different worlds. The world I drew was somewhat heavy metal and Moebius inspired with a potential villainous lair in the background as well as some crystals scattered about the alien planet.

Why do you create art? How would you describe your style in general?

I always like to tell or hint at little stories in my drawings. I guess I'd describe my style as a lot of detailed line work with a little bit of comic book flare.

How did the concept come to you? How long did it take to complete?

I love drawing wreckage and things scattered about, so add in space and time travel (all things I love) and I'll figure out a way to fit everything in. I think the process from conception to finished pencils and pens took about one or two weeks. The edition had a few screenprinted versions so I was in the print studio for a lot of that time.

What do you appreciate most about the show?

Its world building is thoughtful and has very well defined time travel rules while also applying some actual science to a world full of very intelligent and ludicrous characters.

Can you talk about the storytelling power of the art?

I grew up staring at movie covers, working retail jobs like Blockbuster and Virgin Megastore (RIP) and some of the most successful posters always allude to things incomplete or mysterious. With *Smooth Landing*, I tried to pitch my episode with a vehicle we all know from the show crash landed in this obviously alien terrain with our heroes nowhere in sight, leaving the viewer to wonder what could have happened.

Is there a specific moment from the show that resonates with you?

Any time Jerry has something terrible done to him, or an episode that gets a song stuck in my head, like 'Get Schwifty' or 'Goodbye Moonman.' Or jokes about human music.

What was your process for creating this artwork?

I thumbnailed a bunch of different ideas out, but ended up with this one. It seemed to mesh with my style best and it dealt with a lot of topics I love. After the thumbnail ideas phase, I'll draw in pencil and then ink over my pencils. From there, I scan the image into Photoshop and color and revise things accordingly and plan for a minimal color palette, since I screen print my art myself by hand I typically try not to go over four colors.

How do you see this artwork fitting into the *Rick and Morty* universe?

Hopefully someone looks at it and thinks, "I want to see that episode."

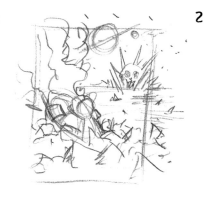

Above: 1) A rough sketch of the composition. 2) The first inks. 3) A close-up of the first inks. 4) A variant color design.

Barry Blankenship is a freelance illustrator and screenprinter from the Pacific Northwest with a background in advertising and creative concepting.
@BarryTheArtGuy

Poster by Barry Blankenship

Felix Tindall
Show Me What You Got
11.5 x 16.5"

What did you want to convey or represent with your art piece?

My piece features the silhouettes of Rick and Morty standing, looking puzzled as they're presented by a monolithic-type alien head thing... with small references to the show and a sci-fi vista in the background. Loosely inspired by a scene in the episode, 'Get Schwifty.' Without relying on the silhouette of Rick and Morty, I wanted to feature another character or element that would be immediately recognizable in the composition. The alien 'head' in this case was something I thought of while exploring ideas. It also happens to be from one of the most iconic episodes of the entire show and one of my favorites as well, so I thought basing my design off the episode was a safe bet.

What is your favorite *Rick and Morty* episode? Is there a specific moment from the show that resonates with you?

My favorite episode has to be 'Total Rickall' from season two because it's extremely funny, unpredictably crazy, and, above all else, super well executed. This show is capable of having some deep and meaningful moments, but I can't say I can relate with a lot of the goings-on in that show. But I do feel like Morty sometimes in general life.

If you could be in a single episode, which would it be?

I'd be in 'Total Rickall' as a random parasite character!

What was your process for creating this artwork? How did you prepare to create the piece?

When approaching a *Rick and Morty* themed artwork, I always intended to recreate or be inspired by a scene or a moment from an episode. When diving into a new piece, I like to visualize the composition and base my design off a scene from an episode of the show. I went back through my favorite episodes and settled on one that stood out to me.

What was your favorite part of creating the artwork?

It was the perfect excuse to watch the show all over again and getting to call it 'research'!

Why do you create art? How would you describe your style in general?

I do what I do for the love of all things pop culture. I'm passionate about the film and video game industry so creating inspired poster art is my way of giving back. Alternative poster art has grown to be a huge sub-culture movement over the last few years and has formed a brilliant and endlessly talented community of artists I am honored to be a part of. In terms of style, I gravitate towards silhouettes and (sometimes excessive!) use of textures. I'm attracted to simple composition, minimalism, contrast, and monochromatic color schemes. It's something I have developed an eye for and ends up being my defining style.

I'm a designer and illustrator based in New Zealand with a passion for video games and movies that inspire me to create. I like posters. Like, a lot. Maybe too much! For as long as I can remember, I have always had some form of interest in the world of design. I think it really kicked off when I took Art & Design during my last year of high school. That was when I became familiar with the Adobe suite and discovered a passion for creating. My persistent love for creating pop culture poster art has helped me create an identity for myself and has further expanded my possibilities as a freelance designer.

Doug LaRocca
You Can Run But You Can't Hide, BITCH!
12 x 18"

What does your piece convey?

It's a three-color, hand-pulled screen print inspired by *Rick and Morty*, Scary Terry, and *Nightmare on Elm Street*.

How did the concept come to you? How long did it take to complete?

I actually had the idea of putting Scary Terry in a *Nightmare on Elm Street* poster well before I was asked to be a part of the show. I was just waiting for the right moment to break it out. Luckily, Gallery 1988 was kind enough to think of me for this project.

How is your Rick and Morty piece similar to, or different from your other works?

I use a lot of the same color themes and line work in my other pieces as well.

What do you appreciate most about the show?

I love *Rick and Morty*! It's very high on the re-watch-ability scale. Not since early seasons of *The Simpsons* have I re-watched a TV show so much. It's the layers and layers of jokes that keeps me coming back for more.

Do you have a favorite character and, if so, what do you like most about them?

I always enjoy when Birdperson shows up to drop his wisdom bombs. I'm excited for his eventual return (please don't be a bad guy for long)!

What excited you most about getting to participate in this exhibition?

It's always more fun to work on a project that you're passionate about. I love the show so when I was asked to submit a piece, I jumped at the chance.

What was your process for creating this artwork?

The poster was originally screen printed for the show. First, I worked up a sketch on paper then scanned it and finished it up in Adobe Illustrator. Next, I printed out transparencies and burned the separations onto screens. Lastly, I hand pulled the three colors (blue, red, and yellow) onto Bristol board to finish the poster.

How has the aesthetic of Rick and Morty informed your piece?

I'm usually hesitant about doing projects based on cartoons with such a distinct aesthetic. It's hard to bring your own style when something is so recognized. But I couldn't pass up a chance to make a *Rick and Morty* print. I tried to be true to the characters while showcasing my own style.

1

2

3

Above: 1) An early sketch with shading. 2–3) Stacks of posters drying after the screen print process.

Doug is an illustrator and designer living in South Philadelphia. He designs party supply packaging by day and paints robots and dinosaurs by night (and sometimes weekends). Doug has been a part of many geeky group shows in places such as Gallery 1988 (LA), Bottleneck Gallery (NYC), and Spoke Art Gallery (SF).

REAL FAKE DOOORS   ♥todd!

I LIKE WHAT YOU GOT!   ♥todd!

Toddbot

Real Fake Doors
I Like What You Got
8 x 8"

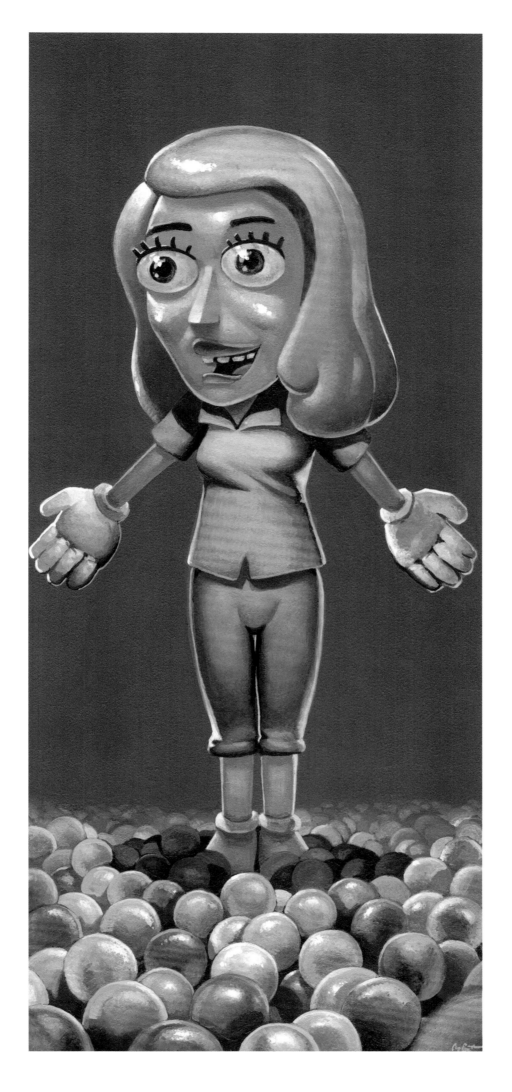

Ashton Gallagher
Welcome to Jerryboree!!!
5.5 x 11.5"

Scott Listfield
Earth Rick C-137
12 x 12"

Scott Listfield is known for his paintings featuring a lone exploratory astronaut lost in a landscape cluttered with pop culture icons, corporate logos, and tongue-in-cheek science fiction references. You've probably seen his work on the internet. Find out more about him at www.astronautdinosaur.com.

What did you want to convey or represent with your art piece?

I paint astronauts. That's kind of my thing. The world that my astronaut explores is one where humans are noticeably absent, but one which is filled with the many bits and pieces we've left behind. Some of that stuff is just trash. But some of what lasts are the things we have ascribed meaning to. Things that might otherwise be forgotten in the non-stop turnover of popular culture. Some bit of detritus that was at some point important to somebody. A junky toy robot, some piece of memorabilia from a long closed fast food franchise, somebody's favorite George Michael album.

I always thought I'd grow up to live in the future. And I have, I guess. But it's not quite the future that the movies and TV shows and comic books of my childhood prepared me for. I thought that I'd be flying around in a spaceship, living on the moon, making life long friends with robots and friendly, dog-like aliens. I spend a lot of time thinking about the chasm between those things while I'm painting. And I can only assume that the creators of *Rick and Morty* have spent a lot of time pondering the very same things.

Also I wanted to paint Rick giving the finger. I guess that's what my painting is about.

What is your favorite *Rick and Morty* episode?

God it's hard to pick just one. I'd probably have to go with 'The Ricklantis Mixup,' where the Rick and Morty from Earth C-137 are largely absent and we get a long look at what the Citadel – a surprisingly complex society built entirely of Ricks and Mortys – looks like. Every scene of this whole damn episode is brilliant. That said, if I'm picking one specific moment from the entire show, I would have to go with Dr. Wong's speech at the end of 'Pickle Rick.' It's just amazing. I'm sure I swore out loud as it was happening the first ten times I watched it.

How has the aesthetic of *Rick and Morty* informed your Piece?

I mean, I literally painted Rick giving the finger into an oil painting. If that's not borrowing the aesthetic of the show, I'm not sure what is. Seriously, though, I didn't just want to drop Rick or Morty into one of my paintings and call it a day. I tried to get at the sense of humor in the show and have my painting feel like it fits in with that sensibility.

Louie Perez III "LPIII"
Lucid Scientific Delusions
30 x 40"

What did you want to convey or represent with your art piece?

Rick and Morty is such a wild ride of a show in all the right (and wrong) ways. I really wanted to capture how psychedelic the show is in all its twisted glory.

How did the concept come to you? How long did it take to complete?

The concept came quite naturally. I knew I wanted to do something that required UV lighting and a system where art was activated by blacklight within the frame. It took me a couple weeks in the Dagobah vision cave…

What do you appreciate most about the show?

Rick and Morty is easily one of my favorite current running shows. It's an intelligent show that can get a laugh without dumbing itself down.

What is your favorite *Rick and Morty* episode?

It's hard to pick a fave episode. Every season they have managed to jump the shark further in a mightier way but 'Vindicators 3: The Return of Worldender' is tops. The idea of Rick defeating a nemesis and then setting up an elaborate *Saw* style trap in a total drunk blackout is frighteningly relatable.

Do you have a favorite character?

Arthricia is fave character of mine.

What was your favorite part of creating the artwork?

I had a lot of fun paying homage to a show with almost zero boundaries aesthetically. I laughed and smiled a lot. That doesn't happen often…

Why do you create art? How would you describe your style in general?

Art is the best way for me to quiet and exercise my mind at the same time. I am not really good at describing myself, and when most people do, it involves a lot of expletives.

How has the aesthetic of *Rick and Morty* informed your piece?

Rick and Morty is a cosmic rollercoaster. I hope I did it a quarter of its credit in weirdness.

What excited you most about getting to participate in this exhibition?

I already loved the show, and being asked to participate was such an honor. Then I showed up on the opening night, and saw that line around the block (a mile down)!? What a feeling for everyone involved! Bravo! Gallery 1988!

How do you see this artwork fitting into the *Rick and Morty* universe?

This work belongs in the 86th parallel dimension of purgatory.

Below: 1) Final paintings before the exhibition. 2) The psychadelic lighting brings out the neon colors. 3) Lights out with UV paint.

Martina D'Anastasio (SineSenze)
Schrödinger's Night
16 x 12"

How did the concept come to you? How long did it take to complete?

I didn't know *Rick and Morty* much before joining the show at Gallery 1988. I found it brilliant and funny, and I wanted to find an episode that would inspire me. When I saw Schrödinger's Cats in 'A Rickle in Time' I said to myself: I wanna paint that! I'm pretty fast when I have an idea in my mind. I started to draw the concept and when I was happy with it, it just took me a week to paint it.

What was your process for creating this artwork?

I'm a pop surrealist/realistic artist and I wanted to combine these two parts of my work in the painting. I repainted the characters with the same colors, using 'flat' and thin brushstrokes to make it look as a frame of that episode – I tried to make each detail as accurate as the original.

Why do you create art? How would you describe your style in general?

I need to paint, I need to draw. My style is realistic but it represents my inner world, full of dreams and tales. It's my way to express my dreamland and bring my imaginary friends to life.

How has the aesthetic of the show informed your art?

I love details. In details you can hide messages, and *Rick and Morty* is a show that always needs a second watch to understand it and enjoy it fully.

What excited you most about getting to participate in this exhibition?

First of all, the importance of the show: *Rick and Morty* is so famous that I couldn't believe to have been chosen to be part of that art show. And after this I had the chance to know many wonderful artists, and the most interesting thing is to see how each one of them portrayed *Rick and Morty* in their own style.

What else about your piece do you think Rick and Morty fans should know?

You should know that I chose to use a thick canvas with no frame for my artwork because I wanted to simulate the different universe levels from the episode on a flat surface, so I also painted some cats on the side of the canvas.

Jared Circusbear
Licensed Character
Merchandise Adventure
3 x 3 x 6"

What did you want to convey or represent with your art piece?

I'm a toy artist, so when considering what to make for the official art show at Gallery 1988, I wanted to pick a moment from the series that would jive with what I do. I thought back to a TV Promotional Ad for season two that featured fake *Rick and Morty* action figures, and knew I had to riff on that! Essentially my piece pays respect to the toy version of Rick seen in that commercial.

What is your favorite *Rick and Morty* episode? Is there a specific moment from the show that resonates with you?

'Total Rickall': I love the highly conceptual episodes, and this one has to be my favorite. It's also the first episode I ever watched and I've been hooked ever since.

If you could be in a single episode, which would it be?

If I could be in any one episode, I'd have to go visit Anatomy Park. You know, to help put a dent in their overhead.

Stephen Andrade
Get Schwifty (Vintage Pulp Edition)
11 x 17"

How did the concept come to you? How long did it take to complete?

I knew I wanted to do something that felt like classic sci-fi iconography, and you can't do much better than giant floating heads from space! After I had the concept it took a little time to figure out the best composition and, once it was locked in, the painting went fairly quickly.

Can you talk about the storytelling power of the art?

The story is pretty straightforward— basically showing the viewer the gist of 'Get Schwifty' – but I also indulged my love of *Rick and Morty*'s supporting cast with the blurb about Birdperson and the inclusion of Mr. Poopybutthole (which gives a clue to the viewer that my take on it takes place in an alternate dimension).

What do you appreciate most about the show?

I love that *Rick and Morty* runs the gamut from vulgar gross-out humor to high concept science fiction to action-adventure, and even manages to include genuine existential questions and (dare I say it?) heart.

What is your favorite *Rick and Morty* episode?

'Interdimensional Cable' is one of my favorites because it embraces the two extreme moods of the series so perfectly. First, there's the inspired improvisational nonsense that makes up the TV shows that the family watches. Then there's the dark, and yet somehow tender, nihilism as Morty shows Summer the graves of his and Rick's alternate dimension doppelgängers. Philosophy and poop jokes all in one great package.

What was your process for creating this artwork? What techniques have you used?

The painting was executed using acrylics, and once that was completed the finished painting was photographed and text and distressed aging was added digitally. As always, I looked at lots of vintage pulp magazine covers to try to capture that same spirit, both in the overall color palette and the text design.

What else about your piece do you think *Rick and Morty* fans should know?

I think it's worth at least thirty brapples.

Stephen Andrade graduated from the Hartford Art School and works as an illustrator and sign painter. He has also worked as a conceptual artist for film, and created the poster for the short horror film *Givertaker*. Stephen also recently created the album cover for *The Eldritch Realm* by the metal band Parius, which has been included in *Heavy Music Artwork's Masterpieces*, a book of the best heavy metal album artwork of 2018. Stephen's works have been shown in galleries in New York and Los Angeles. He lives and works in Western Massachusetts with his wife and daughter and one fat cat. Visit his website at sandradeillustration.com.

Above: Rough sketches plotting out the composition of the piece.

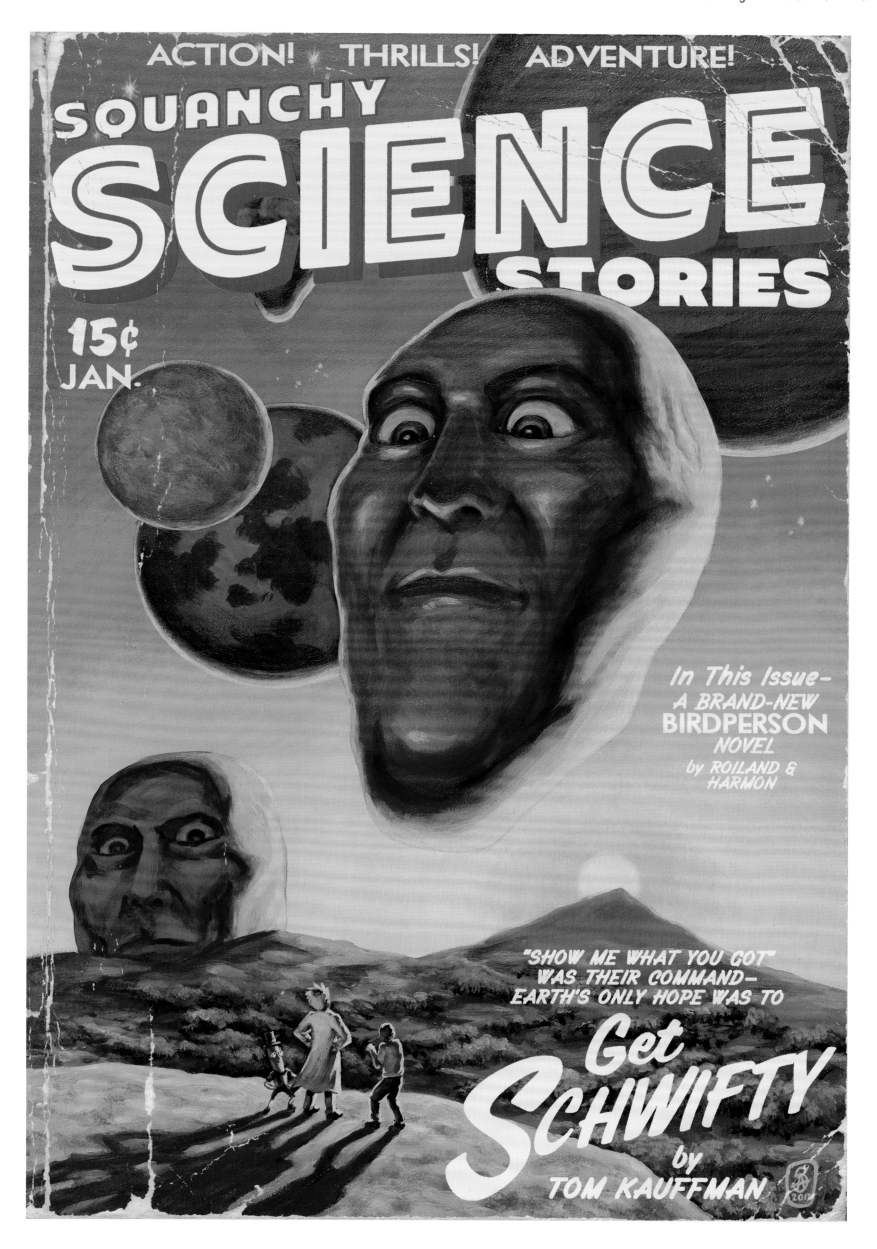

Lawrence Hugh Burns
Snortin' Mortys
8 x 10"

Lawrence Hugh Burns is a full-time illustrator working in New York City. His inspiration is drawn from all aspects of pop culture, but he considers Nintendo and Nickelodeon as some of his most profound influences. When he's not drawing for work, he's drawing for himself and for the sporadic gallery show. Beyond that, he's a man of simple pleasures: a cold beer, a medium-rare steak, and a summer thunderstorm viewed from a front porch. He can be found on Instagram at @lawrence.hugh.burns.

Jeremy Berkley is a graphic designer/illustrator/printmaker based out of East Peoria, IL. His pop culture inspired silk screen prints have been exhibited in art galleries across the country. Most notably the #1 pop culture gallery in the world Gallery 1988: Los Angeles, where he is a regular contributor. You can see his work at: http://www.berkleycc.com/
https://www.instagram.com/jeremy.berkley/
https://www.facebook.com/jeremyberkleyart/

Jeremy Berkley
Get Schwifty
12 x 12"

Brandon Griffith
Le Rick
37 x 27"

Photo Credit: Tommy Williamson

How did the concept come to you? How long did it take to complete?

This was one of a series of LEGO® portraits of two-dimensional characters with very three-dimensional sensibilities. This took roughly four weeks to do from conception to completion.

What excited you most about getting to participate in this exhibition?

Having Dan Harmon critiquing my piece.

Can you talk about the storytelling power of your piece?

This is a man who can do anything and go anywhere, and yet cannot find the wonder of the cosmos and lives every day in constant pain. That's the story I wanted to convey in my piece.

What was your process for creating this artwork?

All my artwork is created using LEGO® bricks. First, I sketched out an image of Rick and then broke up the different sections of his body into layers. Then, I picked the appropriate colors and found unique elements to work into those sections. I take the different layers that I've sketched out and start building off base plates until I find what is the appropriate height and shape. Lastly, I created a LEGO® frame with little Easter eggs from the show for the corners.

How do you see this artwork fitting into the Rick and Morty universe?

I can see it hanging on the walls of the Citadel of Ricks.

What do you appreciate most about the show?

I appreciate its depth, intelligence, and pop culture references reinterpreted in a fresh way.

What was your favorite part of creating the artwork?

The hair – so much fun in designing the hair.

Why do you create art? How would you describe your style in general?

I generally do portraits and characters from pop culture and fiction out of LEGO®. I'm drawn to characters that resonate with me.

What else about your piece do you think Rick and Morty fans should know?

There are approximately 4,700 pieces in this portrait.

Above: Early stages of the mosaic in progress.

Brandon Griffith is best known for his pop art style built using only LEGO® bricks. Drawing heavy influences from pop culture, Brandon takes memorable characters, scenes, and moments from a variety of sources and creates his own imagery. The final pieces are an invitation to look at the work both as a whole and as a deconstructed use of a beloved childhood toy.

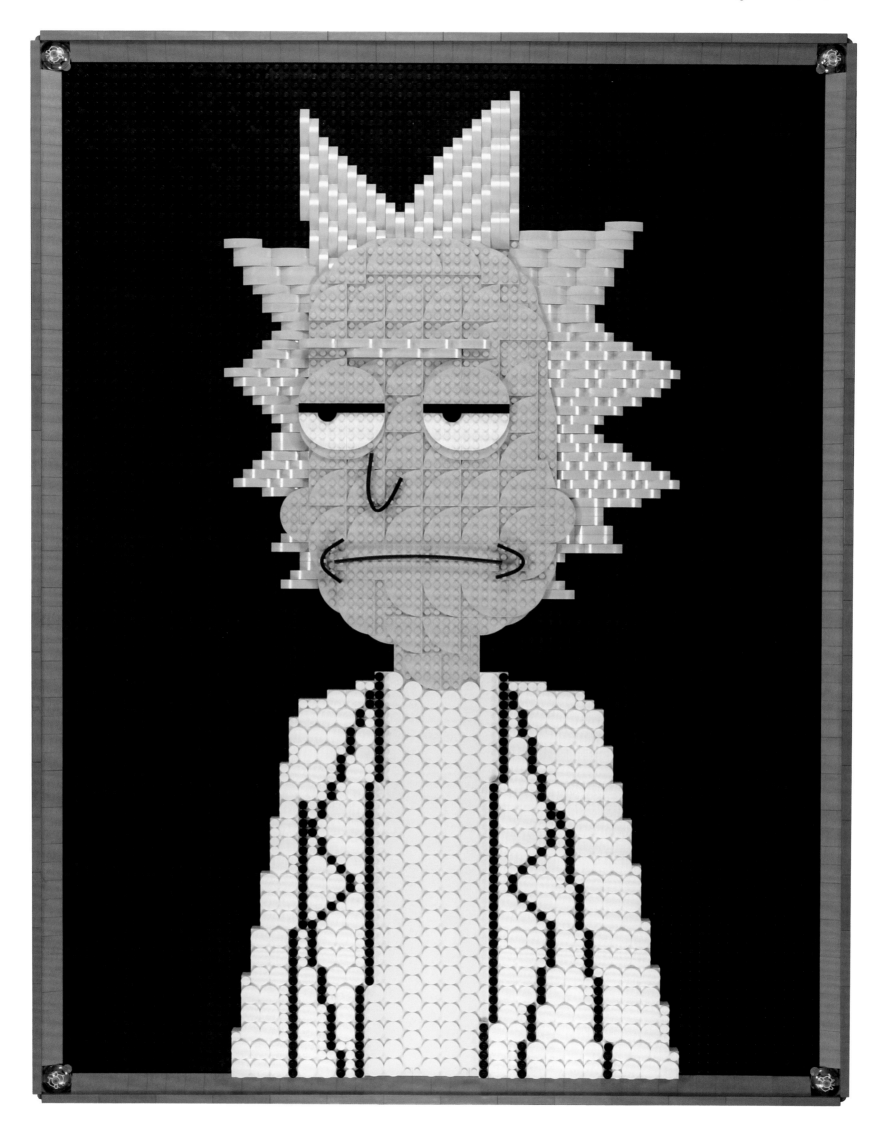

Florian Bertmer

It Takes Strength to be Gentle and Kind

8.5 x 11"

Dan Stiles
Show Me What You Got
18 x 24"

What did you want to convey or represent with your art piece?

I am known for my haunting portraits, and I wanted to express Rick's self-destructive and self-loathing nature.

How did the concept come to you?

I had a completely different concept before starting this one and ended up doing a lot of process work for an illustration I ultimately canned. I decided to simplify my idea and began the portrait instead. It said everything I wanted.

What do you appreciate most about the show?

Honestly, at first, I didn't like the show. But after giving a few episodes a chance, the show is incredibly witty and smart. Each is crafted so well that I've enjoyed watching all three seasons many times over. I also admire how you can see the side effects of previous events. Like for instance, when the house is transported to another dimension and then back again to Earth. The continuing episodes include a large crack circling the house because of its past departure from this universe. That's a small thing, but I love that appreciation for the details.

Ashly Lovett

Rick
Morty
8 × 10"

What was your process for creating this artwork?

I work traditionally with chalk pastel on paper. Not many people choose to use this media, but from the beginning, I found it comes most naturally to me. For my technique, work with general shapes and then slowly tighten up the piece with details. I try my best to design each illustration using expressive marks making engaging eyes. I have a process video of me working on 'Rick' on my YouTube channel at AshlyLovett.

What was your favorite part of creating the artwork?

I loved working with the same color palette used throughout the animated series. A lot of deep blues and psychedelic purples and pinks.

What is your favorite *Rick and Morty* episode?

Season two, 'Total Rickall.' I can only imagine the amount of fun the art department had when coming up with all those 'zany' characters. Another favorite would be season three, 'The Rickshank Rickdemption.' The whole Shoney's, szechuan sauce, and the surprise farting butt gags were brilliant.

What excited you most about getting to participate in this exhibition?

Putting my spin on an existing character is always a fun challenge. And this project gave me a chance to pay homage to a story that I enjoy.

Ashly Lovett is a freelance illustrator and gallery artist working primarily with chalk pastel for the horror and fantasy genre. She is known for her illustrative portraiture with romanticism undertones. She has done licensed work for Jim Henson Company, Adult Swim, Netflix, Focus Features, *Archie Comics,* and *Monty Python,* etc. She has a BA in illustration from Ringling College of Art and Design.

Kevin Tiernan
You Know Me
12 x 36"

What does your Piece convey?

Based on the episode 'Total Rickall,' the two posters unite to form one design – elements like the layout, the portal, and Rick's arm are completed. For color, I stuck to a limited palette of greens and dark grays. Rick and Morty are trapped in a grid of impostor alien parasites.

How did the concept come to you? How long did it take to complete?

The entire process took about a month from concept to print. First, I re-watched the episode to gather character references. My original poster was unbalanced, so I split the whole composition into two pieces. I spent a lot of time figuring out how to make the design flow across both posters. For the variant, I included a few extra characters that didn't make the initial cut.

What was your favorite part of creating the artwork?

Doing research was one of my favorite parts of the process. There are so many funny parasites in the episode. I kept discovering new ones hiding in the background, and it was cool finding ways to interpret all of them.

Why do you create art? How would you describe your style in general?

Art and design have always helped me to be more present. When I work on projects, I can really focus my attention on the moment. Also, poster design makes me feel connected with a community of people who share similar interests. In terms of style, I'm largely inspired by flat minimal design. I've been working on incorporating more texture and gradients.

How has the aesthetic of Rick and Morty informed your Piece?

Rick and Morty is a show that has so much fun energy – the aesthetic definitely informed my thought process. I wasn't focused on making everything perfect, I wanted the designs to be a bit quirky with personality.

What excited you most about getting to participate in this exhibition?

It was exciting to see the general response to the show – not only from people who attended, but also online. This was also my first opportunity to do something official with such a large scale property, and my second show with the gallery. I'm super grateful that I had the chance to participate.

Above: Variant versions of the final artwork showing different expressions and compositions.

Kevin Tiernan is a designer and illustrator with a clean visual style. He's worked in advertising as an art director and creative lead on campaigns for national brands. As a kid, his notebooks were covered with doodles of characters from pop culture, something that's still true today. Passionate about movie posters, Kevin started creating fan art as a hobby and gained experience designing official art over the years. He enjoys playing guitar, collecting records, comics, hiking, and dogs.

Dan Mumford

I'm starting to work up some anxiety about this whole thing
18 x 24"

What did you want to convey or represent with your art piece?

I wanted to try and convey the size and overwhelming nature of that first episode when Morty starts to get really anxious about their situation. I really liked the idea of it being the start of this grand adventure and the slightly scary nature of what stood before them. Having the space cruiser shooting across the top of the piece I thought was quite a fun way of showing that things are never as they seem in *Rick and Morty* too.

Can you talk about the storytelling power of the art?

I always tend to draw things on quite a large scale with any figures in the scene quite small, I mainly wanted to convey the size of what was ahead of them in this weird and unknown landscape. I like for viewers to be able to look at my work and imagine the characters walking off into the distance towards adventure.

What is your favorite *Rick and Morty* episode? Is there a specific moment from the show that resonates with you?

'Lawnmower Dog' is fantastic. I loved the whole concept of that episode, I think it hits on what *Rick and Morty* does so well, crazy concepts executed with heart. It was hard not to be on Snowball's side when you see things from his point of view. It's also a great example of why it's hard to explain what it is *Rick and Morty* does so well, to describe that episode it sounds bizarre, but when you watch it, it's quite a simple idea created beautifully.

What was your favorite part of creating the artwork?

I really enjoyed coloring this piece. It started with the color palette from the show, but from there I amped it up and pushed it further. At the time, I was mainly working with quite monochromatic color palettes in my work, so this was actually the start of me moving into more fully colored pieces. So I remember this piece fondly as the starting point for me experimenting with some new coloring techniques.

Why do you create art? How would you describe your style in general?

Like most artists I think it's a love of creating. Whether it's playing around in worlds already existing in film and TV, or coming up with my own things, there's just something very cathartic about it for me. My style is basically a refining of my love of comic books when I was younger. I'm not quite sure specifically how to describe it, but I like to make things epic and colorful with lots of nice detail.

What excited you most about getting to participate in this exhibition?

Working on this piece for the exhibition was a great opportunity to get involved with a whole world of fans and people that I hadn't been exposed to before. I think the exhibition itself as well showed how huge a fan base *Rick and Morty* has with some incredible artwork throughout.

Over the past ten years, Dan has worked within the pop culture and music scene creating everything from album covers, branding, and screenprints to new interpretations of classic film posters and albums. Clients include Disney, Sony, Iron Maiden, Wizards of the Coast, Icon Motoports, CBS, and many many bands and record labels from around the world.

Erin Hunting
Thanks, Mr. Poopybutthole
11.7 x 16.5"

How did the concept come to you? How long did it take to complete?

I wanted to honor my favorite *Rick and Morty* episode, and since 'Total Rickall' is a stand out fave, it didn't take long to decide what to draw.

What do you appreciate most about the show?

I am a fan of the show and love how different it is to any other show – animated or not – out there at the moment.

If you could be in a single episode, which would it be?

'Total Rickall' of course! Finding out whether or not Mr. Poopybutthole is real or not sounds like an extra fun Sunday night in.

Do you have a favorite character and, if so, what do you like most about them?

Growing up on a healthy diet of horror movies in the 80s makes me appreciate Scary Terry (probably more than I should). 'Lawnmower Dog' was such a fun and brilliant episode too, and Scary Terry pretty easily stole it from the main stars Rick and Morty.

What was your favorite part of creating the artwork?

Drawing all of the different characters as, apart from Rick and Morty, I had never drawn them before.

What was your process? How did you prepare?

My preparation was watching the episode ('Total Rickall') again and then Googling what characters I wanted to fit into the piece. I then started the digital sketching process, trying to fit in as many characters as I could while still having Rick and Morty as the central figures.

Why do you create art? How would you describe your style in general?

I create art both digitally and traditionally. Traditionally I use ink and Copic markers and keep detail to a minimal as it's usually a warm up drawing before I hit my Wacom Cintiq, as I create all of my professional work digitally. For style, I am known for my bright colors and glassy eyes. I would describe it as fairly modern and hopefully fun.

How is your *Rick and Morty* piece similar to, or different from your other works?

I think the level of detail and characters was turned up a notch for this piece, which was unusual, as my personal work doesn't usually include that much detail. It was also one of the reasons I chose to illustrate from this episode too, as I knew it would be fun and a little bit different.

What excited you most about getting to participate in this exhibition?

The fact that it was an official show is always exciting and being asked to be involved in it is always a pretty big deal. And since the show has such a huge appreciation, there was a real buzz about this one in particular.

Erin Hunting is an Australian illustrator who has worked in comics (including an official *Rick and Morty* cover with Oni Press), children's books, visual development in animation, and has also worked with Netflix, Tegan and Sara, Facebook, and many other worldwide identities. She resides in Melbourne, Australia with her cat Louie and is kept inspired by her love of animals, comics, and movies.

Stephen Sandoval

Untitled

18 x 12"

Brendon Flynn is an illustrator and fine artist from Syracuse, NY. His life and art is inspired by, but not limited to, science, mythology, nature, monsters, the nature of monsters, and quality footwear. He received his BFA in illustration from the University of the Arts in Philadelphia. Brendon creates album cover and poster art for heavy metal and rock bands while spreading his questionable influence on gallery walls from coast to coast.

Brendon Flynn
Avoiding Gonorrhea
10 x 8"

Sara Richard
The Roarin' Unities
9 x 12"

What did you want to convey or represent with your art piece?

I love the Art Deco style and I wanted to play around with the idea of a seemingly dignified Gatsby-esque party scene full of flapper girl Unities. But then balance it out with the fact Rick probably only had his pants on a total of five minutes for this classy affair. I love that sort of juxtaposition, which is what I take away from the show.

How did the concept come to you? How long did it take to complete?

I did quite a few thumbnail sketches before landing on this one, I wanted a piece with characters interacting instead of a static portrait. The actual painting process was a few days, as I work on acrylic so it dries pretty quickly and once I start a project I don't get up from my desk too often.

Can you talk about the storytelling power of the art?

I tried to use the interactions and expressions of the Unities to move the eye around the painting. Rick's butt, I feel, adds that perfect punctuation to the whole thing. There are also a few details like Morty and Summer's heads carved into the mountain in the distance to be used as extra fun Easter eggs for the piece.

Do you have a favorite character and, if so, what do you like most about them?

Mr. Poopybutthole. He's a damn treasure to animation. I feel like I quote him the most and I love his positivity despite his betrayal. I'm still sad about not winning that body pillow of him at Comic Con a few years ago.

How did you prepare to create the piece? What techniques have you used?

I like to put on music that relates to the mood of what I'm working on. I think for this one I listened to *The Great Gatsby* soundtrack and *Postmodern Jukebox*. I paint with acrylic on illustration board mostly and I love using metallic paints. I have a ton of Art Deco reference books so those were everywhere while I painted this. Erté, one of my favorite artists, was a huge inspiration in this piece.

If you could be in a single episode, which would it be?

Hands down, 'Total Rickall.' I want to know what Ghost in a Jar's backstory could've been because the fan fiction I've written is probably crazier than it needs to be. Kidding... maybe.

Above: Early sketches of the final artwork showing different ideas for the composition. Note that the background characters change position but the two main figures are constant.

Sara Richard is an Eisner nominated comic artist and illustrator. She is the regular variant cover artist for IDW Publishing's *My Little Pony: Friendship is Magic* series and has done covers for the Oni Press' *Rick and Morty* comics series. Sara is inspired by Art Deco, 80s fashion, and fueled by true crime podcasts and gin & tonic (the secret recipe for artistic success).

Joey Spiotto
Wubba Lubba Dub Dub
8 x 10"

What does your piece convey?

This is an idea of what a *Rick and Morty* children's book would look like, inspired by the classic books from my youth.

How did the concept come to you? How long did it take to complete?

I've been working on a series called *Storytime* for several years now where I take some of my favorite movies, musicians, TV shows, and video games, and reimagine them as children's books.

What do you appreciate most about the show?

I absolutely love *Rick and Morty*. The plotlines of the episodes are so deep and get so weird, and the characters are all so rich. It's just an amazing series and the writing is some of the best sci-fi because it's so far out there.

What is your favorite Rick and Morty episode? Is there a specific moment from the show that resonates with you?

My favorite episode has to be 'Total Rickall' from season two. It's the one where the family is fighting against a parasite that implants fake memories in their heads so they keep introducing more and more insane characters and events. I love it so much.

Do you have a favorite character and, if so, what do you like most about them?

I love Jerry. He's just out there trying (sort of) to do his best. His best is not very good, but he still tries and everyone hates him for it.

What was your favorite part of creating the artwork?

I loved reinterpreting these characters in the classic vintage look of an old children's book illustration. They don't belong in that world, and yet it totally works. I'd read this book to my kids.

What excited you most about getting to participate in this exhibition?

As a huge fan of *Rick and Morty*, I loved being able to put my spin on characters that I love so much. The exhibition was an amazing 'thank you' to all of the people that work on the show. Our creativity as artists is inspired by their creativity in creating that world.

How do you see this artwork fitting into the Rick and Morty universe?

In some alternate dimension, a *Rick and Morty* children's book definitely would exist.

Joey Spiotto is a Los Angeles based illustrator and the creator behind *Alien Next Door*, *Grumpy Unicorn* and the print series *Storytime* where he takes our favorite movies, musicians, TV shows, and videogames and re-imagines them as children's books from our youth. His artwork is regularly featured at Gallery 1988 and he has worked in film, video games, clothing design, toys, and more. You can find him at comic book conventions around the United States or visit him online at jo3bot.com.

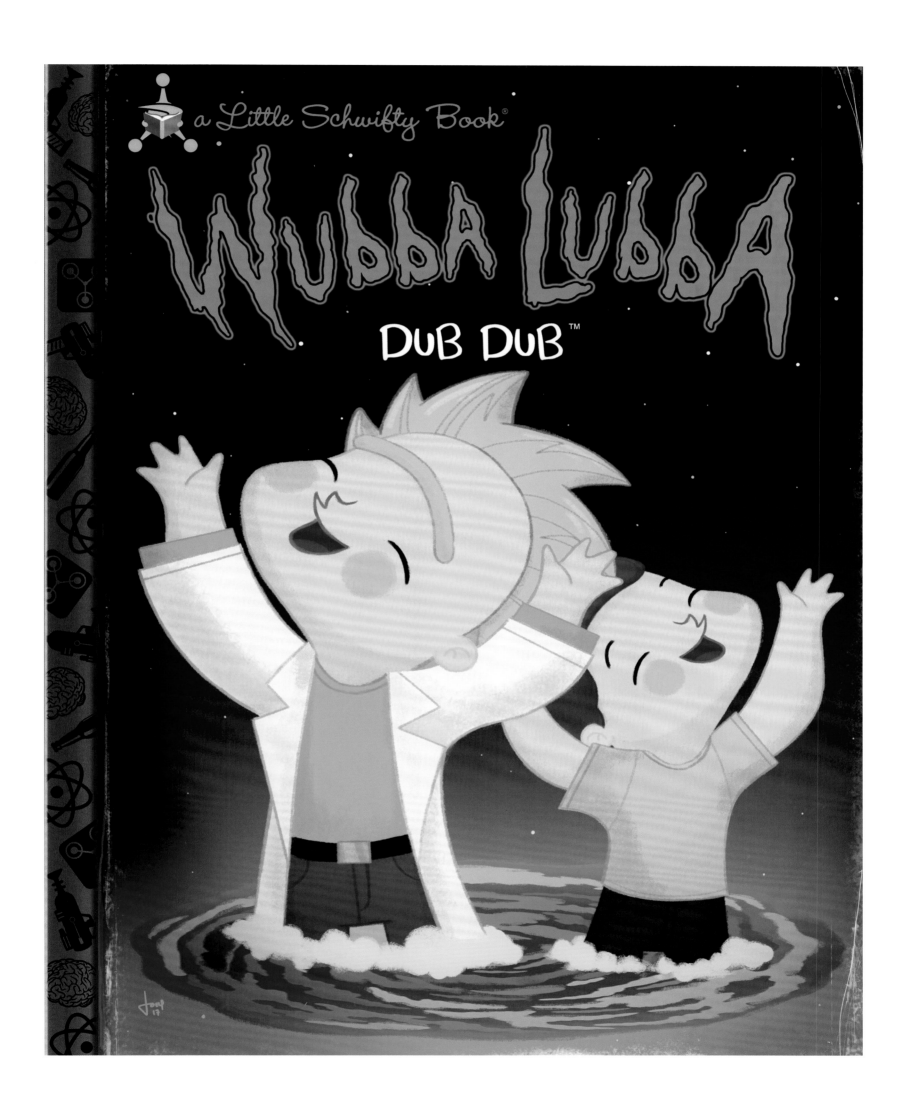

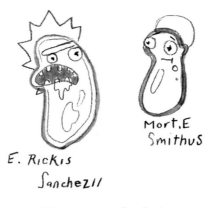

Elisa Wikey
Come Watch TV
8 x 8"

What did you want to convey or represent with your art piece?

I wanted to isolate that quote from Morty specifically. The *Rick and Morty* universe is so expansive already but it does all kind of boil down to "Who gives a shit? Let's go do something fun." I like that. I have to pay bills and deal with my life and be an adult, and then I want to go watch some TV – it resonates.

How did the concept come to you? How long did it take to complete?

'Rixty Minutes' is the episode that has really stuck with me since I first watched it. It was an early front-runner to base my piece on when I started sketching ideas. I wanted to make something that had a nice silhouette from far away but gained details the closer you get to it. I painted it a couple of times to achieve a look I was happy with, so it sat on my desk for a few weeks as I left and came back to it. Squishing all the time together, it probably took eight hours or so.

Can you talk about the storytelling power of the art?

To me, the show is following these two characters who are so embattled inside, trying to find a way to distract themselves from a dark void. Run through a portal, go on an adventure, kill something (probably). It's a simple piece that seems fun on the surface but tries to embody that attempt at escapism. We don't have portal guns but we do have television. It all comes back to that in the end, doesn't it?

Do you have a favorite character and, if so, what do you like most about them?

Rick and Morty together. They're symbiotic when they're a team; different than on their own. They're messed up together. Either them, or Mr. Meeseeks – I'm also always pulling my hair out to solve a problem.

What was your process for creating this artwork? What techniques have you used?

Sketches first, getting ideas out to see which one I keep coming back to. I painted this traditionally with gouache so I needed to test paint colors out to see what they'd look like on the paper. I had to practice the portal to make sure you could tell what it was!

Why do you create art? How would you describe your style in general?

Why not? Someone's gotta do it. I wasn't going to be a doctor or do math for the rest of my life. Why not make things that are fun to look at? Doctors need to look at art, too. My style is, at its core, minimalist and cartoonish. I try and use shapes more than lines.

Above: Rough sketches for different design concepts, representing the characters in the artist's recognizable art style.

My work is influenced by Lowbrow art, cartoons I watched as a kid (and still do), *The Far Side*, comics and graphic novels, Americana, and any culture with a bad attitude. It's been said to flirt with a dangerous sense of humor and is probably fun to look at by children aged two to seventy and a half, the average life expectancy in the world today. Some describe my work as single-panel comics. They're noodley, cute, irreverent, and subversive with a healthy dose of dark humor.

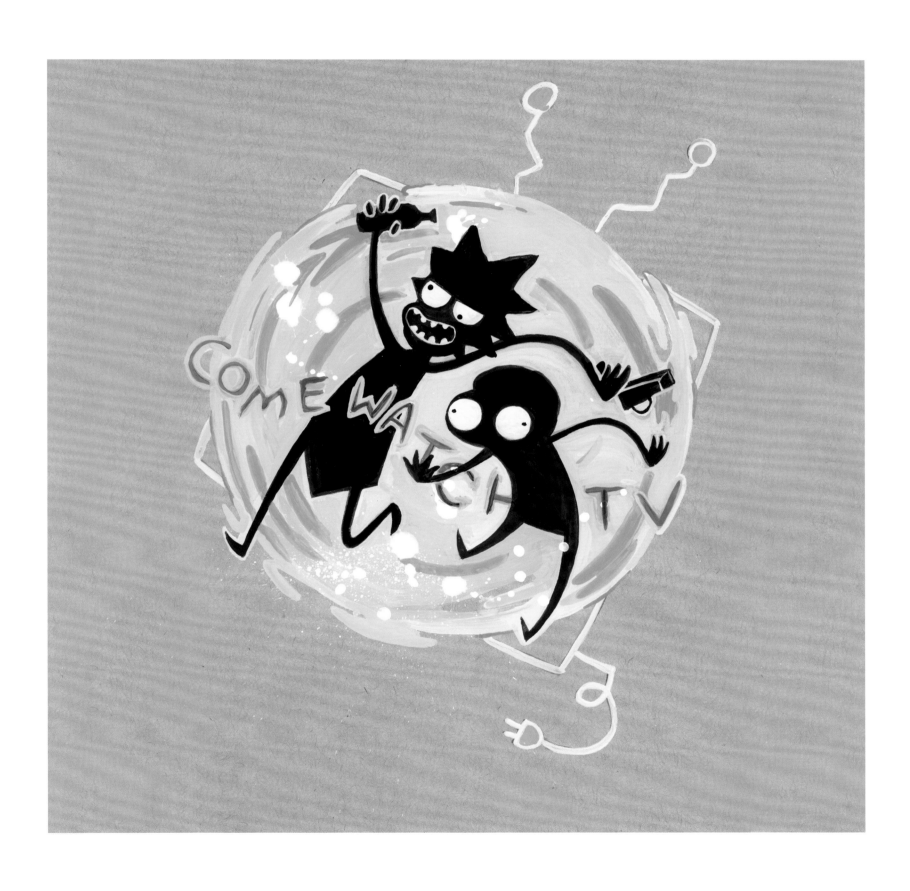

Justine "Steen" Pulles
The Adventures of Mr. Meeseeks in Never Past Bedtime Land
12 x 16"

What did you want to convey or represent with your art piece?

The Adventures of Mr. Meeseeks in Never Past Bedtime Land is a piece featuring my favorite character visiting my favorite part of my favorite episode. I wanted to do something fun and colorful, to offset the darker humor of the show, while also remaining totally plausible. Also, Mr. Meeseeks deserves a fun-filled vacation.

How did the concept come to you? How long did it take to complete?

The concept came to me pretty quickly, but the piece took about ten hours to complete.

What do you appreciate most about the show?

I absolutely adore the creators of *Rick and Morty*, the style of humor and originality portrayed within the writing and characters, and the voices. I appreciate that *Rick and Morty* isn't afraid to get schwifty!

If you could be in a single episode, which would it be?

I'd love to jump into Never Past Bedtime Land, because look at all the giant candy! It looks super inviting, and very similar to dreams I had as a kid about giant lollipops and popsicles that grew on trees.

What excited you most about getting to participate in this exhibition?

I was so excited to be asked to participate in this art show because of how much I admire Dan Harmon and Justin Roiland as people; they inspire me to keep being weirdly confident. The thought that they could see my artwork was just super cool! Plus it was just a bonus and an honor to create artwork based on a show I already love.

What was your process for creating this artwork? What techniques have you used?

I used a combination of Adobe Flash and Photoshop to create the finished piece. I sketched a rough of the piece, and completed Mr. Meeseeks as well as the other characters in Flash, and exported them as separate layers into Photoshop. I knew I wanted the characters to have a crisp, clean line art, and Flash allowed me to do that with vectors, so the characters could be resized if needed without losing quality. I drew and painted the background in Photoshop, and added the character layers before applying the finishing touches to the piece.

What was your favorite part of creating the artwork?

My favorite part of working on this piece was re-watching episodes of *Rick and Morty* as 'research.'

How is your *Rick and Morty* piece similar to, or different from your other works?

The process I used for this piece is similar to my other digital illustrations and what I do working in 2D animation, but it is very different to my portraiture work and paintings, which are much more traditionally influenced, painterly, and tend to have darker color palettes.

What else about your piece do you think *Rick and Morty* fans should know?

I almost worked as a background artist on *Rick and Morty*! I went for the interview, but the timing didn't work out. This piece is my 'would've should've could've.'

Hi! I'm Justine Pulles, but I go by Steen. I'm from Vancouver, BC, Canada, and I'm a professional 2D animation artist and color stylist, illustrator, and painter. I've worked on many cartoons you or your kids have probably seen, including *My Little Pony: Friendship is Magic, Cloudy with a Chance of Meatballs (the series), Littlest Pet Shop, Supernoobs,* and Netflix's *The Hollow.* I am a crazy Disney nerd, cupcake baker, and toy collector, who loves horror, aliens, halloween, unicorns, bunnies, and rainbows. www.artworkbysteen.com.

Taylor Rose
The Ricks Must Be Crazy
11 x 17"

Please describe your piece. What did you want to convey and what does it represent?

This illustration was inspired by my favorite episode 'The Ricks Must Be Crazy.' I wanted to flood the scenes with detail and connect as much multiverse complexity as possible from the episode. I adored the concept and design elements that went into this episode's storytelling and world building, and really wanted to honor that in the piece.

How did the concept come to you? How long did it take to complete?

I was thinking a lot about this episode's world building and how wonderfully the story flows from each newly introduced environment, playing with darker concepts of human intention with each new world. I realized I could use design elements to show both the separation and connectivity of each world and its creators. From start to finish, it probably took in the seventy to seventy-five hour range.

What do you appreciate most about the show?

Rick and Morty has helped carve a wonderfully surreal space in storytelling today. When you get to go on space adventures with burp-fueled dialogue and brightly rendered universes, it really opens up more room to tackle and explore some of our darkest human impulses and curiosities.

What was your process for creating this artwork? What techniques have you used?

This piece was illustrated digitally (I paint on a Cintiq 22HD) I use a lot of digital watercolor and ink brushes, as well as handmade textures that I scan in and layer over in Photoshop. My overall approach was very design based initially. Blocking out each world broadly and simply at first really helped to navigate the best way to connect everything together in the details.

What excited you most about getting to participate in this exhibition?

I was really excited to get to study and showcase the details of 'The Ricks Must Be Crazy' episode, it also became pretty clear that the *Rick and Morty* fandom was really craving and deserving of more fan art, and everyone that took part in the exhibit totally delivered.

What else about your piece do you think *Rick and Morty* fans should know?

I'm so appreciative to the response I've received on this piece over the years. I often spend so much time obsessing over the details in my art, and with this piece in particular it's been amazing to see people really dive in and take the time to absorb all the little Easter eggs in the piece.

Above: The various details within the artwork are represented in the early sketch stages of development.

I grew up in New England spending a lot of time exploring forests or watching cartoons and reading books. Drawing was always a wonderful escape to render my favorite animals, bugs, plants, and characters. I kept at it as a teen and found a lot of purpose and community in high school and college art studies. Today I work full time as a freelance illustrator, still getting to celebrate nature and storytelling through art. Outside of art life, I can usually be found snowboarding or fly fishing, or obsessing over cartoons, fantasy books, and film.

JellyKoe
Anatomy Park
Family Portrait
8 x 10"

Michelle Hiraishi
Gubba Nub Nub Doo Rah Kah

8 x 10"

Oh Sew Nerdy
Get your shit together
What is My Purpose?
4-inch embroidery hoop

What did you want to convey or represent with your art piece?

I work with fabric – specifically Aida cloth. When I was initially approached about doing a piece or two for the *Rick and Morty* art show, these two moments jumped out at me. I usually use quotes and simple items to complete my pieces. The "get your shit together" tirade is one of my favorite moments from the show. I think it also works as a bit of an inside joke for the person viewing it. It isn't beating you over the head with a Plumbus or anything. If you saw it and know *Rick and Morty* you'll get it. The butter-passing robot was so adorable and cute and his existential breakdown of realizing he was built to pass butter was so immediate, funny, and heartbreaking at the same time.

How did the concept come to you? How long did it take to complete?

The concepts for me are usually the quotes that stick out in my head from the show. Usually when I'm watching something I'll jot down a line or quote if I love it and then come back to it once I'm in a stitching mode. I design my stitches on a computer first to get the shape and color correct. Then I'll use the computer pattern to hand stitch everything. The whole process can take up to about four hours, depending on the difficulty of the image and how many colors I'm using.

What is your favorite *Rick and Morty* episode? Is there a specific moment from the show that resonates with you?

Besides the two moments that I stitched for the show, anytime Birdperson is around I absolutely love it. Oh, and Pickle Rick.

If you could be in a single episode, which would it be?

Is it insane that I want to go to Jerryboree? Yeah, probably.

Why do you create art? How would you describe your style in general?

I create it for myself. It's fun that other people like it and enjoy it. I like using cross stitch and fabric as a different medium than you would normally see (especially for pop culture art). Things are usually so dominated by screen prints and digital prints. I think the cross stitch helps my pieces stand out.

How is your *Rick and Morty* piece similar to, or different from your other works?

I really enjoy doing this style of work: 4" embroidery hoops with a quote and an image to connect it. I've done quite a few of these types of stitches and always seem to enjoy how they look aesthetically but how they can convey a message or a feeling with as few components as possible. Literally a few words and a single image.

How do you see this artwork fitting into the *Rick and Morty* universe?

I'd like to think it would be hanging above butterbot's mantle, forever haunting him. Or in whatever dimension cross stitch is the preferred communication medium.

Oh Sew Nerdy (Derek Hoeksema) is a cross stitch and fiber artist from Illinois. He is self-taught and enjoys watching raccoon videos on the internet. His art has been shown in different galleries across the United States and his entire collection is on Instagram. And probably Reddit.

Lawrence Yang
Show Me What You Got
10 x 7"

What did you want to convey or represent with your art piece?

It's meant to be a hypothetical sixth planet to compete in the Cromulon episode – completely populated by Meeseeks. Probably singing a song called 'I'm Mr. Meeseeks, look at me.'

How did the concept come to you? How long did it take to complete?

I'm a huge fan of *Rick and Morty* and knew I wanted to do something related to Cromulons. It took a week or so of sketching, practicing, starting over, and finishing the piece.

What do you appreciate most about the show?

I'm a big fan for the usual reasons – funny, random, dark, smart.

What is your favorite *Rick and Morty* episode? Is there a specific moment from the show that resonates with you?

Cliché, but it's probably 'Pickle Rick' – watching Rick Frankenstein himself a pickle/rat body and kick ass is amazing.

What excited you most about getting to participate in this exhibition?

All the other artists' amazing takes on the *Rick and Morty* universe!

If you could be in a single episode, which would it be?

'Total Rickall,' as Ghost in a Jar.

Do you have a favorite character and, if so, what do you like most about them?

Rick Sanchez. I like him for the same reason I like Sherlock – he knows his shit and can outthink/plan everyone in the room.

What was your process for creating this artwork? How did you prepare to create the piece?

Splashing ink and watercolor around in layers to get the trippy background, then painting with watercolor and gouache on top. To prepare I sketched and painted a few failures before I got a good one out of it.

What was your favorite part of working on the artwork?

Painting the Meeseeks – just imagining them screaming "LOOK AT ME" with the Cromulon looking on made me chuckle.

Why do you create art? How would you describe your style in general?

I create art for fun – it helps keep me sane with everything else going on in my life. Sometimes I have ideas that won't let me go until I get them down on paper.

Lawrence Yang designs by day and paints by night. His ink and watercolor paintings are inspired by traditional Chinese painting and pop culture. Lawrence lives in the Seattle area with his amazing wife, daughter, and imaginary pets Cholo and Billy.

Above: An alternate background design that was created before the final piece was chosen.

Above: A photograph of the piece in progress, showcasing the artist's work area.

Bennett Slater
What is My Purpose?
11 x 14"

What did you want to convey or represent with your art piece?

'What is my Purpose?' follows up with the fate of the one-off character of the butter-passing robot from the episode 'Something Ricked This Way Comes.' I'm sure I don't need to describe the bit, but basically this robot is told by its creator that its only purpose is mundane and disappointing. Something about the nihilistic bluntness of this robot's revelation is both a hilarious punchline and an incredibly tragic reality. I loved the idea that the robot rejects his fate and ventures off on a lifelong pursuit of a deeper meaning.

How did the concept come to you? How long did it take to complete?

The concept came to me fairly quickly – it's where my brain went immediately upon seeing the bit for the first time. The time-consuming part was deciding which *Rick and Morty* bit I wanted to explore. That's the thing with these spear-carrier characters; they get imbued with these morsels of depth, and it leaves me wanting to see so much more. As far as the time this painting took to complete, I'd say a week from planning to completion.

What do you appreciate most about the show?

What I love most about the show is how it is both one of the most visually imaginative shows out there, but also incredibly real and raw in its character moments and voice. The show doesn't pander or talk down to its audience. You can also tell it's written by some hard sci-fi book, movie, and television nerds. It turned Cronenberg into a verb and got millions of people to Google "Jan Michael Vincent."

What is your favorite *Rick and Morty* episode?

OOF. This is Sophie's choice. I think, pound-for-pound, 'Total Rickall' is my favorite. That episode is so rewarding on repeat viewings. It also introduced us to Mr. Poopybutthole.

What techniques have you used? How did you prepare to create the piece?

This was an oil painting on a wood panel. The process and preparation for this piece was pretty straightforward – I knew I wanted the character pose to be the exact moment when the robot's existential bombshell drops. After that, I transferred the drawing to the panel, and began layering on paint.

How is your *Rick and Morty* piece similar to, or different from your other works?

I often incorporate forms of natural growth or decay in my work, so the subject matter of this piece and my process sort of serendipitously came together.

What else about your piece do you think *Rick and Morty* fans should know?

The butter robot is surrounded by butterflies and buttercups. Maybe someone out there didn't make that connection?

I am a Canadian oil painter, currently living in Toronto. Utilizing traditional oil painting methods on wood, my work mixes teachings borrowed from Flemish and Dutch still life disciplines, combined with bold colors and forms from the pop art and surrealist schools. This dichotomy of contrasting artistic disciplines and influences lends itself to the underlying dualities explored in my work.

Jessica Edwards
Where are My Testicles, Summer?
12 x 12"

Studiohouse Designs
Rick and Morty Time All Day Long Forever, All a Hundred Days Rick and Morty
Forever a Hundred Times Over and Over Rick and Morty Adventures Dot Com

18 x 24"

Chris McGuire
Sometimes Science is More Art than Science
11 x 14"

What did you want to convey and what does your artwork represent?

Rick constantly criticizes his family's conventional lifestyle as mundane and pointless, and seems to be searching for some kind of meaning in the adventures he goes on to other worlds, often dragging a confused and somewhat powerless Morty along with him. To illustrate that idea, I showed Rick escaping suburbia with his arm eagerly outstretched, through a portal to the Citadel of Ricks, while Morty is pulled along unwittingly.

What was your favorite part of creating the artwork?

I think illustrating the nebula behind the Citadel of Ricks was surprisingly fun. It was quite calming.

What is your favorite Rick and Morty episode? Is there a specific moment from the show that resonates with you?

My favorite has to be 'Meeseeks and Destroy.' Another great one is 'Pickle Rick.' I thought Rick's story arc where he turns himself into a pickle just to avoid talking about his feelings was a funny way of showing that Rick's weakness is not his intellect but his emotional immaturity.

Do you have a favorite character and, if so, what do you like most about them?

I thought Birdperson was a great character. He had a Spock-like quality which was fun. I was sad to see him go.

What was your process for creating this artwork? How did you prepare to create the piece?

First, I re-watched many episodes of the show, while brainstorming possible concepts for the piece. I then sketched several quick roughs that I showed to my wife, Kristine. Once we agreed on which concept had the most potential, I started work on that idea. I gathered reference images I thought would apply, including some of myself posing as the characters, to give the piece some realism. I completed a detailed drawing with pencil on paper and then scanned it into the computer. From there, I colored everything in Photoshop using a Wacom tablet. Finally, I printed out proofs and made adjustments as needed to make sure the colors matched what I had on screen.

How has the aesthetic of Rick and Morty informed the style of your piece?

The show has a very bold colorful style, so I thought it would be interesting to try working with a softer and more subtle palette that would merge my aesthetic with the imagery from the show.

What excited you most about getting to participate in this exhibition?

The show has a lot of different crazy worlds and concepts so it was great getting to just sit and think about how to play with them inside a single piece.

1

2
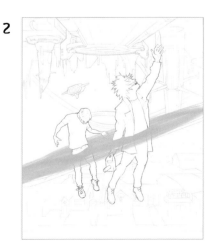

Above: 1) A rough sketch early in the development process maps out the basic composition. 2) The final design before the colors stage.

Chris McGuire graduated from Long Beach State University with a Bachelor of Fine Arts. He works in graphite, watercolor, oil, and digital mediums. His work has been displayed in art galleries in Los Angeles and New York, and he has had the opportunity to work on art and illustration projects for a variety of clients, including Los Angeles Metro, Paramount Pictures, and HBO. He lives and works in Huntington Beach, California.

Derek Deal
Rick Fink
11 x 17"

What did you want to convey or represent with your art piece?

My piece is a mash-up of *Rick and Morty* and the mid century hot rod illustration style of Ed Roth, most well known for his 'Rat Fink' character. I wanted to capture the divergent personalities of the characters while paying a small homage to one of my illustration role models.

How did the concept come to you? How long did it take to complete?

I went through a ton of concepts. Most of which I hated. Then I thought, "What if Rick's spaceship had WHEELS!" I thought that would blow some minds and the rest, as they say, is history. Somewhere between ten minutes and sixteen weeks.

Can you talk about the storytelling power of the art?

The intent was for the piece to feel like it was a freeze frame from a non-existent episode. I guess one where Rick and Morty go back to the early sixties and have to juice up the ship to escape some Kenickie-looking antagonists.

Do you have a passion for *Rick and Morty*? What do you appreciate most about the show?

Yes. I've seen every episode multiple times. I like how it's completely absurdist and irreverent on the surface but has well rounded characters that are complicated and relatable. Also that the story is much deeper than it seems. When I first started watching, I didn't really pick up that there was a narrative through-line that carried through each episode but once I did I was able to go back and re-watch episodes and appreciate them on totally a different level.

What excited you most about getting to participate in this exhibition?

Just being able to play around with these characters was a lot of fun.

What is your favorite *Rick and Morty* episode? Is there a specific moment from the show that resonates with you?

I really love the Tales from the Citadel episode. Its a bit of a departure from the typical format and gets super dark and foreboding toward the end.

Do you have a favorite character and, if so, what do you like most about them?

Hard to pick a favorite but I like Mr. Poopybutthole. I see a lot of potential for his character.

Why do you create art? How would you describe your style in general?

Early on, I figured out that if I made a nice drawing, people would praise me and validate my existence. Now, I actually depend on it to buy Apple products. My style is cartoony, bold, playful, and disposable.

How has the aesthetic of *Rick and Morty* informed your piece?

I wanted the piece to feel like it came right out of the show or comic so I adhered to the *Rick and Morty* aesthetic pretty closely.

Derek Deal is a graphic artist and motion designer based in Orlando, Florida.

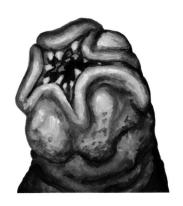

Jason Chalker
Thundersquanch
12 x 18"

What did you want to convey or represent with your art piece?

My piece is a mash-up of *Rick and Morty* with the James Bond *Thunderball* movie poster. Rick Sanchez would be perfect in the Bond universe… if in that universe Bond was genetically spliced with Ernst Stavro Blofeld and Francisco Scaramanga. I think this is a movie the Council of Ricks wouldn't hesitate to fund.

Can you talk about the storytelling power of your piece?

I think it shows the callousness, bravery, and womanizing ways of Rick.

What do you appreciate most about the show?

At its core it's a very intelligent show where nothing is sacred. The character interactions are great and the script writing is top notch.

How is your *Rick and Morty* piece similar to, or different from your other works?

I always try and have some sort of traditional (non-digital) elements to my work. My art normally has a vintage feel to it and having hand drawn/painted elements adds to the authentic look of the piece.

What was your process for creating this artwork?

After coming up with the idea, I roughed out the basics of the piece and then found as much relevant reference material as I could. I then did tight sketches of the three vignettes and finalized the overall layout of the poster. After I was happy with how everything looked, I transferred the drawings to an illustration board and did three individual gouache paintings for the vignettes. After scanning the paintings, I color-corrected them and inserted them into the final layout in Photoshop.

What excited you most about getting to participate in this exhibition?

Getting a chance to (officially) pay homage to one the best animated TV series ever made.

How do you see this artwork fitting into the *Rick and Morty* universe?

I imagine *Thundersquanch* was playing at the multiplex in the Citadel of Ricks when Rick C-137 teleports the aforementioned Citadel into the middle of a Galactic Federal Prison.

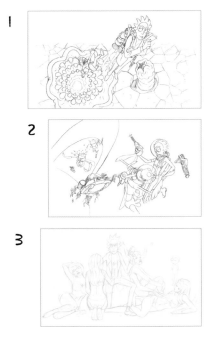

Above: 1–3) Rough sketches of each separate piece of the design.
4) The early sketches in place, plotting out the final composition.

Jason is a multi-disciplined illustrator, animator, and designer based in Detroit. He has done illustration and animation work for a variety of clients such as Topps and Upper Deck on brands like *Mars Attacks*, *Star Wars*, and *Marvel*. Jason was an animator on the Warner Independent film *A Scanner Darkly*. He is also a regular contributor to pop culture art shows around the country.

100% Soft

Sometimes Science is More Art than Science, Morty

16 x 20"

Taylor Blue
Goodbye Moonmen
10 x 20"

Mark Borgions
This TV is for Cartoons and Videogames Only
13 x 19"

What did you want to convey or represent with your art piece?

The poster uses its cues from 'Raising Gazorpazorp,' from the scene where Morty and Morty Jr. argue about purpose in life and fight for the TV remote control.

How did the concept come to you? How long did it take to complete?

I liked the quote "This TV is for cartoons and videogames only." Once I decided to play with that quote, I tried sketching a few poses with respect to the original designs. Since there is no scenery, the illustration did not take all that long to make.

Can you talk about the storytelling power of the art?

I liked the idea that the poster could have a purpose in real life. That it could hang over a TV in someone's home. That it could end a real discussion about who gets to choose what to watch.

If you could be in a single episode, which would it be?

I'd love to hang out with Tiny Rick in 'Big Trouble in Little Sanchez.' I'd like to see those dance moves for real.

What was your process for creating this artwork?

My final pieces are always digital, but they start as sketch on paper. I've learned that going from pencil to vector to bitmap really helps my style.

What was your favorite part of working on the artwork?

I liked interpreting the characters, taking design cues from the originals, respecting the original design details (like Morty's behind the head hair), yet translating it to my own kind of character illustrations. When you work from an illustrated original, where certain design decisions have been addressed in a specific way, I feel you need to respect those things.

Why do you create art? How would you describe your style in general?

I've always liked drawing. I never call it art. I prefer calling it 'my work.' I try to put a certain graphic quality to it, with cues from fifties and sixties low budget animation aesthetics.

How is your *Rick and Morty* piece similar to, or different from your other works?

For gallery work, I always try to create a filmic scene. Not really a poster *per se*. I like to dive into the feeling of a certain shot or story element. I seldom use poster size type like I did here. Yet here, to give it that extra layer of meaning, I decided to put the quote.

How do you see this artwork fitting into the *Rick and Morty* universe?

Since the piece thrives so much on the message, I think it doesn't need a deep knowledge of the *Rick and Morty* world. Yet if you know the scene and the characters, you recognize the dynamic. It would be fun to do a whole series of these.

Above: The varying stages of development. 1) First sketches of the basic outlines. 2) The artist begins to add color to the page using the sketch as a guide. 3) The color layer is finalized.

Mark Borgions (°1967) is an award-winning independent illustrator and animator, working from his studio in Antwerp, Belgium. He is co-author of a best-selling series of audio plays and has illustrated numerous children's books. He designs graphic packages for television and creates animations for clients around the globe. He also creates limited edition prints for pop culture art shows in Europe and the US. He lives happily with a wife, two kids, and a cat.

Alexander Wells
Oh man, Rick! What is this place?
9 x 6.5"

What did you want to convey or represent with your art piece?

When I first watched *Rick and Morty,* my favorite aspect was the crazy, insane world that appeared at the other end of Rick's portals. Poor Morty ended up going to some pretty undesirable places. I wanted to do something where we felt like we were heading into the mind of Rick.

What do you appreciate most about *Rick and Morty*?

I think it's hard for an animated show to pull off a mixture between comical gags and sentimentality. It's a fine line which *Rick and Morty* pulls off well. I'm invested in the characters.

Is there a specific moment that resonates with you?

Ants in my Eyes Johnson gets me every time.

If you could be in a single episode or moment, which would it be?

Being in the Pleasure Chamber would be interesting.

Do you have a favorite character and, if so, what do you like most about them?

Ants in my Eyes Johnson because of the ants in his eyes.

What was your process for creating this artwork? How did you prepare to create the piece?

I usually do several small thumbnails for rough sketches, see which ones I feel work best, and then digitally sketch that out larger. Once I've found something I think works, I start inking over my sketch and then go on to the color stages. I usually pick out a color palette before anything else.

What was your favorite part of creating the artwork?

Getting to watch *Rick and Morty* in the background.

Why do you create art? How would you describe your style in general?

I create art because life is too short to do anything you don't love and I'm passionate about creating work.

How has the aesthetic of *Rick and Morty* informed your piece?

I wanted to lean away from the visual style of the show and try to create something in my own style. I was worried it would look too 'weird,' so I kept it discreet and the idea I picked had most major features covered up so it left it up to the viewer to fill them in.

What excited you most about getting to participate in this exhibition?

I've been a big fan of Dan Harmon for the longest time so I was excited to be involved in anything he's had a hand in!

How do you see this artwork fitting into the *Rick and Morty* universe?

Probably sitting in the background of an interdimensional cable episode. Maybe in a toilet.

What else about your piece do you think *Rick and Morty* fans should know?

No animals were harmed in the making of it.

Ridge Rooms

Rick(s)
Morty(s)
8 x 10"

Ridge Rooms is an illustrator and consumer product designer who combines her film school background and love of mid-century design and advertising to create movie-and-TV-themed artwork with a retro flair. Previously an in-house designer for *Peanuts*, Barnes & Noble, and Pepsi, Ridge relocated from New York City to a sleepy little Victorian tourist town in the Midwest where she owns a pop art boutique called The Mascot Syndicate.

What did you want to convey or represent with your art piece?

I'm kinda obsessed with cartoon families and how weird and fun they can be, and let's face it… *Rick and Morty* has one of the more oddball families in the cartoon universe. I didn't know exactly what I wanted it to look like, so I started with hunting a very traditional frame for the piece, so I could draw something silly that could maybe be a visual clash for that. I came across a pair of oval frames that reminded me of the kind of thing you see on a long hallway of family portraits in old movies, so I decided to do a coordinating pair of portraits for Rick and Morty separately. But with the twist of having a bunch of each of them squeezing into the portrait all at once.

What is your favorite *Rick and Morty* episode?

Probably 'Interdimensional Cable 2: Tempting Fate' because it was the first one I saw and I still remember my reaction. I had not heard of the show and I was at the laundromat and the guy was streaming it on the TV there, and I couldn't turn away for even a second. I was like 'WHAT AM I WATCHING???' I had no understanding of what was even going on in the episode because the washers and dryers were making too much noise, but I was instantly hooked.

What was your process for creating this artwork?

I did some pencil sketching to decide on which of Rick and Morty's expressions to use, then the final was done in colored pencil on colored paper. That's been my favorite combination of media since I first started drawing as a kid. I mostly work on the computer now making prints, but for one-of-a-kind hand-drawn artwork, I love colored pencil on colored paper.

How is your *Rick and Morty* piece similar to, or different from your other works?

I do a few variations of styles depending on what medium I'm working in and/or what type of subject it is, but I often like to do pieces that use very basic elements to tell a visual story. For example, I love working with basic shapes and negative space. For this piece, I used outlines – which I don't always draw – because of the style of the source material, but I still drew it in a very simple way, with a little bit of color for accent. When doing hand-drawings, I almost always use the paper itself as the main color so it's as if the character is part of the page, not on top of it.

What else about your piece do you think *Rick and Morty* fans should know?

I may or may not have hidden something under Morty's hair.

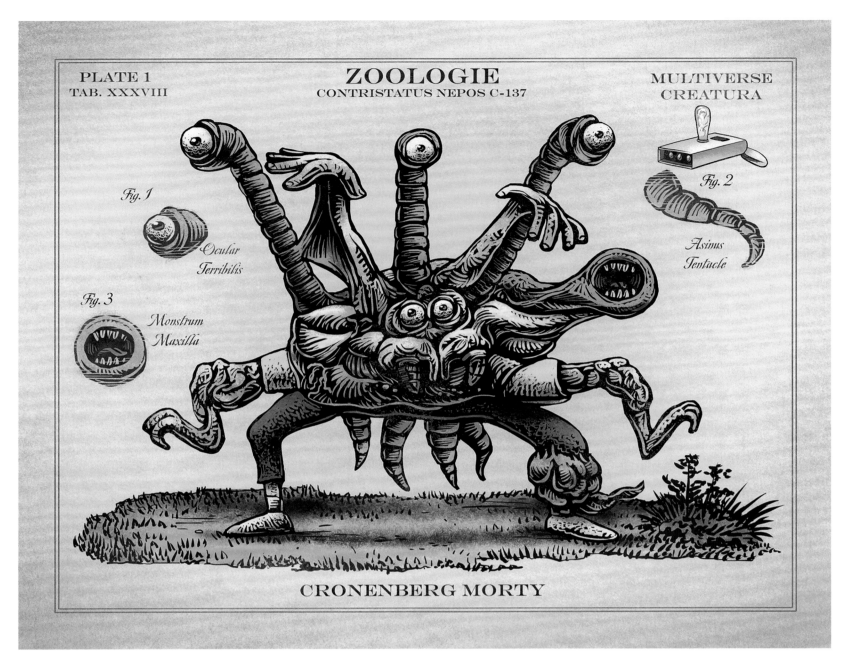

Chet Phillips

Cronenberg Morty
Cronenberg Rick

8 x 10"

Above and Left: Chet Phillips used concept sketches to plan out the composition of each piece.

Andy Stattmiller
Bitch
12 x 24"

What did you want to convey or represent with your art piece?

My piece is a painting of Scary Terry in his underwear. I depicted him in his underwear to show him in a state that he is truly vulnerable and not so scary.

How did the concept come to you? How long did it take to complete?

I like to play with opposites, positive vs. negative concepts. It adds a kind of contrast in the concept, which makes the work more interesting to me. This piece took me around ten hours to paint.

Can you talk about the storytelling power of the art?

A picture is worth a thousand words. I wanted to pay tribute to the show, so finding something that really happened in it was important. I wanted to tell a story with just the character alone, where you can really get the story of what's happening just by his facial expression.

What was your process for creating this artwork?

I first drew him out on the canvas. Then I decided what color would work well with the character for the background. I proceeded to paint Scary Terry, using the brightest colors I could mix. I used acrylic paint for the fill and oil based enamel for the line work. I also used metallic ink for his claws.

Why do you create art? How would you describe your style in general?

I like to stay humorous with my work. So a funny concept is first, then a simple, clean way to execute it. I don't like to 'muddy it up' or overwork things. So starting with a solid drawing before even thinking of painting it is how I go. I never get too realistic, I always need to keep it cartoony while still based in reality, if that makes sense.

How has the aesthetic of *Rick and Morty* informed your piece?

It's a cartoon, but they really go all out with the monsters and detail, which I love! It's also hilarious!

What excited you most about getting to participate in this exhibition?

Just being a part of anything *Rick and Morty* related was awesome! There is so much good stuff to make art of from that show. The hardest part of it all was choosing what to do!

Mike Bilz
Shut Up, Morty!
12 x 12"

What did you want to convey or represent with your art piece?

Rick and Morty dodge laser fire as they escape in their ship. Rick drinks casually as Morty screams, pinned upside down to the roof of the ship. The piece is about perspective: when you first look at the piece you see things from Rick's perspective, and everything seems cool and under control. But if you turn the piece upside down and look at it from Morty's perspective you realize they are flying upside down, Rick is drunk, and everything is very much out of control.

How did the concept come to you?

While playing around with different and ideas for pieces I doodled Morty upside down in the ship screaming and it made me laugh.

What do you appreciate most about the show?

I love that the show can move so effortlessly between brilliant science fiction, heartfelt emotional moments, and absolutely crass nonsense dick jokes.

Do you have a favorite character and, if so, what do you like most about them?

Anyone who tells you that they are a Rick is, by definition, a Jerry.

What is your favorite Rick and Morty episode? Is there a specific moment from the show that resonates with you?

'Pickle Rick' is a nearly perfect episode of television, and a perfect encapsulation of the show and exploration of the characters.

If you could be in a single episode, which would it be?

I wouldn't mind a trip to Blips and Chitz, I've heard Roy 2 is amazing.

How has the aesthetic of Rick and Morty informed your piece?

I tried to keep the rich bright colors of the show, and play up the grungy DIY nature of the sci-fi elements like the ship.

How do you see this artwork fitting into the Rick and Morty universe?

I tried to make something that felt like the show, without referencing any particular episode. I wanted it to feel like one of the lost adventures that happens between episodes.

Growing up, Mike Bilz was the nerdiest punk rocker in San Diego. He spent the majority of his youth watching cartoons, drawing, and eating burritos. Since drawing was really the only one of the three that had any sort of future, he ventured out to Los Angeles to attend Otis College of Art and Design. His work walks the fine line between adorable and disturbing; giving life to the odd little thoughts that permeate his imagination by creating eccentric characters that are both endearing and upsetting.

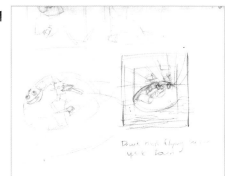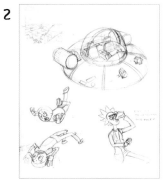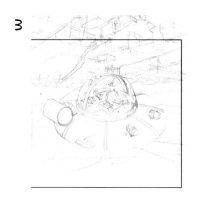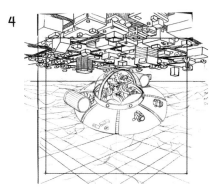

Above: 1) Rough sketches help develop an idea. 2) The outline of the ship and possible positions of the characters are developed. 3) A firmer outline for the design. 4) The final inks for the piece.

Kelly Vivanco
The Real MPB
16 x 7 x ¾"

What did you want to convey or represent with your art piece?

My piece is based on the old-time 'Jumping Jack' style toys that animate when you pull the string. Mr. Poopybutthole's arms and legs flail up and down when the string is pulled and he is double sided so you can choose between the happy and betrayed expressions

How did the concept come to you? How long did it take to complete?

I knew I wanted to create an appreciative piece for a side character with a pivotal role. So many to choose from but Mr. PB worked for what I wanted to make. From concept to construction and painting took about a week to complete.

Can you talk about the storytelling power of the art?

I wanted my piece to be interactive and to mirror the animation of the show in an equally silly 3D manner.

What do you appreciate most about the show?

The endless possibilities and creativity of the storylines. The writing, characters, and world building is top-notch clever.

If you could be in a single episode, which would it be?

Gosh, none of them. I would probably get 'sploded or Cronenberged.

What was your process for creating this artwork? What techniques have you used?

I had an idea of the toy-like quality and interactivity I wanted to do but had to figure out how those toys work. Mr. Google gave me some ideas of the inner workings for 'Jumping Jack' type toys, so I built off those basics and made a mock up with matte board. The final piece was cut out of basswood on a hand saw then a scroll saw, put together with wire and string, then finished with acrylic paints and varnish.

Why do you create art? How would you describe your style in general?

I gotta make stuff or I don't feel right. Normally I paint in an illustrative style; narrative works with characters and animals and made-up environments. I do like to mix it up with animals and humorous pieces once in a while, though. It's good to get out of my comfort zone to try new things, see different timelines and universes.

What excited you most about getting to participate in this exhibition?

Rick and Morty is one of my favorite shows. I would have done a bunch of characters in this format if I had time and got greedy with wall space!

What else about your piece do you think *Rick and Morty* fans should know?

I wish books had animations, then you could see him flail. Maybe in a pop-up version of the book?

Above: Front and back of the marionette-style piece give a different perspective on the beloved character.

California native and current San Diego County resident Kelly Vivanco holds a BFA with honors from LCAD. She enjoys setting whimsy to work in many mediums and pulls inspiration from the natural and imagined world, vintage photographs, children's literature and dreams. Solo and in group exhibitions since 2005 include showings at the California Center for the Arts Museum, The Portsmouth Museum of Art, Thinkspace, Distinction, Gallery 1988, Subtext, Rotofugi, Inner State, Flatcolor, Nahcotta, SCOPE, Antler, The Brand, Art Basel and Orange County Center for Contemporary Arts. Her work is held in collections across the U.S. and abroad.

Nate Bear
Get Down with the Rickness
13 x 19"

What did you want to convey or represent with your art piece?

A lot of fans identify with Rick's preoccupation with alerting his consciousness. But it's a dual edged sword that can unleash creativity and bring you to higher consciousness, but in the case of Rick he also tends to use it as an escape and way to numb his pain.

How did the concept come to you?

I think just saw the overlap of the shadows of Rick's hair and the lotus/mandala shape and thought I could emphasize the trippiness of Rick's mind. And, of course, I wanted to draw a bunch of characters and cool aliens so I stuck those in as the facets of the mandala. Also had to put Morty's butt in there… for reasons…

Can you talk about the storytelling power of the art?

Story? Well uh… yeah… Once upon a time there was this crazy old scientist who wanted to kill the pain…

What is your favorite *Rick and Morty* episode? Is there a specific moment from the show that resonates with you?

The one that always stands out to in my memory is the cop drama episode that takes place in the Citadel of the Ricks. I just love that they can find ways to tell all sorts of stories within the universe they created. I wouldn't mind seeing more side stories like that, because the main C-137 characters aren't the only interesting things in that universe. And the writing team over there can really just pull on any thread and run with it.

What was your process for creating this artwork? What techniques have you used?

The hardest part was figuring out the mandala pattern and getting that to line up with Rick's hair. I think I sketched that like ten times, on different layers in Clip Studio (which is like Photoshop but more toward comic and cartoon art). That was also the most time consuming part when I was trying to finish the piece. Because there are so many facets and I was filling each one with a character drawing.

Why do you create art? How would you describe your style in general?

I create art because I would be an empty shell of a normie if I weren't an artist. Without art I'm nothing but another mediocre loser drifting through space. You can't take this away from me man. It's all I have!

How is your *Rick and Morty* piece similar to, or different from your other works?

It's different in that I don't usually cram so much detail in a single piece. I usually try to keep things simple, but for this piece I really wanted to max it out. The creators of the show go hard on every level from the story to the art and animation, so I wanted to match that.

What else about your piece do you think *Rick and Morty* fans should know?

Not every alien in my piece is from the show. I actually made up a couple. Can you figure out which ones?

1

2

3

Above: 1–2) Rough sketches of Rick and Morty in different scenarios. 3) An early sketch of the final design.

Hi. I'm an illustrator slash designer slash blob of flesh living in New Jersey of all places. I've worked on various projects from animation to toys and t-shirts to editorial and cartoons. I've been lucky enough to get paid to create and somehow pay for daycare and groceries every month.

Matthew Rabalais
No Rest for the Ricked
18 x 24"

What does your piece convey?

A contemplative Rick sits fireside, surrounded by mementos from his past. If you look closely, you can find at least one reference to each episode of seasons one and two. I wanted it to be a piece that raised more questions the longer you look at it. Where is this place? Why did Rick collect these things? How did Rick skin a Garblovian? Why is a tiny Morty swimming in Rick's glass?

How did the concept come to you? How long did it take to complete?

I imagined this secret place where Rick goes to revisit memories and artifacts from his past. It's sort of a 'Museum of Rick' that Rick keeps for himself. The piece itself took about two weeks to complete. I spent a lot of time choosing which objects to fill the room with and how to arrange them. The composition was more difficult than the drawing itself.

What excited you most about getting to participate in this exhibition?

It was kind of a dream come true. I've been a fan of Dan Harmon and Justin Roiland since their Channel 101 shorts. If you'd told me back then that someday I'd have work in an art exhibition based their TV show, I'd never believe you.

Can you talk about the storytelling power of the art?

If this were an episode, I imagine that we're seeing Rick at a pretty low point. He's gone to this place where he can be alone and deal with things in his own way and maybe gain some perspective.

What do you appreciate most about the show?

I've always appreciated the amount of craftsmanship that goes into every episode. While making this piece, I realized just how much time and effort the show's artists put into every little detail.

What was your favorite part of creating the artwork?

I enjoyed drawing in the aesthetic of the show. It was a departure from my normal style and was a really fun exercise to draw a scene within that world.

How is your *Rick and Morty* piece similar to, or different from your other works?

If there's a common thread within my work, it's packing the frame full of references and Easter eggs. In a similar piece, I populated a scene with characters from every John Hughes movie.

Above: The varying stages of the development for this piece, from pencils to value studies.

Matthew Rabalais is a painter and illustrator from Baton Rouge, LA. He enjoys working in both traditional mediums as well as digital. As a lifelong art and film nerd, he has been fortunate enough to create work that satisfies both interests.

Shane Lewis

Beauty is in the Eyes of Rick

8 x 8"

What does your piece convey?

For my piece I wanted to imagine what Rick would look like as a beholder. I was inspired by Dan Harmon's love of D&D, and his show *Harmon Quest,* to make this monster manual Rick mash-up. You can see all of Rick's new found eyes searching for Morty, while he inadvertently drools on him.

How did the concept come to you?

I've always been a big fan of D&D as well, so as soon as I heard about Dan Harmon being a fan I had to jump on the idea. All in all, the piece probably took me sixty-seventy hours including the rough sketch stage and ideation.

Why do you create art? How would you describe your style in general?

I create art because I love the craft and creating something that didn't exist before. My style is a modern take on crosshatching, my biggest influences early on were R. Crumb and Albrecht Durer.

What excited you most about getting to participate in this exhibition?

I've been a big fan of the show from the start, and it's rare that a cartoon's vibe lines up so perfectly with the kind of art I like to make. Also I've been watching Adult Swim/Cartoon Network since their inceptions so it was a dream of mine to create something for one of their franchises.

If you could be in a single episode, which would it be?

'Big Trouble in Little Sanchez' would be my episode of choice. I feel like he could use some accompaniment on his 'dying in the garage' song.

What was your process for creating this artwork? What techniques have you used?

To create my artwork, I make three rough sketches in increasing dark pencil till I'm happy with the layout. Then I take the tightest rough sketch and put a piece of bristol over the top of it on the light table. I then ink the piece using Pilot Precise pens. Once done, I scan it in and start coloring. Once I'm happy with the coloring, then I separate each hue onto its own layer and send it off to the screen printer.

What do you appreciate most about the show?

I love the show, the nihilistic themes and overall dark humor get me every time.

How do you see this artwork fitting into the *Rick and Morty* universe?

My thoughts were that Rick had yet to face a beholder, so hopefully this turns some gears over at Morty HQ and we can see him in all of his Rickholder glory some day on the show.

Shane is a silkscreen poster artist whose creations are inspired by pop culture of the past and present. His works are handcrafted posters made traditionally with pen and ink, which are screen printed in limited editions. Shane's work has been shown in galleries across the U.S. alongside notable contemporary and comic book artists such as Mike Mignola and Alex Pardee. Companies Shane has worked with in the past include Focus Features, WWE, Wizards of the Coast, Gallery 1988, Hero Complex Gallery, *Teenage Mutant Ninja Turtles*, Adult Swim, Netflix, and *Archie Comics*. Shane's work has been recognized by various illustration periodicals including a winning spot in 3x3's annual illustration contest as well as garnering numerous Addys from his work as an advertising art director.

Jesse Riggle

Cronenbergs

9 x 12"

What did you want to convey or represent with your art piece?

I made a painting based on a quick joke at the end of an episode, where Rick and Morty are in a world of mutated monsters lovingly referred to as Cronenbergs. As a life long fan of Cronenberg movies, I found this joke especially funny. I thought it was also fun to see the titular characters re-imagined in a style of the wonderful creature-work done for the show.

What do you appreciate most about the show?

I was a fan of the show after the first episode I watched. I have also been a fan of Dan Harmon since back in his 'Scud' days, so I was excited to hear about this cartoon. I find the absurdist humor quite appealing, and its nice to see something with good art direction being produced.

Do you have a favorite character and, if so, what do you like most about them?

Definitely Jerry, he is so amazingly dense.

How has the aesthetic of *Rick and Morty* informed your piece?

Rick and Morty is visually interesting. The main characters are not particularly refined, in the same way that many modern primetime cartoons are fairly simplistic. However, they really go crazy with backgrounds and especially the monster designs in the show. It makes an interesting dichotomy. I wanted to encapsulate the latter portion as I think it is one of the best parts of the show, visually speaking.

Why do you create art? How would you describe your style in general?

I create art mostly to make myself laugh. I used to describe my art by saying I paint lumpy people, which I think this encapsulates well!

Above: 1) An early pencils stage. 2) A tight sketch features the texture of Birdperson's clothing. 3) An initial color study. 4) The final inks for the piece.

Erin Gallagher
Portrait of Birdperson

11 x 14"

Ryan Brinkerhoff
Wanted by the Council of Ricks
18 x 24"

What did you want to convey or represent with your art piece?

This piece is made to look like a wanted poster put out by the Council of Ricks. My goal for this piece was to get real science-y with it and pack in as many references as I could!

What excited you most about getting to participate in this exhibition?

Rick and Morty is an awesome show with tons of little details. I knew it would make for an interesting piece that a fan would really enjoy.

How did the concept come to you? How long did it take to complete?

I've done similar pieces like this for other movies/TV shows like *Aliens*, *Bob's Burgers*, and *The Fly* – where it looks like a chart or page out of a textbook describing details and characters in a scientific way. Since I wanted to make a poster that highlighted some of my favorite gadgets and characters from *Rick and Morty*, it was an appropriate fit. This took twenty-thirty hours from concept to finished product.

What is your favorite *Rick and Morty* episode? Is there a specific moment from the show that resonates with you?

I like to sing the song from 'Rick Potion #9' to annoy my wife: "I love Morty, and I hope Morty loves me… I'd like to wrap my arms around him and feel him inside me."

If you could be in a single episode, which would it be?

I'd like to head over to Blips and Chitz and play some of those wacky arcade games from the 'Mortynight Run' episode!

Do you have a favorite character and, if so, what do you like most about them?

Sleepy Gary makes me laugh every time.

What was your process for creating this artwork? What techniques have you used?

I sketched a few versions of the basic layout, blocking in the 'arsenal' and the 'known accomplices' sections. Once I had a rough plan worked out, I used Adobe Illustrator to make the final illustration. I had to watch a few crucial episodes to make sure I had the gadgets right, like the dream inceptor and the freeze ray. Then I prepped it for production and selected some colors before sending it off to my screen printer, End Hymns (endhymns.com).

How do you see this artwork fitting into the *Rick and Morty* universe?

My piece is literally made to look like a poster that the Council of Ricks would distribute to other dimensions in search of Rick C-137!

I'm a graphic designer/illustrator with eleven years of experience in the design industry. Having worked in an agency environment and as an in-house designer, I'm constantly pursuing passion projects outside of my nine-to-five job to keep the creativity flowing. I have a love for pop culture and enjoy making posters that showcase my interests, allow me to be creative, and, above all, make people smile!

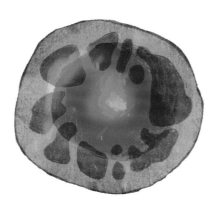

Alice Meichi Li
All the Moonmen
13 x 19"

What did you want to convey or represent with your art piece?

My piece features Morty with his gaseous friend, Fart, from the episode 'Mortynight Run.' I was mostly inspired by the transcendent feel Morty experienced during Fart's Bowie-esque musical number.

Do you have a passion for *Rick and Morty*? What do you appreciate most about the show?

Yes, of course! I appreciate the layers of interpretation involved in the show. It's easy to watch it from a surface level and enjoy the spectacle and humor. But you can then interpret it on a different level, especially starting from the splintering of the dimensions at 'Total Rickall.' Once you realize that the entire episode is taking place in an entirely different reality from the one we as the audience had grown accustomed to, the entire series becomes a different playing field altogether. In a way, this drags the audience into Rick Sanchez's shoes with the realization that every character you were attached to not only is replaceable, but was replaced.

What is your favorite *Rick and Morty* episode? Is there a specific moment from the show that resonates with you?

'Big Trouble in Little Sanchez' is my favorite episode, because both A and B plots were very strong and progressed each character's story arc. Not only is Tiny Rick always fun, but the alien marriage counseling was too real.

If you could be in a single episode, which would it be?

I would be in a pre-cannibalistic Froopyland from 'The ABC's of Beth.' Who wouldn't want to have free rein in a fantasy playground where you could literally never get hurt?

Do you have a favorite character and, if so, what do you like most about them?

I actually really relate to Beth. We're both type-A overachieving personalities with fathers whom we put on pedestals.

Why do you create art? How would you describe your style in general?

I create art because I wouldn't know what to do with myself if I didn't. My style is equal parts traditional and digital media, each to satisfy my desire for order and chaos.

How is your *Rick and Morty* piece similar to, or different from your other works?

I previously worked on a variant cover for *Rick & Morty: Li'l Poopy Superstar* where I had to stay a bit more on-model than I have for this piece. I enjoyed this opportunity to render Morty in a way closer to my typical style.

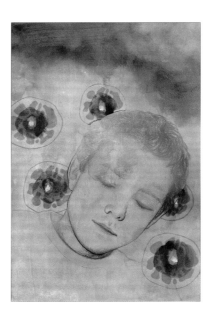

Above: Early stages in the development of the artwork.

Alice Meichi Li is an illustrator who is originally from Detroit and currently living in Jamaica, Queens. Other than being a regular contributor to Gallery 1988, she has contributed art to Dark Horse Comics, Image Comics, *Archie Comics*, and Oni Press – notably cover work for *Rick and Morty: Li'l Poopy Superstar*. You can follow her at @aliceMeichi or visit her site at AliceMeichi.com.

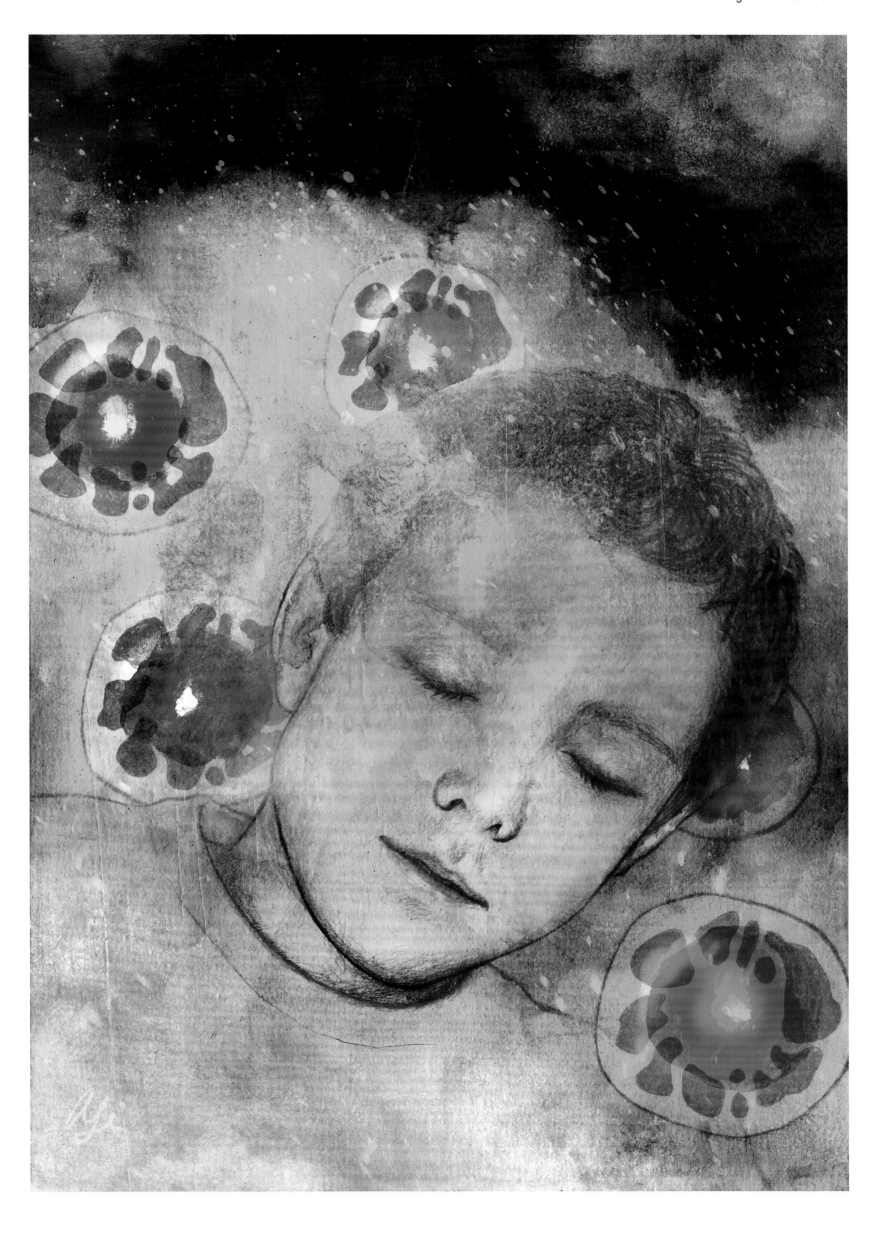

Meagan Hyland
Blips and Chitz
8.27 x 11.69"

What did you want to convey or represent with your art piece?

It's a print of Rick, Morty, and Mr. Poopybutthole enjoying a successful day at the intergalactic video game arcade Blips and Chitz (as seen in season two episode two 'Mortynight Run.') Morty is playing a game that was teased near the end of the episode Roy 2: Dave.

How did the concept come to you? How long did it take to complete?

I love to create fake advertisements for objects and places that only exist within a show's universe so I thought that an ad for Blips and Chitz would be fun to do. The concept came together pretty quickly, so then it was all about ironing out the little details like Morty's expression and what the typography would look like. It took about two weeks on and off to complete.

Can you talk about the storytelling power of the art?

I wanted to show what it would look like to see the Rick and Morty that C-137 Rick and Morty run into at the Jerry Jamboree (the ones who just chilled at Blips and Chitz all day). I wanted to show what their uninterrupted day of fun looked like. And if Mr. Poopybutthole tagged along as well.

What was your process?

I watched a lot of *Rick and Morty*. I find that using references from the show is the best way to capture specific character details like facial expressions and hand movements. I started by sketching on paper with pencil and markers to figure out the layout and what to include before bringing it onto my computer into Adobe Illustrator and playing around with colors and shadows.

What was your favorite part of creating the artwork?

Finding the opportunity to add in a bit of Squanch.

Why do you create art? How would you describe your style in general?

As far back as I can remember, I have always drawn, it's the one thing I do in my life for me. I have a background in graphic design so I always try and find ways to marry my design knowledge into my art by taking something from the subject matter and turning it into an advert or a product that you can hold. Typography would be another thing that is consistent across my work. I can't help but add in a little quote here or there.

How do you see this artwork fitting into the *Rick and Morty* universe?

As a poster used to advertise Blips and Chitz across multiple dimensions in the multiverse.

What else about your piece do you think *Rick and Morty* fans should know?

Mr. Poopybutthole knows that that expression doesn't mean 'Peace among worlds.'

1

2

Above: 1) An early pencils stage plotting out the composition of the piece.
2) A firmer idea of the design is shown here in inks.

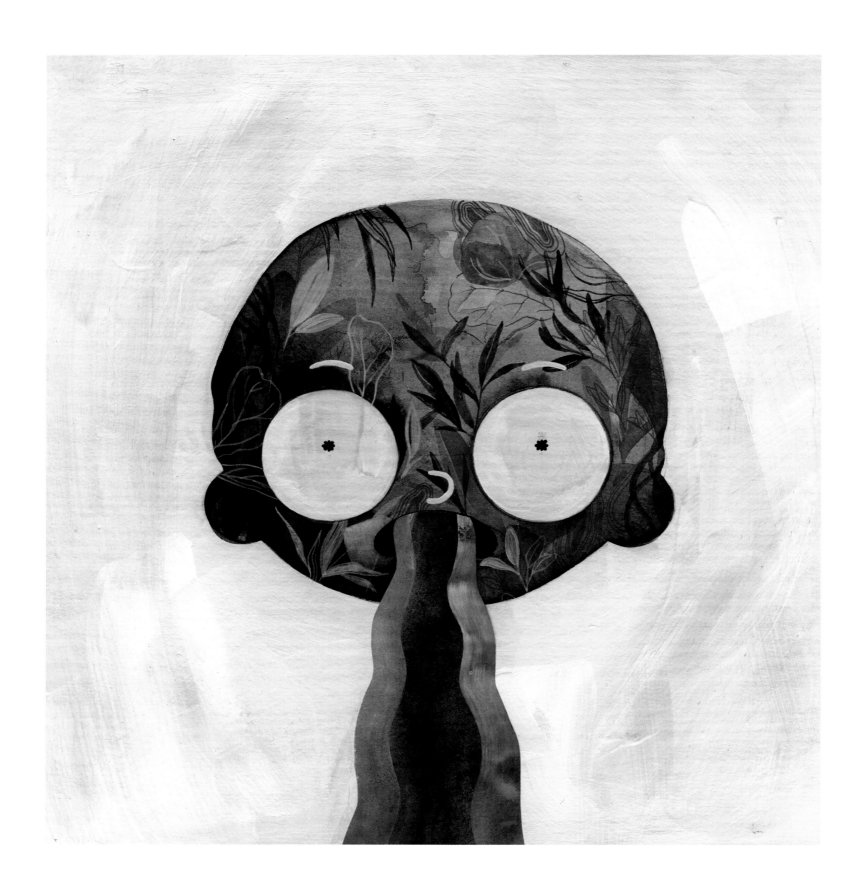

Maggie Chiang
Goodbye Moonmen
10 x 10"

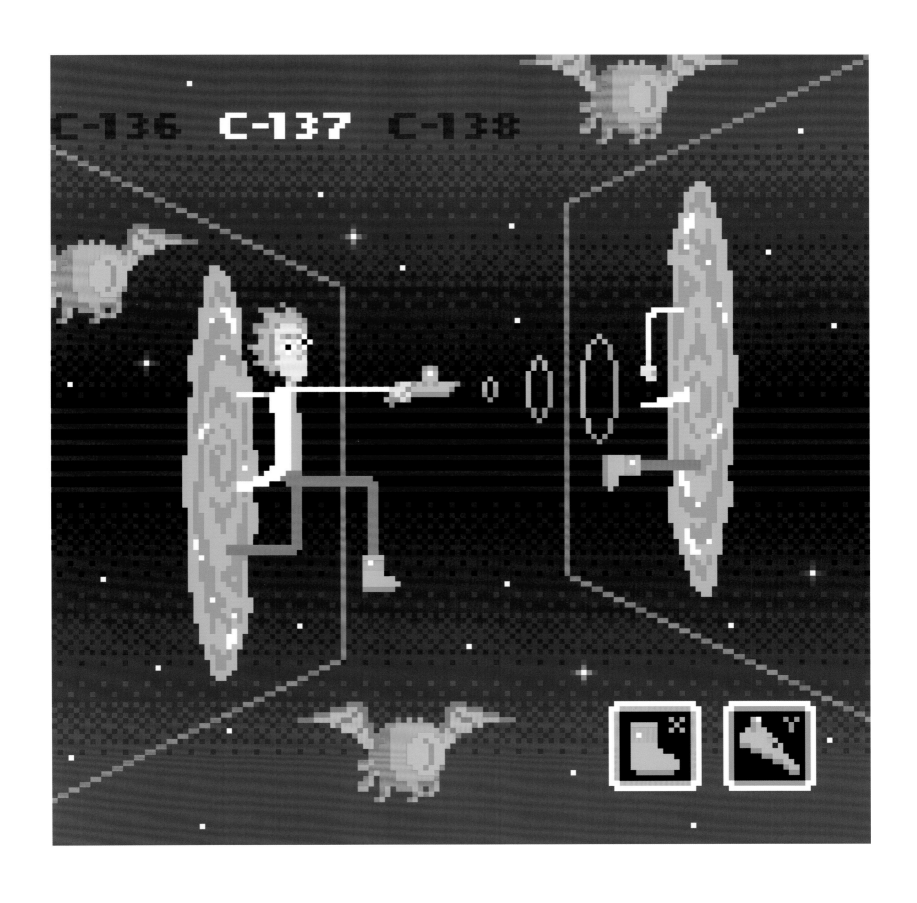

Jude Buffum
C-137
9 x 9"

Cuddly Rigor Mortis

Squanchy
Mr. Meeseeks
Mr. Poopybutthole

7 x 8"

Kristin Tercek has been painting under the name Cuddly Rigor Mortis since 2009. Her family of CRM characters continues to come to life in the form of happy foods, charming botanicals, and animals both real and imagined. Her work has been shown in galleries and museums all over the world from New York City to Los Angeles to Paris to the Disneyland Resort in California. She still can't believe it.

How did *Rick and Morty* inspire me to create these?

Uh, because it's the most awesome show ever. From the first episode, I was hooked. The universe that they created is smart, funny, and thought provoking. All I could do was take a few of my most favorite characters and paint their portraits.

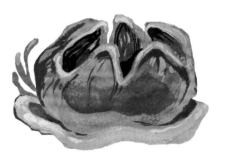

Malisa Suchanya
Moonman Morty
16 x 20"

What did you want to convey or represent with your art piece?

I was inspired by the vast universe that *Rick and Morty* explores. Everything is unforgivably and aggressively existing at the same time, and there is just so much information to take in. I also was inspired by the 'Moonman' song and imagery.

How did the concept come to you? How long did it take to complete?

The concept came rather quickly since I decided to use ideas from a few of my favorite episodes. In 'Total Rickall,' there is an explosion of characters tightly packed into the house and I wanted to recreate that scene, but with characters that are obvious (and some not so obvious) to the *Rick and Morty* universe. This piece took about ten hours to complete.

What excited you most about getting to participate in this exhibition?

I'm just such a huge fan of the show that I couldn't believe I could be a part in creating works in homage to my favorite TV show!!!

What was your favorite part of creating the artwork?

I loved working with an insanely saturated palette and with a large array of characters, it was really fun to try and represent them accurately but with a little hint of my own artistic hand. It was also really great to paint a giant Morty head with a rainbow coming out. It was probably one of my favorite paintings to create!

Why do you create art? How would you describe your style in general?

Art is such an essential part of my existence. I really don't know what I would do if I wasn't pursuing a career in arts or any kind of creative field, to be honest. So I suppose I create art because I see it as one of my main purposes on Earth. My style is pretty whimsical and cute. It can range from something a little more subtle when I work primarily with inks or graphite, but when I'm using colors, I tend to let go and become a lot more playful.

Malisa Suchanya is a Singaporean illustrator and art educator based in San Francisco. Her work focuses on trying to be a reflection to the world, capturing moments that are oftentimes overlooked. Tying in personal experiences, reflections of her environment, and adding a touch of whimsy, her work tends to balance on the tightrope of what is real and what is imagined. Using watercolors, gouache, and graphite as her main mediums, she remain a lover of traditional art in a technological age.

DCAY Design / Sean C. Naylor
Get Riggity-Riggity Wrecked Son
Hand Engraved Stainless Steel Flask

What does your piece convey?

I created a one of a kind, hand engraved flask. It's an item that is just as much a part of Rick as his portal-gun. For the engraving, I decided to use one of my favorite lines from the show.

How did the concept come to you?

For this exhibition, I wanted to create something different than the usual art print. I had previously purchased an engraver with the intent of drawing on metal items, but had not used it up to this point. This exhibition seemed like a great opportunity to try it out.

If you could be in a single episode, which would it be?

I would love to be part of a fake memory in 'Total Rickall.'

Do you have a favorite character and, if so, what do you like most about them?

My favorite characters are always the most obscure. Sometimes just one time joke characters that tend to work their way back into another episode every so often. I'm a big fan of Revolio Clockberg Jr. also known as Gearhead.

What was your process for creating this artwork? How did you prepare to create the piece?

I had never worked with engraving my art before, so I was taking a chance in a very different medium than my other work. I had to practice on small sheets of metal and then a practice flask before I felt ready to create the one for the exhibition.

Why do you create art? How would you describe your style in general?

My art comes from a passion to make things. It might be making a piece that doesn't already exist or putting my own twist on something familiar. For me, if there's no passion behind it, then it's less about art and just becomes work. My style is all over the place. I'm always trying out new looks and testing my capabilities as an artist. I like to add a bit of humor to my work when it fits within the subject or theme.

How is your *Rick and Morty* piece similar to, or different from your other works?

My *Rick and Morty* piece is similar to my other work with the typography aspect. When given the opportunity, I try to implement my own custom type into my art. I thought creating a text-based design would stand out amongst the other pieces in this art show.

What excited you most about getting to participate in this exhibition?

When the exhibition was announced, the show was beginning to blow up. I had just finished watching the first season and became an instant fan. It was very exciting to be asked to be a part of something that was so funny with so much potential. I knew this was a big opportunity.

What else about your piece do you think *Rick and Morty* fans should know?

It's one of a kind!

Howdy. My name is Sean. I'm a graphic designer, illustrator, and all-around creative guy. Born and raised in central Florida (the worst), currently based in southern California (the best!), I create art under the moniker "DCAY." I don't really specialize in one form of art. Whether it's graphic design, hand drawn illustration, digital art, mixed media, or traditional paint on canvas, I like to challenge myself and try new things in my work.

Above: 1) The flask marked up and halfway through engraving.
2) The design for the back of the flask.

Bruce White
Rick Sanchez
11 x 14"

How did the concept come to you? How long did it take to complete?

Originally based on a background image of young Rick with baby Morty. It took maybe ten hours altogether.

Can you talk about the storytelling power of your piece?

Eh... it's a portrait he might have commissioned for himself, or perhaps it was a gift from Birdperson, who understood that giving someone a black velvet painting of themselves was the highest form of flattery on Earth.

What do you appreciate most about the show?

I love this show. I appreciate the realistic characterization of the family dynamic, because most families are fucked up in some way. I also love sci-fi, so this is right up my alley.

What is your favorite Rick and Morty episode?

'The Ricklantis Mixup' is amazing to me because it is so dark.

Do you have a favorite character and, if so, what do you like most about them?

Probably Rick, because he is the smartest man in the universe and also a giant, snarky asshole.

If you could be in a single episode, which would it be?

'Rest and Ricklaxation,' because I am in constant need of a vacation.

Why do you create art? How would you describe your style in general?

I don't know... making art silences the voices in my head. Actually, there is only one voice, which is just mine, and it tells me I am garbage, but having people compliment my work quiets that voice for a few seconds and I can go on a bit longer (is that 'people pleasing?' Probably so).

How has the aesthetic of Rick and Morty informed your piece?

I wanted to do an 'in universe' portrait of Rick on black velvet that he might have hanging in his garage, so I tried to stick close to the animation style of the show.

How is your Rick and Morty piece similar to, or different from your other works?

I usually do more photo realistic portraits, so doing an animated character is a bit more challenging, because they are traditionally so 'flat.' I try to add a bit of depth to the characters.

What excited you most about getting to participate in this exhibition?

That it was an official show, and hopefully it would amuse the creators of the show.

Originating from the swamps of North Carolina, I received my BFA in printmaking from UNC-Chapel Hill in 1995 and started tattooing in 1999. In 2009, I turned to another underappreciated, 'lowbrow' medium: black velvet painting. I feel that working with velvet gives my paintings a degree of visual contrast that cannot be replicated on any other surface. I use this medium to channel my nerdy admiration for many of pop culture's most iconic characters.

Nick Comparone
Jessica and Morty
16 x 20"

What did you want to convey or represent with your art piece?

I wanted to portray the more typical life of Morty as an awkward teenage boy. The outlandish relationship and adventures of he and Rick often overshadow that he is still a daydreaming teenager in love with the popular girl at school. Jessica is no doubt on the move, engaging with Brad or one of her friends in the opposite direction of Morty, left standing there lost in his fantasy world.

What do you appreciate most about the show?

I think the ability to combine an often-adolescent humor with science and philosophy at the level that *Rick and Morty* does is quite fantastic. There are some serious considerations and somber thoughts to be made between the show's fart joke style comedy.

What was your process for creating this artwork? What techniques have you used?

This piece is an eleven-layer stencil and collage on wood panel. After the initial drawing is created, each color is individually hand-cut to create the layers then used to compose the painting. The panel is collaged using various printed materials – patterns, illustrations, and stories – and then coated to be a consistent color. Each stencil, including the black outline, is then spray-painted on to the panel, which is finalized with a brush coat varnish.

What was your favorite part of creating the artwork?

I don't usually paint cartoons, it's not really in my wheelhouse, but once or twice a year something will come up where I'm doing just that. It's refreshing to be reminded that what may seem 'simple' or 'easy' in fact calls for a concentrated precision.

How would you describe your style in general?

My work is almost exclusively portraits. Many of them touch upon the relationship of two characters, portraying them in a single frame. I try to capture in a static image what I believe is the major essence of their relationship or of the character. The medium I use is just my personal way of presenting that.

How has the aesthetic of *Rick and Morty* informed your piece?

I kept to the original presented style of the characters for my piece, in terms of the actual drawing. The almost shaky style, loose line work and colors.

What excited you most about getting to participate in this exhibition?

I think I only partly understood the immense fanbase of *Rick and Morty* when I started this painting. After seeing the turnout and response to this gallery show it was quite exciting to have been able to be involved.

New England born and Pacific Northwest based artist, Nick's work is composed of hand drawn and cut stencils, spray paints, and collage. Giving new life to an overabundance of printed materials, these books, prints, and patterns form the basis of each painting. From layer upon layer of spray paints, the final work emerges in a display of depth and overlaying tones.

Artist Gallery

1. Anthony Petrie
instagram.com/zombiebacons

3. Nan Lawson
instagram.com/nanlawson

2. Jackie Huang
instagram.com/jackiehuangstudios

4. Bryan Brinkman
instagram.com/ryanbrinkerhoff

7. Doug LaRocca
instagram.com/douglaroccaart

9. Ashton Gallagher
instagram.com/ashtongallagher

8. Toddbot
instagram.com/toddbotdotcom

5. Barry Blankenship
instagram.com/barrytheartguy

6. Felix Tindall
instagram.com/f_tindall

10. Scott Listfield
instagram.com/scottlistfield

11. Louie Perez III "LPIII"
instagram.com/louie_perez_3

12. Martina D'Anastasio
instagram.com/sinesenze

13. Jared Circusbear
instagram.com/jaredcircusbear

14. Stephen Andrade

sandradeillustration.com

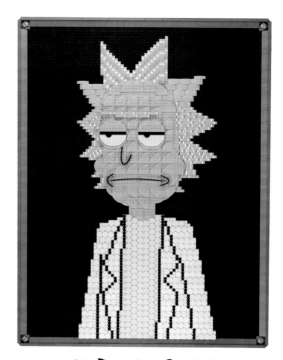

17. Brandon Griffith

instagram.com/brandongriffithart

15. Lawrence Hugh Burns

instagram.com/lawrence.hugh.burns

18. Florian Bertmer

instagram.com/florianbertmer

16. Jeremy Berkley

instagram.com/jeremy.berkley

19. Dan Stiles

instagram.com/danstiles

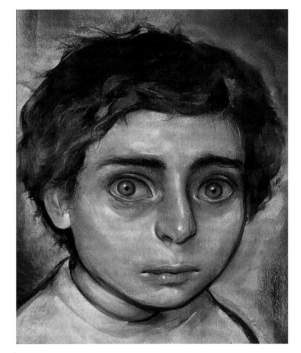

20. Ashly Lovett
instagram.com/ashlylovett

21. Kevin Tiernan
instagram.com/jurassickevin

23. Erin Hunting
instagram.com/erinhunting

22. Dan Mumford
instagram.com/danmumforddraws

24. Stephen Sandoval
instagram.com/artistssandoval

25. Brendon Flynn
instagram.com/b.flynn.art

28. Elisa Wikey
instagram.com/elisawikeydrawsthings

26. Sara Richard
instagram.com/sararichardart

29. Justine "Steen" Pulles
instagram.com/artworkbysteen

27. Joey Spiotto
instagram.com/jo3bot

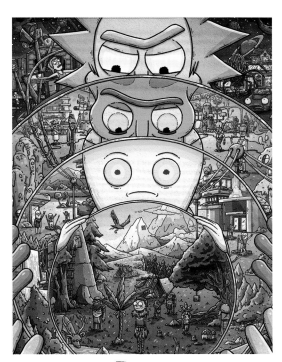

30. Taylor Rose
instagram.com/taylorrosemakesart

31. JellyKoe

instagram.com/jellykoe

32. Michelle Hiraishi

instagram.com/_mhiraishi

34. Lawrence Yang

instagram.com/lawrenceyangart

33. Oh Sew Nerdy

instagram.com/ohsewnerdy

35. Bennett Slater

instagram.com/bennett_slater

38. Chris McGuire

instagram.com/chris_mc_guire

36. Jessica Edwards

instagram.com/jessievirginia

39. Derek Deal

instagram.com/derekdeal

37. Studiohouse Designs

instagram.com/studiohousedesigns

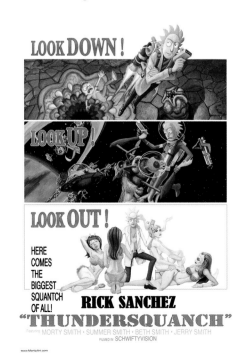

40. Jason Chalker

instagram.com/manlyart

41. 100% Soft

instagram.com/100soft

43. Mark Borgions

instagram.com/handmade_monster

42. Taylor Blue

instagram.com/taylor_blue_art

44. Alexander Wells

instagram.com/alexanderwells

45. Ridge Rooms

instagram.com/ridgerooms

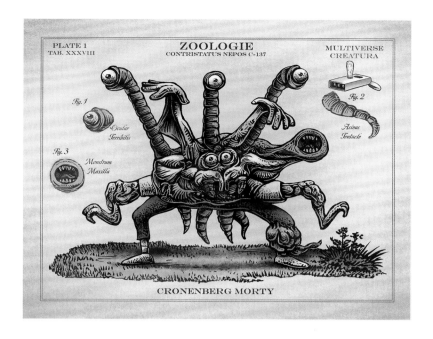

46. Chet Phillips
instagram.com/instachetart

47. Andy Stattmiller
instagram.com/astatt

49. Kelly Vivanco
instagram.com/verpabunny

48. Mike Bliz
instagram.com/mikebilzart

50. Nate Bear
instagram.com/bearbrains

51. Matthew Rabalais
instagram.com/rabalaisart

54. Erin Gallagher
instagram.com/erinillustrates

52. Shane Lewis
instagram.com/shanelewisart

55. Ryan Brinkerhoff
instagram.com/brinkmanatee

53. Jesse Riggle
instagram.com/jessealso

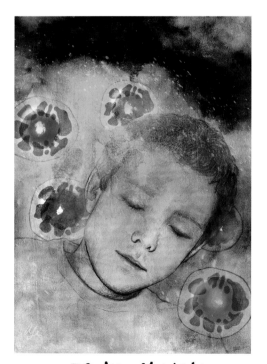

56. Alice Meichi Li
instagram.com/alicemeichi

OXFORD
UNIVERSITY PRESS

Complete
English
Literature
for Cambridge IGCSE®

Mark Pedroz

Oxford excellence for Cambridge IGCSE®

OXFORD

OXFORD
UNIVERSITY PRESS

Great Clarendon Street, Oxford, OX2 6DP, United Kingdom

Oxford University Press is a department of the University of Oxford. It furthers the University's objective of excellence in research, scholarship, and education by publishing worldwide. Oxford is a registered trade mark of Oxford University Press in the UK and in certain other countries

© Oxford University Press 2014

The moral rights of the authors have been asserted

First published in 2014

British Library Cataloguing in Publication Data
Data available

978-0-19-839932-2

10 9 8 7 6 5 4 3 2

Paper used in the production of this book is a natural, recyclable product made from wood grown in sustainable forests. The manufacturing process conforms to the environmental regulations of the country of origin.

Printed in Great Britain by CPI Group (UK) Ltd., Croydon CR0 4YY

Acknowledgements

® IGCSE is the registered trademark of Cambridge International Examinations.

The publisher would like to thank Cambridge International Examinations for their kind permission to reproduce the past paper questions. All other questions and all example answers, marks awarded and comments that appear in this book were written by the author. In examination, the way marks would be awarded to answers like these may be different. Cambridge International Examinations bears no responsibility for the example answers to test-style questions which are contained in this publication.

The publishers would like to thank the following for permissions to use their photographs:

Cover image: Shutterstock.com

p2: Madredus/Shutterstock; **p3:** Photodisc/OUP; **p4:** Alastair Muir/ Rex Features; **p5:** Image dj/Alamy; **p6:** Hill Street Studios/Glow Images; **p7:** Robbie Jack/Crobis; **p7a:** Superstock/Superstock; **p7b:** Ramin Talaie/Corbis; **p7c:** Alvin Langdon Coburn/Archive Photos/ Getty Images; **p7d:** Dylan Martinez/Reuters; **p8:** Alasair Muir/ Rex Features; **p13:** Superstock/Glow Images; **p14:** Bob MacCallum; **p15a:** Simon Annand/AP Images; **p15b:** Bettmann/Corbis; **p16:** C.Miramax/Everett/Rex Features; **p18:** Snap Stills/Rex Features; **p21a:** E.O Hoppe/Corbis; **p21b:** Archive Photos/ Warner Brothers/ Moviepix/ Getty Images; **p24:** Oleg Popov; **p25:** Tony Larkin/Rex Features; **p31:** Macmullan Co/SIPA/AP Images; **p32:** King's Own Royal Regiment; **p33:** Bettmann/Corbis; **p37a:** Frans Lanting/Mint Images/Glow images; **p37b:** British Library/Robana/Rex Features; **p37c:** Wordsworth Editions Ltd; **p37d:** The Random House Group Limited; **p37e:** Rex Features; **p39:** General Photographic Agency/ Hulton Archive/Getty Images; **p41:** Guy Bouchet/Photo Non Stop/ Glow Images; **p42:** EWA Stock/Glow Images; **p43:** Dustin Dennis/ Shutterstock; **p44:** CSA Images/Vetta/Getty Images; **p45:** Sici/The Irish Image Collection; **p46:** DWD-Media/Alamy; **p50a:** Vladis Chern/Shutterstock; **p50b:** Robodread/Shutterstock; **p51:** Czesnak Zsolt/Shutterstock; **p55a:** John Gilbert/The Bridgeman Art Library/ Getty Images; **p55b:** Onslow Auctions Limited/Mary Evans Picture Library; **p56:** New Homes/Britain on View/Getty Images; **p59:** Hulton Archive/Stringer/Getty Images; **p67:** Carl Mydans/Time and Life Pictures/Getty Images; **p72:** Pure Stock/Superstock; **p73:** Wim Claes/Shutterstock; **p77a:** British Library/Robana/Hulton Fine Art Collection/ Getty Images; **p77b:** Rex Features; **p80a:** Snap/ Rex Features; **p80b:** Moviestore Collection/Rex Features; **p82:** Moviestore Collection/Rex Features; **p83:** C.Sony Pics/Everett/ Rex Features; **p88:** Glow Images; **p95:** Chris Mellor/Lonely Planet/ Getty Images; **p101:** Michele Bella/Cubo Images/Glow Images; **p102a:** Moviestore Collection/Rex Features; **p102b:** Moviestore Collection/Rex Features; **p103:** Marilyn Volan/Shutterstock; **p107:** ITV/Rex Features; **p111:** Geraint Lewis/Rex Features; **p120:** 20th Century Fox/Everett/Rex Features; **p127:** ITV/Rex Features; **p133:** Snap Stills/Rex Features; **p139:** Geraint Lewis/Rex Features; **p143:** Popperfoto/Getty images; **p146:** Donald Cooper/ Rex Features; **p148:** Jupiter Images/ Stockbyte/Getty Images; **p149:** Historical/ Glow Images; **p150:** Ttphoto/Shutterstock; **p155:** Bettmann/Corbis; **p160:** Everett Collection/Rex Features; **p162:** Everett Collection/ Rex Features; **p164:** The Print Collector/ Heritage Images/Glow Images; **p169:** ITV/Rex Features; **p175:** Heritage Images/Corbis; **p181:** Daniel Farson/Picture Post/Getty Images; **p186:** Everett Collection/Rex Features; **p192:** Ann Ronan Pictures/Heritage Images/ Glow Images; **p196:** Bettmann/Corbis; **p200:** Visage/Stockbyte/Getty Images; **p201:** PhotosIndia.com/ Uniquely India/Glow Images; **p203:** Hulton-Deutsch Collection/ Corbis; **p205:** Baker Alhashki/Shutterstock; **p208:** Arno Depta/ Pantherstock; **p212:** Olies/Shutterstock; **p214:** Bjorn Wittek/ Panther Media; **p216:** Snap Stills/Rex Features; **p218:** Ann Ronan Pictures/Heritage Images/Glow Images; **p222:** Vidler Steve/Prisma RM/Glow Images; **p226:** Mark Davidson/Alamy; Back Cover: Fox Search/Everett/Rex Features

Artwork by Q2A Media and Phoenix Photosetting

The authors and publisher are grateful for permission to reprint extracts from the following copyright material:

W. H. Auden: "On This Island', from *Collected Poems*, copyright © 1936 by W. H. Auden (renewed 1965), reprinted by permission of Curtis Brown Ltd and Random House, an imprint and division of Random House LLC, all rights reserved.

Alan Ayckbourn: excerpt from *A Small Family Business*, 1987, © Alan Ayckbourn, published by Samuel French Ltd, reprinted by permission of Faber and Faber Ltd.

Alan Bennett: excerpts from *The History Boys*, 2004 © Alan Bennett, reprinted by permission of Faber and Faber Ltd and United Agents.

Sujata Bhatt: 'A Different History' from *Brunizem*, reprinted by permission of Carcanet Press Ltd.

Bruce Chatwin: excerpt from *In Patagonia*, copyright © 1977 by Bruce Chatwin, published by Jonathan Cape, reprinted by permission of The Random House Group Limited and Simon Publishing Group, all rights reserved.

Boey Kim Cheng: 'The Planners' from *Another Place*, published by Time Books, 1992, reprinted by permission of Marshall Cavendish.

Continued on back page.

Contents

 Website Unit 1: Extending your critical skills

Extended essay writing

Reading unseen texts

 Website Unit 2: Revision

**Access your support website at:
www.oxfordsecondary.com/9780198399322**

What's on the website?

English Literature for Cambridge IGCSE® is supported by a website packed full of additional material specially written to support your learning. Everything in the book and on the website has been designed to help you develop your skills and achieve your very best.

Extra chapters

Two extra units designed to stretch your skills and approach assessment with confidence. Unit 1 is an extension unit which tackles unseen texts and extended essay writing. Unit 2 has lots of revision advice to use as you prepare for assessment.

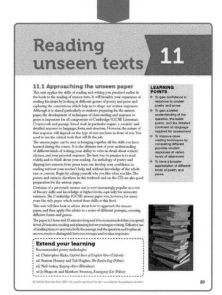

Glossary

A comprehensive revision tool that unpacks the vocabulary and carefully explains tricky terms.

Worksheets

A wide range of activities to cement your understanding and develop your close reading skills. Some relate to specific texts but many can be used to analyse any text you study.

Extracts

Printable copies of all the text extracts in the book for you to annotate.

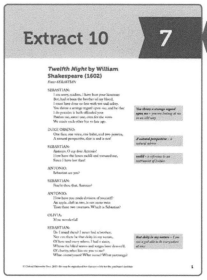

Exam-style questions

These questions, written in the style of exam questions, will help you develop all the skills you need.

Setting off as a literature student

Introduction

Congratulations. You have just begun a voyage of discovery as you begin your **Cambridge IGCSE Literature** course. Up to now you have probably studied a single subject called 'English' or 'literacy' and you have developed your skills in reading (both for specific purposes and for pleasure), writing, speaking, and listening. Your Cambridge IGCSE studies will continue to develop all of those skills, but in order to prepare you for the challenges of further study, you are now likely to be studying for two subjects, 'Language' and '**Literature**'.

This handbook will help you to prepare for Cambridge IGCSE Literature by developing your skills in the **close reading** of different kinds of fictional text and improving your critical writing. It cannot replace the preparation of the set texts that you will work on with your teacher, but it gives you examples of how to improve your response to literature and develop your skills to higher levels. You will be introduced to texts in the three genres of drama, prose, and poetry and to ways of analysing them and writing about them. There will be plenty of activity-based learning, with suggestions of activities you can try, in pairs and in groups, in order to develop your understanding, and there will be a range of extension tasks, both in the book and on the website, for further study and revision work.

How to use this book

The first three units are introductory and build on what you already know about English, working on your reading and writing skills and developing your understanding of how literature texts work. Students and teachers can use different parts of this unit at early stages of the course in order to develop appreciation of genre, structure, and form. There is also an introduction to texts in their historical and cultural contexts.

Unit 4 is central to the course. It explores ways of studying and interpreting set texts through more detailed analysis of the conventions of each genre. Examples are drawn from some of the Cambridge IGCSE set texts, from past or future syllabuses.

KEY TERMS

Cambridge IGCSE Literature = this textbook prepares you for Cambridge IGCSE Literature (English) 0486. It also teaches skills useful for other Cambridge IGCSE qualifications.

literature = writing across the genres of poetry, prose, and drama. Not all literature needs to be fiction. Literature texts are those in which language and the imagination play an especially important role.

close reading = analysis of the words and effects writers use and how they make an impact on their readers.

The website includes two additional units. The first is an extension unit. It further develops your ability through more challenging coursework tasks, revision activities, and a whole chapter on the unseen paper, using past questions to develop an understanding of genre, form, and style.

The second unit on the website is a final revision unit with exam-style questions and suggestions about how to answer them, revision advice, and tips for developing exam technique.

 The website includes two units to allow you to extend your learning.

Activity-based learning

This will follow the principles of **assessment for learning** by encouraging a range of self-directed activities for students, allowing you to explore the meaning of texts, and work creatively to develop personal responses to the language and ideas used by writers. Each unit includes activities under the following headings.

LEARNING POINTS

These set out the objectives for each unit, chapter or section. They provide a clear definition of what you will be learning and which skills you will be practising.

Think ahead

These are activities that explore the world of the text, involving research into culture and background, genre and convention, ideas and themes, and the relationship between a text and its context. They will encourage you to engage with the world of the text before looking in detail at the words.

✎ Check your understanding

These questions aim to achieve basic understanding of how the text works. They can be used as written activities or opportunities for whole-class discussion.

💬 Pair and share

These are opportunities to discuss your response to a text with a partner or as part of a group. They are intended to extend and develop your understanding. You may find that different views and opinions are also possible!

Viewpoints

These are more extended activities in groups, which allow the development of personal response through drama, debate, and structured discussion. Working together to make meaning from texts, you should be able to develop your understanding of how characters and situations are presented by the writers.

Extend your learning

These activities go beyond the surface to explore ideas and attitudes through language, and encourage you to look back on your reading with deeper understanding of words, the writer's choices, and their effect on the reader.

Language links

Through both reading and writing activities there will be opportunities to link your literature work with the skills you are developing in your English language course. There will also be opportunities to write creatively in response to what you have read.

Looking back

You will be encouraged to check what you have learned and to assess the ways in which you have developed your skills as a student of literature by reviewing what you have learned in the current unit and how it builds on skills you have learned earlier in the course.

Practice questions

These questions follow a format similar to those used by Cambridge IGCSE Literature exams, with advice on how to improve your answers. Some questions are identified as past paper questions from the Cambridge IGCSE. All other questions have been written by the author. You will find some 'student-style responses', with helpful comments on their strengths and weaknesses.

Throughout this handbook you will find additional information, and suggestions in boxes on the right-hand side of the page including advice about how to plan and time your answers and glossary terms.

Where this icon occurs, there will be an opportunity to extend activities by referring to the website for text extracts, more worksheets, and more exam-style questions. These will help you to practise your essay writing skills and demonstrate your understanding of the texts.

Individual responsibility for your learning and the development of your ideas will be emphasized throughout: this book will not tell you the answers but it will help you to ask yourself the right questions.

What is literature?

1.1 The Cambridge syllabus

Literature has been described as the best that has been thought and said. Above all the Cambridge syllabus has the aim of encouraging you to 'enjoy the experience of reading literature'. Literature texts have often stood the test of time. They appeal to very different cultures. At university, the study of literature allows you to study a huge range of texts and explore different ways of reading them. At school, your teachers will introduce you to various texts, some chosen by them and others set for examination, in order to introduce the key skills for success in this subject. These are:

- close reading—analysing the effects that writers use in order to make an impact on their readers
- reading in depth—tackling substantial whole texts in order to look at meaning beyond the surface narrative
- writing critically—exploring and evaluating a range of ideas and opinions, and coming to conclusions of your own about them
- writing discursively—learning to argue, finding evidence to support your views, and making an informed personal response to a text.

While language study teaches you a range of practical skills, literature study is more theoretical. Assessment focuses on the way in which students communicate their own response to texts through their essays. Studying literature teaches you to be sensitive to different people and what interests them, to be alert to the ways in which writers express themselves, and to ensure that your own ideas are well supported by close observation of language and form. These are all transferable skills and will be useful to you in your future studies.

LEARNING POINTS
- ▶ To understand the nature of literature as a subject
- ▶ To appreciate the Cambridge IGCSE syllabus assessment objectives

Literature assessment objectives

Now have a look at the assessment objectives (AOs) for the literature course.

AO1   Show detailed knowledge of the content of literary texts in the three main forms (drama, poetry, and prose).

AO2   Understand the meanings of literary texts and their contexts, and explore texts beyond surface meanings to show deeper awareness of

ideas and attitudes.

AO3   Recognise and appreciate ways in which writers use language, structure and form to create and shape meanings and effects.

AO4   Communicate a sensitive and informed personal response to literary texts.

Clearly all these objectives ask you to take a responsible and responsive approach to the reading you are asked to do. You will need to read and think about the books! However, for your understanding to go **beyond the surface** and for your **personal response** to be truly sensitive to the text you will need further qualities. They are:

- confidence in tackling the writer's use of language and ideas
- engagement in the close reading and interpretation of a text
- an innovative and individual approach—your own response should be both truly personal and relevant to the question.

It is the purpose of this book to encourage those further skills, so that your response becomes personal, developed, and critical.

Thinking about assessment

Your teachers will set you various tasks to test your knowledge and understanding of your literature texts. Throughout this book and on the website you will find practice essay questions, in the style of the Cambridge IGCSE but written by the author. You will also find some examples of past Cambridge IGCSE questions. Initially, you will be given plenty of help in structuring and answering practice questions though bullet points and essay plans. Chapters 5, 6 10 and 12 give guidance on how to make your essays more sophisticated.

Throughout the textbook, you are encouraged to assess your own work and those of others, as well as working with your teachers to improve your grades. You will not be achieving high marks right away but you should see yourself improving throughout the course.

> **KEY TERMS**
>
> **beyond the surface** = going beyond the dictionary definition (denotation) of words to explore their deeper connection with the reader (connotations).
>
> **personal response** = your own individual reaction to the text.

Structure of the course

There are three different ways to study the Cambridge IGCSE Literature syllabus, depending on the choice of final examination made by your teachers.

All students do Component 1 (1 hour 30 minutes) and have to answer questions on both a poetry and a prose text. You have a choice of passage-based questions or whole-text essay questions. You cannot take your texts into the examination, but passages and the poems referred to in the questions will be printed on the examination paper.

You then have a choice of:

- Component 2 (1 hour 30 minutes) with two questions on two drama texts (you may not take your text into the exam)
- Component 3 (45 minutes) with one question on one chosen drama text (you may take your text into the examination) plus Component 4 (1 hour and 15 minutes) with one question on a short text of poetry or prose you have not prepared (referred to as unseen)
- Component 3 (drama as above) plus Component 5 (a portfolio of two **coursework** essays).

You can see that all of these exams require close and detailed study of drama, poetry, and prose. The first requirement of the course is to achieve an understanding of the different demands of each of the three genres.

Understanding genre

Literature began with poetry. These were songs and stories recited by bards or storytellers around the fire in ancient days which then became written texts. They were composed in a form of verse to make them easier to remember: lines have set patterns of rhythm and sound.

Lyrics (songs based around emotional experiences) and epics (longer narrative or story) were the first poems to become established as parts of world literature. Before long, actors supplemented the recitals of bards, whether by adopting the parts of characters (called personae or more literally 'masks', as most early drama involved the wearing of masks) or by forming part of a chorus. This was the beginning of drama. Early drama was often in verse too: it helped the actors to remember their parts through structures of rhythm, repetition, and sound effect. Actors wore different masks for the different forms of tragedy and comedy.

However, sometimes both drama and stories were told in prose, keeping more closely to the language, rhythms, and rules of everyday speech.

✎ Check your understanding

Draw up three columns headed prose, poetry, and drama in your exercise book or on paper. Think about the texts you have already studied or know about. Which column do they belong in?

Note: Texts chosen for study in this syllabus must have been originally written in English. Cambridge offer another syllabus called 'World Literature' which includes texts in translation.

How did English literature develop?

It is worth knowing that English literature is not really very old: the language itself comes from a fusion of the languages of the Anglo-Saxons and the Norman French, both heavily influenced by the Viking Norse, and really only becomes recognizable as English from about 1200 CE. The form of the novel is even more recent (indeed the name means 'new'), as prose only became the most common genre for writing a narrative from around 1700 CE. It was the process of colonization and trade during the following years which established English as such a dominant world language: readers of English took their literature all over the world, and the world contributed its stories to what we now call 'English'. This course book will take an international approach to our appreciation of literature, appropriate to Cambridge IGCSE which is studied all over the globe.

The poet Ezra Pound said that 'Literature is news that stays news', in other words it comes out of the society that produced it and always begins as something novel, but over time different readers agree that there is still plenty to learn and understand in these texts long after they have been written. Literature scholars talk about a canon of texts which have remained a part of current thought or culture, and which students might expect to study. However, the texts which make up that canon keep changing, and they probably tell us more about the society we live in than the society that originally produced those texts.

When Shakespeare, for example, wrote his plays (although not his poems) he was probably more concerned about filling the theatres of which he was a shareholder. He probably did not imagine he was writing texts which would become canonical. He seems to have been fairly careless about how his plays were written down. Others collected his plays and studied them after his death. Many modern writers have rather mixed feelings about finding their works on school syllabuses, especially while they are still alive and writing!

English literature moved around the globe and now includes work from writers such as the Indian novelist Anita Desai

First collection of Shakespeare's works

 **Pair and share**

With a partner create a mind map to explore what you understand by the study of 'English'. How does it divide into studies in language and literature? How do we decide the skills we need to demonstrate and develop in each? What makes up a syllabus for each subject? How did English get a 'literature'? Which books have you read which you would call 'literature'?

'Literature is news that stays news.'
Ezra Pound

1.2 How do modern writers see the craft of writing?

Digital communication is rapidly changing the way we think about writing and literature, and you might want to think about what 'English literature' will look like at the end of the twenty-first century.

However, for an example of the ways in which writers saw the craft of literature in the twentieth century, there are few better examples than the poem which follows by Seamus Heaney called 'Digging', which headed his first published volume of poetry in 1966.

Many readers find poetry quite difficult at first. Remember that poetry comes out of song, and needs to be read, or at least 'heard' aloud. Listen for the sounds and 'music' of the poem and reflect on what it makes you feel. A famous poet said that 'poetry communicates before it is understood'. A second reading can push your understanding further: focus on the images, or pictures, the poet creates and how they tell a story.

In this poem the poet tells us that his father is a farmer, seen here planting potatoes, and his grandfather used to cut 'turfs', squares of peat used for heating. Both are traditional activities in the countryside of Ireland. The poet, however, has returned from university and wants to live a life as a writer (he later won the Nobel Prize for Literature).

'Digging' by Seamus Heaney (1966)

Between my finger and my thumb
The squat pen rests; snug as a gun.

Under my window, a clean rasping sound
When the spade sinks into gravelly ground:
My father, digging. I look down

Till his straining rump among the flowerbeds
Bends low, comes up twenty years away
Stooping in rhythm through potato drills
Where he was digging.

The coarse boot nestled on the lug, the shaft
Against the inside knee was levered firmly.
He rooted out all tops, buried the bright edge deep
To scatter new potatoes that we picked
Loving their cool hardness in our hands.

By God, the old man could handle a spade.
Just like his old man.

My grandfather cut more turf in a day
Than any other man on Toner's bog.
Once I carried him milk in a bottle
Corked sloppily with paper. He straightened up
To drink it, then fell to right away
Nicking and slicing neatly, heaving sods
Over his shoulder, going down and down
For the good turf. Digging.

The cold smell of potato mould, the squelch and slap
Of soggy peat, the curt cuts of an edge
Through living roots awaken in my head.
But I've no spade to follow men like them.

Between my finger and my thumb
the squat pen rests.
I'll dig with it.

✏. Check your understanding

1. The poet uses a lot of hard or harsh sounds. List as many words as you can find that sound harsh. Why do these sounds suit the masculine activity of digging?

2. The poem is made up of a series of images, beginning with the poet looking out of his window then working back through his memory, through family legends, and stories. The poem tells a story across three generations. Organize your notes chronologically to explain:

   a. what the poet sees now

   b. how his father worked 20 years before

   c. how his grandfather worked before that.

3. Clearly what the poet is going to do is very different, but he tells us that he will 'dig' with his pen. In what ways might writing poetry be similar to digging? Think about the regular rhythms of work, the hard effort, and finding or planting something precious. How does the poet justify his choice of work?

4. When the poet talks about 'living roots' he is perhaps describing the stories of his family, as well as digging through the soil. How has his writing helped to convey those roots to you?

5. The end of the poem is very similar to the start, but it is also different. Why do you think the image of a spade has replaced that of a gun? Write down the effect of that change on you. This will help you to evaluate or interpret the poem.

💬 Pair and share

How can we turn the poem into a drama? Form a group of three: poet, father, and grandfather. The father and grandfather are worried about what the boy will do with his life after university. What are the questions they have? Why doesn't he want to be a farmer or dig for peat turfs? Discuss the ways in which they might argue or interact.

When writing a script, remember that audiences need to be introduced to each character and their interests. (It helps to give them a name!) It is often easier to start a scene with just two characters and then introduce a third. Give characters some longer speeches in order to explain their points of view and show them telling stories or passing on memories.

Perform your scene to your classmates. Has writing and performing the poem as drama helped you to understand it better? Has it developed your own understanding of the characters, or has it made the poem less intimate and personal?

Extend your learning

Now try turning the poem into a novel. Will you tell the story in the first person or the third person? First try drafting the boy's diary, showing us his ideas as he thinks them through.

This probably does not look very different from the poem. Do you still have a strong sense of the characters and the realism of the situation which you created in your play?

You need to capture the drama of the moment when the boy tells his family what he intends to do, and, like in the play, you may want to use dialogue. However, a novel needs description to capture the realism of the moment and it needs to get inside the minds of the central characters and communicate some of their thoughts. You can do this in the third person just as effectively as in the first person, so now use the third person to give the young writer's thoughts: a novel does not need to sound like a diary.

Re-write your diary or journal entry as a novel, in the third person, but giving the thoughts as well as the spoken words of the characters.

What have you discovered about how prose communicates? How is it different from drama?

⊘ Language links

Heaney uses the **extended metaphor** of digging to pay homage to what his father and grandfather did and to explore what he will do in his adult life. He makes his poem out of a slide show of images or pictures which are briefly but memorably described.

Do you have an idea of the activity that will define your future life? If you don't, perhaps looking at what your ancestors did will help you to think about this, even if it is your intention to rebel against their model, just as Heaney does, and explore a different kind of life.

Use Heaney's style of writing which does not need a set and regular pattern of rhyme or rhythm to write a poem of your own, based on a sequence of images. You might like to illustrate your poem with images. Think about the ways in which sound effects, the contrast of long and short lines, and different kinds of punctuation (pauses) can make your writing more memorable.

Compare your ideas with a friend. Concentrate on the lines which your partner agrees work best. Your poem does not need to be very long, provided it works.

1.3 Making meaning

We now live in a global culture. Not only do sons choose very different lives from their fathers, but English has become a world language, spoken by over a quarter of the world's population. That means it is not always easy to understand one another. Reading literature is about the art of **interpretation**, making sense and meaning out of the language of others. This is a very useful skill, but it isn't always easy, and in our diverse world, people don't always understand one another.

Look at this extract from a short story written by R.K. Narayan in 1970. 'A Horse and Two Goats' describes an encounter between a very old, very poor Indian man called Muni and a rich American. Muni only has two words of English, 'yes' and 'no', and so doesn't realize that the American wants to buy the statue of a horse which he is sitting under. Indeed Muni thinks he may want to question him about a murder. Muni is speaking Tamil in reply to the American's English.

'A Horse and Two Goats' by R.K. Narayan (1970)

Muni felt totally confused but decided the best thing would be to make an attempt to get away from this place. He tried to edge out, saying, 'Must go home,' and turned to go. The other seized his shoulder and said desperately, 'Is there no one, absolutely no one here, to translate for me?' He looked up and down the road, which was deserted in this hot afternoon; a sudden gust of wind churned up the dust and dead leaves on the roadside into a ghostly column and propelled it towards the mountain road. The stranger almost pinioned Muni's back to the statue and asked, 'Isn't this statue yours? Why don't you sell it to me?'

The old man now understood the reference to the horse, thought for a second, and said in his own language, 'I was an urchin this high when I heard my grandfather explain this horse and warrior, and my grandfather himself was this high when he heard his grandfather, whose grandfather...'

The other man interrupted him with, 'I don't want to seem to have stopped here for nothing. I will offer you a good price for this,' he said, indicating the horse. He had concluded without the least doubt that Muni owned this mud horse. Perhaps he guessed by the way he sat at its pedestal, like other souvenir-sellers in this country presiding over their wares.

Muni followed the man's eyes and pointing fingers and dimly understood the subject matter and, feeling relieved that the theme of the mutilated body had been abandoned at least for the time being, said again, enthusiastically, 'I was this high when my grandfather told me about this horse and the warrior, and my grandfather was this high when he himself…' and he was getting into a deeper bog of reminiscence each time he tried to indicate the antiquity of the statue.

The Tamil that Muni spoke was stimulating even as pure sound, and the foreigner listened with fascination. 'I wish I had my tape-recorder here,' he said, assuming the pleasantest expression. 'Your language sounds wonderful. I get a kick out of every word you utter, here' – he indicated his ears – 'but you don't have to waste your breath in sales talk. I appreciate the article. You don't have to explain its points.'

✏ Check your understanding

1. List the words which suggest how frustrated the American is by his inability to understand Muni.

2. Which words tell you how isolated this place is?

3. What is the importance of the horse to Muni?

4. What sort of value does the American place on the horse?

5. What does the American like about Muni's language?

6. What does he fail to understand?

The American cannot appreciate that Muni does not own the mud horse, or that it is part of a very old culture which he does not understand, even though he does respond to its beauty (and wants to take it home). For the American, everything has a price, and it is a price which will be welcome to Muni as he is very poor, although Muni thinks the American is offering him a hundred rupees for his two goats.

As the story goes on, Muni tries to explain that the horse represents 'Kalki' who will come at the end of the world to trample down bad men, and then tells stories about god, avatars, and the plays he used to take part in. The American gets out a large wad of money.

You can see that the meaning of the story goes beyond a language barrier. The American does not just fail to understand the literal meaning of Muni's words but he also can't imagine the values and traditions of a culture much older than his own. These are also 'lost in translation' and there is no one there to interpret them to him. As a reader, we see that making meaning is about interpretation at a deeper level; we need to go beyond literal meanings and understand the kind of world a story comes from, or tells us about. The meaning of an object or a text needs to be connected to the community and culture that produced it.

Pair and share

Cultural understanding is often about values and traditions, not just about money or the acquisition of knowledge.

1. What does your own culture value especially highly?

2. Are there stories you know which support those values?

3. Which myths and traditions should visitors be aware of in order to understand your culture?

Extend your understanding

Different generations and different cultures have different ideas of values and traditions. How do stories preserve traditions for future generations? Write a review of a play you have seen or a story you have read that has told you something about the values and culture of the past. Try to answer the following questions.

1. Who was the story about?

2. What were the values or ideas which it presented?

3. How did it make you think about them?

4. What was the impact of the story on you and what do you remember best about it?

You will now see that interpreting the language and meaning of a story is about understanding ideas and attitudes as well as words.

Looking back

Do you now feel that you have a better idea of what a literature course involves? Here are some questions and activities for you to discuss and write about.

1. Give your own definition of the subject you are studying and its different parts. Explain the kind of literature you most enjoy and why. Remember your teachers may have different ideas about what they want you to study!

2. What are the skills that teachers are looking to reward in this subject?

3. How do poetry, prose and drama differ in form and effect? Which is the most private form and which the most public? Which is the most concentrated and which did you find easiest to write?

4. How does interpretation relate to the meaning of a text? What is meant by going beyond the literal meaning?

5. Why is cultural understanding important alongside an appreciation of language if we are to appreciate literature?

You are now ready to progress to the second unit, where we will explore the skills of reading across these three genres in more detail.

Developing reading skills

Unit 2

The forms of literature

The next two units are designed as an introduction before you begin the detailed study of your set texts. They introduce the features of the three genres you will be studying. They explore ways of linking texts through their structure and choice of subject in order to develop a critical and comparative response to literature.

We will look at the choices writers make about the form and structure of their texts, addressing assessment objective 3. We will explore comedy, the short story, and war poetry.

The texts chosen will introduce you to some short texts from the past, showing some of the traditions of literature in English. You will not need to read these texts in the same close detail as you will your set texts (although some of the texts used here could be your set texts) but by exploring form and structure you will appreciate some of the history and traditions of each genre, while also moving forward in time to consider more contemporary texts.

In this unit, we want you to understand the conventions and forms of texts. This approach to the structure of texts should help you to look at plot and character in new ways. You will also begin to practise close reading and ways of making your response both personal and informed. Units 3 and 4 will develop these skills further.

LEARNING POINTS
- To explore in more depth and understand the ways in which readers respond to the three genres of drama, prose, and poetry
- To appreciate ways in which language, structure, and form shape our response
- To begin to identify writer's effects
- To appreciate how texts are influenced by culture and historical context.

Reading drama

How did drama evolve?

As we saw in chapter 1, ancient literature consisted of lyrical and epic poetry, recited out loud. **Lyrical** poetry was usually like a song with a single speaking voice, expressing emotions, and accompanied by a stringed instrument, like a lyre. **Epic** poetry told

Masked Greek chorus

long stories about the gods and men, with many adventures, battles, and confrontations. There were lots of characters making speeches and many changes of scene or situation, so the poems were divided into books.

Drama emerged out of epic poetry: a theatre audience wanted to hear more about the characters and their stories, and to see these performed. **Drama** introduces a second voice, so that there is **dialogue** between the characters. It introduces more debate, as we can hear and see different viewpoints, and identify with different characters, depending on how they are played. Instead of being told a story, it is presented to us. We, as the audience, can make our own sense of it. While early dramas had a **chorus** to help the audience to make meaning out of the story, we are now used to dramas where we make meaning ourselves. Live theatre is an event, with a sense of performance and with intervals, allowing us to discuss our reaction to characters and events. Most film and television actors began their careers in, and enjoy, live theatre. They like the element of risk and they like the more immediate reactions that a live audience can give.

To write about drama, you will need to imagine the texts on stage. Think about how they could come to life, and how an audience would react to the words. Try to link your reaction to the text of the play. 'The text' refers to the words the actors are given and also the directions which suggest how a scene could be staged.

Ancient drama involved actors in masks. Masks remind us that we are watching a play, and the icons opposite remind us of the two genres of tragedy and comedy. In the European tradition, costume replaced the mask: in medieval times, and in Shakespeare's theatre, costume told audiences a lot

LEARNING POINTS

▶ To appreciate distinct features of dramatic form, especially dialogue

▶ To look at a range of texts from the past and how they can come to life through staging and performance

▶ To look at setting, characterization, and conflict

▶ To explore some of the conventions of comedy, for example, status anxiety and misunderstanding

▶ To look at and question the traditional 'happy ending'.

KEY TERMS

lyrical = a traditional form of poem, which is song-like and expresses a single, but often complex, emotion.

epic = an extended and heroic poem, often containing mythological characters.

drama = text designed for performance.

dialogue = any situation where two or more people are speaking. Dialogue helps to dramatize prose and bring the characters to life.

chorus = in drama, characters who work together, often commenting on the action of a play.

about a character. Drama in the English tradition has also enjoyed combining elements of **tragedy** and **comedy**: there are serious elements in comedy, and comic scenes in tragedies. These can add extra levels of irony as we shall see.

Part of the pleasure of theatre has always come from watching larger-than-life characters, in elaborate costumes, behaving in ways that are much more exaggerated than real life, who we can laugh at, but also understand. Comedy in literature often involves the complications of love, and sometimes also depends on the comedy of class, bringing characters from different parts of society together in a clash of cultures.

We will look at three theatre texts. All of them are comedies and involve people acting outrageously. What do we find funny about this and why?

We will also explore some of the **conventions** of drama. It is much easier to analyse drama when you are aware of how writers make choices about:

- character
- situation and setting
- contrast and conflict
- problems and plot development
- social comedy and conventions involving status
- use of exaggeration and the **surreal** (larger than life) in comedy
- misunderstanding and its consequences, especially plot complication ('**farce**')
- the convention of the happy ending.

One of the building blocks of drama is **duologue**—a dialogue involving just two characters, as opposed to the **monologue** in which only one character speaks. All the texts we will be looking at involve arguments or quarrels. What do we learn about the two characters from their conversation and confrontation?

Mark Rylance in a production of Shakespeare's *Twelfth Night*. In Shakespeare's theatre female roles were played by men. Some modern productions follow this convention.

KEY TERMS

tragedy = a serious and often disturbing play which usually ends in death.

comedy = a play that is funny and usually ends happily.

convention = the ways in which texts are written to meet reader or audience expectations.

surreal = a situation which is beyond the real, taking us into a different way of looking at the 'real' world.

farce = especially exaggerated comedy, which relies heavily on stage conventions.

duologue = a dialogue involving just two characters.

monologue = one character speaking and telling the audience their thoughts.

 See Worksheet 1 on the website for an activity on comedy and tragedy.

Think ahead

Find out the definition of the following terms:

1. drawing-room comedy
2. duologue
3. Gorgon (a mythological beast)
4. earnest (as an adjective)
5. pun
6. irony
7. ward (a legal term)
8. epigram
9. snobbery
10. Victorian

Share your definitions with your classmates.

2.1 Introducing characters: the double act

In *The Importance of Being Earnest* Jack Worthing has just proposed to his girlfriend, Gwendolen, who says that she loves him because his name is Ernest. However, this isn't his real name—it is just the name he uses when he visits London from the country, where he uses his real name, Jack. In the country he pretends to be very mature and respectable, especially in front of his niece Cecily, but says he needs to go up to London regularly to help his wicked brother, Ernest. He has also spoken to Lady Bracknell, Gwendolen's mother, and the aunt of Ernest's best friend, Algernon, and revealed to her that his surname, Worthing, is also made up. He was found in the cloakroom of Victoria station by a rich gentleman who adopted him. Lady Bracknell is appalled: she cannot allow her daughter to marry someone who grew up in a handbag!

Rupert Everett as Algernon and Colin Firth as Jack in a film adaptation of *The Importance of Being Earnest*

The Importance of Being Earnest by Oscar Wilde (1895)

Algernon Didn't it go off all right, old boy? You don't mean to say Gwendolen refused you? I know it is a way she has. She is always refusing people. I think it is most ill-natured of her.

Jack Oh, Gwendolen is as right as a trivet. As far as she is concerned, we are engaged. Her mother is perfectly unbearable. Never met such a Gorgon … I don't really know what a Gorgon is like, but I am quite sure that Lady Bracknell is one. In any case, she is a monster, without being a myth, which is rather unfair … I beg your pardon, Algy, I suppose I shouldn't talk about your own aunt in that way before you.

Algernon My dear boy, I love hearing my relations abused. It is the only thing that makes me put up with them at all. Relations are simply a tedious pack of people, who haven't got the remotest knowledge of how to live, nor the smallest instinct about when to die.

Jack O, that is nonsense!

Algernon It isn't!

Jack Well, I won't argue about the matter. You always want to argue about things.

Algernon That is exactly what things were originally made for.

Jack Upon my word, if I thought that I'd shoot myself … (*A pause.*) You don't think there is any chance of Gwendolen becoming like her mother in about a hundred and fifty years, do you, Algy?

Algernon All women become like their mothers. That is their tragedy. No man does. That's his.

Jack Is that clever?

Algernon It is perfectly phrased! And quite as true as any observation in civilized life should be.

Jack I am sick to death of cleverness. Everybody is clever nowadays. You can't go anywhere without meeting clever people. The thing has become an absolute public nuisance. I wish to goodness we had a few fools left.

Algernon We have.

Jack I should extremely like to meet them. What do they talk about?

Algernon The fools? Oh! About the clever people, of course.

Jack What fools!

💬 Pair and share

1. Which lines do you find shocking?
2. Who do you think is cleverer: Algernon or Jack?
3. Who do we laugh with and who do we laugh at?
4. What are the qualities that make Algernon and Jack attractive and interesting characters?

Comedy is often about 'fooling', that is, playing characters who are a bit larger than life, either cleverer than we really are or less clever. Have a go at performing this duologue together, exaggerating the characters. How funny can you make them?

Check your understanding

Comedy involves exaggeration, featuring outrageous characters who are allowed to say shocking things. In England at the time the play was written, marriage was about your social status and relations were important, not only for status but for the money they might leave you when they died. When he is in the country, Jack lives a very conventional life which he finds boring. In London with Algernon he can go to parties and say witty and outrageous things.

Write or discuss answers to the following questions.

1. Why would Algernon not have been surprised if Gwendolen had turned Jack down?
2. What does that suggest about attitudes to marriage and proposals at that time?
3. Why does Jack call Lady Bracknell a Gorgon?
4. Why does Algernon wish his relations knew when to die?
5. Why is Jack so worried about Gwendolen becoming like her mother?
6. How does Algernon turn this into an **epigram**?
7. Why does Algernon like Jack's epigram about fools and clever people?
8. Who do they think are 'fools'?

Extend your learning

We have seen that double acts provide witty characters who can compete with each other in saying outrageous things. This gives us epigrams, witty sayings you could apply to other situations in life:

- … she is a monster, without being a myth, which is rather unfair …
- Jack: You always want to argue about things. Algernon: That is exactly what things were originally made for.
- All women become like their mothers. That is their tragedy. No man does. That's his.

Writing essays in English literature about the texts you study involves choosing the right quotations and saying something interesting about how they work. As you know, this play is about relatives and relationships, about battles of wit, and about inheritance. Commenting on a quotation is a three-stage process sometimes called the PEA technique that you need to practise.

- Make a *point* (P) about how the quotation illustrates the impact of an aspect of the text or the character on the audience. (Use the hints in the previous paragraph.)
- Use the quotation as *evidence* (E).
- *Analyse* (A) how the language shows a characteristic of the language of the play, in the last case contrast, or to use a more classical term, antithesis.

 # Viewpoints

You can see that a lot of the comedy of this scene comes from characterization. The writer has created two characters who are friends but very different from one another. They contrast very effectively.

1. Who do you find more likeable?
2. Why do you think Algernon felt 'Ernest' the right name for Jack and said 'You are the most earnest-looking character I ever met in my life'?
3. Why does Jack need a friend like Algernon, and why does Algernon need Jack?
4. Can you think of other famous pairs of characters, comic like Laurel and Hardy or 'straight' (that is, serious) like Holmes and Watson? List as many as you can. These are called double acts.
5. How do they contrast? Funny and serious? Clever and foolish (or gullible)?

 See Worksheet 3 on the website for an activity on double acts.

KEY TERM

epigram = a witty and memorable saying.

analyse = give a detailed explanation of the effects of language, based on evidence from the text.

Developing the situation

Analysis helps us to look at how writers use language, but we should also look at their choices of form and structure. The playwright has used two contrasting characters to amuse the audience but also to develop his plot while keeping us entertained.

We have established that in this play the 'town', London, is a place where Jack can be outrageous and have a different name and identity. However, if he is to get married to Gwendolen, whom he loves, he will need her mother's approval. He needs relatives so that he can establish who he really is. This gives us a situation.

There is a further plot complication or problem. Complications help comic plots: they lead to further confusion and misunderstanding (always funny) and involve all the characters in the action that follows. Look at the next passage and how it shows further developments, both of situation and character. It shows the developing contrast between the town and the country.

In the country, Jack has a young ward, the daughter of the rich man who found him, Cecily. She thinks Jack is a very serious person. When Jack gets bored of being serious, he uses an invented friend called 'Bunbury' who lives in town and is always getting in trouble which requires Jack's help (and money), rather like the real life Algernon. Of course, when he gets to London, Jack becomes Ernest, as we have seen, allowing him to live a double life. Algernon rather likes the sound of the innocent young Cecily.

The Importance of Being Earnest by Oscar Wilde (1895)

Algernon By the way, did you tell Gwendolen the truth about your being Ernest in town and Jack in the country?

Jack *(in a very patronizing manner)* My dear fellow, the truth isn't quite the sort of thing one tells, to a nice, sweet, refined girl. What extraordinary ideas you have about the way to behave to a woman!

Algernon The only way to behave to a woman is to make love to her, if she is pretty, and to some one else, if she is plain.

Jack Oh, that is nonsense.

Algernon What about your brother? What about the profligate Ernest?

Jack Oh, before the end of the week I shall have got rid of him. I'll say he died in Paris of apoplexy. Lots of people die of apoplexy, quite suddenly, don't they?

Algernon Yes, but it's hereditary, my dear fellow. It's a sort of thing that runs in families. You had better say a severe chill.

Jack You are sure a severe chill isn't hereditary, or anything of that kind?

Reese Witherspoon as Cecily

Algernon	Of course it isn't!
Jack	Very well then. My poor brother Ernest is carried off suddenly, in Paris, by a severe chill. That gets rid of him.
Algernon	But I thought you said that … Miss Cardew was a little too much interested in your poor brother Ernest. Won't she feel his loss a good deal?
Jack	Oh, that is all right. Cecily is not a silly romantic girl, I am glad to say. She has got a capital appetite, goes for long walks, and pays no attention at all to her lessons.
Algernon	I would rather like to see Cecily.
Jack	I will take very good care you never do. She is excessively pretty, and she is only just eighteen.
Algernon	Have you told Gwendolen yet that you have an excessively pretty ward who is only just eighteen?
Jack	Oh! One doesn't blurt these things out to people. Cecily and Gwendolen are perfectly certain to be extremely great friends. I'll bet you anything you like that half an hour after they have met, they will be calling each other sister.
Algernon	Women only do that when they have called each other a lot of other things first.

 Check your understanding

Wilde called this play 'a trivial play for serious people' and added that its philosophy was that 'we should take all the trivial things of life seriously, and all the serious things of life with sincere and studied triviality'. In other words silly things (like eating lots of cucumber sandwiches or crumpets) are treated very seriously, but the play makes lots of jokes about serious things such as marriage. What do Jack and Algernon have to say about the following?

1. Telling the truth
2. The way to behave towards women
3. Death and illness
4. Education and learning
5. Looking after young people
6. How women behave towards each other

 Viewpoints

1. Do you find the attitudes of Algernon and Jack funny or disturbing?
2. Why doesn't Jack like to tell the truth?
3. What attitude do they seem to have towards women?

Create a table with two columns. Under the headings 'witty' and 'shocking' find quotations to give evidence of their attitudes.

 Pair and share

Using the PEA technique you learned in the previous section, find the most outrageous epigram in this extract and comment on what makes it funny and memorable. Do you agree on what it is?

 See Worksheet 2 on the website for an activity on the conventions of comedy.

KEY TERMS

contrast = when you compare texts, always look at differences (contrasts) as well as similarities.

antithesis = a deliberate contrast of opposites.

Extend your learning

Whatever the underlying attitudes of the two young men, this scene certainly advances the plot and adds extra complications.

- What does it reveal about Algernon's interest in Cecily?
- What kind of man does Cecily think 'Ernest' must be?
- What qualities do 'Bunbury', 'Ernest' and Algernon all have in common?

In a few moments, Jack will give his address in the country over the telephone. Why do you think that Algernon takes good care to write it down and what is he planning? Write a brief sketch of what happens next.

You can see why we call the storyline in a play or novel the **plot**. Writers need to construct a map of the characters and how they are going to combine them. How will they pair them up or contrast them? How will they reveal their hidden secrets and connections (the process of revelation)? How will they handle different locations? How will they add complications and twists? How will they bring all these elements together to achieve a climax?

These are the ways we will develop our understanding of the structure of texts. The purpose of a good first act or first chapter is to set things up.

The contrast between town and country is clearly a very important part of setting in the text. Setting is often a form of **symbolism,** in other words different places stand for different attitudes or ways of life. Compare and contrast town and country attitudes in the duologue.

Drama comes out of a clash of cultures and attitudes. How might they conflict in the next act?

The passage reveals underlying attitudes to marriage, the role of women, and the class system at the time the play was written. In 1895 Queen Victoria ruled over Britain and its Empire, and was called Empress of India. To attack the attitudes of society was subversive; marriage underpinned the values of class and **status**.

To extend your understanding, explore Victorian attitudes in other texts you have read, and read Oscar Wilde's novel *The Picture of Dorian Gray* or his play *The Ideal Husband*. How did marriage underpin the class system?

For comparison, have a look at P.G. Wodehouse's story 'The Custody of the Pumpkin', which we will be exploring further in chapter 3.

Compare:
- attitudes to marriage
- attitudes to class and status
- how Algernon and Jack and the Honourable Freddie both use slang.

2.2 Status and problems

Think ahead

Group activity

Actors often play status games to establish the ways in which their characters relate to each other. For example, you could walk silently around the room after having been assigned numbers from 1 (low status) to 4 (high status) and without talking guess which number applies to each person you meet. Is it a higher number than your own? Or a lower one? Or are you at the same level?

Clearly Algernon has higher status than Jack as he is cleverer and wittier (and has relations). But in the country Jack has higher status than Algernon: he has more money, is more mature, and has a stable situation in life. Britain in the nineteenth century was very class-conscious: money and status mattered a lot, and people were afraid of losing status, or not having a secure identity. We now call this status anxiety.

▶ Are there similar concerns about social status in your country?

▶ Does it matter what car you have (or even if you have a car)?

▶ Does it matter where you live, where you go to school, or how you speak?

These things can be serious as well as trivial, but comedy makes fun of them all. Nowadays, social class may be less important, and you are judged less by who your relatives are, but appearances still matter a great deal. People employ image consultants to tell them how to make the right impression.

Social attitudes did not change greatly in Britain until after the Second World War, hence the success of Shaw's play *Pygmalion* which showed a flower girl Eliza Doolittle learning to pass herself off as a duchess by studying how to change her accent. The most comic moment in the play—which shocked audiences at the time—comes when she says 'Not bloody likely' at the end of a polite tea party. The professor teaching her, Professor Higgins, realizes that he also need to work on the register and content of her speech, and all goes well at the smart ball they attend. Indeed the professor's former pupil thinks she is a foreign princess as she speaks English far too well to be a native! The play was adapted into a musical entitled *My Fair Lady*.

However, then comes the problem of what will happen next. We have seen how comedy comes out of contrasts, misunderstandings, mistakes, and exaggerations. Sometimes comedy comes close to being shocking, outrageous, or disturbing. What happens when the joking is over and characters need to face real life? Shaw asks this more serious question too. Colonel Pickering is the Professor's friend, (another double act) who had made a bet with him that he could not do it.

George Bernard Shaw

Audrey Hepburn as Eliza in *My Fair Lady*

Pygmalion by George Bernard Shaw (1914)

PICKERING. Anyhow, it was a great success: an immense success. I was quite frightened once or twice because Eliza was doing it so well. You see, lots of the real people can't do it at all: they're such fools that they think style comes by nature to people in their position; and so they never learn. There's always something professional about doing a thing superlatively well.

HIGGINS. Yes: that's what drives me mad: the silly people don't know their own silly business. [*Rising*] However, it's over and done with; and now I can go to bed at last without dreading tomorrow.

Eliza's beauty becomes murderous.

PICKERING. I think I shall turn in too. Still, it's been a great occasion: a triumph for you. Good-night. [*He goes*].

HIGGINS [*following him*] Good-night. [*Over his shoulder, at the door*] Put out the lights, Eliza; and tell Mrs. Pearce not to make coffee for me in the morning: I'll take tea. [*He goes out*].

Eliza tries to control herself and feel indifferent as she rises and walks across to the hearth to switch off the lights. By the time she gets there she is on the point of screaming. She sits down in Higgins's chair and holds on hard to the arms. Finally she gives way and flings herself furiously on the floor raging.

HIGGINS [*in despairing wrath outside*] What the devil have I done with my slippers? [*He appears at the door*].

LIZA [*snatching up the slippers, and hurling them at him one after the other with all her force*] There are your slippers. And there. Take your slippers; and may you never have a day's luck with them!

HIGGINS [*astounded*] What on earth—! [*He comes to her*]. What's the matter? Get up. [*He pulls her up*]. Anything wrong?

LIZA [*breathless*] Nothing wrong—with YOU. I've won your bet for you, haven't I? That's enough for you. *I* don't matter, I suppose.

HIGGINS. YOU won my bet! You! Presumptuous insect! *I* won it. What did you throw those slippers at me for?

LIZA. Because I wanted to smash your face. I'd like to kill you, you selfish brute. Why didn't you leave me where you picked me out of—in the gutter? You thank God it's all over, and that now you can throw me back again there, do you? [*She crisps her fingers, frantically*].

HIGGINS [*looking at her in cool wonder*] The creature IS nervous, after all.

LIZA [*gives a suffocated scream of fury, and instinctively darts her nails at his face*]!!

HIGGINS [*catching her wrists*] Ah! would you? Claws in, you cat. How dare you show your temper to me? Sit down and be quiet. [*He throws her roughly into the easy-chair*].

LIZA [*crushed by superior strength and weight*] What's to become of me? What's to become of me?

HIGGINS. How the devil do I know what's to become of you? What does it matter what becomes of you?

LIZA. You don't care. I know you don't care. You wouldn't care if I was dead. I'm nothing to you— not so much as them slippers.

HIGGINS [*thundering*] THOSE slippers.

LIZA [*with bitter submission*] Those slippers. I didn't think it made any difference now.

A pause. Eliza hopeless and crushed. Higgins a little uneasy.

Check your understanding

1. What has Higgins said to Pickering that has upset Eliza so much?

2. How does Shaw show you how angry she is?

3. Why was Higgins asking about his slippers so provocative?

4. Why is the fight so shocking?

5. What is Eliza's status in society now?

6. Who is in charge in this duologue and why?

7. Who gets the most sympathy from you?

Pair and share

The emotions of this scene are certainly very different from the witty conversation of Algernon and Jack. Eliza's emotions are much more raw, her anxieties about her status much more genuine. Now Higgins has won his bet is she a lady or only a servant?

The fight between the two characters is a dramatic way of showing conflict, the kind of clash of emotions and ideas which creates tension and has a powerful impact on the audience.

How does Shaw show his actors how they should communicate this tension? He uses **stage directions** to indicate both movement and how lines should be spoken. He shows Eliza's concern about her status by showing her on the floor beneath Higgins, and then rising up to claw at his face, before being thrown into a chair.

When writing about drama, stage directions as well as the characters' words need analysis, as sometimes characters express themselves as much through gestures and tone as through the words they use. In pairs, complete the table to examine Eliza's feelings.

Quotation	Comment
Eliza's beauty becomes murderous.	This shows her emotions are becoming violent.
flings herself furiously on the floor raging.	Shaw's language demonstrates how physically she feels her anger and despair.
hurling them at him one after the other with all her force.	The word 'hurling' powerfully conveys Eliza's energy and fury.
breathless	
She crisps her fingers, frantically	
gives a suffocated scream of fury	
instinctively darts her nails at his face	
crushed by superior strength and weight	
with bitter submission	Shows Eliza giving in to Higgins's intellect as well as his strength, but the word 'bitter' shows that she is resentful at the way he bullies her.
Eliza hopeless and crushed.	

Is Higgins really unfeeling and a 'selfish brute'? Can you find clues in the stage directions to suggest he is more emotional than he likes to pretend? Explore the effect of the stage directions given for him.

Quotation	Comment
in despairing wrath outside	
astounded	
He pulls her up	
looking at her in cool wonder	
He throws her roughly into the easy-chair	
thundering	
Higgins a little uneasy	

Act out the duologue as a pair, giving plenty of expression to these stage directions.

💡 Viewpoints

The audience's response

This drama is moving towards its climax, with the problems and consequences of the initial plot emerging and becoming more complicated. Eliza has managed to achieve a new status through changing her voice, but now asks 'What's to become of me?' Higgins's reply implies that he thinks status doesn't matter, but do his words and behaviour suggest this? The scene ends with more questions than answers.

Shaw asks for 'a pause', so the scene ends with dramatic tension. The audience need to think about what they are seeing, and not just find it amusing.

Let's evaluate the evidence. Is Higgins a brute and a bully, or someone who challenges the conventions of society (an awkward revolutionary)? What evidence can you and your partner find? Create a table to record you findings like the one below.

Brute and bully	Awkward revolutionary
Throws her roughly	*a little uneasy*

Shaw shows Higgins's pride in what he can achieve:

> HIGGINS. *YOU won my bet! You! Presumptuous insect! I won it. What did you throw those slippers at me for?*

How does the language here show Higgins's lack of interest in Eliza as a person? Analyse the use of sarcasm, imagery, and questions here. Does he show her any respect? Why not?

Higgins is a professor and his main interest in language is academic. He seems to think that image and language matter more than feelings. This makes him witty and a good comic character. However, an audience will notice powerful emotions emerge here, and they are not just comic, but based on serious questions.

Is it possible to change people's identity by changing their image?

Debate this question, drawing examples from the modern world.

Extend your learning

Drama can combine both comic and serious elements. A tragedy can have comic scenes, especially in Shakespeare, and comedy can address serious questions about life.

How has Shaw made sure the characters are well-matched in this scene? Look at more of this scene from the play to explore the ways in which Eliza eventually achieves a kind of victory in her quarrel with Higgins, by making him reveal real emotions.

1. Do real emotions belong in comedy?

2. What happens when an audience stops laughing and starts to think?

Higgins wants to see Eliza as a kind of animal he can experiment and play with: he calls her 'insect', 'cat', and 'creature'. How human do you find him?

Write two paragraphs of character notes for an actor playing Higgins to bring out his contradictions. Using the quotations above, bring out his dark side and his more human side.

Writing techniques

Teachers often ask you questions about the impact of a scene and the writing on an audience. This is sometimes called **dramatic effectiveness**. You will need to use quotations and evidence in order to explore, analyse, and evaluate the way in which a live audience would react to what it sees and hears.

✎ Practice question

Looking back at the scene from *Pygmalion* and the evidence you have gathered, write a short essay (400–500 words) in answer to the following question:

> *How does Shaw make this confrontation a powerful and revealing moment for an audience?*

Remember to refer to details of language and their effect, and to concentrate on *how* the audience respond, rather than just retell *what* happens. Look at the situation, the characters, and what is **revealed** about them, deeper attitudes and suggestions, and the way the action builds to a **climax**, followed by a dramatic pause.

KEY TERMS

revealed = this term is often used to encourage students to go beyond the surface meaning and look at deeper attitudes, especially what words tell us about characters.

climax = the moment audiences and readers will see as the high point to which everything has been building up.

dramatic effectiveness = how well a scene works in live performance; the effect on the audience.

2.3 Quarrels

Think ahead

Our next text also involves a quarrel, this time between a pair of lovers. This is taken from Shakespeare's *A Midsummer Night's Dream*. If you study a Shakespeare text as part of your Cambridge IGCSE course, it is important not to be put off his plays by the verse and the language of his day. He became famous as a writer of comedy, and he uses many of the same conventions of comedy as other writers.

A Midsummer Night's Dream shows many of the elements of traditional drama we have explored already:

- pairs of characters
- a situation caused by marriage conventions
- the problems caused by love
- status and money often determining marriage rather than love
- comedy caused by misunderstandings
- a surreal element, taking us beyond a completely realistic situation
- conflict leading to tension, quarrels, and insults
- exaggeration and larger-than-life characters
- outrageous language and behaviour
- a setting which allows these qualities to be seen.

Read the brief synopsis of the situation which follows and identify these elements.

Sketch out in your notes the love triangle before the fairies intervene: who is in love with whom, and who is left out of the triangle with no one to love her? How has this changed after the fairies' interference?

A pair of lovers in *A Midsummer Night's Dream*

Lysander and Hermia are in love and have run off into the forest outside Athens because Hermia's father has insisted that she must marry Demetrius, who comes from a richer family. Demetrius used to love Hermia's best friend, Helena, and, convinced he is in love with Hermia, follows the lovers into the forest. He is followed by Helena, although he keeps telling her he hates her. They all get lost and fall asleep, at which point the fairies in the forest intervene to try to sort things out with a love potion. Unfortunately Puck, the fairy given this task, has given the potion to the wrong man: now Lysander is in love with Helena and hates Hermia. Helena assumes he is joking and that he and Hermia are making fun of her. Oberon, king of the fairies, now gives the love juice to Demetrius, but he has not yet given the antidote to Lysander. Puck (who enjoys mischief) is now watching the fun … (and so are we). Note that words and phrases that may be unfamiliar to you are explained to the right of the extract.

A Midsummer Night's Dream **by William Shakespeare (circa 1594)**

LYSANDER

> Helen, I love thee; by my life I do;
> I swear by that which I will lose for thee
> To prove him false that says I love thee not.

to prove him false *= prove him a liar*

DEMETRIUS

> I say I love thee more than he can do.

LYSANDER

> If thou say so, withdraw, and prove it too.

withdraw and prove it too *= come and fight me (they have swords)*

DEMETRIUS

> Quick, come,--

HERMIA

>   Lysander, whereto tends all this?

LYSANDER

> Away, you Ethiope!

whereto tends all this *= what does this all mean?*

Away, you Ethiope *= refers to Hermia's dark hair and complexion*

DEMETRIUS

>   No, no, sir:--he will
> Seem to break loose; take on as you would follow:
> But yet come not. You are a tame man; go!

take on as you would follow *= match your words to deeds and fight*

LYSANDER

> Hang off, thou cat, thou burr: vile thing, let loose,
> Or I will shake thee from me like a serpent.
>
> Out, loathed medicine! hated potion, hence!

thou burr *= you sticky plant*

HERMIA

> Why are you grown so rude? What change is this,
> Sweet love?

LYSANDER

Thy love! Out, tawny Tartar, out!
Out, loathed medicine! O hated potion, hence!

HERMIA

Do you not jest?

HELENA

Yes, sooth; and so do you.

LYSANDER

Demetrius, I will keep my word with thee.

DEMETRIUS

I would I had your bond; for I perceive
A weak bond holds you; I'll not trust your word.

LYSANDER

What! should I hurt her, strike her, kill her dead?
Although I hate her, I'll not harm her so.

HERMIA

What! can you do me greater harm than hate?
Hate me! wherefore? O me! what news, my love?
Am not I Hermia? Are not you Lysander?
I am as fair now as I was erewhile.
Since night you lov'd me; yet since night you left me:
Why then, you left me,--O, the gods forbid!--
In earnest, shall I say?

LYSANDER

Ay, by my life;
And never did desire to see thee more.
Therefore be out of hope, of question, doubt,
Be certain, nothing truer; 'tis no jest
That I do hate thee and love Helena.

HERMIA

O me! you juggler! you cankerblossom!
You thief of love! What! have you come by night,
And stol'n my love's heart from him?

HELENA

Fine, i' faith!
Have you no modesty, no maiden shame,
No touch of bashfulness? What! will you tear
Impatient answers from my gentle tongue?
Fie, fie! you counterfeit, you puppet, you!

HERMIA

Puppet! why so? Ay, that way goes the game.

Out, tawny Tartar = another reference to Hermia's dark complexion

Do you not jest? = are you joking?

A weak bond holds you = you don't keep your promises

Therefore be out of hope = give up, have no more hopes about me

you cankerblossom = you insect ruining the flower of love

you counterfeit = you fake

Now I perceive that she hath made compare
Between our statures; she hath urg'd her height;
And with her personage, her tall personage,
Her height, forsooth, she hath prevail'd with him.--
And are you grown so high in his esteem
Because I am so dwarfish and so low?
How low am I, thou painted maypole? speak;
How low am I? I am not yet so low
But that my nails can reach unto thine eyes.

HELENA

I pray you, though you mock me, gentlemen,
Let her not hurt me. I was never curst;
I have no gift at all in shrewishness;
I am a right maid for my cowardice;
Let her not strike me. You perhaps may think,
Because she is something lower than myself,
That I can match her.

HERMIA

                    Lower! hark, again.

HELENA

Good Hermia, do not be so bitter with me.
I evermore did love you, Hermia;
Did ever keep your counsels; never wrong'd you;
Save that, in love unto Demetrius,
I told him of your stealth unto this wood:
He follow'd you; for love I follow'd him;
But he hath chid me hence, and threaten'd me
To strike me, spurn me, nay, to kill me too:
And now, so you will let me quiet go,
To Athens will I bear my folly back,
And follow you no farther. Let me go:
You see how simple and how fond I am.

HERMIA

Why, get you gone: who is't that hinders you?

HELENA

A foolish heart that I leave here behind.

HERMIA

What! with Lysander?

HELENA

                With Demetrius.

LYSANDER

Be not afraid; she shall not harm thee, Helena.

thou painted maypole = *you tall, gaudy pole for dancing around in spring*

shrewishness = *being a difficult woman*

keep your counsels = *kept your secrets*

your stealth unto this wood = *how you crept away secretly to the wood*

he hath chid me hence = *he drove me away with insults*

spurn me = *reject me*

will I bear my folly back = *I will take all my silly ideas (of love) with me*

DEMETRIUS

    No, sir, she shall not, though you take her part.

HELENA

    O, when she's angry, she is keen and shrewd:
    She was a vixen when she went to school;
    And, though she be but little, she is fierce.

She was a vixen = *she was like a cunning, aggressive female fox*

HERMIA

    Little again! nothing but low and little!--
    Why will you suffer her to flout me thus?
    Let me come to her.

LYSANDER

          Get you gone, you dwarf;
    You minimus, of hind'ring knot-grass made;
    You bead, you acorn.

minimus = *thing of insignificant size*

of hind'ring knot-grass made = *made of an annoying weed*

DEMETRIUS

          You are too officious
    In her behalf that scorns your services.
    Let her alone: speak not of Helena;
    Take not her part; for if thou dost intend
    Never so little show of love to her,
    Thou shalt aby it.

You are too officious = *you are trying too hard to impress someone who isn't interested in you (that is, Helena)*

Thou shalt aby it = *you will pay for it (in a fight)*

LYSANDER

          Now she holds me not;
    Now follow, if thou dar'st, to try whose right,
    Of thine or mine, is most in Helena.

to try whose right = *to fight over the right (to Helena)*

DEMETRIUS

    Follow! nay, I'll go with thee, cheek by jowl.

cheek by jowl = *close behind*

[Exeunt LYSANDER and DEMETRIUS.]

HERMIA

    You, mistress, all this coil is 'long of you:
    Nay, go not back.

all this coil is 'long of you = *this trouble is all your fault*

HELENA

          I will not trust you, I;
    Nor longer stay in your curst company.
    Your hands than mine are quicker for a fray;
    My legs are longer though, to run away.

quicker for a fray = *quicker to fight*

[Exit.]

HERMIA

    I am amaz'd, and know not what to say.

[Exit, pursuing HELENA.]

Did you work out the following pattern?

- Lysander loves Hermia who loves him back
- Demetrius loves Hermia but she doesn't love him
- Helena loves Demetrius but he doesn't love her
- No one loves Helena

This becomes the following.

- Helena loves Demetrius but he doesn't love her
- Demetrius loves Hermia but she doesn't love him
- Hermia loves Lysander but he doesn't love her
- Lysander loves Helena but she doesn't believe him

And finally we get this.

- Helena loves Demetrius and he loves her but she doesn't believe him
- Lysander loves Helena but she doesn't believe him
- Hermia loves Lysander but he doesn't love her
- No one loves Hermia

The fairies, like the audience, are watching the lovers' quarrels. As the boys both love Helena (when they used to both be in love with Hermia), they are rude to Hermia. However, Helena thinks that all three are just pretending in order to make fun of her. Why do we find this so amusing? We don't just enjoy the teasing and the insults, there is also something amusing about observing other people who are in love and making fools of themselves. Puck, the mischievous fairy who has accidentally caused these problems, says 'Lord, what fools these mortals be!'

Extend your learning

The forest and the fairies are really a metaphor for our dreams and fantasies, and for the random power of love.

As we have seen, comedy does not need to be realistic. This comedy is quite surreal, using magic and the fantastic to make human beings react in exaggerated ways.

1. What has love done to the relative status of the two girls?

2. How do the jokes referring to height present this to the audience?

3. What has love done to friendships and loyalties, and how has it caused conflict in the play?

✎ Check your understanding

Have some fun collecting the insults hurled at Hermia and Helena.

Create a table to list the insults used about each of the girls. We have given you a few below to start you off. Notice that Hermia is insulted by both Lysander and Helena, and that Helena even insults herself.

The jokes revolve around the fact that Hermia is short and dark and Helena is tall and fair. Hermia tends to get angry while Helena is more self-pitying.

About Hermia	About Helena
you Ethiope	thou painted maypole
thou cat, thou burr	you juggler! you cankerblossom
you dwarf; You minimus	how simple and how fond

Viewpoints

Discuss and debate the following questions.

1. 'What change is this?' Everyone used to love Hermia, and Helena was rejected. What do you think Hermia has learned in this scene about what it feels like to be rejected?

2. Does the audience simply laugh at this scene or is there something uncomfortable in what it tells us about love?

3. What happened to Hermia and Helena's friendship once rivalry in love came along?

4. How does this scene resemble a bad dream?

One way to address these questions is to write an **empathy response**, to imagine you are the character writing down her thoughts, as in a diary.

You are Hermia waking up after this bad dream. Write your thoughts about imagining all your friends had turned against you.

Language links

Empathic responses help you to find the 'voice' of a character, which is also good practice for the reading paper in First Language English.

Pair and share

We have seen the different ways in which characters contrast, develop, and come into conflict. We have looked at tensions between characters, and how arguments over status create drama. We have seen how duologues and pairs of characters can create powerful drama through double acts. How do the dramatists we have studied in this chapter, all masters of the craft of writing, bring these problems to a **resolution**? Discuss these questions with a partner.

2.4 Happy endings?

We will now explore the different ways of concluding comedies. The traditional ending for a comedy is to find a way to get virtually the entire cast on stage, sort out all the misunderstandings through a series of unhappy (and often unlikely) coincidences and marry off the young (and even the not-so-young) couples. Everyone joins in to celebrate the marriages. Can you spot the similarities to the conventions of romantic comedy in films today?

Act 3 of *The Importance of Being Earnest* with most of the cast on stage

Pair and share

One of you is Hermia and the other Helena. Serve up the insults you listed to play insult tennis. Which insults return service and which are an ace? Ask your teacher to play the role of umpire as you throw them at each other. Helena (thanks to Lysander) probably has more weapons.

Now prepare a performance of this scene. Begin by dividing into pairs of 'boys' and 'girls'.

How will the audience react to the outrageous things you say to each other?

KEY TERMS

empathy response = sometimes called 'empathic', this is an opportunity to write the character's thoughts at a particular moment in the text (see chapter 5).

resolution = an ending which sorts out problems and differences, and brings everything together, also called 'closure'.

A traditional ending: bringing everyone together

Jack discovers that he is in fact Algernon's brother (and, incidentally, Gwendolen's cousin and Lady Bracknell's nephew). Algernon gets to marry Cecily because he really is Jack's wicked friend—indeed his brother (even if he is not called Ernest). All that is needed is to find out Jack's real name (which oddly enough no one, not even Lady Bracknell, can remember).

Book of lists from 1890s

> ***The Importance of Being Earnest* by Oscar Wilde (1895) (final scene)**
>
> **Jack.** The Army Lists of the last forty years are here. These delightful records should have been my constant study. [*Rushes to bookcase and tears the books out.*] M. Generals … Mallam, Maxbohm, Magley, what ghastly names they have—Markby, Migsby, Mobbs, Moncrieff! Lieutenant 1840, Captain, Lieutenant-Colonel, Colonel, General 1869, Christian names, Ernest John. [*Puts book very quietly down and speaks quite calmly.*] I always told you, Gwendolen, my name was Ernest, didn't I? Well, it is Ernest after all. I mean it naturally is Ernest.
>
> **Lady Bracknell.** Yes, I remember now that the General was called Ernest, I knew I had some particular reason for disliking the name.
>
> **Gwendolen.** Ernest! My own Ernest! I felt from the first that you could have no other name!
>
> **Jack.** Gwendolen, it is a terrible thing for a man to find out suddenly that all his life he has been speaking nothing but the truth. Can you forgive me?
>
> **Gwendolen.** I can. For I feel that you are sure to change.
>
> **Jack.** My own one!
>
> **Chasuble.** [*To Miss Prism.*] Laetitia! [*Embraces her.*]
>
> **Miss Prism.** [*Enthusiastically.*] Frederick! At last!
>
> **Algernon.** Cecily! [*Embraces her.*] At last!
>
> **Jack.** Gwendolen! [*Embraces her.*] At last!
>
> **Lady Bracknell**. My nephew, you seem to be displaying signs of triviality.
>
> **Jack.** On the contrary, Aunt Augusta, I've now realised for the first time in my life the vital Importance of Being Earnest.

💡 Viewpoints

Do comedies really need happy endings? Where are the suggestions in this scene that Wilde might be saying something more serious about the things we take seriously and the things we laugh at?

In pairs, script an interview with Oscar Wilde after the first performance of this play and ask him some serious questions about what he meant by the title of the play, its action, and its ending. Do you think he will give serious answers?

✎ Check your understanding

1. How do the Army Lists provide some (rather unlikely) realism into the play?
2. How does the writer use names to bring characters together in a happy ending?
3. Do we believe that names are really so important?
4. What does Jack suggest about the relationship between names and being serious or telling the truth?
5. Why is Gwendolen's comment 'I feel that you are sure to change' very revealing?

Another kind of ending: the epilogue

When the 'mechanicals' put on a play for Duke Theseus in *A Midsummer Night's Dream*, he tells them not to bother with an **epilogue** (the last words of the play) 'for your play needs no excuse'. However, Shakespeare decides to end this play with a traditional epilogue, in which one actor addresses the audience directly, once the other characters have left the stage to prepare for their weddings.

KEY TERMS

epilogue = the last words of a literary text, especially a play, after the action is over. An epilogue may be spoken by a named character, or by one of the actors, stepping out of role. These used to be much more common in the past (as were prologues, at the beginning of the play) and were not necessarily written by the author.

Shakespeare gives the last word to the mischievous fairy, Puck, who tells the audience that the actors are really 'shadows' and the whole play only a 'dream'. He asks for their pardon and applause, and daringly promises a better play next time.

PUCK

A Midsummer Night's Dream by William Shakespeare (circa 1594)

If we shadows have offended,
Think but this, and all is mended,
That you have but slumber'd here
While these visions did appear.
And this weak and idle theme,
No more yielding but a dream,
Gentles, do not reprehend;
If you pardon, we will mend.
And, as I am an honest Puck,
If we have unearned luck
Now to 'scape the serpent's tongue,
We will make amends ere long;
Else the Puck a liar call:
So, good night unto you all.
Give me your hands, if we be friends,
And Robin shall restore amends.

Gentles = *ladies and gentlemen*
reprehend = *tell off*

to 'scape the serpent's tongue = *to escape being hissed off the stage*
We will make amends = *we will come up with something better next time*
restore amends = *bring everything to a happy ending*

 Pair and share

Discuss these questions.

1. Why do you think Shakespeare gives Puck, the spirit of mischief, the last word?
2. Why does he want the audience to treat it like a dream?
3. Does he really think he has written a bad play?
4. Why does Puck get to say he has?
5. How will applause (clapping your hands) make it better?

6. Does this help you to understand the nature of comedy?

Puck says that the play is, literally, 'claptrap'—just a piece of amusement. Compare this with Wilde's comment that *The Importance of Being Earnest* was 'a trivial play for serious people'. Do the writers mean this? Why do the writers of comedies draw attention to ways in which they are not realistic?

Extend your learning

You have an opportunity here to evaluate and review what you have learned in this chapter. This task gives you an extended piece of text and an opportunity to look back, compare, and come to your own judgment. You are given less help with this task, as you can use the skills that you developed earlier in the chapter.

Controversially, *Pygmalion* does not have an entirely conventional happy ending. Liza and Higgins will not marry—instead she will marry a young boy called Freddy. The film and musical have slightly different endings. Shaw felt he needed to write an essay to justify his chosen ending. He condemned 'the ragshop in which Romance keeps its stock of "happy endings" to misfit all stories' and wanted to write an ending which was realistic.

However, he struggled with the final lines of the play and several versions exist.

1. Why do you think producers would have preferred to bring the two main characters together?

2. Why do you think the writer resists this idea?

3. What does this tell you about the differences between the social conventions of comedy and those of realism (that is, drama based on real life)?

You now have a chance to evaluate Shaw's ending for yourself.

Annotate your copy of this scene (from the CD-ROM). Explore the impact of the language and the stage directions.

Eliza is now ready for the wedding with which a comedy traditionally ends. However, it isn't the wedding we expected—instead Eliza's father, a dustman, is getting married at the end of the play because he has (accidentally) become a rich celebrity. Freddy, who loves Eliza, is from a higher class than Eliza, but he is not rich, and he certainly isn't as clever as Eliza or Professor Higgins. However, the audience's main interest is in how the relationship between Eliza and Higgins will end. Look out for the change in status in this scene.

Pygmalion by George Bernard Shaw (1914) (final scene)

LIZA. Freddy loves me: that makes him king enough for me. I don't want him to work: he wasn't brought up to it as I was. I'll go and be a teacher.

HIGGINS. What'll you teach, in heaven's name?

LIZA. What you taught me. I'll teach phonetics.

HIGGINS. Ha! Ha! Ha!

LIZA. I'll offer myself as an assistant to that hairy-faced Hungarian.

HIGGINS [*rising in a fury*] What! That impostor! that humbug! that toadying ignoramus! Teach him my methods! my discoveries! You take one step in his direction and I'll wring your neck. [*He lays hands on her*]. Do you hear?

LIZA [*defiantly non-resistant*] Wring away. What do I care? I knew you'd strike me some day. [*He lets her go, stamping with rage at having forgotten himself, and recoils so hastily that he stumbles back into his seat on the ottoman*]. Aha! Now I know how to deal with you. What a fool I was not to think of it before! You can't take away the knowledge you gave me. You said I had a finer ear than you. And I can be civil and kind to people, which is more than you can. Aha! That's done you, Henry Higgins, it has. Now I don't care that [*snapping her fingers*] for your bullying and your big talk. I'll advertize it in the papers that your duchess is only a flower girl that you taught, and that she'll teach anybody to be a duchess just the same in six months for a thousand guineas. Oh, when I think of myself crawling under your feet and being trampled on and called names, when all the time I had only to lift up my finger to be as good as you, I could just kick myself.

HIGGINS [*wondering at her*] You damned impudent slut, you! But it's better than snivelling; better than fetching slippers and finding spectacles, isn't it? [*Rising*] By George, Eliza, I said I'd make a woman of you; and I have. I like you like this.

LIZA. Yes: you turn round and make up to me now that I'm not afraid of you, and can do without you.

HIGGINS. Of course I do, you little fool. Five minutes ago you were like a millstone round my neck. Now you're a tower of strength: a consort battleship. You and I and Pickering will be three old bachelors together instead of only two men and a silly girl.

Mrs. Higgins returns, dressed for the wedding. Eliza instantly becomes cool and elegant.

MRS. HIGGINS. The carriage is waiting, Eliza. Are you ready?

LIZA. Quite. Is the Professor coming?

MRS. HIGGINS. Certainly not. He can't behave himself in church. He makes remarks out loud all the time on the clergyman's pronunciation.

LIZA. Then I shall not see you again, Professor. Good-bye. [*She goes to the door*].

MRS. HIGGINS [*coming to Higgins*] Good-bye, dear.

HIGGINS. Good-bye, mother. [*He is about to kiss her, when he recollects something*]. Oh, by the way, Eliza, order a ham and a Stilton cheese, will you? And buy me a pair of reindeer gloves, number eights, and a tie to match that new suit of mine. You can choose the color. [*His cheerful, careless, vigorous voice shows that he is incorrigible*].

LIZA. [*disdainfully*] Number eights are too small for you if you want them lined with lamb's wool. You have three new ties that you have forgotten in the drawer of your washstand. Colonel Pickering prefers double Gloucester to Stilton; and you don't notice the difference. I telephoned Mrs Pearce this morning not to forget the ham. What you are to do without me I cannot imagine. [*She sweeps out*].

MRS. HIGGINS. I'm afraid you've spoiled that girl, Henry. I should be uneasy about you and her if she were less fond of Colonel Pickering.

HIGGINS. Pickering! Nonsense: she's going to marry Freddy. Ha ha! Freddy! Freddy!! Ha ha ha ha ha!!!!! [*He roars with laughter as the play ends*]

Instead of a happy ending, we see that the pupil has turned the tables on her teacher.

Check your understanding

1. What does Eliza say which makes Higgins so angry?

2. How will Eliza set herself up as a teacher of phonetics (the sounds of languages, the Professor's subject)?

3. Why does Higgins now find Eliza admirable?

4. Why does Shaw bring in Mrs Higgins to say that Higgins always behaves badly in church?

5. How does Higgins show that he is sure Eliza will come back after her father's wedding?

6. How does Eliza show him that he will now struggle to cope without her?

7. Do you think she will come back?

Pair and share

Form a group of three to perform this scene.

Look together at the stage directions.

- How does Shaw make this scene dramatically effective?

- How do various actions support the words of the characters?

- How does he indicate the tone with which the actors speak?

Now make the scene as dramatic and full of contrasts of tone as you can.

Practice question

This kind of question asks you to analyse the writer's methods ('how') and techniques ('writing') and to evaluate Shaw's purpose. Remember to think about the effect on the audience. Think about the decisions he has made about the final scene, his stage directions, and his choice of words:

How successfully does Shaw's writing in this scene show that Eliza is now a more powerful character than Higgins?

Write 300–400 words.

Note that although there will be no bullet points to help you in the drama paper, there is guidance in the unseen paper in the form of bullet points. Use the questions here to structure your response.

1. How do the stage directions in this scene show you how much stronger Eliza is now?

2. How has Eliza's status changed? Why has she developed more than Higgins?

3. What do you think Shaw might be suggesting to his audience about the changing relationships between different classes and between men and women?

4. Where does Eliza show her understanding of how the modern world works?

5. How would the audience react to such a powerful portrayal of Eliza and to her rejection of a traditional 'happy ending' with Higgins?

For more advice about writing critical essays, look ahead to chapter 6.

 Viewpoints

Does this work well as an alternative to the happy ending that Shaw's audience might have expected? Do you agree that a marriage between Eliza and Higgins would never work? Why not? Why have those who have **adapted** the play wanted to soften the ending?

KEY TERM

adapt = rewriting a text to fit a different format, for example, play to film or musical (play with songs).

Looking back

We have explored the ways in which drama is structured and the effect of its form on the audience. We have also suggested that dramatic form changes in response to changes in society.

Write notes in response to the following questions.

1. What kind of characters interest and intrigue an audience most?

2. Why is a contrast a successful way of developing drama?

3. What makes conflict between characters, whether serious or comic, so dramatically effective?

4. What is the traditional way of resolving conflicts in comedy?

5. Why might the more realistic writers of recent times have wanted to quarrel with this tradition?

We will explore dramatic form and its effect on the audience in more detail in chapter 7.

Reading prose texts

3.1 Prose: the novel and short story

'Prose' may not be a term you use very often, but literary texts that are not written in verse are usually called 'prose texts'. Shakespeare's dramas are written in a mixture of verse (like the poetry used by the quarreling friends and lovers in *A Midsummer Night's Dream*) and prose (used by the 'rude mechanicals', the ordinary workers, when they are not trying to act).

Prose really means anything that is not written in verse. When this is explained in Molière's comedy *Le Bourgeois Gentilhomme* to the middle-class gentleman of the title, Monsieur Jourdain, he is amazed to discover that 'I have been speaking prose all my life and did not know it'. By 'prose texts', English literature teachers usually mean novels and short stories.

The novel is, in fact, one of the most recent of literary forms: as we have seen, imaginative literary texts were originally devised to be performed aloud, sung or acted before an audience. In the history of literature, prose only becomes a genre for storytelling once more people can read, books have become much cheaper to produce, and as a result many more people have access to texts.

 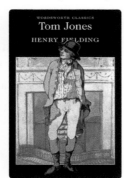 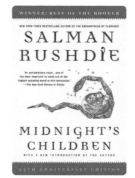

Covers of some prose texts

Today, prose is the literary form we are most familiar with. We read books and stories privately for their plot, for interesting characters, and to take us into an imaginary world different from our own. What is called 'genre fiction', for example, detective stories, thrillers, fantasy novels, romances, Gothic stories, and adventure, is especially popular. These kinds of books are often adapted into films and television series. We are less used to reading prose texts aloud, together, or performing or analysing them, although you have probably done all of these activities in your English classes.

LEARNING POINTS

▶ To develop appreciation of the forms of literature by looking at prose

▶ To explore writer's choices of structure, viewpoint, and characterization through the short story

▶ To appreciate the importance of developments such as conflict and confrontation in identifying key moments in a short story

▶ To explore different forms of closure, including the use of irony and symbolism

▶ To develop further the ways in which our understanding of texts is shaped by their historical and cultural context.

Stories about characters such as Sherlock Holmes are often turned into television series

The set prose text is probably the biggest challenge of your Cambridge IGCSE English Literature course. It involves the detailed study of quite a long text, written for adults not children, with complex characters and a plot (in film usually called the 'storyline'). There is a lot to read, even more that you can analyse, and difficult choices to make about what you should concentrate on. One option in the prose section is to study ten short stories. This is not necessarily an easier option: you have more characters and plots to learn, a variety of different styles and contexts to master, and no single storyline to help you through the text. However, you can learn a lot about how prose works through the short story.

In this unit, we will explore how three writers begin, develop, and conclude their short stories.

Think ahead

When writing a story where is the best place to start?

What are the advantages and disadvantages of beginning your story:

▶ at the beginning
▶ somewhere in the middle and then include a flashback
▶ at the end and then explain how you got there?

What decisions do you need to make before you start?

You need to answer the questions: Where? When? Who? What? How? Why? But not necessarily in that order.

Who is going to tell your story? Consider the advantages and disadvantages of:

▶ a first-person narrative by one of the characters, inside the story and involved in its action
▶ an objective narrator telling the story in the third person, and viewing the action from the outside
▶ a narrator telling the story in the third person but able to enter the minds of the characters and explain their thoughts and viewpoints.

The choice of **viewpoint** is crucial when beginning a story.

KEY TERMS

viewpoint = the person from whose point of view we 'see' the events of the story. This might be a narrator looking at events from outside the story or one of the characters.

characters = characters are people invented by the writer to have a particular effect on the reader. Characterization is the way writers use characters.

 **Language links**

Think about the decisions you have made in your own narrative writing. How have you achieved a striking opening? How have you introduced **characters**, setting, and situation?

Pair and share

With your partner, discuss the kind of books and stories you like.

1. What are the names of your favourite books?
2. Where are they set?
3. Who are your favourite characters?
4. What kind of action is involved?
5. What are the funniest moments?
6. Which are the most exciting?
7. Do you prefer happy or sad endings?
8. What do the writers do to get your attention in the first pages?

 Viewpoints

The essential building blocks of prose writing are:

- action
- **dialogue**
- **description**.

Which do you think is the most important and least important? Why are all three necessary? What is the purpose of description?

Write down three essential purposes for description in writing stories.

What is the function of detail in description and how does it help you to visualize the story?

Think ahead

In chapter 2, we explored the ways in which class and social attitudes towards the end of the nineteenth century influenced comedy and drama. We explored tension, the clash of characters, and the ways in which drama handles conflict (quarrels and fights) and resolution (different kinds of ending).

The first three short stories in this chapter all show generations clashing.

▶ Why might different generations have different attitudes and ways of speaking?

▶ What are the slang words you use that your parents and teachers don't understand?

▶ How do your attitudes differ from theirs?

▶ Who has a better understanding of the way the world is changing?

▶ Which attitudes of older people are you most critical of?

3.2 Opening a short story

Many short stories begin with description which gradually introduces a character. Thomas Hardy begins his short story 'The Son's Veto' with a long descriptive passage which plunges into the middle of the story. A mother and son are described, but we will only find out their names, the nature of their relationship, and how the mother came to be married and living in London later in the story. At first, the woman is described from the outside, but towards the end of this extract, the writer decides to change his viewpoint and to tell us her thoughts. Hardy is using a technique of gradual revelation: the reader becomes more informed about the characters in the story than the characters are themselves, but only in stages.

KEY TERMS

dialogue = any situation where two or more people are speaking. Dialogue helps to dramatize prose and bring the characters to life.

description = this is never just 'setting the scene'. Description is often a metaphor for characters' feelings or the emotional atmosphere the writer wants to create, and not just there to help you imagine the physical environment.

'The Son's Veto' by Thomas Hardy (1894)

To the eyes of a man viewing it from behind, the nut-brown hair was a wonder and a mystery. Under the black beaver hat, surmounted by its tuft of black feathers, the long locks, braided and twisted and coiled like the rushes of a basket, composed a rare, if somewhat barbaric, example of ingenious art. One could understand such weavings and coilings being wrought to last intact for a year, or even a calendar month; but that they should be all demolished regularly at bedtime, after a single day of permanence, seemed a reckless waste of successful fabrication.

And she had done it all herself, poor thing. She had no maid, and it was almost the only accomplishment she could boast of. Hence the unstinted pains.

She was a young invalid lady – not so very much of an invalid – sitting in a wheeled chair, which had been pulled up in the front part of a green enclosure, close to a bandstand, where a concert was going on, during a warm June afternoon. It had place in one of the minor parks or private gardens that are to be found in the suburbs of London, and was the effort of a local association to raise money for some charity. There are worlds within worlds in the great city, and though nobody outside the immediate district had ever heard of the charity, or the band, or the garden, the enclosure was filled with an interested audience sufficiently informed on all these.

As the strains proceeded many of the listeners observed the chaired lady, whose back hair, by reason of her prominent position, so challenged inspection. Her face was not easily discernible, but the aforesaid cunning tress-weavings, the white ear and poll, and the curve of a cheek which was neither flaccid nor sallow, were signals that led to the expectation of good beauty in front. Such expectations are not infrequently disappointed as soon as the disclosure comes; and in the present case, when the lady, by a turn of the head, at length revealed herself, she was not so handsome as the people behind her had supposed, and even hoped – they did not know why.

For one thing (alas! the commonness of this complaint), she was less young than they had fancied her to be. Yet attractive her face unquestionably was, and not at all sickly. The revelation of its details came each time she turned to talk to a boy of twelve or thirteen who stood beside her, and the shape of whose hat and jacket implied that he belonged to a well-known public school. The immediate bystanders could hear that he called her 'Mother.'

When the end of the recital was reached, and the audience withdrew, many chose to find their way out by passing at her elbow. Almost all turned their heads to take a full and near look at the interesting woman, who remained stationary in the chair till the way should be clear enough for her to be wheeled out without obstruction. As if she expected their glances, and did not mind gratifying their curiosity, she met the eyes of several of her observers by lifting her own, showing these to be soft, brown, and affectionate orbs, a little plaintive in their regard.

She was conducted out of the gardens, and passed along the pavement till she disappeared from view, the schoolboy walking beside her. To inquiries made by some persons who watched her away, the answer came that she was the second wife of the incumbent of a neighbouring parish, and that she was lame. She was generally believed to be a woman with a story – an innocent one, but a story of some sort or other.

In conversing with her on their way home the boy who walked at her elbow said that he hoped his father had not missed them.

'He have been so comfortable these last few hours that I am sure he cannot have missed us,' she replied.

'*Has*, dear mother – not *have*!' exclaimed the public-school boy, with an impatient fastidiousness that was almost harsh. 'Surely you know that by this time!'

His mother hastily adopted the correction, and did not resent his making it, or retaliate, as she might well have done, by bidding him to wipe that crumby mouth of his, whose condition had been caused by surreptitious attempts to eat a piece of cake without taking it out of the pocket wherein it lay concealed. After this the pretty woman and the boy went onward in silence.

That question of grammar bore upon her history, and she fell into reverie, of a somewhat sad kind to all appearance. It might have been assumed that she was wondering if she had done wisely in shaping her life as she had shaped it, to bring out such a result as this.

Check your understanding

1. What is it that makes the woman's coiled hair 'a wonder and a mystery'?

2. What does the narrator know that a casual observer would not?

3. What do these facts reveal about the woman's class and status?

4. Why might people watching her find her fascinating?

5. And why might they also be disappointed?

6. What picture does Hardy give of people and attitudes in this part of London?

7. What is revealing about the boy's uniform and the way he addresses his mother?

8. What do the woman's eyes reveal about her temperament?

9. What does the boy's correction of his mother's grammar show?

10. How does her grammar relate to her past life or 'history'?

 Pair and share

Create a table and collect quotations that show some of the characteristics of the woman in the story, who is called Sophie. We have given a few below to start you off. Hardy's language is difficult, so you may need a dictionary to help you.

Quotation	What it reveals about Sophie
a reckless waste of successful fabrication	She has nothing else to do but keep up her appearance which is slightly fake – 'fabrication'
unstinted pains	
challenged inspection	
attractive her face unquestionably was, and not at all sickly	
did not mind gratifying their curiosity	
affectionate orbs, a little plaintive in their regard	
generally believed to be a woman with a story	
did not resent his making it, or attempt to retaliate	
reverie, of a somewhat sad kind to all appearance	

1. How does Hardy manage to suggest that although Sophie's life has been successful in terms of raising her social status, it is not really a happy one?

2. Why might the attitude of her son, Randolph, make this unhappiness greater?

Viewpoints

Should we feel sorry for Sophie, or do we think she has made her own destiny ('shaping her life as she had shaped it')? Use the questions below to assemble your own notes.

Consider the evidence.

1. What makes her seem self-pitying and attention-seeking?

2. Which details make us feel sorry for her and the life she now lives?

There is evidence to make us feel sorry for her as well as think she has created her own situation because Hardy wants us to be interested and not to have made up our minds yet. The description and the snippet of dialogue between Sophie and Randolph make us want to find out more. They have interested us in the whole plot and how it develops.

1. Is the description of her hair a symbol or metaphor?

2. What else seems a 'reckless waste' and 'fabrication'?

3. How has Sophie's change of status affected the relationship she has with her son?

4. Because he was born into a higher class, he already seems to look down on her, in more than one way. Which is the key quotation which shows his attitude towards her?

Extend your learning

Hardy has deliberately chosen to give us a picture of Sophie from the outside, to make us judge her. Look back over the evidence, and then write a **character sketch** of Sophie. What questions does the reader ask about her? What is her status in society and what are her feelings?

Write about 300 words in answer to this question:

> *How does Hardy's language make her appear mysterious and gradually reveal her unhappiness?*

KEY TERM

character sketch = description of how the writer has described and presented a character, using quotations as evidence.

3.3 Developing character and situation

The next extract shows how writers use details of character and situation to develop their plots further.

Think ahead

Like Sophie Twycott in 'The Son's Veto', Lord Emsworth prefers the countryside. What images do you have of 'an English country gentleman' or an 'aristocrat'? Why might they make good comic characters if you exaggerate their characteristics?

Between the wars, England was still a very class-conscious society, but America offered new money and new attitudes.

P.G. Wodehouse's novels are set in an exaggerated and fantastic version of England between the wars and make fun of class-conscious society, eccentric aristocrats, and their clever and cunning servants. In 'The Custody of the Pumpkin', the Earl of Emsworth, owner of Blandings Castle, has, through his new telescope, spotted his party-loving second son, the Honourable Freddie, with a young lady called Aggie. He is horrified to hear they are engaged, and even more horrified to hear that Aggie is American and 'a sort of cousin' of his own gardener, Angus McAllister. Lord Emsworth wants Freddie to marry a rich girl, so he won't have to support him any longer. He therefore dismisses McAllister from his job at Blandings.

English country house

'The Custody of the Pumpkin' by P.G. Wodehouse (1935)

The importance of this pumpkin in the Earl of Emsworth's life requires, perhaps, a word of explanation. Every ancient family in England has some little gap in its scroll of honour, and that of Lord Emsworth was no exception. For generations back his ancestors had been doing notable deeds; they had sent out from Blandings Castle statesmen and warriors, governors and leaders of the people: but they had not – in the opinion of the present holder of the title – achieved a full hand. However splendid the family record might appear at first sight, the fact remained that no Earl of Emsworth had ever won a first prize for pumpkins at the Shrewsbury Show. For roses, yes. For tulips, true. For spring onions, granted. But not for pumpkins; and Lord Emsworth felt it deeply.

For many a summer past he had been striving indefatigably to remove this blot on the family escutcheon, only to see his hopes go tumbling down. But this year at last victory had seemed in sight, for there had been vouchsafed to Blandings a competitor of such amazing parts that his lordship, who had watched it grow practically from a pip, could not envisage failure. Surely, he told himself as he gazed on its golden roundness, even Sir Gregory Parsloe-Parsloe, of Matchingham Hall, winner for three successive years, would never be able to produce anything to challenge this superb vegetable.

And it was this supreme pumpkin whose welfare he feared he had jeopardized by dismissing Angus McAllister. For Angus was its official trainer. He understood the pumpkin. Indeed, in his reserved Scottish way, he even seemed to love it. With Angus gone, what would the harvest be?

Such were the meditations of Lord Emsworth as he reviewed the position of affairs. And though, as the days went by, he tried to tell himself that Angus McAllister was not the only man in the world who understood pumpkins, and that he had every confidence, the most complete and unswerving confidence, in Robert Barker, recently Angus's second-in-command, now promoted to the post of head-gardener and custodian of the Blandings Hope, he knew that this was but shallow bravado. When you are a pumpkin owner with a big winner in your stable, you judge men by hard standards, and every day it became plainer that Robert Barker was only a makeshift. Within a week Lord Emsworth was pining for Angus McAllister.

It might be purely imagination, but to his excited fancy the pumpkin seemed to be pining for Angus too. It appeared to be drooping and losing weight. Lord Emsworth could not rid himself of the horrible idea that it was shrinking. And on the tenth night after McAllister's departure he dreamed a strange dream. He had gone with King George to show his Gracious Majesty the pumpkin, promising him the treat of a lifetime; and when they arrived, there in the corner of the frame was a shrivelled thing the size of a pea. He woke, sweating, with his Sovereign's disappointed screams ringing in his ears; and Pride gave its last quiver and collapsed. To reinstate Angus would be a surrender, but it must be done.

Pair and share

Collect the adjectives and phrases that Lord Emsworth uses to describe the pumpkin, both in paragraphs two and three, and in paragraph five. How do they reveal the extent of Lord Emsworth's obsession?

A pumpkin

Check your understanding

1. What were Lord Emsworth's ancestors famous for?
2. What is the only fame he is interested in?
3. Who is his enemy in the competition?
4. Why has dismissing McAllister caused him a problem?
5. What makes the dream so terrifying for Lord Emsworth?
6. Why is reinstating McAllister a 'surrender'?

Extend your learning

Although this passage is told in the third person, it clearly recreates Lord Emsworth's point of view. How does his language reveal his attitudes? Not only is he obsessed with the prize pumpkin (which is odd enough) but his language is very old-fashioned. Use your dictionary to establish the meaning of some of the odder words in this story.

Lord Emsworth's vocabulary	Modern English equivalent
achieved a full hand	Won everything possible
striving indefatigably	
blot on the family escutcheon	
but shallow bravado	
to his excited fancy	
his Gracious Majesty	
Pride gave its last quiver	
to reinstate Angus would be a surrender	

His language uses old-fashioned vocabulary, and he is also fond of imagery. Can you find metaphors and personification in his language?

Viewpoints

Is Lord Emsworth charmingly old-fashioned, eccentric, and funny? Or deeply sad, out of touch, and mad?

You decide.

1. Which is the better way to view Lord Emsworth?

2. What does the writer want you to think about him?

Write a paragraph supporting each point of view. Make sure you use quotations from the text as evidence to support your view.

Looking at the evidence, what do you think was Wodehouse's opinion of Lord Emsworth?

3.4 Endings

As we have seen, happy endings are a convention in comedy, however unlikely they may seem. However, in the short story endings are often very much more open, and they can come rather abruptly, leaving you to decide what the story was about. The term for this is **closure**. Lord Emsworth is given a happy ending: Freddie marries a rich girl and is off his hands, and he beats Sir Gregory Parsloe-Parsloe with his immensely superior pumpkin, thanks to McAllister. However, nothing ends happily for Sophie in 'The Son's Veto', as her son forbids her a second chance at happiness, showing the power of class snobbery.

> **KEY TERM**
>
> **closure** = the way a text ends; sometimes we say that a text 'resists closure' because it does not end neatly, and problems are not resolved.

Think ahead

Graham Greene's 'The Destructors' was written soon after the Second World War, when London and other major cities were still full of bomb sites.

Draw a timeline showing key world events between 1945 and 1954. The internet is a good resource for finding out what these key events were. Refer to websites such as www.bbc.co.uk/history/british/ or www.britishempire.co.uk/timeline/20century.htm.

Focus on the events that might have made British people feel their world was being transformed or destroyed. In particular look at:

▶ the end of the Second World War

▶ the end of the British Empire

▶ the Cold War.

A house near a bomb site

The gang of young boys who give this short story its title enjoy mischief. While Mr Thomas, or 'Old Misery', is away over the bank holiday, they get into his old house, one of the few left standing around the bomb site and held up by wooden props, and systematically demolish it, led by T. who has assumed leadership through this plan. Even the complication of Old Misery's early return makes no difference. They lock him in his own outdoor 'loo' (a slang word for toilet).

'The Destructors' by Graham Greene (1954)

Mike had gone home to bed, but the rest stayed. The question of leadership no longer concerned the gang. With nails, chisels, screwdrivers, anything that was sharp and penetrating, they moved around the inner walls worrying at the mortar between the bricks. They started too high, and it was Blackie who hit on the damp course and realized the work could be halved if they weakened the joints immediately above. It was a long, tiring, unamusing job, but at last it was finished. The gutted house stood there balanced on a few inches of mortar between the damp course and the bricks.

There remained the most dangerous task of all, out in the open at the edge of the bomb-site. Summers was sent to watch the road for passers-by, and Mr Thomas, sitting on the loo, heard clearly now the sound of sawing. It no longer came from the house, and that a little reassured him. He felt less concerned. Perhaps the other noises too had no significance.

A voice spoke to him through the hole. 'Mr Thomas.'

'Let me out,' Mr Thomas said sternly.

'Here's a blanket,' the voice said, and a long grey sausage was worked through the hole and fell in swathes over Mr Thomas's head.

'There's nothing personal,' the voice said. 'We want you to be comfortable tonight.'

'Tonight,' Mr Thomas repeated incredulously.

'Catch,' the voice said. 'Penny buns – we've buttered them, and sausage-rolls. We don't want you to starve, Mr Thomas.' Mr Thomas pleaded desperately. 'A joke's a joke, boy. Let me out and I won't say a thing. I've got rheumatics. I got to sleep comfortable.'

'You wouldn't be comfortable, not in your house, you wouldn't. Not now.'

'What do you mean, boy?' But the footsteps receded. There was only the silence of night: no sound of sawing. Mr Thomas tried one more yell, but he was daunted and rebuked by the silence – a long way off an owl hooted and made away again on its muffled flight through the soundless world.

At seven next morning the driver came to fetch his lorry. He climbed into the seat and tried to start the engine. He was vaguely aware of a voice shouting, but it didn't concern him. At last the engine responded and he backed the lorry until it touched the great wooden shore that supported Mr Thomas's house. That way he could drive right out and down the street without reversing. The lorry moved forward, was momentarily checked as though something were pulling it from behind, and then went on to the sound of a long rumbling crash. The driver was astonished to see bricks bouncing ahead of him, while stones hit the roof of his cab. He put on his brakes. When he climbed out the whole landscape had suddenly altered. There was no house beside the car-park, only a hill of rubble. He went round and examined the back of his lorry for damage, and found a rope tied there that was still twisted at the other end round part of a wooden strut.

The driver again became aware of somebody shouting. It came from the wooden erection which was the nearest thing to a house in that desolation of broken brick. The driver climbed the smashed wall and unlocked the door. Mr Thomas came out of the loo. He was wearing a grey blanket to which flakes of pastry adhered. He gave a sobbing cry. 'My house,' he said. 'Where's my house?'

'Search me,' the driver said. His eye lit on the remains of a bath and what had once been a dresser and he began to laugh. There wasn't anything left anywhere.

'How dare you laugh,' Mr Thomas said. 'It was my house. My house.'

'I'm sorry,' the driver said, making heroic efforts, but when he remembered the sudden check of his lorry, the crash of bricks falling, he became convulsed again. One moment the house had stood there with such dignity between the bomb-sites like a man in a top hat, and then, bang, crash, there wasn't anything left – not anything. He said, 'I'm sorry. I can't help it, Mr Thomas. There's nothing personal, but you got to admit it's funny.'

✎ Check your understanding

Greene chooses to alternate description and dialogue in this passage.

1. How do the descriptions of the boys demolishing the house show their hard work as 'destructors'?

2. How does the detail of the dialogue reveal Mr Thomas's low status in comparison with the boys?

3. How does the writer show the fall of Mr Thomas's house from the lorry driver's point of view?

4. Why do you think the boys are not there?

5. Which details show the violence and completeness of the 'desolation'?

6. How does the dialogue show the different points of view of Mr Thomas and the driver?

7. Why does the driver laugh? Is he right to laugh?

8. Is this a happy ending? Or an open ending?

Extend your learning

Irony is used by writers when they, and the readers, know things that the characters do not. We often read the details of stories differently once we know the ending. Looking more closely at language, aware of what will happen next, comment on the effects of the following phrases:

a. 'they moved around the inner walls worrying at the mortar between the bricks'

b. 'it was a long, tiring, unamusing job'

c. 'We want you to be comfortable tonight.'

d. 'A joke's a joke, boy.'

e. 'You wouldn't be comfortable, not in your house, you wouldn't. Not now.'

f. 'He was vaguely aware of a voice shouting'

g. 'the sound of a long rumbling crash'

h. 'the whole landscape had suddenly altered'

i. 'the nearest thing to a house in that desolation of broken brick'

j. 'How dare you laugh'

k. 'he became convulsed again'

Symbolism is the use of an extended metaphor to construct a story beneath the surface story. The word 'house' occurs more often than any other in this extract.

1. What might the house stand for or symbolize? (Remember that it is very old, and was left behind when others around it were destroyed by the war.)

2. Could it stand for Britain itself?

3. If so, who are the boys, and who is the lorry driver?

The style in this passage changes. Most of the language is plain and straightforward, especially compared to Lord Emsworth's old-fashioned language. However, the writer adds some poetic touches (similar to language we will explore in chapter 4).

Look at the use of **personification**:

'he was daunted and rebuked by the silence – a long way off an owl hooted and made away again on its muffled flight through the soundless world'.

4. How does this passage contrast the sounds of the human world with the silence of the night?

5. Why do you think Greene chose to mention the sound of a bird of prey?

Explore the significance of the final **simile**:

'the house had stood there with such dignity between the bomb-sites like a man in a top hat, and then, bang, crash, there wasn't anything left – not anything'.

6. What does the top hat image contribute to the reader's ideas about the house?

7. What is the effect of the repetition?

Extend your learning

1. Consider different generations in 'The Son's Veto' and 'Her First Ball'.

2. How do parents and children clash in 'The Son's Veto' and 'The Custody of the Pumpkin'?

3. How do the older and younger generation differ in 'The Custody of the Pumpkin' and 'The Destructors'?

4. How do different cultures clash in 'A Horse and Two Goats', and 'Sandpiper'

5. How does the 'The Rain Horse' portray conflict between man and nature?

6. How do 'My Greatest Ambition' and 'At Hiruharama' portray growing up?

3.5 Structure of the short story

We have looked at the structure of the short story through three examples. All these stories involve older people clashing with younger people and their attitudes.

We have explored how writers use:

- setting when opening their stories
- gradual revelation of character and situation
- use of a character's viewpoint
- and the irony and symbolism implied by a story's ending.

You can use these structural ideas, and some of those in the previous chapter on drama, to look at other short stories.

On the next page we give you some headings that you can use to organize your notes with questions you could ask for each.

 See Worksheet 3 on the website for further help with the structure of short stories.

KEY TERMS

personification = a particular form of metaphor; ideas or objects are given human characteristics and treated as if they were a person.

simile = an explicit comparison using 'like' or 'as'.

SITUATION and CHARACTERS

1. Who are the characters from different generations and why do they clash?
2. What are their different interests?
3. Why are their motivations different?

CONTRAST

What are the differences between:
1. their appearances
2. the ways they speak
3. the ways they react to things
4. things they say or are said about them?

CONFLICT

1. Why do those differences begin to cause problems?
2. What happens as the story develops which shows that the generations are going to clash?
3. What has brought out the difference in their interests, attitudes and way of thinking and speaking?

PROBLEM

Writers of short stories often introduce an additional problem about halfway through the story in order to complicate the plot further.

Can you find an example? How is it linked to the original conflict?

CONFRONTATION

Problems can lead to more arguments before there is a solution or resolution.

1. How have developments in the story brought on a battle between two different characters and ways of speaking as well as thinking?
2. Where do characters confront each other in a dramatic way?

SOLUTION or RESOLUTION

1. Is the problem solved?
2. How has the writer chosen to end the story?
3. What does the reader think about at the end?
4. Are we happy with the ending or disturbed by it?
5. Does the writer have a particular bias or point of view which he wants you to share?
6. Do characters resolve their problems at all?
7. What is the difference between a comic (happy) ending and a tragic (sad) one?
8. Does the ending involve irony or symbolism?

Extend your learning

Refer to the story you are studying and answer these questions.

1. Identify the key pages where characters are introduced and where their differences become obvious.
2. How does the writer's use of language show differences between characters? Collect quotations which illustrate the difference between characters.
3. Where do additional problems complicate the action? Plot the action of your story and make a note of the page where the 'problem' develops.

How has the writer made this a dramatic moment?

4. Look for dialogue which reveals the difference between characters in a striking way. This is clear towards the end of 'The Son's Veto', or when the father and son talk about money in 'The Fly in the Ointment'.
5. Do the differences between characters lead to a confrontation? Or are they left unresolved? For different reasons, there is no clear resolution in 'The Rain Horse' or 'Sandpiper'. This is left for us to work out from the symbolism of the language.

3.6 English literature becomes world literature

After 1945, with the United Kingdom in decline economically and politically, the story of 'English' becomes less connected with the story of England, and more about the English language as something that connects (and sometimes divides) people from many different cultures all over the world. We saw this in chapter 1 when we looked at 'A Horse and Two Goats'. Many twentieth-century texts explore America and the American dream of independence, or the process of independence and rediscovery of identity in **post-colonial** cultures after 1945.

The English language bound these many different cultures together, but has had to diversify in order to respect different identities. The increase in the number of people not born in the British Isles who speak English has changed the nature of 'English' language and literature, just as it has changed notions of culture and identity. Inter-marriage between members of very different communities and people has also influenced how individuals express their sense of who they are. We can read this in their language and stories: many novels and stories now explore the experience of migration and multiculturalism. You might read 'The Third and Final Continent' by Jhumpa Lahiri or Anita Desai's *Fasting, Feasting*.

Statue of Liberty

Gate of India

In the title story of Ahdaf Soueif's *Sandpiper*, a young writer from Britain reflects on her eight years of marriage to her husband, and her experience of living in his homeland of Egypt. She reflects on her visit to another part of Africa, how she fell in love, and on the image of her daughter Lucy, playing by their beach house near Alexandria. Her marriage has become difficult, as this quotation shows.

A Sandpiper

'Sandpiper' by Ahdaf Soueif (1994)

I suppose I should have seen it coming. My foreignness, which had been so charming, began to irritate him. My inability to remember names, to follow the minutiae of politics, my struggles with his language, my need to be protected from the sun, the mosquitoes, the salads, the drinking water. He was back home, and he needed someone he could simply be at home with, at home. It took perhaps a year. His heart was broken in two, mine was simply broken.

✎ Check your understanding

1. What is the effect of the lists in the third sentence?

2. What has the narrator found so difficult about life in Egypt?

3. How has her husband reacted?

4. How does the use of pronouns bring out the rift between the unnamed narrator and her unnamed husband?

5. How does the writer bring out the importance of 'home' for the husband?

6. By contrast what seem to be the feelings of the narrator?

7. Why does it help to know that a sandpiper is a migratory bird, found all over the world? Who is the sandpiper in this story?

Before reading this, you need to know that the narrator has just told, in flashback, the story of how she was nearly killed when the aircraft she was travelling in when visiting Nigeria had to crash land. Soon afterwards, she married her husband.

KEY TERM

post-colonial = the literature which came after the break-up of the British Empire, and other colonial structures.

'Sandpiper' by Ahdaf Soueif (1994)

And in that moment, not only my head, but all of me, my whole being, seemed to tilt into a blank, an empty radiance, but lucid. Then three giant thoughts. One was of him – his name, over and over again. The other was of the children I would never have. The third was that the pattern was now complete: this is what my life amounted to.

When we did not die, that first thought: his name, his name, his name became a talisman, for in extremity, hadn't all that was not him been wiped out of my life? My life, which once again stretched out before me, shimmering with possibilities, was meant to merge with his.

I finished the french plait and Lucy chose a blue clasp to secure its end. Before I let her run out I smoothed some after-sun on her face. Her skin is nut-brown, except just next to her ears where it fades to a pale cream gleaming with golden down. I put my lips to her neck. 'My Lucy, Lucia, *Lambah*,' I murmured as I kissed her and let her go. Lucy. My treasure, my trap.

Now, when I walk to the sea, to the edge of this continent where I live, where I almost died, where I wait for my daughter to grow away from me, I see different things from those I saw that summer six years ago. The last of the foam is swallowed bubbling into the sand, to sink down and rejoin the sea at an invisible subterranean level. With each ebb of green water the sand loses part of itself to the sea, with each flow another part is flung back to be reclaimed once again by the beach. That narrow stretch of sand knows nothing in the world better than it does the white waves that whip it, caress it, collapse onto it, vanish into it. The white foam knows nothing better than those sands which wait for it, rise to it, and suck it in. But what do the waves know of the massed, hot, still sands of the desert just twenty, no, ten feet beyond the scalloped edge? And what does the beach know of the depths, the cold, the currents just there, there – do you see it? – where the water turns a deeper blue.

 Viewpoints

The world has become a smaller place, bringing about new cultural exchanges but also more difficulties. The mysterious and open nature of the way this story ends leaves you, as the reader, with plenty to think about and work out for yourself. We are not directly told what will happen next, although we know plenty about the past. Perhaps this makes this kind of writing especially true to life. You will need to debate the meaning of the ending with a partner.

How do you interpret the imagery of sea, sand and desert in these powerful final paragraphs of the story?

 Check your understanding

1. In the first paragraph, the narrator is still looking back at the moment when she thought she was going to die. What three things did she think of?

2. When she survives, how does the pattern of her thoughts show what mattered most to her at the time?

3. How does repetition and the form of her sentences show this?

4. What do you think she means by a 'talisman'?

5. How did she understand the pattern of life at the time when she realized she would not die?

6. How has the pattern of her life developed since?

7. Why do you think she pays special attention to her daughter when she is thinking in this way?

8. Why is the description of Lucy's skin colour significant here?

9. Why does she call her daughter 'My treasure, my trap?'

10. How does the beginning of the final paragraph bring together the narrator's thoughts about Africa, her daughter, and her marriage?

Pair and share

Compare your answers with a partner. You will need to work together to make sense of the final paragraph. One of you should look at the imagery of the sea and the foam of the waves. The other should explore the imagery that describes the sand or desert. Together you will work out what the description of the two coming together, or clashing, might symbolize.

First, use the quotation and comment technique to explore the meaning of each individual image. You will need to go beyond the surface meaning and look at what is suggested. Some answers have been done for you in the table below.

The sea	
'I walk to the sea … where I wait for my daughter to grow away from me'	Suggests a link between the sea and freedom, growing away from home
'The last of the foam is swallowed bubbling into the sand …'	
'… to sink down and rejoin the sea at an invisible subterranean level …'	Suggests the waves will never become part of the land, they will eventually rejoin the sea
'The white foam knows nothing better than those sands which wait for it, rise to it and suck it in.'	
'But what do the waves know of the massed, hot, still, sands of the desert …'	
'… the depths … where the water turns a deeper blue.'	
The desert sands	
'With each ebb of green water the sand loses part of itself to the sea …'	
'… another part is flung back to be reclaimed once again by the beach.'	Suggests that the sand always returns to the land
'That narrow stretch of sand knows nothing in the world better than it does the white waves that whip it, caress it, collapse onto it, vanish into it.'	Suggests the relationship between sands and seas is sometimes gentle, sometimes violent, and that the sands absorb the water
'… what does the beach know of the depths, the cold, the currents just there …'	

Share your answers and discuss the following questions.

1. Have you both noticed a pattern?
2. What kind of relationship is described?
3. Where do both sand and sea really belong?
4. How do the final questions move beyond the beach where the two meet and explore their very different worlds and senses?
5. How do these images contrast?
6. Which people in the marriage might sand and sea correspond to, and why?
7. What is ironic about this use of symbolism of sand and sea, considering coastal erosion?
8. What is suggested about the past and future of the marriage?

Practice question

You will need to look back at the complete passage and your notes so far.
Write 300–400 words. Use the bullet points which follow the question to
give structure to your response.

- *How does Soueif's writing portray the thoughts and feelings of the narrator
  and make this a powerful ending to her story?*

To help you to answer, you might consider:

- the narrator's thoughts about the feelings which encouraged her to
  marry
- what she feels about her daughter now
- how her language expresses her thoughts about being a foreigner in
  Africa
- how the writer's choice of metaphors and expression show the nature
  of her marriage now
- what the reader feels about the way this story ends, and the way it
  expresses the narrator's deeper thoughts.

When you have written your answer, work with your teacher or a
partner to assess your writing. Have you produced a developed response
to the writing? Have you explored the 'deeper implications'? Have you
provided well-selected textual support? Are you working towards 'critical
understanding'?

Looking back

1. What have you learned about the importance of establishing
   interesting characters and situations?
2. How do problems, clashes, and conflicts contribute to the complexity
   of short stories?
3. How does viewpoint influence the reader's degree of sympathy?
4. Why are good endings often so mysterious or ambiguous?
5. Can you apply a similar structure to novels you have read or studied?

We will explore the structure and language of prose fiction in more detail
in chapter 8.

 Viewpoints

You should now be able to
answer the question you
were asked earlier about
how to interpret the final
paragraph. As we have seen,
making meaning goes far
beyond the literal meaning
of the words, and requires
you to explore metaphor
and imagery. The meaning
of the story is also shaped
by its viewpoint: we only
hear the wife's account of
her marriage. To make your
response personal, relate
your observations about
language to the way you
understand and interpret
character and situation, as
you have learned previously.

How have you come to
understand her thoughts and
feelings? Do you sympathize
with her? What do you
think will happen next?

Reading poetry

The poetry of war

Think ahead

Ancient heroes were portrayed with swords and shields

War is a powerful and emotive subject. It is also one of the traditional subjects of poetry, going back to early epics like Homer's *Iliad* or *Beowulf*, which made fighting and heroic action part of their narrative. Modern warfare brings even greater destruction and fewer opportunities for heroic action: soldiers often seem victims of a system beyond their control. Today, poets use verse to commemorate loss or to express a protest more often than to celebrate heroism or destruction.

1. Why do we hear more now about the problems caused by war than about heroic fighting?

2. Why are war and conflict appealing subjects for literature?

3. What kind of emotions can war poetry excite?

LEARNING POINTS

▶ To explore the distinctive features of poetry texts, linked by theme

▶ To analyse the effects of rhyme, rhythm, and stanza form

▶ To see patterns of words and imagery in poetry

▶ To use details of language and form to understand tone

▶ To interpret the meaning of poems by exploring mood.

4.1 The call to arms

Poetry gives shape to powerful feelings, by applying a strong rhythm and memorable images to the idea of conflict and destruction. British poets John Scott (1731–83) and A.E. Housman (1859–1936) call up the music and the images of the recruiting drum, which in the past was used to literally drum up support for the wars which the British fought abroad, while establishing their Empire. As the military band sounded their drums, young men would be called up to go off to fight, usually in other countries.

As you read the first poem below, try to hear the beat of the drum and to picture the scenes Scott describes.

A poster showing the recruiting drum

'The Drum' by John Scott (1782)

I hate that drum's discordant sound,
Parading round, and round, and round:
To thoughtless youth it pleasure yields
And lures from cities and from fields,
To sell their liberty for charms
Of tawdry lace, and glittering arms:
And when Ambition's voice commands,
To march, and fight, and fall, in foreign lands.

I hate that drum's discordant sound,
Parading round, and round, and round:
To me it talks of ravaged plains,
And burning towns, and ruined swains,
And mangled limbs, and dying groans,
And widows' tears and orphans' moans
And all that Misery's hand bestows,
To fill the catalogue of human woes.

tawdry = *cheap and nasty*

discordant = *harsh, unmusical*

swains = *young men*

bestows = *gives out*

RHYME and SYNTAX

Repetition and pattern are clearly important elements of the poem's structure. Poetic form relies on a number of elements which give the poem its shape and its sound. This poem is clearly divided into two **stanzas**: a stanza is the correct name for a verse paragraph (sometimes just called a verse). This poem also uses one of the most common forms of shaping a pattern in sound: rhyme. When pairs of lines rhyme in this way, we call them rhyming couplets.

Notice that the stanzas also provide the sentence structure or syntax of the poem.

Check your understanding

Look again at the poem.

1. Can you find the full stops?
2. What is the effect of these long-running sentences?
3. Is it easy to stop the flow, or to pause for thought?

A soldier in uniform

You should now learn to mark up the key features of a poem on a paper copy of the text, or on a whiteboard. Here the **rhyming couplets** have been underlined.

> I hate that drum's discordant <u>sound,</u>
> Parading round, and round, and <u>round</u>:
> To thoughtless youth it pleasure <u>yields</u>
> And lures from cities and from <u>fields,</u>
> To sell their liberty for ch<u>arms</u>
> Of tawdry lace, and glittering <u>arms</u>:
> And when Ambition's voice comm<u>ands,</u>
> To march, and fight, and fall, in foreign l<u>ands.</u>

The rhymes make the poem sound insistent and predictable, as if you cannot resist what comes next. In the past, words did not always sound the same as today: pronunciation of English varies a lot, which gives poets a degree of **poetic licence**.

The shading highlights the most often repeated word in the poem. What is the effect of this?

- Now mark up the next stanza in the same way.

RHYTHM

Having looked at rhyme and **syntax**, another important element in this poem is rhythm. The most common form of rhythm is the **iambic** rhythm of weak STRONG, often represented as x/. Rhythms in English poetry usually depend on **stress**, which means the words you place stress or emphasis on when speaking.

> x / x /   x / x /
> I hate that drum's   discordant sound,
> x / x / x / x /
> Parading round, and round, and round:

Pair and share

Notice the weak stress on the first syllable and the strong stress on the last.

1. Does this help you to hear the regular sound of the drum?
2. Look this word up and find out what it means about the sound of the poem.
3. Why does the poet call the music of the drum 'discordant'?
4. Discuss what you think the poet feels about the sound of the recruiting drum and why he feels that way.

KEY TERMS

stanza = the correct name for a paragraph of verse, sometimes called a verse.

rhyming couplets = pairs of lines that rhyme, a common pattern in English verse.

syntax = sentence structure.

poetic licence = the freedom which poets have to break or bend the rules, particularly over patterns of rhyme but also over what is real and what is imagined.

KEY TERMS

stress = where you put the emphasis when reading aloud, sometimes called the 'beat'.

iambic = iambic pentameter is the verse line most commonly used by Shakespeare and other verse dramatists, and very common in longer English poems. It is made up of a line with five beats in it following a weak STRONG rhythm. This is also the rhythm most common in English speech patterns.

Extend your learning

Imagery

Poems are highly visual as well as musical: they set up images as well as a soundtrack. As you have seen in previous chapters, we use the word **imagery** for language which is figurative or non-literal. A comparison, such as a **metaphor** or a simile, is used to create an image related to the object that is being described. Another form of imagery is personification: when an idea is presented as if it were a person. When an idea is personified, it often has a capital letter, so this kind of personification is easy to spot and to imagine.

1. Scott uses personification in the penultimate line of each verse: what do you think Ambition or Misery might sound or look like?

There is another form of personification which is much more subtle.

2. If you look at phrases like 'to thoughtless youth it pleasure leads' and words like 'lures', 'charms' and 'glittering arms', what do they suggest is attracting the young men to military life?

3. Is 'it' the drum? Or a woman?

4. How does this help you to picture the effect the drum has on the young men it is calling to?

 Pair and share

Choice of words and patterns

Diction is another word for a poet's choice of words: Scott chooses words for what they suggest to you as well as what they describe.

1. Why does he use words like 'tawdry' or 'glittering'?

2. What does it suggest about the rewards the men get for agreeing to 'sell their liberty'?

3. Why do they join up, and why do they get less than they expect?

Repetition is the key to the patterns in this poem, imitating the **repetitive** rhythms of the drum. The same technique can have very different effects in different places. Two examples of lists from the poem appear below. Comment on the effects of each.

a. To march, and fight, and *fall*, in foreign lands

b. And burning towns ..., And mangled limbs ..., And widows' tears ..., And *all* that Misery's hand bestows

 Viewpoints

Interpreting the poet's purpose

Notice how sound effects like rhyme and rhythm add to the emphasis here. The word 'and' suggests that everything is connected and follows in a logical sequence. The word 'fall' goes further than just 'fall down'. In the United States, the autumn season is called 'fall' and the word is applied to death. War monuments are sometimes inscribed with the message 'For the Fallen'. Scott is suggesting that death is an inevitable consequence of joining the army. It is all part of the 'catalogue of human woes' that result from following the call of the drum. Do you agree?

Scott does not just use rhyme, a technique English poets borrowed from the French and Italians, but also an older, rougher, and Anglo-Saxon way of linking words together called **alliteration**: To march, and fight, and fall, in foreign lands. It isn't just the word 'fall' which is emphasized here, but also 'foreign'.

1. What do you think Scott might be suggesting about the wars the men were recruited to fight?

2. Do you share his bitter ideas about war?

Practice question

How does Scott's writing memorably convey to you his feelings when he hears the sound of the recruiting drum?

Look carefully at this question. It might help you to answer it if you break it up into different parts.

1. How does Scott's writing	Understanding of the writer's techniques and choice of words
2. memorably convey to you	Analysis of the effect of his techniques on the reader
3. his feelings	Your evaluation of the message of the poem
4. when he hears the sound of the recruiting drum?	Your knowledge of the scene he describes and your appreciation of the poem's sound effects

Now rearrange the different parts of the question so that you can answer it in the most suitable way.

Remember the following formula:

Knowledge > **U**nderstanding > **A**nalysis > **E**valuation

In other words, ask *what* the poem shows, then *how* it works and finally *why* it has an effect on the reader (so part 4, followed by part 1, then 2, concluding with 3).

You should aim to write about 200 words.

Share your work with a partner, as well as your teacher. How clear is your understanding? How thorough and developed your response to language?

4.2 Comparison and contrast

When studying poetry you will often find that you are asked to compare poems on a similar theme. Although comparison is not required as part of the Cambridge IGCSE exam, nor is it necessary in coursework, your teachers may ask you to compare poems on related themes. When teachers use the word 'compare' they mean explore both similarities and differences (sometimes called contrasts, as we have seen).

The next poem by A.E. Housman has many similarities with Scott's.

A.E. Housman

KEY TERMS

metaphor = describing a thing or feeling in terms which apply to something else. The comparison is implicit.

imagery = a general term for techniques and language which create images in the mind of the reader or audience.

diction = the choice of words by the writer (sometimes called 'lexis'). Another useful word is 'connotation' which means what words suggest to the reader (as opposed to the dictionary definition which is the 'denotation').

repetition = any repeated pattern; here we are looking at lists, but repetition could also be a repeated sound or rhyme.

alliteration = patterns of words in which a consonant is repeated at the beginning of each word. In alliterative poetry there are often three such repetitions in each line.

'On the Idle Hill' by A.E. Housman (1896)

On the idle hill of summer,
    Sleepy with the flow of streams,
Far I hear the steady drummer
    Drumming like a noise in dreams.

Far and near and low and louder
    On the roads of earth go by,
Dear to friends and food for powder,
    Soldiers marching, all to die.

East and west on fields forgotten
    Bleach the bones of comrades slain,
Lovely lads and dead and rotten;
    None that go return again.

Far the calling bugles hollo,
    High the screaming fife replies,
Gay the files of scarlet follow
    Woman bore me, I will rise.

powder = *(here) gunpowder, explosive*

hollo = *call out*

fife = *high-pitched flute*

scarlet = *the traditional colour of British military uniforms*

This poem is written in **quatrains**, one of the most common building blocks of English poetry. A quatrain is a four-line stanza. These use alternating rhyme, in other words the last words rhyme *abab* and there is a regular rhythm, just like in Scott's poem, to link the lines together and give the poem its 'logic'.

There is, however, a crucial difference in the rhythm or beat of the poem, isn't there? Housman hears the sound of the drum differently. Instead of weak STRONG he hears a sound which is STRONG weak:

   /   x /x /   x   /   x

On the idle hill of summer,

  / x   /   x   /   x   /

Sleepy with the flow of dreams.

We call this rhythm **trochaic**. A trochee is the opposite of an iamb and has a falling rather than a rising rhythm. Why might this suit the mood of the poem?

KEY TERMS

quatrain = a four-line stanza.
trochaic = verse which follows the opposite pattern: STRONG weak, /x.

✏ Check your understanding

- Mark up your own copy of the poem, as you learned to do earlier.
- Mark in the rhythmic stresses.
- Mark in the rhymes.
- Mark the ways in which sentences follow stanza form.

The rhyme is very different too: there are no rhyming couplets, but instead an alternating rhyme scheme (*abab*). Notice the rhythm of the *b* lines is different: it is cut short or curtailed.

1. Why does he use this effect?
2. What else is cut short or curtailed in the poem?

Pair and share

Tone and mood

Once you have noticed the key differences to the music of the poems, the tone used by the writer, you will notice a lot of similarities in techniques and mood. Mood is the effect of the writing on the reader. It is the atmosphere created by the writer's choices, including tone, and the impact on us as we read.

Your task here is to use the same techniques to analyse this poem. Working together, find the quotations that show Housman's use of poetic techniques, and add a brief comment on their effect on the reader. Some have been done for you.

Technique	Quotation	Effect
Alliteration	sleepy with the flow of streams	
	drumming like a noise in dreams	
Repetition		Creating a sense that war and its consequences are everywhere
	Lovely lads and dead and rotten	
Personification		
Diction	screaming fife	
Use of colour	files of scarlet (note that soldiers still wore red uniforms for parade)	
Stress used for emphasis	**all** to **die**	

Do the words as well as the rhythms of the poem have a different effect on us?

Discuss the answers to the following questions.

1. Is the tone (that is, the music of the poem) very different from the first poem?
2. Which of the two poets we have looked at seems to you to be the more angry or bitter about war?
3. Which creates a rhythm most like a drum?
4. Who has the greater effect on the reader's mood?

Notice there is no right or wrong answer to these questions. Did you and your partner have different views? It is about your *personal* response. This is what we mean by 'mood'. Just make sure you support your opinion with detail, and with appreciation of the poet's 'tone', his choice of voice, and the music of the verse.

 Viewpoints

In pairs, take different positions on the poems.

1. Which do you think is the most powerful in communicating an anti-war message and why?
2. Why do you think both poets choose to use the insistent rhythm of the recruiting drum?
3. Do you find their personal, different messages as relentless as the sound of the drum?

4.3 On the front line

The next poem looks at the situation of being at war, rather than reacting to the sound of men being called to fight. The poet, Wilfred Owen, had first-hand experience of being in the trenches in France in the First World War as an officer, and was killed in 1918. He shows that real war is often about waiting.

This is a much longer poem, so take time to read it carefully twice, paying attention to *sounds* as well as sense. Sentences help you to make sense of the text, but the sounds introduce you to the emotional world of the poem.

'Exposure' by Wilfred Owen (1917)

Our brains ache, in the merciless iced east winds that knive us …
Wearied we keep awake because the night is silent …
Low drooping flares confuse our memory of the salient …
Worried by silence, sentries whisper, curious, nervous,
      But nothing happens.

salient = angle in a fortified trench

Watching, we hear the mad gusts tugging on the wire.
Like twitching agonies of men among its brambles.
Northward incessantly, the flickering gunnery rumbles,
Far off, like a dull rumour of some other war.
      What are we doing here?

The poignant misery of dawn begins to grow …
We only know war lasts, rain soaks, and clouds sag stormy.
Dawn massing in the east her melancholy army
Attacks once more in ranks on shivering ranks of gray,
      But nothing happens.

Sudden successive flights of bullets streak the silence.
Less deadly than the air that shudders black with snow,
With sidelong flowing flakes that flock, pause and renew,
We watch them wandering up and down the wind's nonchalance,
      But nothing happens.

nonchalance = indifference

Pale flakes with lingering stealth come feeling for our faces--
We cringe in holes, back on forgotten dreams, and stare, snow-dazed,
Deep into grassier ditches. So we drowse, sun-dozed,
Littered with blossoms trickling where the blackbird fusses.
      -- Is it that we are dying?

Slowly our ghosts drag home: glimpsing the sunk fires glozed
With crusted dark-red jewels; crickets jingle there;
For hours the innocent mice rejoice: the house is theirs;
Shutters and doors all closed: on us the doors are closed--
    We turn back to our dying.

glozed = *decorated or enhanced*

Since we believe not otherwise can kind fires burn;
Nor ever suns smile true on child, or field, or fruit.
For God's invincible spring our love is made afraid;
Therefore, not loath, we lie out here; therefore were born,
    For love of God seems dying.

loath = *reluctant*

To-night, this frost will fasten on this mud and us,
Shrivelling many hands and puckering foreheads crisp.
The burying-party, picks and shovels in their shaking grasp,
Pause over half-known faces. All their eyes are ice,
    But nothing happens.

puckering = *wrinkling*

 ## Pair and share

Performing the poem

Don't worry about the lines that are difficult: remember that the meaning will become clearer if you give the poem time. Instead perform the poem as a group activity.

1. First think about the title: the men are exposed in their trenches, not just to the hostility of the enemy but also to the winter wind and frost. The poet says the bullets are less deadly than the snow.

2. There are eight stanzas, so work as a class, dividing into eight groups taking a stanza each, and take up your positions in the trenches.

3. Recite the lines, as a chorus, chanting them together. In Ancient Greek drama and many other dramatic traditions, the chorus both comment on and take part in the action.

4. Here there is a lack of action. As you perform, try to communicate the emotions of the men, as they wait through the night, frozen and cold.

5. They should question what they are doing and even begin to hallucinate through exposure.

6. Will anyone at home understand what they are going through?

By performing the poem, you become more familiar with the story, or narrative, the soldiers exposed as much to the cold of winter as to enemy fire, asking what they are doing there, why nothing happens, and whether they are even dead or alive, as their comrades die around them. The language is strong and emotive: it makes an appeal to the reader's emotions. Owen himself said 'the poetry is in the pity'.

Using the terms and techniques you learned in the previous section, you are now well equipped to work your way through this poem. We will look at the structure, rhythm, diction, imagery, tone, and mood in order to explore not only what the poem says, but how it works.

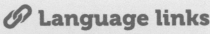 ## Language links

Hearing stress patterns

To hear the rhythm, you need to put an emphasis on the syllable which you stress. You will have done this while performing the poem, even if you did not notice at the time. We especially put stress on those syllables with long vowel sounds. For example:

x   x   / x x   / x x   /   x   /   x   /   x

Our brains ache, in the merciless iced east winds that knive us

A more regular line is:

x   /   x   / x x x   /   x /   x /   x

Like twitching agonies of men among its branches

Do you see how each line has five stresses?

Find the stress pattern in five more lines (perhaps different groups could explore different stanzas) and comment on the effect of the variations in rhythms.

 ## Check your understanding

Structure and rhythm

1. How many stanzas are there? Is there any difference between the first half of the poem and the second?

2. Can you discover a regular rhyme scheme? Compare Owen's choice of stanza form and Housman's choice. What is similar and what is different? What is Owen doing with the last line of each stanza and what is the effect on the reader?

3. How does he use repetition and what effect do you think it has on the reader?

4. It is much harder to find a regular rhythm and beat in this poem than in those of Scott and Housman. Owen is making a point here about the rhythm of the soldiers' lives; what do you think the effect on the reader is meant to be? Why is it so different from the rhythms of the two older poems? What pattern have you discovered?

5. The basic rhythm is iambic (weak STRONG) and there are five beats, or strong stresses, in each of the longer lines, making them iambic pentameters, the verse line most often used by Shakespeare and often thought to be close to the rhythms of English speech. But very few lines actually are very close to this regular pattern.

6. How does the rhythm change in the line below?

   Sudden successive flights of bullets streak the silence

7. Look at the repetition of the sound 's'. What other technique is Owen using here? What is the effect on the reader of this sound effect?

8. What is the rhythmic effect of the short or curtailed lines at the end of each stanza?

Pair and share

Diction

We called the language of the poem emotive: it is made up of language which appeals to the emotions of the reader and stirs them up.

Consider the effect of words or groups of words such as:

- *merciless*
- *knive*
- *agonies*
- *dull*
- *poignant*
- *shivering*
- *shudders*
- *fingering stealth*
- *ghosts drag*
- *love is made afraid*
- *Shrivelling … puckering … shaking.*

Many of the verbs describe the situation of the men suffering from exposure, even if the description is sometimes shifted to the things they see, or imagine they are seeing.

Can you find examples?

 Language links

Imagery

In this poem, personification is again a very important technique.

1. Look for the ways in which various objects are treated as if they were alive or people.
2. Find quotations that personify the flares, the gusts of wind, and the dawn.
3. How does this show the way in which the conditions are the enemy of the soldiers as much as the men on the other side?

4. How does the imagery make the snow sound even more deadly than the bullets in stanzas four and five?

Consider the effect of the words:

> *Pale flakes with fingering stealth*
> *come feeling for our faces*

In reading papers, you are asked to use quotation and comment in order to identify writers' effects and comment on their impact on the reader. Ask yourself what the effects make you feel or imagine.

 Viewpoints

Tone

Whose experience does this poem really describe? The viewpoint changes later in the poem, which changes the way we understand it.

There is a major change in tone in the last four stanzas. Now the poem becomes less realistic and the images are no longer of the men in the trenches. Instead, we enter the imagination of the men. The exposure they are suffering from makes them dream in a 'snow-dazed' way and they imagine returning home, not as real people but as ghosts, no longer welcome.

1. How do the images, the way Owen pictures the home fires, make the idea of home both attractive and unwelcoming?
2. Answer this question by looking closely at the description in stanza six.

Some lines in poems depend on personal response: everyone will have their own idea, based on what they have already read, about what they mean. This is what we mean by the mood of the poem.

 **Pair and share**

In pairs, debate your own ideas of what the following line means:

For God's invincible spring our love is made afraid

1. Now compare your ideas with the rest of the class and try to come to some conclusions about the meaning of this whole stanza.

2. What does it suggest about the kind of sacrifice the men are making, and what do you think the poet wanted his readers to feel about it?

3. How do the horrifying images of death in the final stanza create a final and lingering memory of life and death in the trenches?

4. Look at the use of metaphor. What is meant when the poet says 'all their eyes are ice'? (You can have more than one answer to this question).

Compare your answers with the rest of the class, and discuss the following question:

● *How does this stanza achieve the "pity" which Owen said is the purpose of his poetry?*

Practice question

You can gather all your observations into an essay form by using them to answer this question.

● *In what ways does Owen's writing create a powerful response to the sufferings of soldiers in 'Exposure'?*

As you learned when answering the question on the drum poems, ask *what* the poem shows, then *how* it works, and finally *why* it has an effect on the reader, in order to give your essay structure.

 Pair and share

Perform the poem once again in groups.

1. Can you make your performance more rhythmic and give your audience a sense of the poem's structure?

2. How has the close study of words, imagery, and their effect changed the way you perform the poem?

3. Can you communicate the sense of the poem's more difficult words?

4. How will you accompany your reading with movement and gesture?

5. Can your actions show developments and changes in the poem?

6. Can you give the poem tone?

7. How can you use the words to move your audience to pity (mood)?

Different parts of the class could compete for the most effective dramatic version.

4.4 Behind the lines

As war became a global event in the twentieth century, it was the civilian population behind the lines who suffered as much as the apparently abandoned soldiers on the front line. While the focus of First World War poems was often on the experience of the individual soldier, more recent conflicts have exposed whole communities to war's destructive potential. We will now read a series of poems that explore the damage done by global conflict and the effect on ordinary women and men.

The next poem provides painful images of the suffering of war and creates disturbing and controversial images. It is based on a moment near the beginning of the Second World War when Western Europe must have seemed on the point of collapse and people would do anything to survive.

'Road 1940' by Sylvia Townsend Warner (1940)

Who do I carry, she said,
This child that is no child of mine?
Through the heat of the day it did nothing but fidget and whine,
Now it scuffles under the dew and the cold star-shine,
And lies across my heart as heavy as lead,
Heavy as the dead.

Why did I do it, she said.
What have I saved for the world's use?
If it grow to hero it will die or let loose
Death, or to hireling, nature already is too profuse
Of such, who hope and are disinherited,
Plough and are not fed.

But since I've carried it, she said,
So far I might as well carry it still.
If we ever should come to kindness someone will
Pity me, perhaps as the mother of a child so ill,
Grant me even to lie down on a bed;
Give me at least bread.

Refugees transport their belongings in a handcart

hireling = *agricultural labourer*
profuse = *overgenerous*

In this poem, the poet imagines the thoughts of a woman in wartime who has picked up an abandoned child and is taking it with her to safety. To analyse this text, you might consider:

- the way the poet shows the woman's feelings about the child and her action in attempting to save the child
- how the poet shows the woman's thoughts and feelings about the future
- the impact the poem as a whole has on you.

Check your understanding

The first bullet point asks about the way the poet shows the woman's feelings about the child and her action in attempting to save the child.

This is a 'what' question that can be answered by writing about the effect which her thoughts and feelings have on you as you read them. You can use a table like the one that appears below to prepare your response.

1. What has the woman done?
2. Why did she pick up a stranger's child?

Words from the poem	What it shows
no child of mine	
it did nothing but fidget and whine	
lies across my heart heavy as lead	This simile suggests that the woman feels that the child is a burden, not only on her body but also her emotions, as the heart is seen symbolically as the home of feelings.
If it grow to hero it will die or let loose/Death or to hireling, nature already is too profuse/Of such	Here too the woman is thinking about the future of the child: if is does not grow to be a death-doomed hero, it will simply be a 'hireling', little better than a slave to others. She thinks there are too many such people already.
I might as well carry it still	The woman expresses a wish to continue bearing the child, perhaps more for what it can do for her than because of what she can do for it.

 Pair and share

The second bullet point asks how the poet shows the woman's thoughts and feelings about the future. This is a 'how' question. In filling in your responses to the quotations, you have already looked at how the poem works and the way the woman thinks about the future. Not only is the child 'heavy as the dead', reminding her of the past, but it also makes her think about a grim future of heroes and hirelings.

What does this suggest about the future world she sees emerging from war and conflict?

With your partner, discuss a response to these lines:

> *nature already is too profuse*
> *Of such, who hope and are disinherited,*
> *Plough and are not fed.*

1. What does Townsend Warner suggest about the relationship between work and ownership, or about ordinary people's chances of being fed?

2. Why do you think she suggests that a 'hero' is not the answer?

3. Do you think the baby is a boy or a girl? Does it make a difference?

Notice the syntax, or sentence structure, of the poem. It begins with questions to which the woman gives her own answers.

4. Do you agree with her? By forming your own personal response you are beginning to evaluate and judge the poem.

5. Does the poet want us to admire or pity the woman? To agree with her, or be disturbed by her action and attitudes?

6. Is she doing the right thing for the wrong reasons? What do you feel about this?

Shape your own response to these questions. This shows you how you can use a question and answer technique to create your own ideas, based around the words of the poem.

 ## Viewpoints

The last bullet point asks about your personal response to the whole poem or the impact the poem as a whole has on you. You will need to produce an argued viewpoint of your own.

To answer this question, you need to bring your observations together. A good way of doing this is to concentrate on the impact of the final stanza and the final lines. The poet imagines finding some kindness or sympathy, and imagines that carrying the child will help her to obtain her immediate needs, whatever the uncertainty of the future.

> *Pity me, perhaps as the mother of a child so ill,*
> *Grant me even to lie down on a bed;*
> *Give me at least bread.*

What is the impact of hearing the repetition in the last three lines? Instead of questioning, the woman is now pleading, using imperatives: pity, grant, give.

She sounds like a beggar: do you find her pitiful or repulsive? Or a little of both?

What do you make of the repetition of the word 'me'? Is this moving, or proof of her self-pity? Sympathy for the woman would be based on a lie 'as the mother of a child so ill'.

The repetitions and voice of the poem give it tone. The mood is what you, as a reader, feel like after reading it.

If you feel sympathy, you are feeling pity, the emotion Owen aims for in his poem. You understand her feelings and feel sorry for them, even if you could not imagine having similar feelings yourself.

If you feel empathy, you know what it feels like to be in that woman's shoes, and to see the world from her position, even if you do not agree with it, or have never been so unfortunate yourself.

1. Which is the more powerful feeling for you as a reader?

2. Which one fits this poem best?

Pair and share

Below are examples of responses candidates could have given to a question on the impact of this poem. Read them and then discuss which answer you agree with the most.

Student A

This poem had a big impact on me from the way the persona is thinking. She should not question herself for saving a baby, it would have been morally wrong to leave it for dead. Another thing is that at the end of the poem the persona thinks only about herself and using the baby, so I feel that this woman is not suitable to take care of a baby because she only thinks about herself.

Student B

At the beginning of the poem we aren't sure of how nice the lady is and whether or not she's prepared to carry the baby all the way to safety but by the end of the poem, the lady takes on a motherly role and we really feel for her.

Student C

The poem strikes me as rather contradictory, where the woman hates, yet cares for the child. Still, this poem speaks of care, no matter how the woman complains, she still picked the child up, and cared for it, saving its life. The poem has an impact on me, relating to time. Time is the solution to her hatred of the child, as the first two stanzas explain hate, and regret, while the last two explore concealed emotions of love and care.

Student D

The overall impact that the poem had on us is shocking; the poem shows several ideas, and how they are changed by conflict. We see the direct story of a woman saving a baby; we see her reasons, which include survival; and we see the persona's outlook on life, and how it changes due to conflict. All three ideas have the potential to shock, as they are so negative compared to our 'rosy' ideas about life. After reading the poem, our outlook changes and we value the things around us more.

4.5 Extend your learning

If you want to read similarly disturbing but thought-provoking accounts of the effect of war on ordinary people in the mid-twentieth century, you could read:

- *The Siege* by Helen Dunmore
- *The Joy Luck Club* by Amy Tan.

Poems are meant to encourage debate and argument and like novels will stimulate discussion as they won't give away their meaning straight away.

This poem was written in the 1920s and uses many of the techniques you have already explored in this unit.

> **'There Will Come Soft Rains' by Sara Teasdale (1920)**
>
> There will come soft rains and the smell of the
>   ground,
> And swallows circling with their shimmering
>   sound;
> And frogs in the pools, singing at night,
> And wild plum trees in tremulous white,
> Robins will wear their feathery fire,
>
> Whistling their whims on a low fence-wire;
> And not one will know of the war, not one
> Will care at last when it is done.
> Not one would mind, neither bird nor tree,
> If mankind perished utterly;
> And Spring herself, when she woke at dawn,
> Would scarcely know that we were gone.

Practice question

Write a detailed personal response, using quotation and comment, in answer to the question which follows. You should allow yourself 45 minutes and aim to write about 300–400 words.

- *How does the poet's language help you to imagine what a post-war future could be like?*

To help you answer this question, you might consider:

- the ways in which the natural world is portrayed in the future
- how the poet shows the destruction of the human world by war
- how the whole poem affects you as a response to war.

Check your understanding

Review your work and mark it together. Swap written responses and use the checklist here to help you give a mark to each other's work. Look and see if your partner has addressed questions 1 to 7, and then evaluate the essay by using questions 8 and 9.

1. What is the effect of the rhyming couplets and verse form?

2. What is the effect of the alliteration of 's' and 'w' sounds?

3. What is suggested by the description of the smells and sounds of nature?

4. What does the imagery suggest about nature's response to the war?

5. How does the poet use personification to show Spring's response to the war, and what does she mean by it?

6. What is implied by the third line from the end? What has happened to the human world?

7. Why does nature not care?

8. Is there an argued personal response, exploring the implied meaning of the poem?

9. How well supported is that response by quotation and comment on the language and effects used by the writer?

4.6 What do we now know about poetry?

We have explored the importance when writing about poetry of the following elements of poetic form:

- rhyme and rhythm
- syntax (sentence structure)
- repetition (word patterns)
- diction (choices of words)
- imagery (metaphors, similes, and personification)
- tone (the 'voice' and music of the poem)
- mood (its effect on the reader, and your personal response).

Modern-day war relies on heavy machinery

We will now apply these tools to a final poem and use them to shape a personal response which interprets the overall effect on the reader.

The final poem brings the subject of war even more up to date. This poem was written during the first Gulf War (after the invasion of Kuwait by Iraq in 1991 and the bombing of Iraq by the USA and Great Britain). The poet based her response on clips from news broadcasts and newspaper reports that she read at the time. The images include seabirds and sea creatures suffering because of the pollution caused by the destruction of oilfields and also the human victims of war, both soldiers and civilians.

'Lament' by Gillian Clarke (circa 1991)

For the green turtle with her pulsing burden,
in search of the breeding-ground.
For her eggs laid in their nest of sickness.

For the cormorant in his funeral silk,
the veil of iridescence upon the sand,
the shadow on the sea.

> *cormorant, tern, gull, wader* = *types of seabird*
>
> *iridescence* = *a surface of shimmering colours*

For the ocean's lap with its mortal stain.
For Ahmed at the closed border.
For the soldier in his uniform of fire.

For the gunsmith and the armourer,
the boy fusilier who joined for the company,
the farmer's sons in it for the music.

> *fusilier* = *rifleman*

For the hook-beaked turtles,
the dugong and the dolphin,
the whale struck dumb by the missile's thunder.

> *dugong* = *large aquatic mammal*

For the tern, the gull and the restless wader.
the long migrations and the slow dying
the veiled sun and the stink of anger.

For the burnt earth and the sun put out,
the scalded ocean and the blazing well.
For vengeance, and the ashes of language.

Check your understanding

1. This poem does not rhyme. What gives the poem its rhythm?
2. The sentences are very short (none run over into the next stanza) and not quite complete. What is the effect of this form of syntax?
3. What are the patterns of repetition that give this poem its shape?
4. The words of the poem are highly descriptive. Which elements of diction strike you as especially memorable or unusual and what is their effect?
5. What is the effect of imagery such as 'their nest of sickness', 'the cormorant in his funeral silk', the 'shadow on the sea', 'the stink of anger', and the 'ashes of language'?
6. What happens to the tone of the poem as you read it? Do the words and images become harsher?
7. What mood is conveyed to you? What does the poem make you feel about the effects of modern warfare?

A seabird covered in oil

 See the worksheet on mood and tone.

 ## Viewpoints

Which single word would you apply most strongly to the emotions portrayed in this poem? Discuss the options with a partner.

Extend your learning

To explore your understanding of this poem further, look ahead to chapter 6, which will help you to write an essay based on this text.

Looking back

1. What have you learned in this chapter about changing patterns and forms in poetry?
2. What have you learned about the ways in which the writer's choices of diction and imagery influence the tone of a poem?
3. How does the tone of a poem influence the mood of the reader?
4. What have you learned about changing responses to war and its impact?

We will explore the forms and language of poetry in more depth in chapter 9.

Developing writing skills

Preparing to write

This unit will explore and develop different ways of writing about and responding to literature, preparing you for essay writing by looking at how we can use reviews, notes, commentary, character study, empathy, and passage-based work.

Are you ready to write?

Writing a response to literature

5

5.1 Writing a review

How have you shown your understanding and appreciation of your reading in English lessons? How many of the following have you already written, either as part of this course, or in the last two years?

▶ Answers to comprehension questions

▶ Reviews of books you have read or plays you have seen

▶ Short play scripts or interviews using characters from texts you have read

▶ Letters or diaries in the voice of a character from a text

▶ Character sketches

▶ Discursive essays looking at a question and debating it, supported by evidence from the text

You will see the similarity with work you are also doing in English language. You may not yet have practised all of these styles of writing, but they prepare you well for the most difficult task in the list, the last one. In a literature exam, you will answer the question set by writing a complete essay (about 2–3 sides or 500–700 words). This could be in response to a particular extract from your text, or in answer to a more discursive question. We call this criticism, not because your opinions are expected to be negative, but because your reaction should be based on evidence from the text.

LEARNING POINTS

▶ To learn to write notes on your reading

▶ To explore the language used in a text

▶ To explore characters and their actions.

Writing techniques

Good responses include:

● relevance to the task set

● a planned argument

● detailed support from the text

● analytical comment on language

● an evaluative personal response, with conclusions based on evidence.

While comprehension answers allow you to explore the evidence to support an opinion about a text, and help you to feel sure you understand what is happening, they don't give you much scope to express your opinions. A personal response in literature means having views of your own about a text, but you must support them with details from what you have read or seen performed, so that your comments are fair and justified.

 ## Viewpoints

In everyday life, you will find plenty of reviews of plays, films, and books. They appear in newspapers, magazines, and especially on the internet, on the websites of booksellers such as Amazon, or film websites like www.imdb.com.

Although you will not be asked to write a review in a Cambridge IGCSE exam or piece of coursework, reviews will help you to construct personal responses, which are a key element of the course.

Which reviews do you pay attention to, and which ones do you not? What do you think makes a review:

- readable
- authoritative
- reliable
- fair
- helpful?

You will probably conclude that reviewers need to express themselves clearly and concisely; know what they are talking about; provide evidence to show that they have done their research; avoid too much bias and consider other peoples' opinions as well as their own; and that they make useful recommendations to their readers ('if you liked x, you would like y').

 ## Pair and share

In chapter 2, you read three extracts from *The Importance of Being Earnest* in detail, and you interviewed the writer after the first performance. Now plan a review in which you express your opinions about the play.

All writing requires planning, and it is often a good idea to share your plan with a partner. You will notice that many bullet points in this chapter follow a 'rule of five'. It can help to look for five areas which you plan to write about. With your partner, look back at chapter 2 and find details to fit the following five points.

1. Find a starting point. This should show the overall impression the play made on you. What kind of play is it? Comment on setting and characters.

2. Develop your review through your choice of details. You have learned how problems and confrontations allow plots to develop in interesting ways. How do characters conflict with each other and get into quarrels?

3. Look at form and structure. How does the play's form as a comedy influence the ways in which the action goes on to a resolution?

4. Look at language. What makes the play funny? Give examples of the more outrageous things characters say or do. Can you look back and find some of Wilde's witty epigrams?

5. Make a recommendation. Remember you should not give the whole plot away in a review (this is sometimes called a 'spoiler'). You can hint at the direction the plot is going in. Instead describe what kind of person would enjoy this play and why.

The Times newspaper

Viewpoints

You are a reviewer for the London newspaper *The Times* in 1895 when Mr Wilde is at the height of his success. Can you recommend this play to your readers? Use the five-part plan you have just worked on in order to write a 300-word review, set out in newspaper format, with five short paragraphs that explain how the play works and why it is so popular.

Extend your learning

Search online for reviews of both theatre and film performances of *The Importance of Being Earnest*. The play is still very popular with both amateur and professional actors. Can you find a performance near you?

There are two well-known film adaptations of *The Importance of Being Earnest*, one by Anthony Asquith (1952) and another by Oliver Parker (2002). Watch either or both of these adaptations.

Write a review giving examples of:

1. the director's choices of setting and actors
2. what worked especially well
3. what did not work
4. how successfully the film caught the spirit of the play
5. whether you would recommend the film to your classmates.

5.2 Writing notes and commentary to explore language

The next text you will write about is a prose text, *The Strange Case of Dr Jekyll and Mr Hyde*. Written just a few years earlier, it was just as successful as *The Importance of Being Earnest* when it first appeared. It also deals with the theme of a double life. We're going to look at how to write good notes about a text and how to comment on the writer's techniques, as you will need to do while reading set texts.

A poster advertising the 1952 adaptation of *The Importance of Being Earnest*

There are many film and stage adaptations of this story; it is very well known. However, the novel itself uses the techniques of gradual **revelation** and **flashback** which we began to explore in chapter 3. We see the viewpoints of several characters and hear more than one narrative voice, so the full story only emerges in the final chapter, which is Henry Jekyll's full confession. In the confession, Jekyll, regarded as a good and respectable doctor, reveals that he actually is Mr Hyde. He has taken a drug to turn himself into someone else so that he can do evil deeds.

In the extract below, very soon after the beginning of the novel, a man called Enfield describes a dingy and sinister-looking door, which we only later discover is a secret back entrance to Dr Jekyll's laboratory, where his experiments take place. He also describes meeting a very unpleasant man, who turns out to be Mr Hyde, who disappears through that door and emerges with a cheque made out in the name of Dr Jekyll.

 See Worksheet 1 on the website for more help with this text.

The Strange Case of Dr Jekyll and Mr Hyde by Robert Louis Stevenson (1886)

Two doors from one corner, on the left hand going east the line was broken by the entry of a court; and just at that point a certain sinister block of building thrust forward its gable on the street. It was two storeys high; showed no window, nothing but a door on the lower storey and a blind forehead of discoloured wall on the upper; and bore in every feature, the marks of prolonged and sordid negligence. The door, which was equipped with neither bell nor knocker, was blistered and distained. Tramps slouched into the recess and struck matches on the panels; children kept shop upon the steps; the schoolboy had tried his knife on the mouldings; and for close on a generation, no one had appeared to drive away these random visitors or to repair their ravages.

Mr. Enfield and the lawyer were on the other side of the by-street; but when they came abreast of the entry, the former lifted up his cane and pointed.

"Did you ever remark that door?" he asked; and when his companion had replied in the affirmative. "It is connected in my mind," added he, "with a very odd story."

"Indeed?" said Mr. Utterson, with a slight change of voice, "and what was that?"

"Well, it was this way," returned Mr. Enfield: "I was coming home from some place at the end of the world, about three o'clock of a black winter morning, and my way lay through a part of town where there was literally nothing to be seen but lamps. Street after street and all the folks asleep – street after street, all lighted up as if for a procession and all as empty as a church – till at last I got into that state of mind when a man listens and listens and begins to long for the sight of a policeman. All at once, I saw two figures: one a little man who was stumping along eastward at a good walk, and the other a girl of maybe eight or ten who was running as hard as she was able down a cross street. Well, sir, the two ran into one another naturally enough at the corner; and then came the horrible part of the thing; for the man trampled calmly over the child's body and left her screaming on the ground. It sounds nothing to hear, but it was hellish to see. It wasn't like a man; it was like some damned Juggernaut. I gave a view halloa, took to my heels, collared my gentleman, and brought him back to where there was already quite a group about the screaming child. He was perfectly cool and made no resistance, but gave me one look, so ugly that it brought out the sweat on me like running. The people who had turned out were the girl's own family; and pretty soon, the doctor, for whom had been sent put in his appearance. Well, the child

prolonged and sordid negligence = *left neglected and dirty for a long time*

distained = *lost its original colour*

mouldings = *decorations*

replied in the affirmative = *said yes*

some place at the end of the world = *he is exaggerating and means a distant part of London*

stumping along = *describes the man as having a small and squat appearance and a clumsy way of walking – this describes Mr Hyde*

like some damned Juggernaut = *like an enormous image or avatar carried in a procession in India. According to English observers, worshippers would throw themselves in front of it*

a view halloa = *a foxhunting shout at the beginning of a chase*

was not much the worse, more frightened, according to the Sawbones; and there you might have supposed would be an end to it. But there was one curious circumstance. I had taken a loathing to my gentleman at first sight. So had the child's family, which was only natural. But the doctor's case was what struck me. He was the usual cut and dry apothecary, of no particular age and colour, with a strong Edinburgh accent and about as emotional as a bagpipe. Well, sir, he was like the rest of us; every time he looked at my prisoner, I saw that Sawbones turn sick and white with desire to kill him. I knew what was in his mind, just as he knew what was in mine; and killing being out of the question, we did the next best. We told the man we could and would make such a scandal out of this as should make his name stink from one end of London to the other. If he had any friends or any credit, we undertook that he should lose them. And all the time, as we were pitching it in red hot, we were keeping the women off him as best we could for they were as wild as harpies. I never saw a circle of such hateful faces; and there was the man in the middle, with a kind of black sneering coolness – frightened too, I could see that – but carrying it off, sir, really like Satan. 'If you choose to make capital out of this accident,' said he, 'I am naturally helpless. No gentleman but wishes to avoid a scene,' says he. 'Name your figure.' Well, we screwed him up to a hundred pounds for the child's family; he would have clearly liked to stick out; but there was something about the lot of us that meant mischief, and at last he struck. The next thing was to get the money; and where do you think he carried us but to that place with the door? – whipped out a key, went in, and presently came back with the matter of ten pounds in gold and a cheque for the balance on Coutts's, drawn payable to bearer and signed with a name that I can't mention, though it's one of the points of my story, but it was a name at least very well known and often printed. The figure was stiff; but the signature was good for more than that if it was only genuine. I took the liberty of pointing out to my gentleman that the whole business looked apocryphal, and that a man does not, in real life, walk into a cellar door at four in the morning and come out with another man's cheque for close upon a hundred pounds. But he was quite easy and sneering. 'Set your mind at rest,' says he, 'I will stay with you till the banks open and cash the cheque myself.' So we all set off, the doctor, and the child's father, and our friend and myself, and passed the rest of the night in my chambers; and next day, when we had breakfasted, went in a body to the bank. I gave in the cheque myself, and said I had every reason to believe it was a forgery. Not a bit of it. The cheque was genuine."

"Tut-tut," said Mr. Utterson.

"I see you feel as I do," said Mr. Enfield. "Yes, it's a bad story. For my man was a fellow that nobody could have to do with, a really damnable man; and the person that drew the cheque is the very pink of the proprieties, celebrated too, and (what makes it worse) one of your fellows

Sawbones = *nineteenth-century slang for a doctor*

apothecary = *dispensing chemist*

wild as harpies = *like fierce avenging creatures, half-woman and half-bird*

like Satan = *like the devil (traditionally seen as arrogant and bold)*

screwed … stick out … struck = *all terms derived from gambling or bargaining over money*

Coutts = *a very respectable bank used by the Queen and other eminent people*

the figure was good for more than that = *the man whose name is on the cheque is worth plenty of money and has good credit*

apocryphal = *as if from an unauthorized part of the Bible, in other words something fraudulent or improper*

damnable = *belongs in hell*

the very pink of proprieties = *as respectable as it is possible to imagine*

who do what they call good. Black mail I suppose; an honest man paying through the nose for some of the capers of his youth. Black Mail House is what I call the place with the door, in consequence. Though even that, you know, is far from explaining all," he added, and with the words fell into a vein of musing.

capers = *pranks or misdeeds*

a vein of musing = *silent thoughts (about things he doesn't want to talk about)*

Dr Jekyll and Mr Hyde as they have been portrayed in film adaptations

✎ Check your understanding

The purpose of this chapter is to help you to make more effective notes while you are getting to know a new text, so that you can collect the details which will help you to write an essay.

Remembering the 'rule of five', you will begin by finding five things which the reader finds out about in this scene. On your own copy, highlight and mark up the parts of the text which tell you about:

1. the sinister door
2. the way the man knocks over the child
3. the reactions of Enfield, the Scottish doctor, and the women in the crowd to the man
4. how the man buys everyone's silence
5. what Enfield finds especially sinister about the cheque, and the man's connection with the person who wrote it.

Now divide up your exercise book or notes into five sections with a column for each of the bullets above. Using the **PEA technique**, look for evidence from the writing which shows that the impression the story makes is a dark and mysterious one.

Base your response around a selection of three short quotations for each bullet. Some of the work has been done for you.

	Door	Knocking over child	Reactions to the man	Buying silence	The mysterious cheque
Point		There is a sharp contrast between the girl's distress and the man's calmness		At first the man reacts as though he could not care about any of their feelings	
Evidence			'one look, so ugly that it brought out the sweat on me like running'		
Analysis	Suggests the building has its own sinister life				Shows that for Enfield the situation looks like a fake
Point					But the man remains calm and looks down on the others
Evidence	'The door, which was equipped with neither bell nor knocker, was blistered and distained'	'it was hellish to see … like some dammed Juggernaut.'	'I saw that Sawbones turn sick and white with the desire to kill him.'		
Analysis				The language suggests he is very familiar with that strange back door	
Point	It is a dirty and disturbing place			He returns with both cash and a cheque for a large sum of money, drawn from the bank account of a well-known man	
Evidence		'I collared my gentleman'			'the person that drew the cheque is the very pink of proprieties'
Analysis			This suggests that the women would happily torture him to get their revenge		

Pair and share

Enfield suggests two explanations of what he saw. One of them relates to the supernatural, and the other assumes that something criminal is going on.

Did you notice how often Enfield's language makes reference to the supernatural? Using the glossary that accompanies the text, go back over it, and with your partner, note down the terms which refer to devils, gods, and demons.

What might Jekyll have done which is allowing Hyde to blackmail him? Discuss and jot down a short note (just a sentence) to sum up your conclusions.

Why does he give a rational explanation to his friend Utterson, who is a lawyer, while hinting at another supernatural explanation which he really thinks is impossible?

As he doesn't spell out all of his suspicions you will need to work them out. One of you should imagine you are Utterson and the other can be Enfield.

Individually, write down a short note about the story of what might lie behind the door. Now compare your notes. Do you have the same ideas? Or different ones?

 Viewpoints

Looking back over your notes, you should now be able to write a short commentary to address the following five questions.

1. Why is this a sinister and appropriate setting?
2. Why is the character of the unnamed man so disturbing and mysterious?
3. Why does there appear to be something supernatural about him?
4. What is so suspicious about his relationship with the man who signs the cheques?
5. Why does this hint at the kind of scandal professional men like Utterson and Enfield particularly hate?

Support your comments with quotations and comments on the writing. Remember that the opening of a novel wants the reader to ask questions: there is no need to give all the answers!

Extend your learning

Find out more about the **Gothic** genre. Explore websites such as www.litgothic.com or www.victorianweb.org. Are there modern stories and films which also use elements of the Gothic genre? Examples of these are:

1. semi-ruinous locations
2. midnight settings
3. challenging the norms of society
4. suggestions of criminality
5. hints of transgressive sexuality
6. elements of the supernatural.

Why is the Gothic still such a popular and interesting genre?

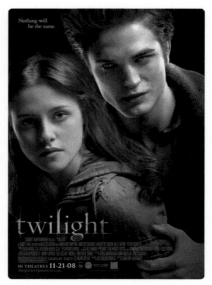

Twilight could be seen as modern Gothic literature

5.3 Exploring character through empathy: *The Merchant of Venice*

The plays of William Shakespeare are not just popular in school classrooms; they remain popular in theatres all over the world. As we saw in chapter 2, it is important not to let the difficulties of his language get in the way of your appreciation of character and action. One way of doing this is to use your own language to express the feelings of characters.

We can respond to characters by recreating their voices through empathic writing. This is a good way for you to find your way into text imaginatively; actors need to do this when creating a character.

Think ahead

▶ To write empathically, you need good idea of exactly what is happening at that moment in a text.

▶ You must create a voice as similar as possible to that of the character at that moment in the play.

▶ When first reading Shakespeare's plays, the language of the past can often be a barrier, as can the verse. However, by putting the emotions of characters into your own words and language, you can get inside the meaning of the text, without letting language get in the way.

▶ You can also show that you understand both the literal meaning of Shakespeare's words, and the emotional impact of his metaphors.

This scene from Act One Scene One of *The Merchant of Venice* is a private duologue between Antonio (the 'Merchant') and Bassanio, two men who are close friends. Antonio is rich and Bassanio is very good-looking.

Bassanio explains that he owes a lot of money, especially to Antonio, but he thinks that if Antonio gives him one more loan, it will enable to him to put on a show which will impress a young heiress called Portia. She has been left vast amounts of money, and if he could marry her that would solve all his financial problems. Antonio explains that he would do anything for Bassanio, but as all his money is currently invested in a fleet of ships, all he can do for Bassanio at the moment is to raise money on his credit with the money markets in Venice.

Perhaps there is more to this scene than either friend will quite admit. Does Bassanio feel guilty at risking his friend's money and credit in this way? Is Antonio worried about Bassanio's recklessness? What makes Bassanio so confident that he can win the rich young lady? Why does he use so many images which are related to money? Is this to show Antonio that he knows what he is doing? How does he really feel about Antonio borrowing the money, and exposing himself to risk?

Jeremy Irons and Joseph Fiennes in the 2004 adaptation of *The Merchant of Venice*

Shakespeare does not really tell us the answers to these questions, as he wants the audience to think about them, and he wants the character of Bassanio to be a slightly puzzling one. Is he really selfish and overconfident, and an adventurer who manipulates people? Or is he just a rather spoilt child, an example of what he calls 'pure innocence'? Even if he's 'innocent', he seems to do whatever he feels he should, without always thinking through the consequences.

Actors playing Bassanio have choices, and their choices are determined by what Bassanio will be like later in the play (if you know the whole play, you can suggest this in your empathy work). Should the audience like him? Or should we be suspicious?

The Merchant of Venice by Shakespeare (circa 1597)

BASSANIO

'Tis not unknown to you, Antonio,
How much I have disabled mine estate,
By something showing a more swelling port
Than my faint means would grant continuance:
Nor do I now make moan to be abridged
From such a noble rate; but my chief care
Is to come fairly off from the great debts
Wherein my time something too prodigal
Hath left me gaged. To you, Antonio,
I owe the most, in money and in love,
And from your love I have a warranty
To unburden all my plots and purposes
How to get clear of all the debts I owe.

ANTONIO

I pray you, good Bassanio, let me know it;
And if it stand, as you yourself still do,
Within the eye of honour, be assured,
My purse, my person, my extremest means,
Lie all unlock'd to your occasions.

BASSANIO

In my school-days, when I had lost one shaft,
I shot his fellow of the self-same flight
The self-same way with more advised watch,
To find the other forth, and by adventuring both
I oft found both: I urge this childhood proof,
Because what follows is pure innocence.
I owe you much, and, like a wilful youth,
That which I owe is lost; but if you please
To shoot another arrow that self way

something showing a more swelling port = *I have been spending more than I can really afford*

Nor now do I make moan to be abridged/From such a noble rate = *I am not complaining about the need to cut my expenses back*

prodigal = *extravagant*

gaged = *in debt to others*

warranty = *guarantee*

extremest means = *all my money*

when I had lost one shaft = *When I lost an arrow when playing with my bow (why do you think Bassanio chooses to use this image?)*

Which you did shoot the first, I do not doubt,
As I will watch the aim, or to find both
Or bring your latter hazard back again
And thankfully rest debtor for the first.

ANTONIO

You know me well, and herein spend but time
To wind about my love with circumstance;
And out of doubt you do me now more wrong
In making question of my uttermost
Than if you had made waste of all I have:
Then do but say to me what I should do
That in your knowledge may by me be done,
And I am prest unto it: therefore, speak.

BASSANIO

In Belmont is a lady richly left;
And she is fair, and, fairer than that word,
Of wondrous virtues: sometimes from her eyes
I did receive fair speechless messages:
Her name is Portia, nothing undervalued
To Cato's daughter, Brutus' Portia:
Nor is the wide world ignorant of her worth,
For the four winds blow in from every coast
Renowned suitors, and her sunny locks
Hang on her temples like a golden fleece;
Which makes her seat of Belmont Colchos' strand,
And many Jasons come in quest of her.
O my Antonio, had I but the means
To hold a rival place with one of them,
I have a mind presages me such thrift,
That I should questionless be fortunate!

ANTONIO

Thou know'st that all my fortunes are at sea;
Neither have I money nor commodity
To raise a present sum: therefore go forth;
Try what my credit can in Venice do:
That shall be rack'd, even to the uttermost,
To furnish thee to Belmont, to fair Portia.
Go, presently inquire, and so will I,
Where money is, and I no question make
To have it of my trust or for my sake.

---

or to find both/Or bring your latter hazard back again = I will either find both 'arrows' or return your second gamble to you

wind my love about with circumstance = you are talking around the problem instead of trusting me

I am prest = I have no choice but to

richly left = her father has died and left her a lot of money

Cato's daughter, Brutus' Portia = a very famous Roman's daughter who married the 'honourable' Brutus, the tragic hero of Shakespeare's play Julius Caesar. Shakespeare's audience would have recognized these references and seen them as proof of Bassanio's good education and high status – despite his lack of money!

renowned suitors = well-known people want to marry her

Colchos' strand = the shores of Colchos where Jason had to sail with his argosy to win the Golden Fleece (why do you think Bassanio chooses this heroic legend as a comparison for his mission to Belmont?)

a mind presages me such thrift = in my imagination this would be an investment that would bring in a profit

that shall be rack'd = he will stretch his credit as far as it can possible go

to have it of my trust = Antonio will raise the money on the basis of his good reputation and what people think of his ability to pay it back

Pair and share

The glossary terms provided are to help you understand the literal meaning of the imagery used by Bassanio and Antonio, as well as to help you with difficult words. Read the scene twice with a partner, first in order to appreciate their relationship, and then in order to make sense of their language.

 Viewpoints

Why do you think Bassanio has such a roundabout way of putting his request to Antonio? What are the emotions he wants to show, and what does he want to hide? Discuss with your partner.

 Check your understanding

To create Bassanio's voice, you need to identify key aspects of his character. In the extract, which phrases show that he is:

a. arrogant and extravagant
b. loving towards his friends
c. highly thought of by others
d. child-like and innocent
e. impressed by good behaviour as well as good looks and money
f. well-educated and brave
g. desperate for money
h. very confident about his ambitions.

Where did you find the reason why he thinks he has a very good chance with Portia? If he thinks she likes him, why does he still need the money to make a good show?

To answer the last question, you need to appreciate that Shakespeare's society, just like our own, was very preoccupied with status. Actors use this term in order to establish who should stand where on the stage, and how they should move, act, and react. Clearly Portia is of very high status, but it is less clear whether Antonio or Bassanio has the higher status, despite Antonio's money.

 Pair and share

In pairs, you could now act out this scene, trying to establish who really has the status here, the man asking for the money, or the one who wants to give it to him.

1. Who would stand upstage (often the more powerful position)?

2. Who looks up to whom?

3. Who is sitting and who is standing?

4. Try changing positions several times in the scene to show how power and status shift and change.

Remember it is only Scene One, so it is good dramatic practice to leave the audience confused and intrigued. They will want to find out the answers as the play goes on!

💡 Viewpoints

In the same way, in your re-creative response you don't need to answer all the questions: it is better to leave some aspects of Bassanio's character ambiguous and uncertain. The audience should be wondering if Bassanio is really the right person for Portia to marry.

You will need to capture Bassanio's voice and complicated character, as we have seen, and also his characteristic choice of images. Have you noticed how many of his words and images relate to money, investment, and profit? This is interesting and amusing as Bassanio doesn't make much money himself!

However, he also makes lots of reference to his childhood, to heroism (Jason and the Golden Fleece), and to virtue. What image does this create of him? You need to capture his contradictions, without needing to resolve them. Compare this with the ways in which Stevenson introduced the mystery of the relationship between Dr Jekyll and Mr Hyde without wanting to solve it.

💬 Pair and share

Your written response will work if it sounds like Bassanio. Actors call this process thought tracking. Your writing should sound as if it really is Bassanio talking to us.

If you find this difficult, you could begin by getting help from your friends. Take up the role of Bassanio and sit in the hot seat. Your friends can ask you questions, but you need to answer in character. If you think a question is cheeky, you don't need to give a straight answer. Bassanio might be asked questions like:

1. How much do you really owe Antonio?
2. Are you really Antonio's friend or just using his money?
3. What did you spend all his money on?
4. Why don't you have any money of your own?
5. Do you think it is an honourable thing to do to marry a woman for her money?
6. Isn't this a bit of a waste of your good education?
7. Why do you think Portia likes you so much?
8. What makes you confident that this is a good plan?
9. Aren't you worried about where Antonio will get the money from?
10. Do you really think you will be able to pay him back?

Try to answer the questions as far as possible from evidence in the play, although you can invent some back story if it sounds plausible. Shakespeare tells us nothing, for example, about Bassanio's family background.

Extend your learning

You will need to remember the importance of cultural background. In Shakespeare's society, when a woman was married to a man he gained control of all her money and could spend it as he wished. If a young man was of very high status (a gentleman) he would be dishonouring himself by working for money. Gentlemen were higher in status than merchants, so marrying a rich young woman would help Bassanio to keep his status as a gentleman, whereas going to find 'a proper job' would not. It cost a lot of money to behave like a gentleman: you needed expensive clothes, money to travel, and lots of servants, including clowns and musicians. Rather like celebrities today, you proved your status by having a large entourage: when Bassanio travels to Belmont later in the play, he takes various friends and servants with him. However, Antonio will be left behind in Venice to pick up the bill.

Pair and share

Now write your response to the question below, remembering the rule of five.

You should aim to write about 500 words.

Plan your writing by using five paragraphs.

Think about five different aspects of the scene.

● *You are Bassanio at the end of Scene One. Antonio has just explained to you that he will need to raise the money for your trip to Belmont from the money markets. Write your thoughts.*

The following questions will help you to structure your response.

1. What does Bassanio feel about Antonio having to borrow this money?

2. Why does he think that his present plan will solve all their problems?

3. Look at Bassanio's past and how it tells him to act in the future.

4. Look at his relationship with Antonio and how he feels it will develop next.

5. Look at his relationship with Portia: why does he feel sure it promises a golden future?

5.4 Exploring character through critical use of quotation

As we have seen, there is plenty you can write about the opening of a text, even before you know how it will end. You can look at the writer's descriptive language and techniques, and explore characterization. Here is a passage from early on in another famous novel, in a very different style.

Jane Austen's *Pride and Prejudice* is more than a novel about dating Regency-style. Although her novels are especially famous for their strongly drawn, contrasting characters and the social comedy of her witty dialogue, there is also a deeper moral interest in the ways in which relationships reflect a rapidly changing society. Her characters are from a background of wealth and privilege, but some are much wealthier than others. In particular, Elizabeth Bennet, from whose viewpoint most of the novel is told, and her elder sister Jane need to marry wealthy men, as they will inherit very little from their parents. Here Mr Darcy, the friend of the wealthy Mr Bingley, the new tenant of Netherfield Hall, is introduced for the first time, and he makes a poor impression on the society of the small English town of Meryton. For more about the novel, see 'The Republic of Pemberley' at www.pemberley.com.

Elizabeth Bennet and Mr Darcy met at a dance

Pride and Prejudice by Jane Austen (1813)

Mr. Bingley was good-looking and gentlemanlike; he had a pleasant countenance, and easy, unaffected manners. His sisters were fine women, with an air of decided fashion. His brother-in-law, Mr. Hurst, merely looked the gentleman; but his friend Mr. Darcy soon drew the attention of the room by his fine, tall person, handsome features, noble mien, and the report, which was in general circulation within five minutes after his

pleasant countenance = *happy face*

air of decided fashion = *looking as fashionable as possible (these sisters are also referred to as Mrs Hurst and Miss Bingley)*

noble mien = *aristocratic appearance*

entrance, of his having ten thousand a year. The gentlemen pronounced him to be a fine figure of a man, the ladies declared he was much handsomer than Mr. Bingley, and he was looked at with great admiration for about half the evening, till his manners gave a disgust which turned the tide of his popularity; for he was discovered to be proud, to be above his company, and above being pleased; and not all his large estate in Derbyshire could then save him from having a most forbidding, disagreeable countenance, and being unworthy to be compared with his friend.

ten thousand a year = *refers to his annual income in pounds – a very large sum in today's money (and twice as much as Mr Bingley)*

Derbyshire = *a county in the North of England*

Mr. Bingley had soon made himself acquainted with all the principal people in the room; he was lively and unreserved, danced every dance, was angry that the ball closed so early, and talked of giving one himself at Netherfield. Such amiable qualities must speak for themselves. What a contrast between him and his friend! Mr. Darcy danced only once with Mrs. Hurst and once with Miss Bingley, declined being introduced to any other lady, and spent the rest of the evening in walking about the room, speaking occasionally to one of his own party. His character was decided. He was the proudest, most disagreeable man in the world, and every body hoped that he would never come there again. Amongst the most violent against him was Mrs. Bennet, whose dislike of his general behaviour was sharpened into particular resentment, by his having slighted one of her daughters.

Netherfield = *the very large country house that Mr Bingley is renting*
amiable = *friendly, even lovable*

violent against him = *Mrs Bennet speaks in strong terms about her disapproval*
slighted = *insulted*

Elizabeth Bennet had been obliged, by the scarcity of gentlemen, to sit down for two dances; and during part of that time Mr. Darcy had been standing near enough for her to overhear a conversation between him and Mr. Bingley, who came from the dance for a few minutes, to press his friend to join it.

"Come, Darcy," said he, "I must have you dance. I hate to see you standing about by yourself in this stupid manner. You had much better dance."

"I certainly shall not. You know how I detest it, unless I am particularly acquainted with my partner. At such an assembly as this it would be insupportable. Your sisters are engaged, and there is not another woman in the room whom it would not be a punishment to me to stand up with."

engaged … stand up with = *both these terms refer to having a dancing partner*

"I would not be so fastidious as you are," cried Bingley, "for a kingdom! Upon my honour, I never met with so many pleasant girls in my life as I have this evening; and there are several of them you see uncommonly pretty."

"*You* are dancing with the only handsome girl in the room," said Mr. Darcy, looking at the eldest Miss Bennet.

"Oh! she is the most beautiful creature I ever beheld! But there is one of her sisters sitting down just behind you, who is very pretty, and I dare say very agreeable. Do let me ask my partner to introduce you."

"Which do you mean?" and turning round, he looked for a moment at Elizabeth, till catching her eye, he withdrew his own and coldly said, "She is tolerable; but not handsome enough to tempt *me*; and I am in no humour at present to give consequence to young ladies who are slighted by other men. You had better return to your partner and enjoy her smiles, for you are wasting your time with me."

Mr. Bingley followed his advice. Mr. Darcy walked off; and Elizabeth remained with no very cordial feelings towards him. She told the story, however, with great spirit among her friends; for she had a lively, playful disposition, which delighted in any thing ridiculous.

Check your understanding

1. Whose point of view are we introduced to in the first paragraph and how can you tell?

2. How does the contrast between Mr Bingley and Mr Darcy make Mr Darcy seem especially disagreeable?

3. How does status play a role in Mr Darcy's pride, and in the prejudice against him?

4. Who expresses the strongest opinions against Mr Darcy?

5. How does the narrative use time shifts? Where does the flashback occur?

6. How does the reported dialogue fit in with what we have been told about Mr Darcy?

7. Why are Mr Darcy's comments especially hurtful to Elizabeth?

8. What is Elizabeth's opinion of Mr Darcy, and how does she turn what he has said about her to her advantage?

Pair and share

Put Mr Darcy on trial for the crime of appalling rudeness. One of you will be counsel for the prosecution and the other will be counsel for the defence, suggesting he is embarrassed, convinced he is surrounded by people after his fortune, and worried that Mr Bingley will make fools of them. Can you read between the lines and find good reasons for Mr Darcy's anxiety?

You each need to gather quotations as evidence.

1. Which phrases show Mr Darcy's rudeness?

2. Which phrases show he is aloof but noble?

3. Which phrases show how much gossip there is about him?

4. Which phrases show he is right to be suspicious?

To extend your ideas about him in role play, you and a partner can imagine and act out one of the following scenes:

● what Elizabeth and her sister will say about the ball in Meryton afterwards

● the conversation between Bingley and Mr Darcy.

In either case, as you have learned, the conversations will be supported by quotation or spoken in the kind of language used by and about the characters in the extract.

Viewpoints

You can see that the narrator adopts the viewpoint of the prejudiced people around Darcy, who have formed opinions within five minutes of finding out how rich he is. She deliberately does not tell us much about Darcy's real feelings, which he is bad at expressing. How might this create irony? Why might the real meaning of the scene be almost the opposite of what it appears to be?

Write comments which show the effect on the reader of the following things said about Mr Darcy:

1. *his fine, tall person, handsome features, noble mien*
2. *his having ten thousand a year*
3. *a fine figure of a man*
4. *he was discovered to be proud*
5. *unworthy to be compared with his friend*
6. *he was the proudest, most disagreeable man in the world*

Can you account for the apparent contradiction? Why do opinions about him change so decidedly? Could they change again?

Write comments which show the effect on the reader of the following things which Mr Darcy says:

a. *You know how I detest it [dancing], unless I am particularly acquainted with my partner.*
b. *… there is not another woman in the room whom it would not be a punishment to me to stand up with.*
c. *She is tolerable; but not handsome enough to tempt me; and I am in no humour at present to give consequence to young ladies who are slighted by other men.*

Do these phrases confirm the prejudice against him? Or can you find reasons why he might be behaving so badly towards Elizabeth?

✎ Check your understanding

Key terms

Revise the meaning of the following terms. You can use the glossary on the website or refer back to earlier chapters.

- status
- contrast
- flashback
- dialogue
- viewpoint
- irony
- character sketch.

Extend your learning

Write a character sketch of Mr Darcy on his first appearance. You might begin like this:

'Tall, handsome, rich but proud, Darcy makes a very bad impression on Elizabeth and everyone around her. However, the reader is led to think there is more to him than meets the eye …'

Write about 500 words including quotations. You should illustrate your sketch with lots of examples of what is said about Mr Darcy and what he says himself, with comments on their effect on the reader.

Looking back

You should now appreciate that the key to good writing about literature relies on sticking to the following principles.

- Make sure you plan your writing effectively so that you have something relevant and well supported to say.

- Find quotations and make reference to the language used by characters.

- Use the PEA (point, evidence, analysis) technique to ensure that you are making analytical points about the writer's use of language, especially in descriptive passages.

- Engage with characters and their viewpoints while being aware that you should treat them with suspicion: the character's viewpoint is not the same as the author's.

- Appreciate the language used by characters and try imitating it.

- Explore the voice of the narrator and the ways in which dialogue sometimes conceals as well as reveals.

- Keep a good set of notes, tracking important introductions and developments of both character and setting, so that you can compare and contrast ideas when you write critical essays.

In chapter 6, we will apply these ideas to writing a critical essay based on a single poem. You should then be able to use the same writing techniques to write effective reviews, notes, commentaries and essays when writing about your set texts in class.

In chapter 10, you will go on to develop your writing skills further, but first we will explore the structure of the 'critical essay', the format your teachers will want you to use for coursework and in all your writing as you develop a deeper understanding of your texts.

Writing an essay

6.1 Writing a critical essay

We will return to the last poem in chapter 4, on page 72. This time we will focus on producing a continuous piece of writing. This time we will use a question from a Cambridge IGCSE past paper. As we have seen, you will first need to read the question carefully and apply it to the text. The question is:

- *In 'Lament' (by Gillian Clarke) explore how the poet's words vividly convey feelings of bitterness.*

Cambridge IGCSE English Literature, 0486, Paper 12, November 2011, Q20

Think ahead

Remind yourself of what you have already learned about this poem and how it was written, and have a look at Gillian Clarke's very helpful website www.gillianclarke.co.uk. What can you find out about the first Gulf War and US actions after the invasion of Kuwait?

LEARNING POINTS

- ▶ To build on the skills developed in the previous chapter to write a complete essay
- ▶ To write about a single poem in depth and detail
- ▶ To use quotation to show close analysis of language
- ▶ To use research to develop an evaluative approach
- ▶ To compare different student responses and look at the success criteria.

'Lament' by Gillian Clarke (circa 1991)

For the green turtle with her pulsing burden,
in search of the breeding-ground.
For her eggs laid in their nest of sickness.

For the cormorant in his funeral silk,
the veil of iridescence upon the sand,
the shadow on the sea.

For the ocean's lap with its mortal stain.
For Ahmed at the closed border.
For the soldier in his uniform of fire.

For the gunsmith and the armourer,
the boy fusilier who joined for the company,
the farmer's sons in it for the music.

For the hook-beaked turtles,
the dugong and the dolphin,
the whale struck dumb by the missile's thunder.

For the tern, the gull and the restless wader.
the long migrations and the slow dying
the veiled sun and the stink of anger.

For the burnt earth and the sun put out,
the scalded ocean and the blazing well.
For vengeance, and the ashes of language.

Check your understanding

Remember that your first priority when writing is to produce a relevant response which addresses the key term in the question.

1. What do you understand by the term 'bitterness'?

2. Why is it different from 'sadness' or 'regret'?

3. How could you associate that term with the title of the poem?

4. What kind of sound conveys bitterness?

5. What kind of images would a poem expressing bitterness focus on?

6. How would emotions of bitterness develop? Would they change? Or simply become stronger over time?

Now begin to draw up a plan. How could you show that the poem does the following?

- It begins by lamenting and showing distress at damage the poet can do nothing about.

- It continues with increasingly powerful feelings about the senselessness and damage of war.

- It ends with an expression of anger and despair.

Divide the poem into four sections to show how it develops; this will help your paragraph planning.

Then think of a strong opening statement. This needs to give an **overview** of the poem, mention the key term of the question, and explain how both your argument and the poem will develop. Remember to mention the writer's name, and the effect of the poem on the reader.

Compare your opening sentences with those of others in the class.

a. Which one gives the strongest sense of an overview of the poem?

b. Which one gives a powerful sense of the writer's purpose?

c. Which one most clearly answers the question?

d. Does anyone's opening do all of these?

 # Pair and share

What do you and your partner think of the three opening paragraphs which follow? Compare them, look at the comments, and compare these statements with your own.

Student A

'Lament' is a poem written by Gillian Clarke in which she explores and describes the ways in which humans have destroyed, polluted, and killed our planet and its inhabitants.

Comments

This answer can only get better. At the moment, the question is not addressed very directly, nor is there very clear knowledge of the poem and its context. However, the triplet 'destroyed, polluted, and killed' our planet and its inhabitants does show some understanding of the writer's purpose and the poem's development and that it will go on to link the natural world, animals, and humans.

Student B

Gillian Clarke vividly conveys a feeling of bitterness in the poem 'Lament' through her portrayal of the theme of the lack of respect humans have for nature, and the amount of respect and responsibility they should have when it comes to nature. She also conveys a feeling of bitterness through her use of enjambment, metaphors and diction.

Comments

This certainly addresses the terms of the question and begins to define a response when talking about 'responsibility'. This comment shows some clarity of understanding. When using technical terms, it is better to introduce them as part of your analysis, rather than to simply list them. If you mention a literary device, make sure you comment on how it is being used.

Student C

Gillian Clarke shows increasing bitterness and anger in her 'Lament' for all the damage done in consequence of war in the Gulf. A series of powerful images shows that man and the natural world are united in suffering, and the future for the world portrayed in the poem is bleak. The poem's harsh sounds become a crescendo of bleak feelings about the future, culminating in a very dark final couplet.

Comments

This answer shows knowledge of who wrote the poem and why, of the structure of the whole poem, and of its visual and sensory effects. It addresses the language of the question and suggests that the most bitter part of the poem is the way it ends. The candidate has set up a strong opening statement with an argument to prove in the rest of the essay.

You can see how a good introductory paragraph will help you to position what you want to say in the rest of your essay.

Viewpoints

Consider the way Clarke constructs her own viewpoint and portrays her emotions in this poem. It is literally a 'bird's eye view': she is looking down on the world of the poem and lamenting what she sees.

1. What makes the poem list-like?
2. Why might the poet be at a distance from what she describes?
3. Does this limit her ability to intervene or change anything?
4. What effect does this have on the reader?
5. How would this fit the idea of seeing everything from the outside, unable to change or alter things? Why is this appropriate to the idea of a 'lament' or **elegy**?

A 'bird's eye view' allows us to look down on the world

 See Worksheet 1 for further help with this poem.

Writing about language

As we have seen, poems work through a combination of sensory effects, using sound patterns and images (or pictures in words). Let's begin with the sounds. Which sound effects would best convey bitterness: soft or harsh?

Using the skills you developed in chapter 4, identify the sound patterns which link the groups of words in the table that follows. Then comment on the effect of combining these particular words through their sounds. What does this make the reader feel? Remember that commenting on sound effects is worthwhile if you can link the effect to its meaning.

KEY TERMS

elegy = a poem which responds to loss, often to death and expresses mourning and perhaps consolation.

overview = in an essay, an overall evaluation of the impact of the whole text in front of you, in response to the question.

Sound pattern	Identified as	Effect on reader of words and sounds
For … for … for … funeral		
Burden … breeding		
Sand … shadow … sea		
Mortal … closed … soldier		
Fusilier … farmer … for the music		
Dugong … dolphin … dumb		
Tern … wader … long … slow		
Sun … stink … sun … scalded		
Burnt … blazing		
Scalded … ashes … language		

You can see that sound effects such as alliteration and assonance create a certain tone, which conveys emotion to the reader and thus affects our mood. Although the observations in the poem appear to be made from a distance, the poet's feelings are very strongly engaged, and it is probably right to talk about 'bitterness' when emotions are stirred up about a situation you are powerless to change.

Why is the title 'Lament' especially appropriate? What can you now say about the 'funeral music' of the poem, and the bitter feelings it expresses?

 Pair and share

As we have seen, poems are made up of images as well as sounds. They are like a slideshow, accompanied by music. Now you and your partner have a better sense of the poem's harsh music, try to link this to the very specific collection of pictures we are presented with. There is at least one strong visual image in each stanza, sometimes two.

Divide the first two stanzas between yourself and your partner, and come up with:

- a short quotation to illustrate the image

- a comment on what is unusual, disturbing, or sinister about the details.

You should, for instance, bring out the 'nest of sickness', the 'funeral silk', and the 'whale struck dumb'. What is being suggested about the damage done by the war? What kind of images are created and why would they accompany sad funeral music?

Now look together at examples of students writing about images in this poem, followed by comments on each.

Student A

Clarke conveys a feeling of bitterness through her use of metaphors and diction. The metaphor that I particularly like says that we should lament for the 'cormorant in his funeral silk' which is a metaphor which talks of how oil spills affect the cormorant in particular. The oil on the cormorant's feathers looks rather silky and it is referred to as 'funeral silk' because the oil is the cause of its death.

Comments

This shows understanding of the writer's purpose and choices, and gives some personal response. However, the candidate tends to explain rather than explore. The metaphor is identified, and its shock element is implicit, but there is no explicit comment on the effect on the reader.

Student B

After an oil spill the seabirds are coated in a thick layer of oil which entraps them and slowly leads them to their death. Even the sand is covered in oil, showing how our actions have widespread, negative consequences. The author remarks on the oil spill and refers to it as 'wearing a funeral silk'. This is powerful as it gives you the image of a poor gull trapped in black oil, unable to move, slowly dying as if it were a human, wearing a tux in a coffin.

Comments

This is a specific, detailed, and developed set of comments. There is explanation but also a link between the destruction and human actions. The image of the gull 'wearing a tux in a coffin' is especially memorable and suggests how deliberately incongruous and disturbing the metaphor is.

Following student B's example, find some striking and individual things to say (in two or three sentences) about the effect of the images in your chosen stanzas on the reader.

Look at what our two students go on to say:

Now compare your sentences with those of your partner. Are you bringing out the meaning of each image, and how we interpret not just its meaning but also its deeper implication?

Student A

This could liken to the shadow of death and informs me as the reader on just how much the oil affects the life at sea. It also obviously refers to the fact that the oil literally looks like a shadow on the sea's surface. These metaphors and use of diction convey a feeling of bitterness because it tells me as the reader just how badly some creatures are affected because of humans.

Student B

By saying 'shadow on the sea' it shows us how our mistakes are bigger than even the ocean, that we are overshadowing something so vast and beautiful. By placing a full stop after that line the author is emphasizing her message and forcing us to stop and take it all in.

Comments

Once again, student B has more to say about the effects of the choice of image, even though student A provides explanation and identifies the features of language. There is a stronger sense of the tone of the poem, the writer at work, and the impact on the careful reader in student B's answer.

As you and your partner work through the stanzas, you should be developing a sense of the mood of the poem and the ways in which it gets darker.

What does the poem go on to suggest about the following?

1. The effect of war on human beings
2. Why the soldiers joined up
3. The impact of missile warfare on rare and endangered species
4. How nature seems to be set upside down by the destruction of bombing

The work you have done together should have given you plenty of examples of the poet's growing despair at the 'slow dying' she sees through all these images.

 **Viewpoints**

Essays need arguments. You need something powerful and original to say. One of the problems with writing without a plan is that you discover something interesting to say much too late in your essay. A lot of weaker essays begin by saying things which are obvious. However, if you have an overview of the direction of the text as a whole, and a strong sense of where you are heading, then your essay will be much more effective.

As the final part of your preparation for writing the essay we set at the beginning of the chapter, you will need to decide on what to say about the final stanza. Then you will know where your essay is heading.

Poems, extracts from plays or prose, and also good essays don't just stop. As we have already seen, writers make very specific choices about where they begin and how they end their texts. When extracts are selected for comment and analysis in exams, the right place to end the extract has been carefully thought about. You can write your essay much more effectively if you know how you want it to end, and it is much easier to write your conclusion if you have a clear understanding of the writer's last word on the subject.

Let's explore the final stanza again:

> *For the burnt earth and the sun put out,*
> *the scalded ocean and the blazing well.*
> *For vengeance, and the ashes of language.*

There are several powerful images here, so these three lines pack in more details than any of the previous stanzas. They also express a much stronger sense of destruction. Destruction here is not just local but global: 'the sun put out'. Notice how destruction extends to each of the four elements: earth, air, water, and fire. It is almost an image of the end of the world. Some religious texts call this 'apocalypse' or 'Armageddon'. However, the reference to the 'blazing well' makes it clear that the destruction is man-made and is associated with fighting over oil and destroying the oil fields.

The final line is a separate sentence.

1. Why does the writer mention 'vengeance'?
2. What does this suggest about the consequences of war and destruction?
3. Why do you think the writer makes 'the ashes of language' the last thing she says?
4. Why might it be especially poignant to talk about the destruction of words in a poem, and especially a poem set in the Persian Gulf, one of the places where civilization and written language originated?

Having some answers to these questions should allow you to build your writing towards a powerful conclusion.

You will want to conclude in the following way.

- Return to the key term in the question (in this case 'bitterness').

- Suggest how the text has developed (showing increasing bitterness and desperation).

- Comment on the writer's purpose and choices (to demonstrate through analysis how the destruction of war affects everyone and everything, and will have lasting consequences which will bring destruction not peace).

- Comment on the effect on the reader (the tone of the poem influences the reader's mood and understanding of the subject).

- Don't be afraid to voice your personal views (the end of an essay is the best place to use the pronoun 'I'): good answers conclude with an evaluation.

Now you have an excellent set of notes, and have highlighted and found things to say about a range of quotations. You are ready to write the essay:

- *In 'Lament' (by Gillian Clarke) explore how the poet's words vividly convey feelings of bitterness.*

You should write about 700 words. Stick to a five-paragraph plan and make sure you leave plenty of time for a full conclusion.

When you have finished, look again at your essay and consider the following questions:

Have you:

- kept your answer relevant throughout?
- shown clear critical understanding (why the text was written)?
- explored deeper implications (gone beyond surface meaning)?
- responded sensitively and in detail to the writer's effects (used analysis)?
- integrated well-selected references to the text (used short quotations within your sentences)?
- constructed a developed argument working towards a personal response (an original argument, moving stage by stage towards your conclusion)?

Extend your learning

To write a more extensive, argued essay about warfare and its impact, use the techniques of analysis and comment you have learned in this chapter to write a longer essay covering two of the poems in chapter 4. A 1,000-word essay on two poems would be highly suitable for coursework submission.

A suitable title would be:

- *How do different poets powerfully convey to you the destruction and damage done by war through their choices of language and form?*

Remember the following points.

- Refer to just two poems in detail.
- Identify the emotions and tone of the poems.
- Support your answer throughout with close reading of the language and the effect of the writers' choices of detail.
- Make a personal evaluation of the impact of each poem on you.

Looking back

We have seen that effective essay writing in this subject requires:

- analysis of the key terms of the question
- an overview of the structure of the text
- a plan
- selection of relevant details based on the writer's choice of words
- a conclusion which allows you to evaluate the effect of the whole text.

So far, we have only applied these skills to writing about a poem. What problems would you encounter when using them to write about an extract from a play or prose text which you have studied, or when answering a discursive question about a character or theme from a whole text?

Essentially, your only problem will be one of selection. Once you have studied a whole text in close detail, there will be far too much that you *could* say in answer to a question, so your plan will need to involve choosing the right details from the passage to make your points, or choosing three, or at most four, incidents from the whole text which you can refer to in detail in order to construct your argument, whether it is about a character, a theme of the text, or a technique which the writer uses. It is better to say a lot about a little, rather than too little about a lot.

So far, we have explored a number of extracts and poems in order to develop an understanding of literary criticism and personal response. It is now time to move on to a detailed study of the texts your teachers have chosen, which are set for examination or for coursework.

As you work through your set texts, you will write a variety of essays, initially on extracts and sections of the texts, and eventually on the whole text. This unit should have helped you to understand critical writing better, to plan your essays more effectively, and to have confidence in making comments about quotations.

In the next unit, you will develop a deeper appreciation of the structure and language of texts in each genre, moving towards the point when you will feel confident in writing your own evaluation of your chosen texts.

Set texts—an introduction to close reading

How to read set texts

The next three chapters are designed to help you with your detailed study of set texts. As those texts change frequently from year to year, we will focus on genre and ways of appreciating the form and structure of literary texts. In this unit you will find a range of extracts, along with exercises, activities, and practice essay titles.

The aim is to develop and expand the skills you acquired in units 2 and 3. You will find a strong concentration on the structure of texts, encouraging you to ask questions about how writers put their texts together while you are reading your own set texts.

In the questions and activities you will find a greater emphasis on close reading of the language of the texts and on extended written responses. You need to be familiar with the terms introduced in unit 2 and with the style of critical writing introduced in unit 3.

Through close reading of passages, we shall explore the generic features of different forms of writing, and the different ways in which you can construct written arguments about them, and express an informed personal response in classwork and assessment. Units 5 and 6 will extend these skills further and apply them to the preparation of a coursework folder and revision.

LEARNING POINTS

▶ To extend knowledge and understanding of drama, prose, and poetry texts

▶ To explore the distinctive elements of structure and form in each of the three genres and suggest ways of applying them to set texts

▶ To appreciate ways in which set texts are shaped by traditions and conventions within each genre

▶ To develop close analysis of the writers' use of language and effects

▶ To begin to explore the type of questions that could appear on an exam paper, and the detail required for exam and coursework responses.

Studying drama

Structure of drama

Drama texts are perhaps the most approachable of all texts in a classroom situation. They need to be read out aloud, just like poems. Their structure is much more obvious than that of prose texts: plays need an effective beginning (or opening scene) and ending (or climax), and often need to be divided into two halves to allow for an interval. The action, therefore, often develops to an exciting point about halfway through the play, before needing to pick up dramatic momentum once again.

LEARNING POINTS

▶ To understand the distinct features of drama texts, using practical theatre techniques

▶ To appreciate how plays are structured

▶ To explore audience response in relation to dramatic form and structure

▶ To evaluate the impact of texts in performance and their overall effect on an audience.

Many plays are written to be performed in theatres like this

Plays need to make sense to an audience hearing the text for the first time, so they are not usually as dense as poems. They rarely take longer than a single evening to perform (although there are epic dramas too!) so they are easy to read out in full in class, unlike the prose texts which require homework reading.

Plays always make more sense when performed, so there is plenty of scope when you are preparing a drama set text to engage with the text through movement and through visual elements: this can appeal to those who struggle with lots of words. For these reasons it is a good idea to begin exploring drama set texts early in the course.

Drama is also the most enjoyable way of exploring character, through performance and through writing, as we have seen in unit 3. Performing drama allows you to submerge your own ideas in the thoughts and feelings of that character, creating the kind of empathy crucial for literary understanding.

However, studying texts in a literature classroom is a different process from studying them in a drama classroom: the concentration needs to be on the language of the text and on the dramatist's craft. Instead of seeing the drama text from the viewpoint of the performer, as in drama or theatre studies, literature asks you to approach texts from the viewpoint of the audience. You need to explore the structure and writing of the text as designed for an emotive effect.

Audiences go to the theatre to experience a work emotionally, in a very powerful way. The ancient Greek philosopher Aristotle called the effect of tragedy catharsis, in other words a powerful emotional response created by the chemistry of empathy, which could stir up, but perhaps also help to understand, such feelings as pity and fear. The ancient Greeks enjoyed comedy too: both tragedy and comedy take audiences out of themselves and take them into different worlds and ways of seeing them, however, they can also make us reflect critically or satirically on our own world. Above all, theatre is a communal and live experience; the interaction of performers and audience, and the greater risks involved, have meant that theatre retains its popularity even in the age of film.

I hope you will have a chance to see your set texts performed live, or to perform them yourselves. If not, there are many good film versions of most of the texts set for study in Cambridge IGCSE Literature. However, remember that a film is only an interpretation based on the personal response of the director. One reason why there are many versions of good drama texts and why they keep on being performed is that you can interpret them in different ways. Recent excellent reinterpretations of Shakespeare's texts have moved the action to American high schools, Bollywood, and the culture of street gangs.

This chapter is structured around the shape of a play, and the building blocks of drama. These are:

- situation
- characters
- conflict
- soliloquy or monologue
- resolution.

These building blocks allow you to follow the plot lines of the plays you are studying and the presentation of the characters in them.

Many of Shakespeare's plays have been made into films – sometimes there are many different versions of the same play

'Why do you act? You act for an audience. In the theatre, you're in their presence. Film stars don't know what it is to have an audience.' Interview with Sir Ian McKellen in *The Daily Telegraph* (November 2012)

7.1 Introducing situation

It is important for dramatists to establish both characters and situation at the beginning of a play.

Alan Ayckbourn's comedy *A Small Family Business* does this in an especially amusing way. He begins the play with extensive stage directions. Jack, described as a 'forceful, energetic man of 45', is coming home to a surprise party. A successful businessman, he has just given up his job to take over the management of the family business, belonging to his wife's family. He fully intends to run a straightforward and profitable business, and he has no idea how corrupt and illegal the 'small family business' is. Indeed they are heavily involved with Italian organized crime, and Jack gradually, and at first quite innocently, finds himself involved in corruption, scandal, and eventually murder. However, Ayckbourn treats all these serious themes through the conventions of comedy, especially family-based farce, so the audience have plenty of entertainment, even if the play does have a serious side.

At the beginning of the play, we meet Jack, who doesn't know his family are throwing a party for him

Think ahead

Which is the most important thing for an audience to know from the start of a play?

- ▶ Who the characters are
- ▶ Where the action takes place
- ▶ The kind of play it is
- ▶ The play's themes and ideas

The answer is really all of these. This particular production needs to introduce:

- ▶ the family of Poppy, Jack's wife
- ▶ the idea of family and business matters getting hopelessly entangled
- ▶ Jack as a character who appears powerful, but is in fact manipulated by others.

The stage directions tell us that the action takes place on a set resembling a family house, opened out for us to look into. In the course of the play, the same set will serve as several different houses, to show how closely the family is linked, but at first the audience will assume that it is Jack's house.

Poppy's family are hiding at the back of the sitting room as Jack comes in the door, in order to make the party a surprise. They are:

- ▶ Ken, Jack's father-in-law
- ▶ Desmond, his brother-in-law
- ▶ Harriet, Desmond's wife
- ▶ Yvonne, her sister and Ken's secretary
- ▶ Cliff, Jack's younger brother
- ▶ Anita, Cliff's wife
- ▶ Tina and Sammy, Jack and Poppy's two daughters
- ▶ Roy, Tina's husband
- ▶ Umberto, an Italian businessman.

So this is going to be a busy play, with many different characters! If you were studying the play, you would need all of this information in your notebook. However, part of the playwright's skill is to introduce all of this information to the theatre audience through the action of the play. Although modern audiences have a programme to say who is who, it is easier to introduce characters through their dialogue.

This scene comes just after the beginning of the play. Poppy has switched off all the lights and we hear Jack arrive. What follows is essentially a duologue (two characters talking) interrupted by background stage whispers. Already the audience, aware of the family gathering in the darkened sitting room, knows much more about what is happening than Jack does, introducing both comedy and irony.

A Small Family Business by Alan Ayckbourn (1987)

Jack: [*a horrid thought*] We're not meant to be going out?

Poppy: No, no.

Jack: Thank God for that. I don't want to see anyone else. Not today.

He goes into the hall.

Anita: [*softly*] Oh, dear, what a shame.

Tina: Sssh!

Poppy: Make us both a drink, will you?

Poppy hangs his coat up in the hall.

Jack: [*calling back to her as he does so*] I drove back past the factory this evening …

Poppy: What's that?

Jack: On my way home just now I drove back past my new office. Do you know, I suddenly felt very excited.

He has returned to the kitchen doorway.

Poppy: I'm glad.

Jack: We're going to the stars with this one, darling, we really are. This is going to be the one.

Poppy: It will be if you have anything to do with it …

Jack: [*holding her*] No, no. Not me. Us. You and me.

Poppy: [*not really believing this*] Yes.

They kiss.

Jack: Come on, what are you dressed up for, then?

Poppy: No reason. I just felt like it.

Jack: Trying to take my mind off my work, were you? Eh?

Poppy: [*coyly aware of her audience next door*] Don't be silly.

Jack: Sammy upstairs?

Poppy: No, she's out tonight.

Jack: Just us, is it?

Poppy: Yes. There's nobody here.

Jack: I see.

Poppy: Go on. Make us a drink.

Jack: [*taking her hand and starting to lead her*] First of all, follow me.

Poppy: Where are we going?

Jack: [*heading for the stairs*] Not far, I promise. Not far.

Poppy: [*alarmed*] Jack, no, we can't. Not now.

Jack: I fancy it right now, I don't mind saying …

Anita: [*sotto*] Oh, my God …

Poppy: No, we can't. Really. Jack.

Poppy pulls away from Jack and remains at the foot of the stairs. Jack continues to retreat upstairs.

Jack: Come on.

Poppy: No. [*more firmly*] Come on. No. I'm going in here. [*Indicates the sitting room.*] I want a drink.

Jack: Poppy …

Poppy: [*opening the door*] I'll be in here.

Jack: Poppy, if I have to come down and fetch you ...

Poppy: Bye-bye.

Poppy goes into the sitting room and closes the door. She crowds in with the rest of her guests.

Jack: Poppy!

Poppy: [*calling girlishly*] Woo-hoo! [*to the others*] I'm ever so sorry. This is so embarrassing.

Tina: [*hissing*] Mum. What are you playing at?

Poppy: It's the only way I can get him in here.

Jack: [*calling*] Woo-hoo! I'm going to have to come in there and get you, Poppy ...

Cliff: This'll be entertaining.

Anita: It's all right, Poppy, we'll shut our eyes.

Poppy: Sssshh!

Jack: Poppy! If I have to come and fetch you, Poppy ... You know what that means, don't you? [*starting to take off his jacket*] It means rough trade. Rough. Rough. Poppy.

[*Throws his jacket over the banisters and starts to descend, treading heavily.*] Right. Here come the Vikings. You hear him coming, Poppy? [*Takes off his tie and starts to unbutton his shirt.*] It's Erik the Hairy, coming for you.

Anita giggles.

Roy: Eric the Who?

Poppy: Oh God, I want to die. I really want to die.

Jack: [*in a strange Norwegian accent*] Nordsky! Nordsky! Where she hidey-hole the little Angley-Sexey girl? Here he come, Hairy Erik with his meatey axey – *He opens the sitting room door, slowly reaching round for the light switch as he does so.* [*calling softly*] Angley-Sexey Girl! Come for a little pillage. Look who's here. Look who's here ... [*switching on the light*] Look who's ... Oh, for crying out loud!

✎ Check your understanding

1. The whole play shows that confusing the private world of the family and the public world of business can be both very embarrassing and very funny. How does this extract set up this idea?

2. Who do you think is more embarrassed by the end of the scene, Jack or Poppy?

3. How does Ayckbourn suggest to you that Jack is a powerful and confident character?

4. *Anita*: [*sotto*] Oh, my God ...

   Tina: [*hissing*] Mum. What are you playing at?

   Poppy: It's the only way I can get him in here.

   Cliff: This'll be entertaining.

   Roy: Eric the Who?

   What do their brief comments reveal to us about the characters of Anita, Tina, Cliff and Roy?

5. There are a lot of other characters on stage in this scene. They are Ken, Desmond, Harriet, Yvonne, Samantha, and Umberto. We do not hear their voices, but the actors will need to react in character and the audience will see those reactions, especially once the lights go on! Is the reason why they do not talk excitement, amusement, or embarrassment? What directions would you give to each character?

Writing techniques

When writing about drama texts pay very careful attention to what has just happened before the extract, and how action in the extract sets up things which will happen later in the play. Be aware of who is on stage, including the characters who are silent. The audience will notice their reactions.

💡 Viewpoints

Look at the scene from Poppy's point of view.

Much of the comedy here comes from the fact that Poppy knows her family are in the sitting room and Jack does not. Similarly, she may know a bit more about her family business than he does. Look closely at what she says to him. When does she hide the truth from him, or reveal a bit more than he understands?

● What does this extract reveal?

> *Poppy:*   [*calling girlishly*] Woo-hoo! [*to the others*] I'm ever so sorry. This is so embarrassing.

Notice the importance of the stage directions here and how they reveal the two very different voices she uses.

1. Why might Poppy be playing a double game here? What would she confess to in the hot seat?
2. Why do you think Ayckbourn uses the game of 'Viking pillager' to show Jack and Poppy playing around?
3. What do you think this shows the audience about Jack?
4. Who is really in control of this game?

Pair and share

Using the idea of a hot seat, individual students can assume the part of one of the characters, speaking or non-speaking, and be questioned by the class. What do they remember of that evening and what were their feelings at the time?

Extend your learning
Begin to evaluate the scene

Which parts of the duologue do you find most amusing and why?

Playwrights will often use sexual **innuendo**, hinting and suggesting comically how men and women relate to each other. This is not meant to offend, but it works on the audience's embarrassment, as well as that of the characters, and we often react with a laugh. However, it also reveals a psychological truth about family relationships, and the roles we play within families, which is more serious and thought-provoking. The comedy comes as much from what is suggested (but we don't see) as from what actually happens.

Extend your learning
Comparison

Compare this scene with the opening scene of your own set text and begin to evaluate how your text works.

How does the playwright do the following?

1. Introduce a situation
2. Show you who is who
3. Give distinct voices to different characters
4. Engage the audience's reaction
5. Establish the tone and genre of the play

7.2 Developing complex characters

Think ahead

We will move on to explore further the development of distinctive and complex characters through duologue. In chapter 2, we saw that duologue and double acts help to reveal what is distinct about characters. They encourage audience reaction, especially in comedy. However, they also prompt us to think about why characters are different and distinctive. So far, we have looked at comedies. Willy Russell's *Educating Rita* is certainly a very funny play too, but it has a more serious side, and in this chapter we will explore the ways in which drama can be comic and tragic at the same time. How does the play you are studying do the following?

1. Develop the audience's understanding of the main characters
2. Show relationships between the main characters
3. Introduce key themes
4. Balance comedy and seriousness
5. Keep the audience interested in what might happen next

Rita is a hairdresser who has begun an Open University degree course and her tutor, Frank, is a heavy-drinking and disillusioned lecturer at the local university. Rita speaks non-standard English, with a heavy Northern English accent. Rita has rushed out of work to tell Frank about her first experience of a Shakespeare play. As well as confronting the audience with the contrast between Rita's enthusiasm and Frank's cynicism, the playwright (like Shaw in *Pygmalion*) also interests us in whether their double act will develop into something more. Could this turn into a deeper relationship?

Julie Walters and Michael Caine in *Educating Rita*

Educating Rita by Willy Russell (1985)

Rita [*she produces a copy of 'Macbeth'*] Look, I went out an' bought the book. Isn't it great? What I couldn't get over is how excitin' it was.

[*Frank puts his feet up on the desk*]

Rita Wasn't his wife a cow, eh? An' that fantastic bit where he meets Macduff an' he thinks he's all invincible. I was on the edge of me seat at that bit. I wanted to shout out an' tell Macbeth, warn him.

Frank You didn't did you?

Rita Nah. Y' can't do that in a theatre, can y'? It was dead good. It was like a thriller.

Frank Yes. You'll have to go and see more.

Rita I'm goin' to. Macbeth's a tragedy, isn't it?

Frank nods

Rita Right.

Rita (*smiles at Frank and he smiles back at her*) Well I just – I just had to tell someone who'd understand.

Frank I'm honoured that you chose me.

Rita (*moving towards the door*) Well, I better get back. I've left a customer with a perm lotion. If I don't get a move on there'll be another tragedy.

Frank No. There won't be a tragedy.

Rita There will, y'know. I know this woman; she's dead fussy. If her perm doesn't come out right there'll be blood an' guts everywhere.

Frank	Which might be quite tragic –
	He throws her an apple from his desk which she catches
	But it won't be a tragedy.
Rita	What?
Frank	Well – erm – look; the tragedy of the drama has nothing to do with the sort of tragic event you're talking about. Macbeth is flawed by his ambition – yes?
Rita	(*going and sitting in the chair by the desk*) Yeh. Go on.

(She starts to eat the apple)

Frank	Erm – it's that flaw which forces him to take inevitable steps towards his own doom. You see?

Rita offers him the can of soft drink. He takes it and looks at it

Frank	(*putting the can down on the desk*) No thanks. Whereas, Rita, a woman's hair being reduced to an inch of stubble, or – or the sort of thing you read in the paper that's reported as being tragic, 'Man Killed by Falling Tree', is not a tragedy.
Rita	It is for the poor sod under the tree.
Frank	Yes, it's tragic, absolutely tragic. But it's not a tragedy in the way that Macbeth is a tragedy. Tragedy in dramatic terms is inevitable, pre-ordained. Look, now, even without ever having heard the story of Macbeth you wanted to shout out, to warn him and prevent him going on, didn't you?

	But you wouldn't have been able to stop him would you?
Rita	No.
Frank	Why?
Rita	They would have thrown me out the theatre.
Frank	But what I mean is that your warning would have been ignored. He's warned in the play. But he can't go back. He still treads the path to doom. But the poor old fellow under the tree hasn't arrived there by following any inevitable steps has he?
Rita	No.
Frank	There's no particular flaw in his character that has dictated his end. If he'd been warned of the consequences of standing beneath that particular tree he wouldn't have done it, would he? Understand?
Rita	So – so Macbeth brings it on himself?
Frank	Yes. You see he goes blindly on and on and with every step he's spinning one more piece of thread which will eventually make up the network of his own tragedy. Do you see?
Rita	I think so. I'm not used to thinking like this.
Frank	It's quite easy, Rita.
Rita	It is for you. I just thought it was a dead excitin' story. But the way you tell it you make me see all sorts of things in it. (*After a pause*) It's fun, tragedy, isn't it?

 Check your understanding

You should be able to see that this is a key scene in Rita's education about the criticism of literature. As Frank explains, words in literary criticism often have a more precise meaning than in everyday life. What does he tell you about the concept of tragedy? How is it linked to fate, or the concept of the inevitable, and who is most aware of this in the theatre?

Answer the following questions to track the development of the scene.

1. What does Rita find enjoyable about the experience of theatre?
2. Which comment shows that she is beginning to understand the concept of **dramatic irony**, even if she doesn't yet know the term?

3. What shows her understanding of conventions in the theatre?

4. What does Frank's choice of the word 'honoured' show?

5. Why, according to Frank, is a tragic event not a tragedy?

6. Why is Macbeth's fate inevitable, according to Frank?

7. How is this linked to the audience's reactions to the drama?

8. How does the tragic **hero** treat the warnings of his doom?

9. Can you link this to the way a tragedy is constructed?

10. Why would an audience laugh at Rita's phrase 'It's fun, tragedy'?

 ## Pair and share

Discuss the characterization of Frank and Rita before producing a dramatic paired reading of their duologue.

1. What are the contrasts which make Rita and Frank so interesting as characters?

2. What is lively and surprising about her attitudes and stories?

3. What qualities does she have which make her different from Frank's other students?

4. As Frank is an alcoholic, there are certain tragic elements in his own character (notice he refuses Rita's soft drink). What are they?

5. Like Shaw, Willy Russell uses stage directions to show the dynamic between the characters. Can you see ways in which they are getting closer?

Present the scene to your class dramatically, with actions and movement as well as words.

Pay particular attention to each stage direction and explore what is implied, as well as explicit. Why does Frank offer Rita an apple? What might this gesture imply? (Look up the story of Adam and Eve and the Tree of Knowledge).

Afterwards, each character should answer questions from the rest of the class in the hot seat. In drama, once a character is in the 'hot seat' they must tell the truth as their character sees it, and explain to the audience what they are feeling at that particular moment.

 ## Viewpoints

We have seen that literature texts raise debates and ask us questions which are not completely resolved. In the theatre this creates suspense or tension. This will keep the audience interested: in a performance, this scene takes place about 15 minutes before the interval. Discuss and debate the questions below.

1. Will Rita's education be an entirely good thing?

2. She wants to learn the technical terms so that she can speak about literature in the same way as Frank's other students. However, if she achieves this, what will be lost?

3. Can you compare her to Eliza in *Pygmalion* (in chapter 2)?

4. By changing her vocabulary, and her way of thinking, Rita is also likely to change her language and her social status. Why might that cause problems?

5. Alcoholism is not a choice. What seems to be Frank's attitude to his own fate?

6. Why does this create a sharp contrast between his character and that of Rita?

7. How does this scene, therefore, sow the seeds of further developments and deeper contrasts between the characters?

Extend your learning

Have another look at Frank's explanation of the difference between the tragic and tragedy. Is the drama text you are studying a tragedy or a comedy? Or does it mix elements of the two? We have seen that there are serious elements to comedy, and there are also possible laughs in tragedies. Both forms use plenty of irony. When writing about plays, we use the term dramatic irony (when the audience knows something that a character does not).

1. Can you link this term to the moment when Rita wanted to warn Macbeth about Macduff (the man who is fated to kill him)?

2. How might an audience react to a character's fate?

3. What are the theatre conventions which stop an audience warning the character of his fate?

4. Why, according to Frank, do tragic characters fail to listen to any warnings in the play?

5. Can you link this idea to the way the writer has deliberately crafted the play?

6. What do these flaws in tragic characters suggest to you about human nature?

 See Worksheet 2 for further help in looking at what makes a tragedy.

7.3 Playing: plays within plays

Willy Russell's play shows how the engagement of the audience is crucial in both tragedy and comedy. Their laughter and their sense of irony create the drama. Rita's lively and fresh reaction – 'It's fun, tragedy, isn't it?' – is just what a writer would want, and it certainly provokes even more interest in her from Frank. You will also have noticed that she reacts to Shakespeare's play as a theatrical experience. She does not worry too much about the language or the history, but enjoys the way in which the audience's emotions are engaged. What is 'tragic' in real life could be 'fun' in the theatre.

Plays often refer to other plays, or to the conventions of playing, to remind audiences of the difference between plays and real life. Nothing is an accident in a play: a thinking audience will be able to anticipate things which are inevitably going to happen. One way in which writers sometimes show their awareness of the audience and of theatricality is to refer to other plays in their own drama (like Willy Russell's use of *Macbeth*), or to have characters play-acting as part of the drama (like Jack in *A Small Family Business*).

Think ahead

In chapter 2, we saw that theatre is not quite like real life. Even when scenes have a strong element of realism, as in the scene we have just read, they are written to be performed to an audience, and to provoke their reaction. Plays from the past often show exaggerated characters who are larger than life.

1. What have you found most difficult about studying a Shakespeare text?
2. Where have you seen instances of his writing combining tragedy and comedy?
3. Shakespeare's plays are highly theatrical. Often the characters in his plays find that they are themselves acting parts, wearing disguises, or behaving in exaggerated ways. Can you think of examples?

In the scene which follows, Prince Henry (who will eventually be the famous hero King Henry V) has been asked to see his father, the King. He knows he will be told off for wasting his time with jokers, thieves, and drunkards. At the moment, he is still with these friends. The chief of them, Jack Falstaff, is a huge fat man, a knight who behaves like a robber. To prepare the Prince for the meeting with his father, Falstaff has been pretending to be the King, and has told him to reject all his wicked friends apart from one – Falstaff himself. This has amused the rest of Falstaff's gang, all gathered in the Eastcheap Tavern, the bar where they like to spend their time. Now the Prince says he will play the King, and Falstaff must be the Prince. Falstaff and Prince Henry form a great comic double act, one fat and one thin, one old and the other young, and both Falstaff's gang and the audience enjoy the way they tease each other and love play-acting. However, there are signs that this particular game may be more serious: we as the audience know the Prince does intend to leave Falstaff and prove to his father that he is going to change and prove himself a suitable future king. He has told us this in a soliloquy. Falstaff, of course, does not realize this.

Falstaff

Henry IV Part One by **William Shakespeare (circa 1597)**

PRINCE HENRY

Dost thou speak like a king? Do thou stand for me, and I'll play my father.

FALSTAFF

Depose me? If thou dost it half so gravely, so majestically, both in word and matter, hang me up by the heels for a rabbit-sucker or a poulter's hare.

PRINCE HENRY

Well, here I am set.

depose = *remove from the throne (Henry's father deposed the previous king, so this is a sensitive subject)*

a poulter's hare = *Falstaff means if Henry can play being a King half as well as Falstaff has done, Henry can call him a baby hare or rabbit (both of them very thin)*

FALSTAFF

And here I stand: judge, my masters.

PRINCE HENRY

Now, Harry, whence come you?

FALSTAFF

My noble lord, from Eastcheap.

PRINCE HENRY

The complaints I hear of thee are grievous.

FALSTAFF

'S blood, my lord, they are false: nay, I'll tickle ye for a young prince, i' faith.

PRINCE HENRY

Swearest thou, ungracious boy? Henceforth ne'er look on me. Thou art violently carried away from grace: there is a devil haunts thee in the likeness of an old fat man; a tun of man is thy companion. Why dost thou converse with that trunk of humours, that bolting-hutch of beastliness, that swollen parcel of dropsies, that huge bombard of sack, that stuffed cloak-bag of guts, that roasted Manningtree ox with the pudding in his belly, that reverend vice, that grey iniquity, that father ruffian, that vanity in years? Wherein is he good, but to taste sack and drink it? Wherein neat and cleanly, but to carve a capon and eat it? Wherein cunning, but in craft? Wherein crafty, but in villainy? Wherein villainous, but in all things? Wherein worthy, but in nothing?

FALSTAFF

I would your grace would take me with you: whom means your grace?

PRINCE HENRY

That villainous abominable misleader of youth, Falstaff, that old white-bearded Satan.

FALSTAFF

My lord, the man I know.

PRINCE HENRY

I know thou dost.

FALSTAFF

But to say I know more harm in him than in myself, were to say more than I know. That he is old, the more the pity, his white hairs do witness it; but that he is, saving your reverence, a whoremaster, that I utterly deny. If sack and sugar be a fault, God help the wicked! If to be

judge, my masters = this means that they are both in their positions to play King and Prince and that the others in the Eastcheap Tavern are the audience who will judge their performance

I'll tickle ye for a prince = Falstaff says the rest of this line to those watching: he says he will play the Prince in a funny way

a tun of man is thy companion = Henry (playing the King) says that the Prince is possessed by a devil in the shape of a man as big as a barrel

with the pudding in his belly = These are all insults relating to Falstaff's fatness: he is full of disease, alcohol, and huge dinners

that grey iniquity = Falstaff is an old devil who embodies evil

sack = sherry, Falstaff's favourite drink

capon = a male chicken

whom means your grace = Falstaff, as Prince, asks who the 'King' is talking about

whoremaster = brothel keeper

old and merry be a sin, then many an old host that I know is damned: if to be fat be to be hated, then Pharaoh's lean kine are to be loved. No, my good lord; banish Peto, banish Bardolph, banish Poins: but for sweet Jack Falstaff, kind Jack Falstaff, true Jack Falstaff, valiant Jack Falstaff, and therefore more valiant, being, as he is, old Jack Falstaff, banish not him thy Harry's company, banish not him thy Harry's company: banish plump Jack, and banish all the world.

PRINCE HENRY

I do, I will.

then many an old host that I know is damned = *if being old and drunken is evil, then lots of old men who run bars are going to hell*

then Pharoah's lean kine are to be loved = *in Joseph's dream interpretation in the Hebrew Bible, the lean kine (cows) in the Egyptian Pharaoh's dream are a bad omen*

banish Peto, banish Bardolph, banish Poins = *these names all refer to other members of Falstaff's gang*

✎ Check your understanding

We have seen the importance of audience reaction in drama. All of the questions below are about the way an audience reacts to particular words and lines. Remember that this was still fairly recent history for Shakespeare's audience. They would have know that Prince Henry will eventually be a great king, and that he will banish Falstaff, so they would be very aware of the irony in the scene.

1. How will members of the audience react to Falstaff's suggestion that the Prince won't be half as good at playing the King as he was?

2. What will they notice the Prince does when he says 'here I am set'?

3. What do they know about Falstaff's claim that the accusations against the Prince are 'false'?

4. How would they react to the great collection of insults which the Prince throws at Falstaff?

5. Why would they find Falstaff's first reaction so funny?

6. Why might they find Falstaff's defence of himself moving?

7. How do Falstaff's final lines here appeal to the audience for approval?

8. How might they find an element of tragedy in the Prince's final line?

Pair and share

You will remember that insults can be part of the fun of Shakespearean drama. When we read *A Midsummer Night's Dream* in chapter 2, we heard a quarrel between a tall person and a short one. Here a fat person is insulted by a thin one. Collect the different insults that the Prince uses which refer to Falstaff's fatness and greed (Worksheet 3 is useful for this exercise). Can you think of insults for Falstaff to use in retaliation?

Now find a text of the play, either online or in print, and compare the insults the characters use with those you have invented. You can find them in Act 2 Scene 4, around line 200.

This is prose, not verse. However, you might want to emphasize particular words or syllables in order to give the longer speeches rhythm. Refer to Shakespeare's text and consider the following questions.

1. Which words would you stress? Highlight these words on your copy of the text.

2. How does alliteration help you to see the pattern of words? Use a different colour to note the repeated sounds.

3. Practise reading the words out and highlight the stressed syllables.

Both of the longer speeches by the Prince and Falstaff are brilliant examples of persuasive writing, which you may also be studying as part of your English language course. The Prince's speech (pretending to be 'the King') is made up of a series of rhetorical questions and Falstaff's speech (pretending to be 'the Prince') is a series of answers, and instructions.

Repetition and tricolon (lists of threes) are good structural principles for persuasive speeches. Who do you think the Prince has learned these tricks from? You and your partner can divide these speeches between you.

'Prince Henry' needs to look at the rhythm of the questions.

1. Why do they get shorter and shorter?

2. How can you build up the insults and questions and make them increasingly provocative?

3. How serious is the Prince when he is accusing Falstaff? Is he angry? Or just trying to get a laugh from Falstaff's rather disloyal gang?

How does Falstaff imitate the rhythms and patterns of the Prince's speech in this scene? 'Falstaff' needs to answer the Prince's persuasive accusations that he is good for 'nothing'.

4. Where does he defend being old, being drunk, and being fat?

5. Which words does he use which suggest that he is good? Highlight them and emphasize them in your performance.

6. How do the rhythms of his speech also become stronger and more persuasive?

7. What is the effect of the repeated 'banish … banish' phrases? How might Falstaff's gang react to the idea that the Prince should banish the rest of them?

8. How will you deliver Falstaff's last line? Is he confident? Pleading? Slightly afraid of the Prince?

Act out the duologue, dramatizing both the fun and the tension between Falstaff and the Prince. Will the Prince say his final lines out loud, or as an aside? If Falstaff hears them how will he react? This is a comic scene, but do you think you introduce an element of tragedy? Consider what might be inevitable about this scene, and what kind of catastrophe this would predict for Falstaff. Why would the audience see the scene with a degree of dramatic irony?

Who do you find most persuasive: the Prince or Falstaff? Perform your duologue to your classmates and take a vote. Or try acting it out in two different ways, one of which will make us feel the Prince is right and Falstaff is just trying to cover up his villainy, and the other making the audience feel that the Prince is too harsh and we should feel sorry for Falstaff.

Viewpoints

Falstaff is a very controversial character and he gives the audience plenty to talk about.

1. Do you sympathize with Falstaff in this scene?

2. Do you find the Prince's behaviour cold? Or realistic?

3. Falstaff is funny, and makes everyone around him have fun. Why might that be a bad thing for a King?

Audiences will always have mixed views about the rejection of Falstaff (which will not happen until the end of the second Henry IV play). Some find the Prince too calculating and manipulative. This play is designed to produce strong personal responses.

Rejecting Falstaff is essential for the Prince. He needs to leave the world of comedy behind if he is to take his place in history. This will be tragic but inevitable for Falstaff. You can see that the ways in which playwrights develop characters is also determined: in their case the conventions of the genre, and the audience's expectations and responses will determine what happens next. Actors talk about the journey their character is on. As characters grow, develop, and change, they will need to come into conflict and sometimes leave their mentors behind. Frank knows that eventually Rita will have to leave him and have other teachers. If all the things which brought them together are no longer there, they are likely to conflict.

7.4 Conflict

We have explored how dramatists present the audience with contrasting characters who will need to engage and often clash with each other if they, and the plot, are going to develop. Alan Bennett's brilliant school-based drama *The History Boys* is based around the clash between two teachers who are preparing the boys for their university entrance exams. They will need to answer a special entrance paper to study history at Oxford. Hector is a traditionalist literature teacher who has encouraged them to memorize poems and filled them with cultural knowledge. The much younger Irwin, in his first teaching job, is here encouraging them to question the assumptions behind what they have learned, and to construct original arguments. The other characters are all schoolboys. They have written essays for Irwin on the First World War, which he has just marked.

The History Boys **by Alan Bennett (2004)**

| Irwin | So. Our overall conclusion is that the origins of the Second War lie in the unsatisfactory outcome of the First. |
| Timms | (*doubtfully*) Yes. (*with more certainty*) Yes. |

Extend your understanding

1. How do characters in your set drama text grow or develop?

2. Can you plot their 'journey' on a timeline?

3. Where will they inevitably come into conflict or challenge others?

4. Does your play depict these conflicts as comedy or tragedy?

5. How successfully does the writer you are studying combine laughter and seriousness?

6. Who does the audience sympathize with?

7. How do they react to conflict and tension between characters?

8. Is the direction of the play inevitable?

Others nod.

Irwin	First class. Bristol welcomes you with open arms. Manchester longs to have you. You can walk into Leeds. But I am a fellow of Magdalen College, Oxford, and I have just read seventy papers all saying the same thing and I am asleep …
Scripps	But it's all true.
Irwin	What has that got to do with it? What has that got to do with anything?
	Let's go back to 1914 and I'll put you a different case.
	Try this for size.
	Germany does not want war and if there is an arms race it is Britain who is leading it. Though there's no reason why we would want war. Nothing in it for us. Better stand back and let Germany and Russia fight it out while we take the imperial pickings.
	These are the facts.
	Why do we not care to acknowledge them? The cattle, the body count. We still don't like to admit the war was even partly our fault because so many of our people died. A photograph on every mantelpiece. All this mourning has veiled the truth. It's not so much lest we forget as lest we remember. Because you should realize that so far as the Cenotaph and the Last Post and all that stuff is concerned, there's no better way of forgetting something than by commemorating it.
	And Dakin.
Dakin	Sir?
Irwin	You were the one who was morally superior about Haig.
Dakin	Passchendaele. The Somme. He was a butcher, sir.
Irwin	Yes, but at least he delivered the goods. No, no, the real enemy to Haig's subsequent reputation was the Unknown Soldier. If Haig had had any sense he'd have had him disinterred and shot all over again for giving comfort to the enemy.
Lockwood	So what about the poets, then?
Irwin	What about them? If you read what they actually say as distinct from what they write, most of them seem to have enjoyed the war. Siegfried Sassoon was a good officer. Saint Wilfred Owen couldn't wait to get back to his company. Both of them surprisingly bloodthirsty.

Bristol … Manchester … Leeds = all very good universities but not as famous as Oxford and its Colleges

the cattle = Irwin is referring to Wilfred Owen's 'Anthem for Doomed Youth', 'What passing bell for those who die as cattle'

Cenotaph and Last Post = the way in which the British commemorate their war dead

Haig = First World War general: British commander on the Western Front

Somme … Passchendaele = major battles on the Western Front

Sassoon and Kipling = were other poets who wrote about the war as well as Wilfred Owen (see chapter 4)

Poetry is good up to a point. Adds flavour. But if you want to relate the politics to the war, forget Wilfred Owen and try Kipling.

Akthar   Thanks a lot.

Irwin   'If any question why we died

Tell them because our fathers lied.'

In other words …

Timms   Oh no, sir. With respect, can I stop you? No, with a poem or any work of art we can never say 'in other words'. If it is a work of art there are no other words.

Lockwood   Yes, sir. That's why it is a work of art in the first place.

You can't look at a Rembrandt and say 'in other words', can you, sir?

Irwin is puzzled where all this comes from but is distracted by Rudge.

Rudge   So what's the verdict, sir? What do I write down?

Irwin   You can write down, Rudge, that 'I must not write down every word that teacher says.'

You can also write down that the First World War was a mistake. It was not a tragedy.

And as for the truth, Scripps, which you were worrying about: truth is no more at issue in an examination than thirst at a wine-tasting or fashion at a striptease.

Dakin   Do you really believe that, sir, or are you just trying to make us think?

Scripps   You can't explain away the poetry, sir.

Lockwood   No, sir. Art wins in the end.

The bell goes.

 Check your understanding

1. Why does Irwin want the boys to produce arguments which are different?

2. Why doesn't he seem to care about the truth?

3. He is also challenging ideas of tragedy and inevitability. How is he suggesting the First World War came about?

4. What does he suggest 'remembrance' encourages people to forget?

5. What does he mean by saying that General Haig 'delivered the goods'?

6. Why does he suggest that we shouldn't trust First World War poets like Wilfred Owen (see chapter 4)?

7. What do you think he likes about the lines by Rudyard Kipling?

8. How do Timms and Lockwood change the terms of the argument?

9. Look at the stage direction which follows and the introductory notes. Where do the boys' ideas about art come from?

10. How does Irwin turn his ideas into epigrams (see chapter 2)?

11. How does Scripps turn this into an argument about art versus history?

12. Who do you think has won this argument?

Viewpoints

Sarcasm and provocation are important parts of Irwin's teaching style. The way he says things is controversial as well as his views.

1. Use the PEA technique to find examples of the harsh way Irwin puts things and explain why his choice of words is so provocative.

2. Look more closely at his language. Give examples of the ways in which he uses short sentences. Find examples of how his short sentences make him sound especially sure of himself or full of authority.

3. How successful are the boys at challenging or undermining that voice of authority? How do they use their own knowledge to do so?

4. Is it true that there are no words which can replace the statement made by a work of art? Why would that provide problems for literary criticism?

Pair and share

This time it isn't clear that the teacher has won the argument. Look over the lesson carefully and think about what you agree and disagree with. Dakin is clearly very impressed by Irwin's arguments, Lockwood less so.

Script and perform your own duologue between Dakin and Lockwood, discussing Irwin's teaching and his beliefs.

1. What do you find challenging about the way he teaches?

2. Do you agree with the views he expresses about truth and about poetry?

3. What about his views about tragedy versus accident?

4. Do you think he will help you to get a university place at Oxford?

Extend your learning

In drama, extreme and controversial characters are often more dramatically effective than those who are reasonable.

1. Are there examples of extreme characters in the texts you are studying?

2. What has made them behave provocatively?

3. How do other characters react and respond to them?

4. What is the audience's response?

5. What problems will the character's outrageous expressions cause for him later in the play?

7.5 Confrontation and climax: use of characters in chorus

So far we have explored characters through duologues and conversation. However, drama also involves bigger set pieces. We will look at two American dramas which contain big courtroom scenes, where the reactions of all of those present will influence the audience's judgments of the principal characters, and where characters will also have an audience of their own to play up to (just as we saw Falstaff and Irwin do). In the case of the famous play *The Crucible* by Nobel Prize-winning American dramatist Arthur Miller, the trial closes the penultimate scene and produces the climactic dramatic moment of the play, and the downfall of the play's flawed hero, John Procter.

Think ahead

1. What do you understand by a witch hunt?

2. Why are courtroom scenes especially powerful places for the confrontations which bring drama to a climax?

3. Can you think of courtroom scenes in films and plays you have seen?

4. What is the role of supporting characters in large (or set piece) scenes? Think about the role of the family in Ayckbourn's comedy?

5. How will the comments of other characters influence the audience's judgment and evaluation?

 See Worksheet 5 for an exercise on judging a character in one of your own set texts.

The play is set against the background of the Salem witch trials in Massachusetts in 1692–93. Abigail Williams, a teenager, has had an affair with Proctor, but in an attempt to cover this up has accused his wife Elizabeth of witchcraft, an accusation which the highly religious community believes. In this culture, anyone who is found guilty of witchcraft is put to death unless they sign a confession. A court has been set up, presided over by Judge Danforth and Reverend Hale, a priest and witchfinder. Proctor has confessed his affair and one of the girls, Mary, has confessed that the girls are lying. Danforth, not believing them, summons Elizabeth and questions her under oath about her husband's affair, but she has denied this, in order to protect him. Ironically, this has endangered everyone, as Danforth now believes Abigail even more strongly. Abigail pretends that Mary has been possessed by the devil, who haunts her in the shape of a bird, and goes on (with the other girls) to accuse Proctor and others of devil worship, having frightened Mary into joining in. The language of the play is archaic (deliberately old–fashioned): it fits the setting of seventeenth-century New England.

Daniel Day-Lewis in a film adaptation of the play

The Crucible by Arthur Miller (1953)

PROCTOR: Elizabeth, tell the truth, Elizabeth!

DANFORTH: She has spoken. Remove her. (*Hale crosses R. following Elizabeth.*)

PROCTOR: (*Cries out.*) Elizabeth, I have confessed it!

ELIZABETH: Oh, John! (*Goes out.*)

PROCTOR: She only thought to save my name!

HALE: Excellency, it is a natural lie to tell; I beg you, stop now; before another is condemned!

DANFORTH: She spoke nothing of lechery, and this man lies!

HALE: (*He cries out in anguish.*) I believe him! I cannot turn my face from it no more. (*Pointing at Abigail.*) This girl has always struck me false! She … (*Abigail with a weird cry screams up to ceiling.*)

ABIGAIL: You will not! Begone! Begone, I say! (*Mercy and Susanna rise, looking up.*)

DANFORTH: What is it, child? (*She is transfixed—with all the girls, in complete silence, she is open-mouthed, agape at ceiling, and in great fear.*) Girls! Why do you …?

MERCY: It's on the beam!—behind the rafter!

DANFORTH: (*Looking up.*) Where!

ABIGAIL: Why …? Why do you come, yellow bird?

PROCTOR: Where's a bird? I see no bird!

ABIGAIL: (*To ceiling, in a genuine conversation with the 'bird' as though trying to talk it out of attacking her.*) My face? My

to save my name = *Proctor means that Elizabeth told a lie to save his reputation*

she spoke nothing of lechery = *she did not say that Proctor had an affair*

I cannot turn my face = *Hale cannot ignore his belief that Proctor told the truth*

Mercy and Susanna rise = *they are joining Abigail's act of pretending the devil is in the room*

face?! But God made my face; you cannot want to tear my face. Envy is a deadly sin, Mary.

MARY: Abby!

ABIGAIL: (*Unperturbed, continues to 'bird.'*) Oh, Mary, this is a black art to change your shape. No, I cannot, I cannot stop my mouth; it's God's work I do ….

MARY: Abby, I'm here!

PROCTOR: They're pretending, Mister Danforth!

ABIGAIL: (*Now she takes a backward step, as though the bird would swoop down momentarily.*) Oh, please, Mary!—Don't come down ….

> *this is a black art to change your shape* = Abigail is accusing Mary of being a witch in league with the devil

ANN: Her claws, she's stretching her claws!

PROCTOR: Lies—lies—

ABIGAIL: (*Backing further, still fixed above.*) Mary, please don't hurt me!

MARY: (*To Danforth.*) I'm not hurting her!

DANFORTH: Why does she see this vision?!

MARY: (*Rises.*) She sees nothin'!

ABIGAIL: (*As though hypnotized, mimicking the exact tone of Mary's cry.*) She sees nothin'!

MARY: Abby, you mustn't!

ABIGAIL: (*Now all girls join, transfixed.*) Abby, you mustn't!

MARY: (*To all girls, frantically.*) I'm here, I'm here!

GIRLS: I'm here, I'm here!

DANFORTH: Mary Warren!—Draw back your spirit out of them!

MARY: Mister Danforth …!

GIRLS: Mister Danforth!

DANFORTH: Have you compacted with the Devil? Have you?

MARY: Never, never!

GIRLS: Never, never!

DANFORTH: (*Growing hysterical.*) Why can they only repeat you?!

PROCTOR: Give me a whip—I'll stop it!

MARY: They're sporting …!

GIRLS: (*Cutting her off.*) They're sporting!

MARY: (*Turning on them all, hysterically and stamping her feet.*) Abby, stop it!

GIRLS: (*Stamping their feet.*) Abby, stop it!

MARY: (*Screaming it out at top of her lungs, and raising her fists.*) Stop it!!

GIRLS:	(*All raising their fists.*) Stop it!! (*Mary, utterly confounded, and becoming overwhelmed by Abigail—and the girls'—utter conviction, starts to whimper, hands half raised, powerless—and all girls begin whimpering exactly as she does.*)
DANFORTH:	A little while ago you were afflicted. Now it seems you afflict others; where did you find this power?
MARY:	(*Staring at Abigail.*) I… have no power.
GIRLS:	I have no power.
PROCTOR:	They're gulling you, Mister!
DANFORTH:	Why did you turn about this past two weeks? You have seen the Devil, have you not?
PROCTOR:	(*Seeing her weakening.*) Mary, Mary, God damns all liars! (*Mary utters something unintelligible, staring at Abigail who keeps watching the 'bird' above.*)
DANFORTH:	I cannot hear you. What do you say? (*Mary utters again unintelligibly.*) You will confess yourself or you will hang!
PROCTOR:	Mary, remember the angel Raphael … do that which is good and …
ABIGAIL:	(*Pointing upward.*) The wings! Her wings are spreading! Mary, please, don't, don't …! She's going to come down! She's walking the beam! Look out! She's coming down! (*All scream. Abigail dashes across the stage as though pursued, the other girls streak hysterically in and out between the men, all converging.—and as their screaming subsides only Mary Warren's is left. All watch her, struck, even horrified by this evident fit.*)
PROCTOR:	(*Leaning across the table, turning her gently by the arm.*) Mary, tell the Governor what they …
MARY:	(*Backing away.*) Don't touch me … don't touch me!
PROCTOR:	Mary!
MARY:	(*Pointing at Proctor.*) You are the Devil's man!
PARRIS:	Praise God!
PROCTOR:	Mary, how …?
MARY:	I'll not hang with you! I love God, I love God—
DANFORTH:	(*To Mary.*) He bid you do the Devil's work?
MARY:	(*Hysterically, indicating Proctor.*) He come at me by night and every day to sign, to sign, to …
DANFORTH:	Sign what?
PARRIS:	The Devil's book? He come with a book?

> **gulling you** = *fooling you, taking you in*

122

MARY:	(*Hysterically, pointing at Proctor.*) My name, he want my name; I'll murder you, he says, if my wife hangs! We must go and overthrow the court, he says …!
PROCTOR:	(*Eyes follow Mary.*) Mister Hale …!
MARY:	(*Her sobs beginning.*) He wake me every night, his eyes were like coals and his fingers claw my neck, and I sign, I sign ….
HALE:	Excellency, the child's gone wild.
PROCTOR:	Mary, Mary …!
MARY:	(*Screaming at him.*) No, I love God; I go your way no more, (*Looking at Abigail.*) I love God, I bless God…. (Sobbing, she rushes to Abigail.) Abby, Abby, I'll never hurt you more! (*All watch, as Abigail reaches out and draws sobbing Mary to her, then looks up to Danforth.*)
DANFORTH:	What are you! You are combined with anti-Christ, are you not? I have seen your power, Mister, you will not deny it!
HALE:	This is not witchcraft! Those girls are frauds! You condemn an honest man!
DANFORTH:	I will have nothing from you, Mister Hale! (*To Proctor.*) Will you confess yourself befouled with hell, or do you keep that black allegiance yet? What say you?
PROCTOR:	I say … God is dead!
PARRIS:	(*Crossing L. toward door.*) Hear it, hear it!
PROCTOR:	A fire, a fire is burning! I hear the boot of Lucifer, I see his filthy face. And it is my face and yours, Danforth. For them that quail now when you know in all your black hearts that this be fraud. God damns our kind especially, and we will burn, we will burn together!
DANFORTH:	Marshal, take him and Corey with him to the jail!
HALE:	(*Crossing D.L.*) I denounce these proceedings! I quit this court! (*Hale EXITS.*)
PROCTOR:	You are pulling heaven down and raising up a whore.
DANFORTH:	(*Shocked.*) Mister Hale, Mister Hale!
CURTAIN	

we will burn together = *Proctor says something evil is happening in Salem, but it is the work of human beings not of the devil. Danforth refuses to understand him*

Check your understanding

1. Why do Hale and Danforth take different views about who is lying at the beginning of the scene?

2. How does this affect the audience (who know Abigail is lying)?

3. How do the stage directions indicate an atmosphere of growing hysteria?

4. Why does Abigail begin pretending to see the devil? What does she want to draw attention away from?

5. What does Abigail pretend the 'bird' is doing to her?

6. What is the effect of the girls' repetitions?

7. What does Danforth believe is happening? Why is he described as 'hysterical'?

8. List the words which show that Mary has completely broken down with fear of being accused of witchcraft.

9. Why does she make her 'confession'?

10. What is the effect on stage of the girls screaming and rushing around?

11. Where do we see Danforth 'leading the witness' by putting words into her mouth through the way he asks questions?

12. What is Mary accusing Proctor of doing?

13. Why does Proctor appeal to Hale?

14. Why do Danforth's questions not give Proctor a chance to tell the truth?

15. What does Proctor mean by 'God is dead'?

16. What does Danforth think he means?

17. What do all the exclamation marks towards the end of the scene suggest about its tone? Is anyone listening to anyone else?

18. How does Miller's language make the end of this scene especially powerful and shocking?

Pair and share

You and your partner have been sent to Salem a few months after the trials and executions have ended and have been asked to compile a report on why a miscarriage of justice has occurred. Examine the transcripts of the trial and prepare your evidence. Then, thinking about two of the following points each, argue in front of the class and explain:

1. why Abigail is guilty of perjury (lying in court)

2. why Mary changed her evidence

3. why John Proctor was misunderstood

4. why Danforth handled the situation badly.

Viewpoints

When groups become hysterical or full of prejudice, it is difficult to carry out justice effectively. Think of examples from your own knowledge or experience. Can you find evidence of trials being influenced by prejudice?

How effective is Miller's drama in re-creating this atmosphere of prejudice? How do both the words and the reactions of his characters reinforce that idea of prejudice?

Consider the following question:

- *How does Miller's writing make this scene so powerfully dramatic?*

Use these questions to shape your response.

1. How does Miller's overall theme make this such a powerful and disturbing scene?

2. Why are Proctor's confrontation with Abigail and Danforth's with Hale both so provocative?

3. How does Miller show the cunning of Abigail's deceptions?

4. How does he demonstrate the hold Abigail has over the other girls, especially Mary?

5. What qualities in the writing make Proctor's use of language so powerful and what does it make the audience reflect on?

Extend your learning

Consider the following questions with regard to a drama text you are studying.

1. What is the contribution that the more minor characters make to the text?
2. How do contrasting characters and opinions contribute to the **tension**?
3. What is the most dramatic scene and why?
4. How does the writing involve the audience in making judgments about characters?
5. Do any of the scenes have especially effective final lines?

KEY TERMS

tension = conflict between characters, felt by the audience.

soliloquy = a verse monologue, especially in Shakespeare's plays, where a character speaks his thoughts – always to himself or herself.

7.6 Using monologue to reveal character

When we studied *Henry IV Part One*, it was clear that part of the dramatic irony came from the fact that the audience always knew that Prince Henry would eventually leave Falstaff. Shakespeare's audience would have known this from history and legends – this was already a famous story before he wrote his play. However, they also knew this because Prince Henry told them so in a soliloquy. In a **soliloquy** or monologue, a character tells the truth – or at least his or her version of the truth – directly to the audience, giving us their thoughts and telling us things they have not revealed to other characters. It is a little like the empathic exercises we looked at in chapter 5 when you wrote down your thoughts. Let's look at how the Prince reveals his idea of becoming a reformed character. Notice that Shakespeare now has the Prince speaking in verse, the 'higher' style favoured by more high born and serious characters. When he was play-acting and fooling with Falstaff, he spoke in prose.

Henry IV Part One **by William Shakespeare (circa 1597)**
PRINCE HENRY:

I know you all, and will awhile uphold
The unyoked humour of your idleness:
Yet herein will I imitate the sun,
Who doth permit the base contagious clouds
To smother up his beauty from the world,
That, when he please again to be himself,
Being wanted, he may be more wonder'd at,
By breaking through the foul and ugly mists
Of vapours that did seem to strangle him.
If all the year were playing holidays,

the unyoked humour of your idleness = *your uncontrolled and pointless jokes*

vapours = *clouds or gases*

To sport would be as tedious as to work;
But when they seldom come, they wish'd for come,
And nothing pleaseth but rare accidents.
So, when this loose behaviour I throw off
And pay the debt I never promised,
By how much better than my word I am,
By so much shall I falsify men's hopes;
And like bright metal on a sullen ground,
My reformation, glittering o'er my fault,
Shall show more goodly and attract more eyes
Than that which hath no foil to set it off.
I'll so offend, to make offence a skill;
Redeeming time when men think least I will.

foil = *opposite. In drama a foil is a character who is the opposite of the main character, so Falstaff is the foil for Prince Henry*

Check your understanding

The Prince's soliloquy is made up of a series of similes and metaphors. Find the quotations which make the following comparisons.

Explanation	Quotation
The Prince is like the sun, waiting to emerge from behind the 'clouds' of his gang of unruly companions.	
We enjoy holidays much more because they don't happen as often as work days.	
So we prefer surprises to the predictable.	
When the Prince becomes a reformed character, it will be like paying back more than the money you owe.	
Or showing people's predictions were wrong.	
I'll glow more brightly surrounded by dull things, and appear more precious.	
Until then, I'll carry on behaving badly in order to make my change even more of a surprise.	

Viewpoints

Do you think this is a clever way to behave? Or is it dishonest and sly? Debate the issue with your classmates, think about whether you approve of this kind of behaviour, and take a vote on the Prince. Has he found a clever way to make himself popular? Or is he just using his 'friends' for his own ambitions?

Extend your learning

Consider the following questions with regard to a text you are studying.

1. How has the writer balanced monologue, duologue, and crowd scenes or set pieces?
2. Is there a place where characters reveal their inner thoughts to the audience or to each other?
3. Is the audience aware of examples of dramatic irony which some of the characters do not understand?
4. How is tension sustained and where does it break out into confrontation or climax?
5. Where is the setting for that confrontation or climax?

We have looked at ways in which characters are revealed and their impact portrayed through their dynamic relationship with others. We have also seen the creation of dramatic tension through clashes between characters and their ideas, or ways in which characters are brought into closer relationships and understandings. We have explored ways in which elements of comedy and tragedy may be present in the same work. Proud characters will express themselves in outrageous, provocative, and often funny ways. Nevertheless, hubris (the pride which goes before a fall) often brings on nemesis (unavoidable destruction).

In the play you are studying, where have you found examples of the following?

1. Tension
2. Provocation
3. Revelation
4. Hubris
5. Nemesis

Shakespeare's play *Richard III* is set out as a tragedy on the opening page. The audience would have known that Richard was doomed to meet a violent death on the battlefield. However, this tragedy, like that of Macbeth, gains its power from the increasing number of those close to him that Richard murders, beginning with his own brother and culminating with his young nephews, who had a better claim to the throne than Richard himself. Rather surprisingly, nevertheless, Richard keeps part of the audience's sympathy for much of the play. This is because however much he lies to other characters, he is quite honest with the audience, sharing his feelings in the form of soliloquies and asides. He takes us into his confidence. However, by the end of the play, his murderous acts have outraged the country, and his nemesis Henry Tudor has arrived in Britain to challenge his reign. Richard has just had a dream in which the ghosts of all those he has killed appeared to curse him and tell him he will lose the next day; the ghosts then visit Henry Tudor (known as 'Richmond') and tell him he will win.

Sir Laurence Olivier stars as Richard III in the 1955 film

Richard III by William Shakespeare (circa 1592)

The Ghosts vanish

KING RICHARD III starts out of his dream

KING RICHARD III

Give me another horse: bind up my wounds.
Have mercy, Jesu!—Soft! I did but dream.
O coward conscience, how dost thou afflict me!
The lights burn blue. It is now dead midnight.
Cold fearful drops stand on my trembling flesh.
What do I fear? Myself? There's none else by:
Richard loves Richard; that is, I am I.
Is there a murderer here? No. Yes, I am:
Then fly. What, from myself? Great reason why:
Lest I revenge. What, myself upon myself?
Alack, I love myself. Wherefore? For any good
That I myself have done unto myself?
O, no! alas, I rather hate myself
For hateful deeds committed by myself!
I am a villain: yet I lie. I am not.
Fool, of thyself speak well: fool, do not flatter.
My conscience hath a thousand several tongues,
And every tongue brings in a several tale,
And every tale condemns me for a villain.
Perjury, perjury, in the high'st degree
Murder, stern murder, in the direst degree;
All several sins, all used in each degree,
Throng to the bar, crying all, Guilty! Guilty!
I shall despair. There is no creature loves me;
And if I die, no soul shall pity me:
Nay, wherefore should they, since that I myself
Find in myself no pity to myself?
Methought the souls of all that I had murder'd
Came to my tent; and every one did threat
To-morrow's vengeance on the head of Richard.

Enter RATCLIFF

RATCLIFF

My lord!

KING RICHARD III

'Zounds! who is there?

---

soft = *quietly*

fly = *run away*

a thousand several tongues = *a thousand different tongues*
brings in a several tale = *brings in a different story*
perjury = *lying*

'Zounds = *a curse*

RATCLIFF

> Ratcliff, my lord; 'tis I. The early village-cock
> Hath twice done salutation to the morn;
> Your friends are up, and buckle on their armour.

The early village-cock/Hath twice done salutation to the morn = a cockerel has crowed twice

KING RICHARD III

> O Ratcliff, I have dream'd a fearful dream!
> What thinkest thou, will our friends prove all true?

will our friends prove all true? = will our allies stay loyal?

RATCLIFF

> No doubt, my lord.

KING RICHARD III

> O Ratcliff, I fear, I fear,—

RATCLIFF

> Nay, good my lord, be not afraid of shadows.

KING RICHARD III

> By the apostle Paul, shadows to-night
> Have struck more terror to the soul of Richard
> Than can the substance of ten thousand soldiers
> Armed in proof, and led by shallow Richmond.

armed in proof = fully armed

✎ Check your understanding

In the soliloquy, Richard appears to be arguing with himself. Does he really want his enemy dead, or is his true enemy himself, and what he has done?

1. As he wakes up ('starts') what is Richard dreaming about?
2. Why does he personify conscience and call it a coward?
3. What does the word 'afflict' mean?
4. How does the writing make Richard's midnight fears come to life?
5. Why can't Richard believe that he is afraid of himself?
6. Why does he contradict himself?
7. How could he revenge himself on himself?
8. Why does he imagine his conscience has so many tongues and so much to say?
9. Which words does he use which show he imagines he is on trial?
10. What do the ghosts seem to want from him?

Look at how the scene continues through the duologue with Ratcliff.

11. How does Ratcliff's way of speaking, the morning before the big battle, create more tension?
12. What is Richard really afraid of?
13. What is the meaning of Ratcliff's answer to this?
14. Why is Richard still not reassured?
15. How does this scene change the audience's reaction to Richard?

Pair and share

What will Ratcliff tell another of Richard's supporters about the King? Why might their optimism about the battle be changing? Dramatize a short scene in which Ratcliff tells a friend in a duologue about what he has seen and heard and why it disturbs him.

Now have some fun with the soliloquy itself. Although these are meant to be Richard's private thoughts, what we really see is that he is arguing with himself. Mark up your copy of the speech. Which parts should be said by Repentant Richard, and which parts by the old Reckless Richard? Reckless Richard did not believe in conscience, ghosts, or God. He thought you made your own fate through violent action. He felt no need to repent.

Dramatize the soliloquy by getting two actors to represent Richard's two voices. What effect does this have, and who wins the argument?

 Viewpoints

There is no creature loves me;
And if I die, no soul shall pity me:
Nay, wherefore should they, since that I myself
Find in myself no pity to myself?

Why has Richard stopped congratulating himself on the murders he committed to obtain and hold on to the crown?

How might the audience's view of him be changing? Do we have any pity or sympathy?

It helps to remember what Richard has done. While his early victims were other politicians who have themselves committed terrible deeds or were guilty of betrayal, the murder of the young princes is different: most in the audience lose any pity for Richard at this moment (compare with the murder of Macduff's family in *Macbeth*).

Let's look at how different students have reacted to this soliloquy.

Student A

Shakespeare has made Richard afraid of himself. He feels like the ghosts that came to him were real. He started by asking for forgiveness from God. Richard is really scared of the war and what it is going to do to him. When he says 'O coward conscience', we can see that Richard does not trust himself at that moment.

Student B

When Richard wakes up from his frightening dream of the ghosts of his victims, he is shaken and very afraid. His immediate exclamation, 'Give me another horse!' is an allusion to the final scene in which he cries out 'A horse! My kingdom for a horse'. William Shakespeare here conveys Richard as a frightened man – what we as the audience were never used to. It also shows that Richard's fear for his life now is as intense as it will be when he comes to his violent end in the battlefield.

Comments

This shows sound understanding. This student knows what has just happened and sees that Richard is perhaps his own conscience, beginning to want forgiveness from a God he has always denied exists until now. A quotation is well integrated into the sentence.

Comments

This student rightly sees this moment as the true climax of the play. Richard is already anticipating the play's tragic conclusion, and the student sees the playwright at work here, showing the audience a new side to Richard's character. There is a very strong sense of the writer's choices, always the sign of a very strong answer.

Student A

His selfish thoughts then creep into his head. He tells himself that he loves himself. This is a way of boosting his own confidence. 'Is there a murderer here? No!' This phrase is dramatic because he asks himself a question and then answers it abruptly. The 'No' came with an exclamation as if he is being defensive about what he said. This then changes his mind to telling us that there is a murderer which is him. He then makes us think he is a threat to himself. 'Lest I revenge'. This is ironic knowing Richard. He loves himself too much to bring any sort of pain upon himself. He says it in the next line that 'I love myself'. Richard has too much pride in him to think of killing himself or bringing harm to himself.

Comments

This is a good answer, showing good knowledge and understanding, and integrating some well-chosen textual support. There is appreciation of what is dramatic about the language and form of expression, and what an audience will find ironic, although there is a tendency to narrate the story instead of giving direct analysis of the effect of the writer's choices.

Student B

Richard has never known love and so when he says 'Alack I love myself' it is only an attempt to cling to any hope that he is good, at least to himself, but still that is not true. He therefore goes on to say 'I rather hate myself'. It is as if Richard dismisses all the good qualities, easily replacing them with his evil characteristics. This shows that Richard is in conflict with himself. He is confused and afraid but the truth still remains clear and he states it clearly when he says 'I am a villain'.

Comments

This is an even better answer. The choice of quotations brings out Richard's inner contradictions and there is strong understanding of why he is like this – he is someone who has never known what love is. There is appreciation of Richard's tone; the student's words 'dismisses', 'conflict', and 'states it clearly' show that for the student Richard is always fighting, even if his enemy is himself.

Student B

The conflict with his conscience is like a trial and his conscience is confessing against him, accusing him of all the crimes of his lies. Richard will not 'flatter' by trying to defend himself. It is made clear here that Richard cannot deny the truth about himself that his conscience now reveals to him. 'My conscience hath a thousand several tongues and every tongue brings in a several tale', the sins that Richard has committed are numerous and they are the most gruesome and brutal of sins. This is shown by the repetition of the word 'degree' which just emphasizes the brutality of Richard when victimizing people. The audience is moved almost to pity when Richard says with finality 'I shall despair. There is no creature that loves me.' This is the plain truth and the dramatic thing is that Richard makes it an unwavering declaration. Though the audience may be moved, to Richard it is a plain truth stated emotionlessly. It is also as if he accepts defeat now and will not care, whatever will happen to him next. He is not as resourceful as he once was and it disappoints the audience somewhat to see him like this.

Comments

This becomes a model commentary on this scene. Notice the student's excellent integration of short quotations from the text and commentary on the dramatic effect of the language. There is a constant sense of the impact on the audience, as well as detailed comment on the choice of words, their repetition, and their emotive power. The student notices that the audience might feel a pity for Richard which he never really feels for himself. There is also a very interesting final and personal response to the way Richard has deteriorated as a character and how this changes the audience's reaction. There is a very strong appreciation of three things we have emphasized in this chapter:

- the craft of the playwright and the shape of the play
- the character's journey during the drama
- changes in the audience's response to and evaluation of characters.

Extend your learning

Does your drama set text have a principal character who learns something about himself/herself? Is this a moment of comedy, enlightenment, or nemesis? As we have seen, serious self-knowledge is a strong element in tragic drama, when a character becomes aware of their fate, and perhaps the extent to which they have caused it through their own actions.

For your own drama set text, consider the following questions.

1. At what point does the fate of a principal character appear inevitable?

2. Is this the moment of climax in the drama?

3. How self-aware is the principal character? Does he or she convey thoughts through monologue? Or duologue?

4. Can we trust the principal character's self-assessment? Or does the audience know more (irony)?

5. What are the contradictions within that principal character and how have they caused conflict?

6. Does the audience react with empathy, sympathy, or pity? Or does the character remain purely comic?

7.7 Confrontation

Self-recognition is just one form of turning point in drama. Whereas Richard's true nemesis is arguably himself, a more conventional way of dealing with contrasting characters and their conflict is through a central dramatic showdown. The turning point leads to a decisive shift in power or status: perhaps a character who was the underdog now emerges triumphant, or a tragic figure sees the inevitability of his destiny. Certainly there will be a decisive shift in the feelings of the audience. This moment in a play is sometimes called the reversal of fortune. In the Middle Ages, fortune was seen as a wheel, with the king on top, and someone being crushed at the bottom. The goddess Fortune is a personification of fate or destiny, so, as in tragedy, the change is inevitable, and only partly under the character's control. The turning of fortune's wheel is a decisive moment in drawing the action to its climax.

A depiction of the Wheel of Fortune

Think ahead

Look at the structure of the drama text you are studying. Can you identify a turning point?

1. Where does the wheel of fortune turn in your text?
2. Whose fortune goes down?
3. Who emerges on top?
4. Why does this happen?
5. Where do the sympathies of the audience lie?
6. Do they change too?
7. How does the change in fortune relate to the fate of the characters?
8. What does the reversal of fortune suggest about the themes of the play?
9. How has the writer dramatized this: through action, duologue, or monologue?
10. How does this prepare the audience for the play's climax?

Not everyone will agree about where the turning point lies. In *Richard III*, it could be the death of the princes (which happens offstage, like many key moments) or the moment Richard orders their deaths, or it might not come until later, perhaps in the soliloquy above. In *A Midsummer Night's Dream* it comes when Oberon and Puck bring the lovers back into their correct pairings and remove the effects of the love juice from Titania, bringing the madness of the night to an end. These are all points you can debate and discuss.

In *Inherit the Wind*, the famous politician Matthew Harrison is leading the prosecution of a local schoolteacher Bertram Cates for teaching the theory of evolution. He believes that every word of the Christian Bible is literally true. Against him in court is his old friend Henry Drummond who is now cross-examining the politician as a witness against his own case. As you read the text, notice the way in which the writers want the audience reaction to mark the turning point of the drama: the reactions of those in the courtroom and on the jury should help the theatre audience to see that this is the key moment when the moment of the play shifts, and Brady's strong literal defence of the Bible begins to collapse, as his own egotism is exposed. Up to this point, Drummond's cross-examination has been quite comic (for example, asking who Cain's wife was) but it now takes a much more serious turn.

A scene from *Inherit the Wind*

Inherit the Wind by Jerome Lawrence and Robert E. Lee (1955)

Drummond (*fiery*) I must be allowed to examine the one witness you've left me in my own way.

Brady (*with dignity*) Your Honor, I am willing to sit here and endure Mr Drummond's sneering and his disrespect. For he is pleading the case of the prosecution by his contempt for all that is holy.

Drummond I object, I object, I object.

Brady On what grounds? Is it possible that something is holy to the celebrated agnostic?

Drummond Yes! (*his voice drops, intensely*) The individual human mind. In a child's power to master the multiplication table there is more sanctity than in all your shouted 'Amens!' 'Holy, Holies! and Hosannahs!' An idea is a greater monument than a cathedral. And the advance of man's knowledge is more of a miracle than any sticks turned to snakes, or the parting of waters! But we are now to halt the march of progress because Mr Brady frightens us with a fable? (*Turning to the jury, reasonably*) Gentleman, progress has never been a bargain. You've got to pay for it. Sometimes I think there's a man behind the counter who says, "All right, you can have a telephone; but you'll have to give up privacy, the charm of distance. Madam, you may vote; but at a price; you lose the right to retreat behind a powder-puff or a petticoat. Mister, you may conquer the air, but the birds will lose their wonder, and the clouds will smell of gasoline." (*Thoughtfully, seeing to look beyond the courtroom*) Darwin moved us forward to a hilltop, where we could look back and see the way from which we came. But for this view, this insight, this knowledge, we must abandon our faith in the pleasant poetry of Genesis.

Brady We must not abandon faith! Faith is the important thing!

Drummond Then why did God plague us with the power to think, Mr Brady? Why do you deny the one faculty which lifts man above all other creatures on the earth: the power of his brain to reason. What other merit have we? The elephant is larger, the horse is stronger and swifter, the butterfly more beautiful, the mosquito more prolific, even the simple sponge is more durable! (*Wheeling on Brady*) Or does a sponge think?

Brady I don't know. I'm a man, not a sponge.

(*There are a few snickers at this: the crowd seems to be slipping away from Brady and aligning itself more and more with Drummond*)

Drummond Do you think a sponge thinks?

Brady If the Lord wishes a sponge to think, it thinks.

Drummond Does a man have the same privileges that a sponge does?

Brady Of course.

Drummond (*Roaring, for the first time: stretching his arm toward Cates*) This man wishes to be accorded the same privilege as a sponge! He wishes to think!

(*There is some applause. The sound of it strikes Brady exactly as if he had been slapped in the face.*)

Check your understanding

1. Why does Brady appear to be in complete control at the beginning of this scene?

2. Why does he claim that Drummond's questioning of the Bible (for example, asking who Cain's wife was) has not worked?

3. How does Drummond change his tone to indicate that he does take some things seriously?

4. How do Lee and Lawrence use stage directions to indicate this change in tone?

5. What is the subject of his long speech and how does it relate to Cates's freedom to teach the science of evolutionary theory?

6. What are the metaphors he uses to make science sound miraculous?

7. What techniques does he use to appeal directly to the audience?

8. The next stage of his argument depends on an analogy to other forms of progress. How does he make comparisons with other gains and losses as a result of progress and technology? Is there really a comparison between Darwin's science and technological progress?

9. How does Drummond use the 'rule of three' to describe the theories of Darwin?

10. How does he suggest that faith is not enough to satisfy human intelligence?

11. What are the effects of his comparisons of 'man' to different creatures, including the sponge?

12. Why does Brady's reaction have a comic effect? He was attempting to make a joke, but why does the joke appear to be on him?

13. How does the argument about the sponge reflect the different arguments of Drummond and Brady?

14. What is the significance of Drummond's gesture towards Cates? What does he claim the defendant in the trial represents?

15. Why has he now begun to win round his audience? What fundamental general principle has he successfully appealed to? Would this work for the theatre audience too?

16. How does the confrontation between Drummond and Brady (who were once good friends) show the difference between faith and the power to ask questions? Why has Brady appeared to run out of answers?

17. What does the final stage direction suggest about Brady's vanity? Why is he no longer able to dominate and direct the crowd?

 ## Pair and share

At what point does Brady begin to lose the argument? Both men are celebrated lawyers and think highly of themselves as well as of their arguments. Act out this scene with a partner.

1. How can you present Brady's convictions powerfully?

2. How does Drummond make sure that his own views can also be taken seriously?

3. Where is the turning point at which Drummond appears to be winning the argument?

4. Why is Brady not able to fight back?

Now perform the scene, using the rest of the class as your jury. Look at them and speak persuasively to them, in order to try to change their views. You will notice that while Drummond can move around, Brady is stuck in the witness box, which limits his movement and makes him seem rather rigid. What does this suggest about his arguments too?

Extend your learning

Look further at how this play develops, or watch the famous film adaptation starring Spencer Tracy.

1. What does it reveal about the conflict between science (especially Darwinism) and religion (creationism)?
2. Where are these arguments still being rehearsed today?
3. What are your own views?

Write an essay on the turning point in the play you are studying.

1. Does everyone agree where it is?
2. What is your own view and why?
3. How does it change the way the audience see the characters and action?
4. Was it inevitable that things would turn in this way?
5. How does this prepare the audience for the play's climax?
6. What does it make us think about?

7.8 Everything is connected: how plays end

We will now look at the ways in which two texts end, drawing the lines of their plots into a satisfactory conclusion. As we have seen, plays are driven by audience expectation and theatrical convention. In chapter 2 we explored the comic convention of the happy ending. Shakespeare's comedies are superbly staged in order to bring everyone together at the end and to suggest fairytale marriages which ensure characters 'live happily ever after' but there is often a bitter element here too. Not everyone is included in the 'happy ending'. What happens to Antonio at the end of *The Merchant of Venice*?

Think ahead

1. How does the play you are studying bring characters together at the end?
2. Will the consequences be comic, tragic, or a mixture?
3. Is that accident (coincidence) or fate (destiny)?
4. Are some characters excluded from the play's resolution?
5. What do you think will become of them?

We will look at extracts from two plays. One is mainly comic, the other tragic.

 Viewpoints

Notice that the turning point (what the Greeks called *peripeteia*) in the drama involves the character losing the sympathy of the audience.

1. Make a note of all the stage directions. How do they give directions to both the principal characters and the onstage audience who are listening to them?
2. How does Drummond's change of tone affect the mood of the courtroom audience at the beginning of the scene?
3. How do you think the mood of the onstage audience affects the audience in the theatre?
4. Why do we sympathize more with Drummond?
5. Are there any reasons for sympathizing with Brady?
6. How has the shift in the audience's sympathies also affected the way they think about teaching evolution?

Shakespeare's *Twelfth Night* was written towards the end of his great comic period and it has some darker elements. Indeed at the very end of the play, the clown will sing a song which is later repeated by the Fool in the tragedy *King Lear*. Various comic consequences have resulted from the confusion between two twins washed up on the shore of Illyria, each thinking that the other was dead. The girl, Viola, has disguised herself as a boy (Cesario). Olivia, a countess, has fallen in love with 'Cesario', to the disappointment of Duke Orsino, who loved her himself and used Cesario as a servant to deliver messages of love to her. Now the boy twin, Sebastian, has arrived, and he is now mistaken for 'Cesario'. Unlike his sister, he quickly agrees to marry Olivia (who is very beautiful as well as rich) and he has no trouble beating up the foolish Sir Andrew and Olivia's wicked uncle Sir Toby, who has been trying to marry her to Sir Andrew, as a way of getting money. Sir Toby and others have also played a cruel trick on Malvolio, Olivia's chief servant, convincing him that Olivia is in love with him, just for a laugh. Malvolio has ended up being locked up as a madman.

Twelfth Night by William Shakespeare (1602)

Enter SIR ANDREW

SIR ANDREW

For the love of God, a surgeon! Send one presently to Sir Toby.

presently = *right away*

OLIVIA

What's the matter?

SIR ANDREW

He has broke my head across and has given Sir Toby a bloody coxcomb too: for the love of God, your help! I had rather than forty pound I were at home.

a bloody coxcomb = *a bleeding head*

OLIVIA

Who has done this, Sir Andrew?

SIR ANDREW

The count's gentleman, one Cesario: we took him for a coward, but he's the very devil incardinate.

devil incardinate = *Sir Andrew means the devil incarnate (made flesh)*

DUKE ORSINO

My gentleman, Cesario?

SIR ANDREW

'Od's lifelings, here he is! You broke my head for nothing; and that that I did, I was set on to do't by Sir Toby.

'Od's lifelings = *a mildly blasphemous oath*

I was set on to do't = *I was set up or made to do it*

VIOLA

Why do you speak to me? I never hurt you:
You drew your sword upon me without cause;
But I bespoke you fair, and hurt you not.

> *I bespoke you fair* = I said nice things to you

SIR ANDREW

If a bloody coxcomb be a hurt, you have hurt me: I
think you set nothing by a bloody coxcomb.

Enter SIR TOBY BELCH and Clown

Here comes Sir Toby halting; you shall hear more:
but if he had not been in drink, he would have
tickled you othergates than he did.

> *halting* = limping
>
> *he would have tickled you othergates* = he would have beaten you (if he were not drunk)

DUKE ORSINO

How now, gentleman! how is't with you?

SIR TOBY BELCH

That's all one: has hurt me, and there's the end
on't. Sot, didst see Dick surgeon, sot?

> *sot* = fool

CLOWN

O, he's drunk, Sir Toby, an hour agone; his eyes
were set at eight i' the morning.

SIR TOBY BELCH

Then he's a rogue, and a passy measures panyn: I
hate a drunken rogue.

> *passy measures panyn* = this is a strange drunken insult (no one is sure what it means!)

OLIVIA

Away with him! Who hath made this havoc with them?

SIR ANDREW

I'll help you, Sir Toby, because we'll be dressed together.

SIR TOBY BELCH

Will you help? An ass-head and a coxcomb and a
knave, a thin-faced knave, a gull!

> *coxcomb* = (here) fool
>
> *gull* = gullible fool
>
> *let his hurt be look'd to* = look after his injury
>
> *Exeunt* = they all go out (together or separately?)

OLIVIA

Get him to bed, and let his hurt be look'd to.

Exeunt Clown, FABIAN, SIR TOBY BELCH, and SIR ANDREW

Check your understanding

1. Why is the 'Cesario' who Sir Andrew has just met not a 'coward' but perfectly capable of beating Sir Andrew up when he thinks he is being insulted?

2. Why is he so shocked to see 'Cesario' next to the Duke?

3. Why does Viola deny having done anything to hurt Sir Andrew?

4. How can we tell that Sir Toby is drunk and that he is angry when someone stands up to him?

5. Why is the Clown's reaction ironic?

6. Why does Sir Toby now reveal his true feelings about Sir Andrew?

7. What difference does it make if Sir Andrew and Sir Toby leave separately?

8. Although this scene is funny, why might some in the audience feel the darker elements are stronger?

So a case of mistaken identity has caused all sorts of problems, as so often happens in comedy. Shakespeare is tying up the various different strands of his plot, but he is also making it clear that although there will be a happy ending for some, it will not be so for everyone. Some characters will not get married or join the final circle of happiness, some of the jokes have got out of hand, and some of the comic characters are no longer as funny as we once thought they were. Many call this play 'bittersweet'. Let us see what happens next.

Actors playing the twins in *Twelfth Night*

Twelfth Night **by William Shakespeare (1602)**

Enter SEBASTIAN

SEBASTIAN

> I am sorry, madam, I have hurt your kinsman:
> But, had it been the brother of my blood,
> I must have done no less with wit and safety.
> You throw a strange regard upon me, and by that
> I do perceive it hath offended you:
> Pardon me, sweet one, even for the vows
> We made each other but so late ago.

DUKE ORSINO

> One face, one voice, one habit, and two persons,
> A natural perspective, that is and is not!

SEBASTIAN

> Antonio, O my dear Antonio!
> How have the hours rack'd and tortured me,
> Since I have lost thee!

You throw a strange regard upon me = *you are looking at me in an odd way*

A natural perspective = *a natural mirror*

rack'd = *a reference to an instrument of torture*

ANTONIO

Sebastian are you?

SEBASTIAN

Fear'st thou that, Antonio?

ANTONIO

How have you made division of yourself?
An apple, cleft in two, is not more twin
Than these two creatures. Which is Sebastian?

OLIVIA

Most wonderful!

SEBASTIAN

Do I stand there? I never had a brother;
Nor can there be that deity in my nature,
Of here and every where. I had a sister,
Whom the blind waves and surges have devour'd.
Of charity, what kin are you to me?
What countryman? What name? What parentage?

that deity in my nature = *I am not a god able to be everywhere at once*

VIOLA

Of Messaline: Sebastian was my father;
Such a Sebastian was my brother too,
So went he suited to his watery tomb:
If spirits can assume both form and suit
You come to fright us.

So went he suited to his watery tomb = *that is what he looked like when he drowned*

SEBASTIAN

A spirit I am indeed;
But am in that dimension grossly clad
Which from the womb I did participate.
Were you a woman, as the rest goes even,
I should my tears let fall upon your cheek,
And say 'Thrice-welcome, drowned Viola!'

VIOLA

My father had a mole upon his brow.

SEBASTIAN

And so had mine.

VIOLA

And died that day when Viola from her birth
Had number'd thirteen years.

SEBASTIAN

O, that record is lively in my soul!

He finished indeed his mortal act
That day that made my sister thirteen years.

VIOLA

If nothing lets to make us happy both
But this my masculine usurp'd attire,
Do not embrace me till each circumstance
Of place, time, fortune, do cohere and jump
That I am Viola: which to confirm,
I'll bring you to a captain in this town,
Where lie my maiden weeds; by whose gentle help
I was preserved to serve this noble count.
All the occurrence of my fortune since
Hath been between this lady and this lord.

do cohere and jump = *all prove together*

SEBASTIAN

[*To OLIVIA*] So comes it, lady, you have been mistook:
But nature to her bias drew in that.
You would have been contracted to a maid;
Nor are you therein, by my life, deceived,
You are betroth'd both to a maid and man.

nature to her bias drew in that = *that was things working out according to nature*

DUKE ORSINO

Be not amazed; right noble is his blood.
If this be so, as yet the glass seems true,
I shall have share in this most happy wreck.

To VIOLA

Boy, thou hast said to me a thousand times
Thou never shouldst love woman like to me.

VIOLA

And all those sayings will I overswear;
And those swearings keep as true in soul
As doth that orbed continent the fire
That severs day from night.

that orbed continent = *the sun*

DUKE ORSINO

Give me thy hand;
And let me see thee in thy woman's weeds.

VIOLA

The captain that did bring me first on shore
Hath my maid's garments: he upon some action
Is now in durance, at Malvolio's suit,
A gentleman, and follower of my lady's.

thy woman's weeds = *in your woman's clothes*

in durance = *under arrest (this is a reminder of Malvolio's existence!)*

✎ Check your understanding

1. Who is the 'sweet one' whom Sebastian is addressing?

2. Why is she lost for words?

3. Why does the Duke think that the existence of two 'Cesarios' is like a miracle?

4. Antonio's presence is important. He is the sailor who saved Sebastian's life, so he knows his true identity. Why is he also confused?

5. How will Olivia say the lines 'most wonderful'?

6. How should a director stage this scene to ensure that Viola and Sebastian see each other as late as possible?

7. Why can't the twins themselves quite believe that the scene is real?

8. How does Shakespeare use coincidence to achieve **recognition** between the twins?

9. Why does Viola now feel confident enough to admit that she is a woman?

10. What does Sebastian mean by 'nature to her bias drew in that'?

11. How does this ending ensure that both couples will live happily ever after? (You might compare it with the 'happy ending' of *The Importance of Being Earnest* in chapter 2).

12. Why does the mention of Malvolio remind the audience of a part of the play which has not ended so happily and what is the effect of this?

💡 Viewpoints

Do we really believe that Orsino can so easily switch from loving Olivia to loving Viola?

Are we confident that Olivia, who fell in love with 'Cesario' when he was played by Viola, will really be happy with the much more masculine Sebastian?

> *And all those sayings will I overswear;*
> *And those swearings keep as true in soul*
> *As doth that orbed continent the fire*
> *That severs day from night.*

1. How does Viola's language here make sure that we believe in the poetry of this moment, even if we are not sure that it is 'realistic'?

2. What simile does she use?

3. Why does she refer to her 'soul'?

4. What does she mean by suggesting that love has more to do with the 'soul' than the body, or its gender?

5. Do you agree?

It depends how you treat comedy: romance is always close to being a fairytale and therefore not to be confused with realism. In the fairytale world, as we saw with *A Midsummer Night's Dream* in chapter 2, all is well which ends well, whatever the confusions in the middle part.

However, there are very realistic (and more cruel) aspects of the comedy in *Twelfth Night*, and they are acted out by humans, not by fairies. There is no happy ending for Sir Toby or for Malvolio.

a) Do you prefer comedy to have a fantasy element?

b) Or should it be close to real life?

c) If comedy is realistic, do we learn something from it?

Comedy which teaches us something about real life, or makes fun of things which we normally take seriously is often called satire. Satirical endings are rarely as happy as comic ones. Satire often has the effect of shocking an audience, as well as making them laugh.

Extend your learning

Answer these questions with reference to the set text which you are studying.

1. What is learned or recognized by the audience at the end of the play?
2. Is the ending happy, sad, or bittersweet?
3. Would you classify the play as comedy, tragedy, tragic-comedy, or **satire**?
4. How realistic do you find the ending?
5. Is it important for audiences to use their imagination, or should they expect an ending which is close to real life?
6. Are the 'loose ends' all tied up at the end of the play? Or are there discordant elements, which don't fit in with that sense of harmony?
7. What does the audience feel like at the end?
8. Why did the writer want to leave them with that particular feeling?

 See Worksheet 6 for a further activity to help you consider the journey of the audience.

KEY TERM

satire = using comedy and irony to mock convention, provoke the audience and teach lessons about life, often by shock effects.

7.9 Recognition

We have seen that recognition is an important element at the end of a drama. Characters recognize something about themselves or about others, and realize something that perhaps we in the audience realized much earlier. However, not everyone wants to recognize what a play appears to be telling them, and not all characters share in the revelations, recognitions, and reconciliations at the end of a comedy. Characters are even less likely to achieve recognition or reconciliation at the end of a tragedy.

In a serious or tragic play, we should expect disturbing, discordant elements, and tears not laughter. If everything is connected up and explained, it might not be in the way characters like, and they will often learn uncomfortable things about themselves.

Let us explore a well-known example from mid-twentieth-century British drama.

Priestley's *An Inspector Calls* is noticeable for having two endings. The first comes when the Inspector closes his notebook, shuts the case, and makes a powerful speech which will provoke the audience, as well as the Birling family. It makes the message to the audience very clear and obvious. The play is set in 1912, before the First World War, but was first staged in 1946, just after the Second World War. It therefore makes very clear the collapse of the class-based culture of Britain that existed before the twentieth century (as we saw in chapter 2). It clearly blames that collapse on the ways in which that culture ignored and blamed the poor, represented here by Eva Smith, who lost her jobs because of Mr Birling and Sheila Birling, became the pregnant mistress of Eric Birling, and finally was turned down by Mrs Birling's charity committee.

A scene from *An Inspector Calls*

An Inspector Calls by J.B. Priestley (1946)

Eric	Come on, don't just look like that. Tell me – tell me – what happened?
Inspector	(*with calm authority*) I'll tell you. She went to your mother's committee for help, after she'd done with you. Your mother refused that help.
Eric	(*nearly at breaking point*) Then – you killed her. She came to you to protect me – and you turned her away – yes, and you killed her – and the child she'd have had too – my child – your own grandchild – you killed them both – damn you, damn you –
Mrs Birling	(*very distressed now*) No – Eric – please – I didn't know – I didn't understand –
Eric	(*almost threatening her*) You don't understand anything. You never did. You never even tried – you –
Sheila	(*frightened*) Eric, don't – don't –
Birling	(*furious, intervening*) Why, you hysterical young fool – get back – or I'll –
Inspector	(*taking charge, masterfully*) Stop! *They are suddenly quiet, staring at him.* And be quiet for a moment and listen to me. I don't need to know any more. Neither do you. This girl killed herself – and died a horrible death. But each of you helped to kill her. Remember that. Never forget it. (*He looks from one to the other of them carefully.*) But then I don't think you ever will. Remember what you did, Mrs Birling. You turned her away when she most needed help. You refused her even the pitiable little bit of organized charity you had in your power to grant her. Remember what you did –
Eric	(*unhappily*) My God – I'm not likely to forget.
Inspector	Just used her for the end of a stupid drunken evening as if she was an animal, a thing, not a person. No, you won't forget. (*He looks at Sheila.*)
Sheila	(*bitterly*) I know. I had her turned out of a job. I started it.
Inspector	You helped but you didn't start it. (*Rather savagely, to Birling.*) You started it. She wanted twenty-five shillings a week instead of twenty-two and sixpence. You made her pay a heavy price for that. And now she'll make you pay a heavier price still.
Birling	(*unhappily*) Look, Inspector – I'd give thousands – yes, thousands –
Inspector	You are offering the money at the wrong time, Mr Birling. (*He makes a move as if concluding the session, possibly shutting up notebook, etc. Then surveys them sardonically.*) No, I don't think any of you will forget. Nor that young man, Croft, though he at least had some affection for her and made her happy for a time. Well, Eva Smith's gone. You can't do her any more harm. And you can't do her any good now, either. You can't even say, 'I'm sorry, Eva Smith.'
Sheila	(*who is crying quietly*) That's the worst of it.
Inspector	But just remember this. One Eva Smith has gone – but there are millions and millions and millions of Eva Smiths and John Smiths still left with us with their lives, their hopes and fears, their suffering and chance of happiness, all intertwined with our lives, and what we think and say and do. We don't live alone. We are members of one body. We are responsible for each other. And I tell you that the time will soon come when, if men will not learn that lesson, then they will be taught it in fire and blood and anguish. Good night.

This is an extremely powerful and effective piece of writing. It is full of tension and forms a strong climax to the play. All the different strands of the story are now connected, and they all condemn the Birling family for their selfishness. The Inspector becomes a mouthpiece for the writer's view on society – 'we are members of one body' – which are conveyed directly in the rhetoric of the Inspector's speech.

Check your understanding

1. Look at the stage directions first. How do they show the contrast between the emotions of the Birling family and those of the Inspector?

2. Do the stage directions also suggest that the older Birlings have slightly different feelings to the younger ones?

3. Why has the writer given Eric such broken sentences? What does he want the actor to show about him?

4. What does the audience see about the relationship between Eric and his mother?

5. How does the Inspector use language in order to take control? What do we notice about his sentences and the pace of his speech?

6. Why does he keep repeating the pronoun 'you' to Mrs Birling?

7. What is interesting about her reaction?

8. What does Birling not understand when the Inspector says he must 'pay'?

9. How does the Inspector underline the tragedy of Eva's death?

10. How does he use Eva's death as a metaphor?

11. Where does he use patterns of three to give his speech rhetorical power and shape?

12. What kind of future does he seem to be predicting? How does this add to the supernatural element of his character?

Viewpoints

Debate and discuss the questions which follow:

1. Why do you think the Birlings are shocked and surprised by the Inspector's message?

2. What do you think were their views about society?

3. Why do you think Priestley wanted us to notice such a big difference between the older and younger Birlings?

4. Look back at chapter 3 and the way we explored conflict between generations. Is Priestley saying something about a changing world?

5. What would an audience in 1946 think about these characters from 1912?

6. Why would they criticize their attitudes?

The dramatic effectiveness of the play depends on its impact on the audience.

7. Why would the play have made such a powerful impression after the Second World War?

8. Do rich people still feel little responsibility for the poor?

9. How well would this play work today, or outside the UK?

10. Is it just a 'period piece' or can it work for today's audiences?

For further research, look at www.aninspectorcalls.com. This is a record of the Stephen Daldry production which was so successful in 1992 that it had a year on Broadway, a major revival in 2009, and finished a UK tour in 2012. Clearly audiences still find that the play can have plenty to say to them.

However, the first extract is not quite the end of the play. Mr Birling phones around and proves the 'Inspector' was not a real police officer and that no suicidal young woman called Eva Smith had been brought to the hospital ('Infirmary'). He tries to convince the others in his family that it makes everything all right, even though they have confessed that all the events the Inspector asked them about did really happen. What does this suggest to the audience about the 'truth' of theatre?

At the very end of the play, the phone suddenly rings. This kind of ending to a play is sometimes called a **coda** (or tail). In this case the tail has a sting.

Daldry production of *An Inspector Calls*

An Inspector Calls **by J.B. Priestley (1946)**

Birling   (pointing to Eric and Sheila) Now look at the pair of them – the famous younger generation who know it all. And they can't even take a joke –

The telephone rings sharply. There is a moment's complete silence. Birling goes to answer it.

Yes?...Mr Birling speaking...What? – here-

But obviously the other person has rung off. He puts the telephone down slowly and looks in a panic-stricken fashion at the others.

Birling   That was the police. A girl has just died – on her way to the infirmary – after swallowing some disinfectant. And a police inspector is on his way here – to ask some – questions –

As they stare guiltily and dumbfounded, the curtain falls.

KEY TERMS

coda = tail end after the main action, like an epilogue (see chapter 2).

anti-climax = something which contrasts with the climax expected.

Extend your learning

1. Why follow the climax of the play with what at first seems an '**anti-climax**'?

2. Was the Inspector a ghost? (He is called Inspector Goole.)

3. What game did Priestley play with realism here?

4. Why did he want the play to have a fantasy element?

5. How do the stage directions show the effect of taking that fantasy away?

6. How much attention is he suggesting the Birlings would pay to a warning which was 'art' rather than 'reality'?

7. What is he suggesting to the audience about the relationship between theatre and real life?

8. How has he successfully played games with our understanding of time?

Looking at the way your own set play ends answer the following questions.

a) Does it conclude with a climax? Or is there an element of anti-climax?

b) Is your play entirely realistic, or is there a sense of fantasy or magic?

c) We have seen that dramatists sometimes end their plays with an epilogue or coda. How does this help the audience to reflect on what they have seen?

d) What do you think is the lingering impact of the ending on the audience? What will it make them think about?

e) Does the ending fit audience expectations, or will it surprise them?

f) Will the audience feel comfortable or uncomfortable at the end of the play?

Looking back

We have looked closely at extracts from dramas of different periods to accompany your study of your set text, in order to develop your appreciation of dramatic effectiveness. This phrase refers to the impact drama makes on a live audience in the theatre. As we have seen, this depends on the structure of the text, as well as the language and humour or tension of the scenes portrayed.

To reinforce your understanding, look back at the extracts we have studied. Audience expectations and the conventions of theatre are provoked in different ways in the scenes we have studied. We are often surprised. Write notes on what you have observed about the following.

1. The ways characters and situations are introduced
2. How we learn from the ways in which characters develop and differ
3. How playing and performing in theatre can be serious as well as comic
4. How drama comes from a clash of ideas as well as a clash of characters
5. How the turning point of a drama changes the audience's sympathies
6. How confrontation builds to a climax or catastrophe
7. How resolutions do not always bring everything together
8. How audiences are encouraged to evaluate and think about the ways in which plays end

Can you apply these ideas to your own set text? Draw plot lines for your play, showing the sequence of developments in the play.

Don't just map the journey that the main character or characters have been on, although this is always useful. Map the journey the audience has made, and bring out the moments when they have been surprised.

For further advice on working with your drama text, look at chapter 12.

Studying prose texts

In chapter 3, we looked at how to study prose texts by exploring the structure of the short story. Novels follow a similar structure to short stories, but on a much larger scale. Reading the class novel will look at first like the most daunting challenge of your course, and it is certainly a good idea to begin your preparation early. You will certainly notice more about the novel when you re-read it, knowing how the narrative will end, so this chapter will help you to make both a first reading and a re-reading of the prose text chosen for your course.

The emphasis in this chapter will be on language as well as structure. Once again, a lot of the work will be based on looking closely at extracts, as will much of the work you and your teachers do while you are reading your set texts. This enables you to look more closely at the techniques used by prose writers. However, you will also need your own notes to track your progress through the prose text, including:

- A brief note on what happens in each chapter.

- Notes on the principal characters as they are introduced.

- Quotations to accompany those characters – what they say and what is said about them. (Add the page numbers so that you can find them again.)

- Notes about the principal themes and ideas of the novel as they emerge: these may be based around different settings, different periods of time or the kinds of relationships which emerge.

In chapter 10, you will find advice for re-reading set texts and improving your essay writing skills for prose.

LEARNING POINTS

▶ To understand and appreciate how narrative texts work through description, dialogue and development

▶ To analyse the significance of the narrative voice or viewpoint

▶ To explore prose writers' use of mystery and tension

▶ To explore and evaluate different kinds of narrative closure.

8.1 Openings

Think ahead

Writers need to capture the reader's attention quickly at the beginning of a piece of prose fiction, whether a novel or short story. When you begin your set prose text you are at the beginning of a long journey and the writer needs to convince you that it will be an interesting one. It is common to begin a story 'in media res', which is a Latin term meaning 'in the middle of things' – in other words to plunge the reader into the middle of some action and for them to discover the background or backstory gradually later, through narration or flashback. A reader, just like a theatre audience, likes to be plunged into the action right away. Readers like to have a sense of where the writing is set, and what kind of writing (genre) they will be reading, but they also like a sense of mystery. While they want to be introduced to interesting characters, they also want to see them doing something immediately. The explanations can always come later.

Write a short review (200 words) of a novel or short story you have read for yourself recently (not part of your course or on the syllabus). Write down what you liked about its:

▶ Action

▶ Characters

▶ Genre

▶ Setting

Share your review with the class. What kind of stories are most popular? Action? Gothic? Fantasy? Realistic? Comic? Detective stories? Ghosts? Vampires? What kind of characters are most appealing, and why?

The novels or stories you will study in depth for the Cambridge IGCSE Literature course may not be the same type that you read for fun or to relax – although you may notice that they have certain characteristics in common with them. Novels for study need a certain kind of depth and engagement with the real world – their main purpose cannot be simply to escape from the everyday. They also need a certain complexity both of language and ideas in order to help you to meet the assessment objectives which you know are so important to your course. They therefore need to be substantial and canonical texts, which we study either because of their influence and impact, or because of the ways in which they engage with the culture which produced them. However, we also hope that you will find them well-written and entertaining!

Charles Dickens (1812–1870) was one of the most successful of all English novelists. He lived in the Victorian period, a period of enormous technological, economical and political change. During his lifetime, London was one of the largest cities in the world, and Britain the wealthiest and most powerful country. The novel had become an enormously popular form, so Dickens's fame quickly spread across the globe. Despite his fame and success, Dickens was a restless man, uncomfortable both with himself and with his society. His early novels had helped to interest Victorian society in social reform, but Dickens's sympathies remained with outsiders and his writing is very sympathetic to the victims of social and technological change.

Charles Dickens

'The Signalman' (1866) was written during the latest and darkest phase of Dickens's writing. Although he continued to write comically, he was increasingly drawn towards ghost stories and more Gothic material. It is part of a longer text called *Mugby Junction*, which is set on an imaginary railway line, full of haunting mysteries, more like a dreamscape than the real world. However, Dickens was also reflecting on real recent railway crashes (he had been involved in such a crash himself in 1865) and on the dangers of rapid technological change.

The extract below introduces us to two mysterious characters, the signalman himself and the narrator, both of whom we can only find out about by reading on. The setting is a deep cutting leading to a dark railway tunnel, with a signal box in front of it.

'The Signalman' by Charles Dickens (1866)

"Halloa! Below there!"

When he heard a voice thus calling to him, he was standing at the door of his box, with a flag in his hand, furled round its short pole. One would have thought, considering the nature of the ground, that he could not have doubted from what quarter the voice came; but instead of looking up to where I stood on the top of the steep cutting nearly over his head, he turned himself about, and looked down the Line. There was something remarkable in his manner of doing so, though I could not have said for my life what. But I know it was remarkable enough to attract my notice, even though his figure was foreshortened and shadowed, down in the deep trench, and mine was high above him, so steeped in the glow of an angry sunset, that I had shaded my eyes with my hand before I saw him at all.

"Halloa! Below!"

From looking down the Line, he turned himself about again, and, raising his eyes, saw my figure high above him.

"Is there any path by which I can come down and speak to you?"

He looked up at me without replying, and I looked down at him without pressing him too soon with a repetition of my idle question. Just then there came a vague vibration in the earth and air, quickly changing into a violent pulsation, and an oncoming rush that caused me to start back, as though it had force to draw me down. When such vapour as rose to my height from this rapid train had passed me, and was skimming away over the landscape, I looked down again, and saw him refurling the flag he had shown while the train went by.

I repeated my inquiry. After a pause, during which he seemed to regard me with fixed attention, he motioned with his rolled-up flag towards a point on my level, some two or three hundred yards distant. I called down to him, "All right!" and made for that point. There, by dint of looking closely about me, I found a rough zigzag descending path notched out, which I followed.

The cutting was extremely deep, and unusually precipitate. It was made through a clammy stone, that became oozier and wetter as I went down. For these reasons, I found the way long enough to give me time to recall a singular air of reluctance or compulsion with which he had pointed out the path.

When I came down low enough upon the zigzag descent to see him again, I saw that he was standing between the rails on the way by which the train had lately passed, in an attitude as if he were waiting for me to appear. He had his left hand at his chin, and that left elbow rested on his right hand, crossed over his breast. His attitude was one of such expectation and watchfulness that I stopped a moment, wondering at it.

I resumed my downward way, and stepping out upon the level of the railroad, and drawing nearer to him, saw that he was a dark sallow man, with a dark beard and rather heavy eyebrows. His post was in as solitary and dismal a place as ever I saw. On either side, a dripping-wet wall of jagged stone, excluding all view but a strip of sky; the perspective one way only a crooked prolongation of this great dungeon; the shorter perspective in the other direction terminating in a gloomy red light, and the gloomier entrance to a black tunnel, in whose massive architecture there was a barbarous, depressing, and forbidding air. So little sunlight ever found its way to this spot, that it had an earthy, deadly smell; and so much cold wind rushed through it, that it struck chill to me, as if I had left the natural world.

Before he stirred, I was near enough to him to have touched him. Not even then removing his eyes from mine, he stepped back one step, and lifted his hand.

This was a lonesome post to occupy (I said), and it had riveted my attention when I looked down from up yonder. A visitor was a rarity, I should suppose; not an unwelcome rarity, I hoped? In me,

he merely saw a man who had been shut up within narrow limits all his life, and who, being at last set free, had a newly-awakened interest in these great works. To such purpose I spoke to him; but I am far from sure of the terms I used; for, besides that I am not happy in opening any conversation, there was something in the man that daunted me.

He directed a most curious look towards the red light near the tunnel's mouth, and looked all about it, as if something were missing from it, and then looked it me.

That light was part of his charge? Was it not?

He answered in a low voice,--"Don't you know it is?"

The monstrous thought came into my mind, as I perused the fixed eyes and the saturnine face, that this was a spirit, not a man. I have speculated since, whether there may have been infection in his mind.

In my turn, I stepped back. But in making the action, I detected in his eyes some latent fear of me. This put the monstrous thought to flight.

"You look at me," I said, forcing a smile, "as if you had a dread of me."

"I was doubtful," he returned, "whether I had seen you before."

"Where?"

He pointed to the red light he had looked at.

"There?" I said.

Intently watchful of me, he replied (but without sound), "Yes."

"My good fellow, what should I do there? However, be that as it may, I never was there, you may swear."

"I think I may," he rejoined. "Yes; I am sure I may."

Check your understanding

One of the first things you need to establish is who is speaking or telling the story. In the case of this extract, it is deliberately a little confusing at first. Gradually a narrative viewpoint is established. Answer the following questions in order to see how the first few paragraphs establish character and situation.

1. Who speaks the first words and what is odd about the reaction they get? (If you read on in the story, you will find that the words themselves gain an extra significance by the time you reach the ending).

2. Where is the narrator when he sees the signalman? Remembering the work you have done on drama texts, how does this help to establish his status?

3. Just as in poetry, prose writers can use repetition to draw the reader's attention to particular words. Which words are repeated in the first main paragraph?

4. Although there is dialogue, it is entirely one-sided. What is the effect of this on the reader?

5. What is the effect of the train rushing past at speed 'as though it had force to draw me down'?

Description

 ## Pair and share

After introducing character and situation, the writer then focuses the reader's attention on the cutting. Here the choice of words, or diction, is significant, not just because they describe things very precisely, but also because of what they make the reader feel. We are in an uncomfortable, dark, damp, eerie place in the glow of a setting sun, with a red lamp glowing in the distance – almost the setting of a Gothic horror story.

Comment on the **implication** of these choices of descriptive words: what associations do they have for you? Some of the work has been done for you, so do the rest with your partner.

Adjectives	Associations
clammy	nasty to touch
oozier	unpleasantly slimy
sallow	
dismal	
jagged	
crooked	
gloomy	
barbarous, depressing and forbidding	
earthy, deadly	like a graveyard
cold	freezes your soul as well as body
chill	
lonesome	

Do you agree that the description makes it sound as if the narrator is descending into a grave or tomb, rather than a railway cutting? We are not surprised that when he finally meets the signalman he thinks he is seeing a ghost, not a man:

> 'The monstrous thought came into my mind, as I perused the fixed eyes and the saturnine face, that this was a spirit, not a man.'

Curiously, the signalman seems to have the same idea, and is not sure whether the narrator is real, or some dreadful ghost:

> 'I detected in his eyes some latent fear of me.'

He seems to think that he has seen the narrator before. He hints that he has seen him inside the tunnel, near the red light. The narrator wonders if the signalman is quite sane, but the reader is certainly interested enough to want to know more: this is what is called development, the process of gradual revelation which keeps the reader interested.

Development

 Viewpoints

When the two men talk, we are not surprised to find that the dialogue is very awkward and uncertain. Read it aloud in pairs, as if it were a playscript, bringing out how uncomfortable the two men are with each other. Each wonders if the other is something monstrous, 'saturnine' or mad. Only at the very end of the passage is some kind of trust established.

The reader cannot help being curious about some of the story's mysteries:

1. What do you think the signalman is so afraid of, and why can't he trust the narrator at first?
2. What does the narrator tell us about himself and why does that also make him mysterious?

The story is told in retrospect and with hindsight – in other words looking back after the events have happened. Like many of the stories in the collection, it has a distinctive and unusual narrating voice. Discuss and debate the effect on the reader of the strange conversation between the two men:

1. What is the effect of the use of the past tense?
2. In what ways might this introduce a certain bias or manipulation into the way the story is told?
3. Notice that the narrator says, 'I have speculated since, whether there may have been infection in his mind'. What do you think he means?
4. In what ways do comments like this unsettle the reader, but also make us curious to read on?
5. Is the signalman mad, or is it the narrator who seems the more unsettling character?
6. If the descent into the cutting was like a descent into a graveyard, or dungeon, what might the train tunnel represent?

Debate with your partner whether you think this is a realistic story, a ghost story or an **allegory**.

Remember that prose writers can use symbolism just as extensively as poets. Dickens, like other short story writers in the collection, may be suggesting something about modern technology and its victims. In allegory, everything could stand for something else.

Extend your learning

Read on and finish the short story. How well does the opening set up later developments, and the tragic conclusion?

8.2 Setting

One of the main purposes of literature is to take our imagination into a world very different from our own, to help us to image what it was like to go through more extreme situations than we have encountered. Helen Dunmore is a British poet and novelist who writes for both children and adults. However, her subject in *The Siege* is a very serious and grim one indeed, the terrible siege of Leningrad (now called St. Petersburg) from 1941–44, which was a key struggle in the Second World War. The early pages of the novel need to establish the following:

- characters we care about and find interesting
- a narrative viewpoint we can share
- a realistic sense of place and time
- an understanding of the context of battle for survival which the women in this extract will be engaged in
- a sense of anticipation and suspense, as we wait for what we know will happen.

Think ahead

1. Find out what you can from encyclopedias (printed or online) about the Siege of Leningrad. Why was it an important turning point in the Second World War?

2. Find out about Stalin and Communism. What were the lives of ordinary Russians like in cities like Leningrad in the 1930s?

3. Why were the Russians right to be so afraid of the consequences of a German invasion? Find out what the Nazis thought about the Russian people and what their intentions were when they invaded Russia.

4. What was the Communist attitude towards women? Why did they form an important part of the workforce?

5. What were the powers of a 'Commissar' under Stalin? In the passage you will notice the women are afraid of a character called Arkady Konstantinovich. What authority might he have over them?

Now read the passage, which describes the women preparing the defences of Leningrad, called the Luga line, in the warm summer of 1941. The reader will be aware of the appalling hardships they will later face. Some of the details of this passage prepare you for shocking descriptions later in the novel.

The Siege by Helen Dunmore (2001)

"All right, girls, you've reached your target here. We're moving on. You're being assigned to fortifications at the railway station. Get going!"

Little Katya, on Anna's right, scrabbles out of the trench like a kid who's afraid she's taken more than her turn in the sandpit. She's terrified of getting things wrong and drawing attention to herself. She doesn't realize that it's precisely her nervous quickness to obey orders which makes her stand out. But then she's only fifteen, so what can you expect?

"It's all right, Katinka, there's no big rush. Here, have a swig of my tea."

"Are you sure? Don't you want it yourself?"

"I'm offering it to you."

Katya's brought nothing with her. Only herself, and her small, rather delicate hands which have certainly never held a spade before these past weeks. She was crimson with shame when her period started and she hadn't 'got anything'. Anna had to sort her out with some borrowed rags, and show her how to wash them in the stream. Katya's blood unrolled and ran away with the clear water. Luckily, in this weather everything dries quickly. Anna rinses out her own sweat-sodden shirt and underwear every night, and sleeps in her jacket.

Katya takes a small, polite sip of the cold tea.

"Go on, have some more. The sugar will give you energy."

But by now Arkady Konstantinovich is looking for blood.

"Do you ladies think this is a tea party?" he scorches them. "Get your backsides over here now! Get in line."

They stumble over the rough ground. It's a couple of kilometers to the station, but at least they're not digging. A change of positions is as good as a rest. With your spade slung over your shoulder, a different set of muscles takes its turn to ache.

Not a tea party… Anna glanced at Katya, at Evgenia beyond her, at the whole line of them tramping forward, boots caked with earth, hands wrapped in rag bandages, sunburnt faces streaked with mud and sweat. Hair is tucked into scarves, or plaited and pinned out of the way. As their line

Katinka = affectionate diminutive version of Katya

advances under the trees, shadow dapples them. Evgenia's red hair sparks, then dims as she goes on into the shade of a fir tree. What a lot of different colours there are in hair, when you look at it. Rust, copper, black. Evgenia's sleeves are rolled up, showing strong, creamy arms which the sun has splashed with freckles. As she works, her strength and bulk become grace. No one can dig out a section of trench faster than Evgenia. She doesn't hurry, she doesn't grunt with effort. She makes her way look like the only possible way of digging a trench. Why is it that some people make you want to watch them, while others – like Katya – have the effect of chalk squeaking up a board?

Katya is pretty, unlike Evgenia. Her fair hair can't help escaping from its plait and curling around her small face. It's one of those rosebud faces which don't stand up well to dirt and exhaustion. Her eyes are frightened. She stiffens when she hears shell-fire, and she's terrified of enemy planes. No wonder, when the first thing she saw on her way here was a girl about her own age, stitched to the ground by bullets. She hadn't made it into the ditch with the others. "*They just left her there,*" Katya told Anna. "*They didn't even put anything over her. We all had to file past her.*"

"It's all right, Katinka," Anna soothes her now. "They're miles away. You can tell from the sound of the engines."

Katya give her a pitiful, grateful smile. At least it's as easy to cheer her up as it is to frighten her. She ought to be at school, frowning over her geometry like a good girl. Instead, she's here, along with every Leningrader who's capable of holding a spade, and plenty who aren't. God knows how many thousands there are altogether. You only see your own bit, but no doubt there are thousands of Annas and Katyas and Evgenias, stretching the length of the Luga line.

Everything becomes normal so quickly. It's normal to get up at dawn, and queue for the hastily dug latrines, and not mind if someone else is peeing alongside you. It's normal to sluice your face in a stream, bundle your hair in a headscarf, gobble down a couple of slices of bread and stumble to work. Your eyes are bleary, your back aches, your arms ache, the muscles in your neck burn. But just get going, and you'll soon warm up. That's the way to deal with stiffness, Evgenia says. Work your way through it.

Just keep on digging and don't give yourself time to think about it.

It's normal to run for cover at the sound of aircraft. It's normal to see someone who didn't move fast enough, sprawled in a ditch. Sprawled there, they look as if they're still running for shelter, deep into the earth. But when you pick them up they have a strange, warm floppiness and their heads fall back.

There are two realities now. There are summer trees, flights of startled birds, the smell of honeysuckle in the depths of the night. This is the old reality, as smooth as the handle of a favourite cup in your hand. And then there's the new reality which consists of hour after hour of digging, and seconds of terror as sharp as the zig-zag of lightning. Lightning that's looking for you, seeking out warm flesh on the bare summer fields.

✏️ Check your understanding

1. Which characters are introduced in this passage?

2. Which tense has the writer chosen, and what is the effect of this?

3. Whose viewpoint does the reader share?

4. Which are the details which show that Katya (or Katinka) is vulnerable?

5. How does the dialogue reveal the harshness of the women's lives? How does the women's journey from the trenches to the railway station give Anna an opportunity to think?

6. How do her descriptions of them develop a strong contrast between Katya and Evgenia?

7. What qualities do these words bring out in Evgenia: '…*her strength and bulk become grace*'?

8. What is revealed about Katya in these passages:
   - '…*one of those rosebud faces which don't stand up well to dirt and exhaustion*'

   - '*She ought to be at school, frowning over her geometry like a good girl*'

9. How do the descriptions create two different ideas of Russian women?

10. How would you characterize Anna?

11. How do the sentences beginning 'it's normal…' bring out the day-to-day reality of the women's lives?

12. In what ways have the women been forced to lose their femininity?

13. Which details bring out the horror of being under attack?

14. What are the 'two realities' and why are they so different?

Pair and share

The setting is created through the writer's choice of words, especially verbs and adjectives. With your partner, copy the table below and fill in the boxes which ask you to comment on the effect of the writer's choices.

Verbs	Effect
scrabbles	
tramping	
splashed	
squeaking	
stitched	
sluice	
gobble	
stumble	
sprawled	

Adjectives	Effect
nervous	
sweat-sodden	
sunburnt	
red	
rosebud	
pitiful	

The larger number of verbs tells you that we appreciate the setting through action as much as description. The women have to live a life of action and their lives reveal the hardship of preparing for war.

Dunmore is also a poet, and both poets and novelists use imagery to help you to imagine things you have not seen.

Can you find interesting uses of similes and metaphors?

Discuss together the effect of the following:

1. *'Sprawled there, they look as if they're still running for shelter, deep into the earth.'*

2. *'…as smooth as the handle of a favourite cup in your hand'*

3. *'…as sharp as the zig-zag of lightning'*

In what ways does the writer's use of imagery create striking contrasts?

Which technique is used in the phrase which follows?

'Lightning that's looking for you, seeking out warm flesh on the bare summer fields.'

How does this image bring out the sinister idea of the war seeking out its innocent victims?

Together, where can you find references to injury, blood and pain? What does this suggest about the fate of the women?

Viewpoints

Why do you think the writer chose to concentrate here on the thoughts and experiences of women? How does this help to develop your understanding of the impact of the World Wars of the twentieth century on ordinary lives? How does the writing bring out the way in which the women's normality has been distorted?

The writing prepares us for more horrors to come. There are two references to dead bodies:

   '…stitched to the ground by bullets'

and

   '…when you pick them up they have a strange, warm floppiness'

What do these unusual descriptions suggest about the reality of sudden death in war? How is death treated by the people in the story? Why is this so shocking for Katya? Does Anna seem to have a different viewpoint?

Notice the final contrast between the two realities: the warmth of summer and the shock of being under attack. How has Anna adapted to extraordinary circumstances? How does the writing suggest that her viewpoint is going to be an interesting one? Why do you think the writer chose her viewpoint, and not Evgenia's or Katya's?

Together prepare an interview with Anna, after the war is over, about the weeks of preparation before the big attack. You can decide for yourselves what will happen to Evgenia and Katya. Use your own words for Anna, but create a voice which will fit what we know about her character.

Think ahead

We have just seen how the previous passage gives Anna's viewpoint or perspective. The thoughts, reflections, experiences and judgments on other people are all Anna's. What is the effect of seeing events through the eyes of a particular character? Are their judgments always reliable? Review the different forms of prose narrative. Which one of the following does your set text use?

▶ A first-person narrator

▶ An omniscient narrator (someone who knows everything and stands outside the narrative)

▶ The viewpoints of various different characters (often called a limited viewpoint)

How reliable are the narrators or viewpoints? How sympathetic do you find the person who tells or 'sees' the story? Do you find it easy to put yourself in their place? How would you describe their voice? Do they take you inside the story, because it happened to them? Or do they remain slightly outside the story, as if looking in? What are the benefits of a detached narrative? Or one which shows complete involvement?

Narrative (story-telling) depends on memory, which also raises the question of reliability, and the border between reality and fantasy. How does your text handle the passing of time, and does that make you ask questions about the reliability of the narrator? What are the limits and limitations of the viewpoint which you are presented with?

Write a paragraph about the narrator or narrators of your set text and evaluate their characteristics and the ways in which they involve you, as the reader, in the events of the story.

Extend your learning

Consider the writer's use of setting in the early chapters of your own set text.

1. From whose viewpoint are descriptions introduced?

2. How does the description prepare us for later events?

3. How does the writer use setting to introduce a world very different from our own?

4. How does the writer use characterization to create interesting and contrasting characters?

5. What have you learnt about the details of those characters' day-to-day lives?

6. In what ways have you already been shocked or surprised by aspects of the lives and situation of characters in your set text?

7. How would you characterize the atmosphere the writer has created?

8. Why do you think the writer chose this particular setting?

8.3 Viewpoint

Amy Tan's *The Joy Luck Club*, written in 1989, has several different narrators, all women from the Chinese American community in San Francisco, USA. The younger generation tells stories about their childhoods in America and their marriages; their mothers, now very elderly, reveal stories about their pasts in China, and how they came to America during the turbulent years of the mid-twentieth century. Just like in *The Siege*, there are shocking stories about war and about the treatment of women in authoritarian societies. In this extract Ying Ying is beginning to tell her story, and goes back to her childhood in China in 1918.

 See Worksheet 3 for more on how writers can show us events of the past.

The Joy Luck Club by Amy Tan (1989)

For all these years I kept my mouth closed so selfish desires would not fall out. And because I remained quiet for so long now my daughter does not hear me. She sits by her fancy swimming pool and hears only her Sony Walkman, her cordless phone, her big, important husband asking her why they have charcoal and no lighter fluid.

Sony Walkman = fashionable portable music device in 1980s

All these years I kept my true nature hidden, running along like a small shadow so nobody could catch me. And because I moved so secretly now my daughter does not see me. She sees a list of things to buy, her checkbook out of balance, her ashtray sitting crooked on a straight table.

And I want to tell her this: We are lost, she and I, unseen and not seeing, unheard and not hearing, unknown by others.

I did not lose myself all at once. I rubbed out my face over the years washing away my pain, the same way carvings on stone are worn down by water.

Yet today I can remember a time when I ran and shouted, when I could not stand still, it is my earliest recollection; telling the Moon Lady my secret wish. And because I forgot what I wished for, that memory remained hidden from me all these many years.

But now I remember the wish, and I can recall the details of that entire day, as clearly as I see my daughter and the foolishness of her life.

In 1918, the year that I was four, the Moon festival arrived during an autumn in Wushi that was unusually hot, terribly hot. When I awoke that morning, the fifteenth day of the eighth moon, the straw mat covering my bed was already sticky. Everything in the room smelled of wet grass simmering in the heat.

Earlier in the summer, the servants had covered all the windows with bamboo curtains to drive out the sun. Every bed was covered with a woven mat, our only bedding during the months of constant wet heat. And the hot bricks of the courtyard were crisscrossed with bamboo paths. Autumn had come, but without its cool mornings and evenings. And so the stale heat still remained in the shadows behind the curtains, heating up the acrid smells of my chamber pot, seeping into my pillow, chafing the back of my neck and puffing up my cheeks, so that I awoke that morning with a restless complaint.

There was another smell, outside, something burning, a pungent fragrance that was half sweet and half bitter. "What's that stinky smell?" I asked my amah, who always managed to appear next to my bed the instant I was awake. She slept on a cot in a little room next to mine.

Amah = nursemaid, servant to a child

"It is the same as I explained yesterday," she said, lifting me out of my bed and sitting me on her knee. And my sleepy mind tried to remember what she had told me upon waking the morning before.

"We are burning the Five Evils, "I said drowsily, then squirmed out of her warm lap. I climbed on top of a little stool and looked out the window into the courtyard below. I saw a green coil curled in the shape of a snake, with a tail that billowed yellow smoke. The other day, Amah had shown me that the snake had come out of a colourful box decorated with five evil creatures: a swimming snake, a jumping scorpion, a flying centipede, a dropping-down spider and a springing lizard. The bite of any one of these creatures could kill a child, explained Amah. So I was relieved to think we had caught the Five Evils and were burning their corpses. I didn't know the green coil was merely incense used to chase away mosquitoes and small flies.

An image from the 1993 film

Check your understanding

1. What does Ying Ying think is wrong with her daughter's life in the USA in the 1980s?

2. Why does she think her daughter ignores her?

3. Why does she think they are both lost and silent?

4. How does she explain the reason for her silence and for not telling her full story before?

5. In what ways was she different when she was a child?

6. How does she create suspense about what the Moon Lady said to her?

7. How does her description recreate a child's experience of a warm, humid climate?

8. Which details of her life reveal that she had quite a privileged childhood?

9. How does her language recreate smells and other senses?

10. What intrigued the child about the incense burner?

11. How does the child's understanding of the world take the reader into the mysteries of legend and fairy tale?

12. What does this suggest about the identity of the Moon Lady and her secret, and the way the story will use the supernatural?

Pair and share

It is always easier to understand how a passage of prose works by dividing it into sections. Discuss this with a partner and divide the passage into Ying Ying's thoughts and feelings as an old woman, her description of the morning of the moon festival, and her other memories as a young child.

How do her memories of her early life differ from modern culture today?

Script and perform an interview in which Ying Ying explains how different China was in 1918 to the USA today.

1. Why do you think Ying Ying has kept silent and not had this kind of conversation with her daughter?

2. What experiences might she have had that mean she does not usually talk about her memories?

3. How does this create a sense of mystery and suspense for the reader?

4. Why does she have a strong belief in the supernatural and fate?

Viewpoints

As we have seen, the use of narrators and multiple viewpoints can lead to lots of debate about the meaning and reliability of a story or narrative.

1. In this novel, Amy Tan uses seven different narrators. Why do you think she did this?

2. What will be the effect of having stories from both the mothers and the daughters?

3. How reliable a narrator do you think Ying Ying is, in the passage above?

4. Which aspects of her story sound more like a fairy tale, or allegory?

5. Which aspects sound very realistic?

When you tell (narrate) a story, you often change details or the order of events in order to make your account more dramatic and more interesting, or in order to project your own personality and role in the story. All of this helps to involve your listener.

Language links

What are the qualities which make reading a story about the past different from reading a factual, historical account?

Debate the advantages and disadvantages of fictional and non-fictional accounts, and then write a discursive essay entitled:

'Facts or fiction? Explore the advantages and disadvantages of historical fiction based on real events.'

Extend your learning

How does your own set text handle factual and real-life elements to the story? Do you find the historical aspect of the story convincing and realistic? How has the story engaged your interest in what has happened in the past?

Write an essay on how past events are presented to you in the opening chapters of your novel. Think about:

*   the way the narrator presents past events
*   how realistic the setting and description are
*   how a sense of anticipation or mystery is created.

8.4 Mysteries

Think ahead

We can see that the viewpoint, as well as the setting, of a narrative can involve and interest the reader and make them curious about what happens next. We are interested in experiences and places very different from our own, and the writing helps to engage our imagination, so that we can picture the scene and begin to share the feelings of the characters. A sense of mystery helps to keep the reader turning the pages.

In your own set text:

1. what has remained unexplained after the initial chapters?

2. what do you want to find out more about?

3. can you begin to predict what will happen?

4. are there clues in the text and its narrative voice?

5. how does your text handle memory and the passing of time?

The Australian, Joan Lindsay's famous novel *Picnic at Hanging Rock* is also based on real-life events. Set in 1900, it describes the disappearance of three boarding-school girls and their teacher, Miss McCraw, after a St Valentine's Day picnic, when they decide to climb the mysterious rock. Only one of them was found, alive but with no memory of what had happened. There were only a few witnesses, all of them part of the story, such as a young Englishman on holiday in Australia, the Hon Michael Fitzhubert, and a fourth girl, Edith Horton, a 15-year-old boarder who is looked down on and bullied by the others, went only part of the way up the Rock, and who is mentioned in the extract. This passage describes the frustrations of the search.

Picnic at Hanging Rock by Joan Lindsay (1967)

Out at the Hanging Rock the long violet shadows were tracing their million-year-old pattern of summer evenings across its magnificent spectacle of gilded peaks slowly darkening upon a turquoise sky, the police party climbed into the waiting vehicle and was driven swiftly towards the familiar comforts of the Woodend Hotel. Constable Bumpher for one had had a bellyful of the Rock and its mysteries and was looking forward with understandable pleasure to a couple of beers and a nice juicy steak.

An image from the film adaptation

In spite of glorious weather and congenial company, it had proved a thoroughly unrewarding day. In view of the belated evidence of the girl Horton – if evidence it could be called – the search had been immediately intensified, including the recall of the bloodhound, who had been furnished with a piece of calico from Miss McCraw's underwear. There seemed no reason to doubt that Edith had actually seen and passed the mathematics teacher making her way up to the Rock in white calico drawers. The vague wordless encounter, however, remained unsubstantiated; nor was it ever established if Miss McCraw had experienced an equally fleeting vision of the terrified girl. Some slight disturbance of the bushes and bracken towards the western end of the rock face had been noted as early as last Sunday morning. It was now thought possible they might have been part of the track taken by Miss McCraw after leaving the rest of the party after lunch. It petered out almost at once; strangely enough, at much the same level of striated rock as certain other faint scratchings and bruisings of the undergrowth at the eastern end where the four girls may have begun their perilous ascent. All day long the bloodhound had sniffed and fossicked its delicate way through thick dusty scrub and sun-baked rocks and stones. The dog, who had proved equally unsuccessful at picking up the scent of the three missing girls earlier in the week, was greatly hampered by the well-meaning army of voluntary searchers having effaced the first elusive imprints where a hand had rested perhaps on a dusty boulder, a foot on springy moss. The animal, however, did raise some false hopes during Thursday afternoon, by standing for nearly ten minutes growling and bristling on an almost circular platform of flat rock considerably further towards the summit, whereon the magnifying glass disclosed absolutely no signs of any disturbance more recent than the ravages of Nature over some hundreds or thousands of year. Bumpher, scanning his meagre notes in the failing light of the cab, had hoped that part or all of the teacher's purple silk cape would have been found stuffed into a hollow log maybe, or under a loose rock. "Beats me what the old girl could have done with it! Considering hundreds of people have been traipsing about in the scrub ever since Sunday last. Let alone the dog."

Check your understanding

Annotate your copy of the passage while answering the following questions:

1. In what ways are the descriptions of the first sentence both beautiful and sinister?

2. How does the writer contrast the human world and the world of nature?

3. How is this made more comical in the second sentence, by making reference to Constable Bumpher and his thoughts?

4. Which words reveal that the next paragraph is a flashback?

5. What are the two reasons why the police and searchers were more optimistic when they began their search in the morning?

6. Which words suggest that they were trying to separate fact from fantasy in Edith Horton's statement?

7. What does the evidence of the tracks suggest?

8. In what ways might this evidence be a metaphor for the difficulties of the search?

9. Which word tells you about how dangerous they thought the girls' climb was?

10. Which words memorably describe the actions of the bloodhound?

11. Why was the dog's work made more difficult by the crowd of searchers?

12. How do Bumpher's words at the end of the passage confirm this problem?

13. Which adjective sums up how difficult it would be to find the forensic evidence?

14. How did the dog briefly raise some false hopes?

15. How do we know that Bumpher is writing up his notes later in the day?

16. What had Bumpher hoped to find?

 Pair and share

Some of the texts you study might reflect on differences between the natural and the human world. We have seen the ways in which this comparison is set up in the first sentence of the extract.

In your pairs, one of you should collect descriptions of the natural world, and the other should collect descriptions of the world of Constable Bumpher and the behaviour of the searchers. Make out a list of quotations to show these two different kinds of description, then discuss and answer the questions which follow:

1. Which world does the dog belong to?

2. What have you noticed about different portrayals of the passing of time?

3. Which of the two worlds is easier to interpret and understand?

4. Which phrases suggest that the human world is unlikely to come up with any answers?

5. Which phrases suggest the ways in which the natural world does not care about the humans and their concerns?

6. What is the overall effect of this comparison on the reader?

 See Worksheet 4 for more on narrative and the natural world.

It is natural and understandable for human beings to want to solve mysteries and find certainties, and readers often want to do this when reading literary texts. However, in 1817 the poet John Keats wrote about what he called Negative Capability, which he defined as:

> "…when a man is capable of being in uncertainties, mysteries, doubts, without any irritable reaching after fact and reason."

This would not be a good quality in a detective, whose job it is to find evidence and details which would fit a hypothesis. Sometimes being a student or critic of literature is like being a detective: you need to collect evidence, especially in the form of quotations, to fit your argument or hypothesis about a text. However, in the matter of interpretation, sometimes the literary critic needs negative capability: we will not always find the answers or solve all the mysteries, and we can make mistakes by searching too hard.

Look back at the quotations you have collected. What do they suggest about the mystery of the Hanging Rock? Could we view the whole incident as a metaphor for man's relationship with the natural world, which we think we can conquer and colonize, but we never really master? Discuss your interpretation with your partner and then share with others in your class.

John Keats

💡 Viewpoints

1. Whose viewpoint do we share during the narrative? This is not an easy question, so debate it with your partner. Is this a limited viewpoint, and if so, what are its limits?

2. Why would the style of this extract be very different from the conversations between the girls, or the confused memories of the witnesses?

3. We never find out much more about what happened. Why do you think the mystery is so interesting, and what might possibly have happened?

🔗 Language links

Explore other similar mysteries, such as the Flannen Island mystery, or the case of the Marie Celeste. Write your own narrative based around one of these disappearances or a story of your own. You can either focus on 'what really happened' or on 'the search'.

Extend your learning

1. How does your own set text handle mysteries and their solution?

2. How reliable have you found the narrators and how limited are their viewpoints?

3. Are there mysteries in your text which are not likely to be solved? What are the different possible reactions of readers?

8.5 Irony

One theme of this chapter has been unreliable narrators and limited viewpoints. Another has been mysteries and different ways of interpreting them, and the descriptive passages of prose narratives. We have learnt that a lot depends on the point of view of the narrator who is describing what we 'see'. We will now look at the function of irony and surprise in narrative. They can act similarly to 'turning points' in the drama which we looked at in the previous chapter. They are moments when we, or the characters, begin to see things very differently. In prose, these surprises have a particular impact not just on the characters but also the ways in which their viewpoints (what they see and their thoughts and feelings) are presented to us.

1. Can you identify such a turning point in your own set text?
2. Does it involve a character seeing things differently?
3. Or does it involve the reader seeing the character in a different way?
4. What is the nature of the revelation?
5. Do things change in the book as a result?

In the famous extract which follows, by the nineteenth-century novelist Jane Austen whom we have already encountered in chapter 5, the character of Catherine Morland, a girl of 17, has been invited by the clever and handsome Henry Tilney to stay at his family home, Northanger Abbey. Catherine has read a lot of Gothic fiction and strongly believes in the supernatural, so she quickly puts together a fantasy, based on false evidence, that Henry's father (General Tilney) murdered his mother. In this passage, Henry catches her doing her 'detective work' and she is surprised into revealing her fantasies. The other characters mentioned are Henry's older brother Frederick and younger sister Eleanor, and Isabella, Catherine's friend who encouraged her reading of fantasy and tendency to exaggerate, confusing her sense of what was real and what was fiction. The passage begins at what Catherine thinks is a 'forbidden door' (see chapter 5 for another example of this convention in Gothic fiction).

Northanger Abbey by **Jane Austen (1803)**

It was done; and Catherine found herself alone in the gallery before the clocks had ceased to strike. It was no time for thought; she hurried on, slipped with the least possible noise through the folding doors, and without stopping to look or breathe, rushed forward to the one in question. The lock yielded to her hand, and, luckily, with no sullen sound that could alarm a human being. On tiptoe she entered; the room was before her; but it was some minutes before she could advance another step. She beheld what fixed her to the spot and agitated every feature. She saw a large, well–proportioned apartment, an handsome dimity bed, arranged as unoccupied with an housemaid's care, a bright Bath stove, mahogany wardrobes, and neatly painted chairs, on which the warm beams of a western sun gaily poured through two sash windows! Catherine had expected to have her feelings worked, and worked they were. Astonishment and doubt first seized them; and a shortly

dimity = a lightweight cotton fabric

succeeding ray of common sense added some bitter emotions of shame. She could not be mistaken as to the room; but how grossly mistaken in everything else! — in Miss Tilney's meaning, in her own calculation! This apartment, to which she had given a date so ancient, a position so awful, proved to be one end of what the general's father had built. There were two other doors in the chamber, leading probably into dressing–closets; but she had no inclination to open either. Would the veil in which Mrs. Tilney had last walked, or the volume in which she had last read, remain to tell what nothing else was allowed to whisper? No: whatever might have been the general's crimes, he had certainly too much wit to let them sue for detection. She was sick of exploring, and desired but to be safe in her own room, with her own heart only privy to its folly; and she was on the point of retreating as softly as she had entered, when the sound of footsteps, she could hardly tell where, made her pause and tremble. To be found there, even by a servant, would be unpleasant; but by the general (and he seemed always at hand when least wanted), much worse! She listened — the sound had ceased; and resolving not to lose a moment, she passed through and closed the door. At that instant a door underneath was hastily opened; someone seemed with swift steps to ascend the stairs, by the head of which she had yet to pass before she could gain the gallery. She had no power to move. With a feeling of terror not very definable, she fixed her eyes on the staircase, and in a few moments it gave Henry to her view. "Mr. Tilney!" she exclaimed in a voice of more than common astonishment. He looked astonished too. "Good God!" she continued, not attending to his address. "How came you here? How came you up that staircase?"

"How came I up that staircase!" he replied, greatly surprised. "Because it is my nearest way from the stable–yard to my own chamber; and why should I not come up it?"

Catherine recollected herself, blushed deeply, and could say no more. He seemed to be looking in her countenance for that explanation which her lips did not afford. She moved on towards the gallery. "And may I not, in my turn," said he, as he pushed back the folding doors, "ask how you came here? This passage is at least as extraordinary a road from the breakfast–parlour to your apartment, as that staircase can be from the stables to mine."

"I have been," said Catherine, looking down, "to see your mother's room."

"My mother's room! Is there anything extraordinary to be seen there?"

"No, nothing at all. I thought you did not mean to come back till tomorrow."

"I did not expect to be able to return sooner, when I went away; but three hours ago I had the pleasure of finding nothing to detain me. You look pale. I am afraid I alarmed you by running so fast up those stairs. Perhaps you did not know — you were not aware of their leading from the offices in common use?"

"No, I was not. You have had a very fine day for your ride."

"Very; and does Eleanor leave you to find your way into all the rooms in the house by yourself?"

"Oh! No; she showed me over the greatest part on Saturday — and we were coming here to these rooms — but only" — dropping her voice — "your father was with us."

"And that prevented you," said Henry, earnestly regarding her. "Have you looked into all the rooms in that passage?"

"No, I only wanted to see — Is not it very late? I must go and dress."

"It is only a quarter past four" showing his watch — "and you are not now in Bath. No theatre, no rooms to prepare for. Half an hour at Northanger must be enough."

She could not contradict it, and therefore suffered herself to be detained, though her dread of further questions made her, for the first time in their acquaintance, wish to leave him. They walked slowly up the gallery. "Have you had any letter from Bath since I saw you?"

she is referring to an earlier conversation with Eleanor

he had too much wit... = the General was too clever to leave obvious clues

"No, and I am very much surprised. Isabella promised so faithfully to write directly."

"Promised so faithfully! A faithful promise! That puzzles me. I have heard of a faithful performance. But a faithful promise — the fidelity of promising! It is a power little worth knowing, however, since it can deceive and pain you. My mother's room is very commodious, is it not? Large and cheerful–looking, and the dressing–closets so well disposed! It always strikes me as the most comfortable apartment in the house, and I rather wonder that Eleanor should not take it for her own. She sent you to look at it, I suppose?"

"No."

"It has been your own doing entirely?" Catherine said nothing. After a short silence, during which he had closely observed her, he added, "As there is nothing in the room in itself to raise curiosity, this must have proceeded from a sentiment of respect for my mother's character, as described by Eleanor, which does honour to her memory. The world, I believe, never saw a better woman. But it is not often that virtue can boast an interest such as this. The domestic, unpretending merits of a person never known do not often create that kind of fervent, venerating tenderness which would prompt a visit like yours. Eleanor, I suppose, has talked of her a great deal?"

"Yes, a great deal. That is — no, not much, but what she did say was very interesting. Her dying so suddenly" (slowly, and with hesitation it was spoken), "and you — none of you being at home — and your father, I thought — perhaps had not been very fond of her."

"And from these circumstances," he replied (his quick eye fixed on hers), "you infer perhaps the probability of some negligence — some" — (involuntarily she shook her head) — "or it may be — of something still less pardonable." She raised her eyes towards him more fully than she had ever done before. "My mother's illness," he continued, "the seizure which ended in her death, was sudden. The malady itself, one from which she had often suffered, a bilious fever — its cause therefore constitutional. On the third day, in short, as soon as she could be prevailed on, a physician attended her, a very respectable man, and one in whom she had always placed great confidence. Upon his opinion of her danger, two others were called in the next day, and remained in almost constant attendance for four and twenty hours. On the fifth day she died. During the progress of her disorder, Frederick and I (we were both at home) saw her repeatedly; and from our own observation can bear witness to her having received every possible attention which could spring from the affection of those about her, or which her situation in life could command. Poor Eleanor was absent, and at such a distance as to return only to see her mother in her coffin."

"But your father," said Catherine, "was he afflicted?"

"For a time, greatly so. You have erred in supposing him not attached to her. He loved her, I am persuaded, as well as it was possible for him to — we have not all, you know, the same tenderness of disposition — and I will not pretend to say that while she lived, she might not often have had much to bear, but though his temper injured her, his judgment never did. His value of her was sincere; and, if not permanently, he was truly afflicted by her death."

"I am very glad of it," said Catherine; "it would have been very shocking!"

"If I understand you rightly, you had formed a surmise of such horror as I have hardly words to — Dear Miss Morland, consider the dreadful nature of the suspicions you have entertained. What have you been judging from? Remember the country and the age in which we live. Remember that we are English, that we are Christians. Consult your own understanding, your own sense of the probable, your own observation of what is passing around you. Does our education prepare us for such atrocities? Do our laws connive at them? Could they be perpetrated without being known, in a country like this, where social and literary intercourse is on such a footing, where every man is surrounded by a neighbourhood of voluntary spies, and where roads and newspapers lay everything open? Dearest Miss Morland, what ideas have you been admitting?"

They had reached the end of the gallery, and with tears of shame she ran off to her own room.

Check your understanding

1. Which word in the first sentence suggests that something terrible is about to happen?

2. Which verbs in the second sentence suggest Catherine's nervousness?

3. How does the writer create suspense as the 'forbidden door' is opened?

4. Why does the room turn out to be a surprise for Catherine?

5. Which phrases suggest that she is already beginning to get embarrassed?

6. How does she explain to herself what has happened?

7. Why is she in a hurry to get back to her own room?

8. Whose footsteps does she think she hears?

9. Who actually catches her in the room and why is this so embarrassing for Catherine?

10. What does Henry seem to think about the room?

11. Why is he curious about Catherine's reasons for being in the room?

12. How does she try to change the subject?

13. What is peculiar about the way Catherine speaks about Henry's father and mother?

14. Why does she not want Henry to ask her any more questions?

15. Henry likes language to be exact. When Henry talks about Isabella why does he make fun of the idea of a 'faithful promise'? Why is that term a tautology or form of exaggeration?

16. Which phrases suggest he is testing her out when he does ask her questions?

17. What fact does Catherine exaggerate when speaking about the death of Henry's mother, Mrs Tilney?

18. How does Henry's language make clear the facts of his mother's death?

19. What does he mean by 'we have not all, you know, the same tenderness of disposition'? What does he imply about his father's temper?

20. Why does Henry say that the crimes which Catherine has imagined could never happen in England?

 # Pair and share

This is a text which clearly divides into two parts, the first made up entirely of description, from Catherine's (rather biased) viewpoint, and the second of dialogue. We will explore the ways in which description is influenced by viewpoint and the drama of the dialogue.

The comic effect of the first part of the text depends on a series of contrasts. Together, search for and find the matching quotations to bring out these contrasts (the first is done for you):

Gothic fiction (Catherine's imagination)	Reality
'without stopping to look or breathe, rushed forward' she rushed at the door	But it opened *with no sullen sound that could alarm a human being*
She saw something which 'fixed her to the spot and agitated every feature'	But it was…
In her anxiety, Catherine expected 'to have her feelings worked'	But the feelings she actually felt were…
She expected a Gothic torture chamber with 'a date so ancient, a position so awful'	Instead she realizes it is…
She thinks the General has covered up his crimes and then is frightened as 'the sound of footsteps, she could hardly tell where, made her pause and tremble'	It turns out to be…
She is astonished and asks Henry 'How came you up that staircase?'	He replies very matter-of-factly that it is…

What is the effect of these contrasts and what do they suggest about Catherine's viewpoint?

Now dramatize the dialogue and prepare a performance in pairs to share with your partners. Remember that Catherine is a rather innocent teenage girl, and Henry a well-educated man in his twenties, who enjoys reading Gothic fiction too, but has seen enough of the world to be rather clearer about the difference between fact and fiction.

1. Have you noticed changes in Catherine's feelings and emotions?

2. Where do they occur and how are they expressed through her language?

3. Try two different readings of Henry's role in the duologue: one in which he appears to be very angry, and one in which he appears to be very amused. Which worked better?

4. Now try a reading in which he appears to Catherine to be angry, but is actually quite amused.

5. Why would this last reading fit the atmosphere of the extract best?

Pair and share

As we have seen, drama depends upon conflict and tension which leads to a climax. What has created the tension between Catherine and Henry? (Remember there may be more than one answer!) Where is the climax of the passage?

As in drama there is also irony: this is when the reader (or audience) know more than the characters do, especially when they read the text (or see the play) for a second time, aware of how things will end:

1. Looking over the description again, where can the reader tell that Catherine does not fully believe her own fantasies even before Henry points out her errors?

2. Looking over the dialogue again, how can we tell that Henry isn't being entirely serious even when he seems to be telling Catherine off?

3. Can you and your partner find the clues that show Henry and Catherine are already deeply in love, even if they don't admit it?

4. What do the conventions of romantic comedy suggest will happen once the jokes, misunderstanding and ironies are over? (Check chapter 2!)

Viewpoints

When Henry speaks about England, it is with the confidence of a nineteenth-century English gentleman, sure of his rational judgment and of his nation's powerful place in the world as it was at that time. What is he suggesting about the kinds of worlds portrayed in a lot of fiction at that time? What is the writer, Jane Austen, suggesting about fantasy and realism in fiction?

- Do you prefer writing which is fantastic, or writing which is realistic?

- What are the advantages and disadvantages of both kinds of writing?

- In what ways do readers' expectations differ, depending on whether the text uses realism or other conventions such as fantasy, the Gothic or science fiction?

Actors play Catherine Morland and Henry Tilney in a 2007 adaptation

🔗 Language links

If you are also studying the Cambridge IGCSE First Language English course, you will know it makes a very clear distinction between descriptive writing (which must be, or appear to be, non-fiction) and narrative writing, which must be a story.

1. How do the literature texts which you have read deliberately blur this distinction?

2. How are the descriptive passages in the text related to the character of the narrator?

3. How do literature texts blur fact and fiction?

With this in mind, choose one of the following writing activities:

Write a story of your own in which a character discovers that they have made a very embarrassing mistake.

OR

Describe the experience of looking around a place which you know you should not be in.

Extend your learning

How does your own set text handle irony? Are there situations and emotions the characters experience which the reader knows are based on a mistake?

Characterization

Think ahead

This chapter has focused less on character than you might have expected. Although we take an interest in characters from the very beginning of a piece of prose fiction, and they can often keep us involved in the story, there is a danger in writing too much about characters when preparing for your exams. We need to beware of treating characters as if they were real people, and writing their diaries or dramatizing their stories as if they had a life outside the text we are studying. Although this kind of exercise can be fun, and the idea of the empathic response comes out of it, we always need to be aware that a character is a construct. Their thoughts, and especially their language, are the creation of the writer. It is therefore better to think about characterization, the way writers present characters, rather than the characters themselves.

Similarly we should beware of thinking about characters as straightforwardly good or evil. Nor can we always easily label characters as heroes or villains. Sometimes we call the main character of a novel or play the hero or heroine, even if he or she isn't always particularly heroic. For example, it would not be wrong to call Catherine Morland the heroine of *Northanger Abbey*, even though the brave things she does are rather different from what she imagines she is doing when she enters the 'forbidden room'.

It is better to think about characters as sympathetic (if it is easy for the reader to share their feelings) or unsympathetic (if we see them from outside, so we don't really share their feelings, or find it hard to side with them).

1. Which characters in your text are sympathetic?
2. Which are unsympathetic?
3. Which are complex?
4. Which are relatively straightforward (or 'flat') characters?
5. How do the complex characters change, or what is revealed about them?
6. What do the 'flat' characters contribute to the story?

The next two passages are about two very different characters, one relatively flat and unsympathetic, the other more complex and the 'hero' of the book named after him.

8.6 Surprise

In this extract from a Pulitzer Prize-winning novel by the Canadian writer Carol Shields, a nasty surprise awaits a fairly nasty character – you may feel he gets what he deserves. The passage is told from the viewpoint of his new bride, who may also surprise you by her thoughts and feelings. The story is set in Europe in the twentieth century, between the two World Wars, and Harold and his bride Daisy are on their honeymoon in France.

The Stone Diaries by Carol Shields (1993)

He manages in the space of an hour to rent an immense car, a Delage Torpedo, black as a hearse with square rear windows like wide startled eyes. Grasping the steering wheel, he seems momentarily revived, singing loudly and tunelessly, as if a great danger had passed, though his tongue whispers of gin: Daisy, Daisy, give me your answer true. I'm half crazy all for the love of you. He shoots out through the Paris suburbs and into the countryside, honking at people crossing the road, at cows and chickens, at the pale empty air of France. They hurtle down endless rural avenues of trees, past fields of ravishing poppies and golden gorse, and eventually, after hours and hours, they reach the mountains.

Delage Tornedo = a French luxury saloon car

hearse = a vehicle for carrying a coffin at funerals

"Daisy, Daisy…" = a poplar song at the time the story is set

She keeps pleading with him to stop, whimpering, then shouting that he oughtn't to be driving this wildly and drinking wine at the same time, that he is putting their lives in danger. He almost groans with the pleasure of what he is hearing, his darling scolding bride who is bent so sweetly on reform.

They stop, finally, at the sleepy Alpine town of Corps, their tires grinding to a halt on the packed gravel, and register at the Hotel de la

Poste. A hunched-looking porter carries their valises up two flights of narrow stairs to an austere room with a sloping ceiling and a single window which is heavily curtained.

valises = suitcases

Daisy lies down, exhausted, on the rather lumpy bed. Her georgette dress, creased and stained, spreads out beneath her. She can't imagine what she's doing in this dim, musty room, and yet she feels she's been here before, that all the surfaces and crevasses are familiar, part of the scenery sketched into an apocryphal journal. Sleep beckons powerfully, but she resists, looking around at the walls for some hopeful sign. There is a kind of flower-patterned paper, she sees, that lends the room a shabby, rosy charm. This, too, seems familiar. It is seven o'clock in the evening. She is lying on her back in a hotel room in the middle of France. The world is rolling over her, over and over. Her young husband, this stranger, has flung open the window, then pushed back the shutters, and now the sun shines brightly into the room.

georgette = a thin silk dress material

apocryphal = invented

And there he is, perched on the window sill, balanced there, a big fleshy shadow blocking the sunlight. In one hand he grasps a wine bottle from which he takes occasional gulps; in his other is a handful of centimes which he is tossing out the window to a group of children who have gathered on the cobbled square. He is laughing, a crazy cackling one-note sound.

centimes = French coins of small value

She can hear the musical ringing of the coins as they strike the stone, and the children's sharp singing cries. A part of her consciousness drifts toward sleep where she will be safe, but she stares sternly at the ceiling, the soiled plaster, waiting.

At that moment she feels a helpless sneeze coming on – her old allergy to feather pillows. The sneeze is loud, powerful, sudden, an explosion that closes her throat and forces her eyes shut for a fraction of a second. When she opens them again, Harold is no longer on the window sill. All she sees is an empty rectangle of glaring light. A splinter of time passes, too small and quiet to register in the brain; she blinks back her disbelief, and then hears a bang, a crashing sound like a melon splitting, a wet injurious noise followed by the screaming of children and the sound of people running in the street.

She remembers that she lay flat on the bed for a least a minute before she got up to investigate.

✎ Check your understanding

1. Which tense is used throughout and what is the effect of this?
2. Whose viewpoint do we share and how do you know this?
3. Which details make Harold's behaviour while driving appear especially dangerous?
4. How does he react to Daisy's fears?
5. What seems strange and slightly sinister about the hotel which they arrive at?
6. What does the description suggest that Daisy feels like?
7. What is odd, even supernatural, about the bedroom?
8. How does their behaviour on reaching the room highlight the differences between the husband and his wife?
9. What does the description of Harold at the window-sill reveal about his wife's feelings?
10. What do you think are Daisy's motions as she leans back on the bed?
11. What appears to be the effect of her sneeze?
12. What is sinister about the writer's description of the accident?
13. What is surprising about Daisy's reaction?
14. What do you think she feels about Harold's death?

Pair and share

The power of the writing depends not just on its shock and surprise effect, but also on the ways in which, when we look back, the tragedy seems to be inevitable and something Daisy almost predicted. Re-read the passage with a friend, exploring all the hints of something bad which is about to happen. Then fill in the table, commenting on the effects of the writer's choice of details. Notice how often the writer uses the technique of simile. The first quotation and comment is done for you, but afterwards you will need to supply the explanation of the effect on the reader which best fits the quotation.

Quotation	Effect
black as a hearse	A dark colour and a simile which reminds us of death give the reader a premonition of disaster to come
windows like wide startled eyes	
as if a great danger had passed	
I'm half crazy	
he is putting their lives in danger	
almost groans with the pleasure	
A hunched-looking porter	
this dim, musty room	
she feels she's been here before	
looking around at the walls for some hopeful sign	
This, too, seems familiar	
The world is rolling over her, over and over	
Her young husband, this stranger	
a big fleshy shadow blocking the sunlight	
he grasps a wine bottle from which he takes occasional gulps	
a crazy cackling one-note sound	
she stares sternly at the ceiling, the soiled plaster, waiting	
an explosion that closes her throat	
an empty rectangle of glaring light	
a crashing sound like a melon splitting	
a wet injurious noise	
the screaming of children and the sound of people running	
she lay flat on the bed for a least a minute before she got up to investigate	

Now discuss the questions which follow and reach agreed conclusions, which you can report back to the class:

1. What do you think the language you have explored reveals about Daisy's attitude to Harold, and her likely feelings about his death?

2. How do these phrases suggest ideas of dèjà vu or the supernatural?

3. Do you think Harold's fate is inevitable? Do you feel he deserves it?

4. Why is Daisy a more complex character than Harold, and what elements in the characterization make Harold rather 'flat'?

5. Who does the writer encourage the reader to sympathize with, and how?

Viewpoints

Many of the effects of the writing depend on the contrast between the beautiful descriptions of the French landscape and evening sunlight, and Daisy's horror at Harold's behaviour and the shock of his sudden death. How many examples of this contrast can you find?

What is the effect on the reader of this contrast?

What does it also suggest about Daisy's likely response to Harold's death?

Explore the reactions of two students:

Student A

I wondered if something was going wrong because Daisy feels like she had been here before. But then the story mentioned that she laid in her bed and then she started to see her husband at the window pane but she stood up Harold was no longer in the window she just see the rectangular window and flashback. She remember that when lay flat on the bed for at least a minute before she got up to investigate. I knew it something was going wrong.

Comment

This is a response showing basic narrative understanding. The student understands and retells the story but does not use quotation or comment on the language. It is essential to move away from paraphrase (just saying what happens) to analysis (exploring the writer's use of language) to get into the higher bands.

Student B

In the hotel room the writer clearly conveys the tension in their relationship. Daisy is so fed up with her husband that she was more worried and intrigued with some things in her bedroom than her husband's situation of being totally drunk...in the ending she shows that Daisy was not so worried about Harold and what might have happened to him: "She blinks back her disbelief" "She lay flat on the bed for at least a minute before she got up to investigate" And to build up the feeling that things would go wrong, the author makes use of short, emotionless and direct sentences.

Writing techniques

Use a highlighter pen to pick out key phrases in the text when re-reading it, in order to identify the phrases you will want to quote and comment on in your answer. This will also help you to think about and plan your response before you begin writing.

Comment

This is a stronger response: this student does use quotation and begins to comment on language, but the quotations and comments are not well integrated within the sentences, nor does the student look far beyond the surface meaning of the words.

Your task:

What advice would you give these two students in order to help them improve?

Write your own reaction to the final three paragraphs of the original, making sure you incorporate short quotations within your sentences in order to show:

- Daisy's anger with Harold
- her reaction to the moment when she sneezes and he falls
- the coolness of her response to the accident.

Why do you think Daisy does not seem to blame herself for Harold's death? Do you think she is right not to feel guilty?

8.7 Sympathy

Think ahead

In contrast, it would be useful to look at a character we are encouraged to feel sympathetic towards, and who has a good experience rather than a bad one. George Eliot (1819–1880) was one of the great successors to Jane Austen and Charles Dickens. Like Austen, she concentrated her writing on small, largely rural communities, but like Dickens, she drew her characters from a wide social range. Silas Marner, a weaver, has moved to the village of Raveloe after being accused of theft and thrown out of a religious community (Lantern Yard). The true thief was his best friend, who also stole the girl Silas loved. In the circumstances, it is not surprising that once he is in Raveloe Silas keeps away from his neighbours and concentrates on building up a stock of gold. He is very short-sighted and is prone to fits ('catalepsy' or a form of epilepsy), and does not know what has happened just before losing consciousness, which superstitious people have believed to be a sign that he is bad or 'half-crazy'. One winter his gold is stolen, forcing him to meet his neighbours in the Rainbow Inn and he finds them surprisingly sympathetic. He soon has a surprise gift he does not expect…

Extend your learning

Consider the following questions in response to the set text you are studying:

1. Where do surprises and shocks occur in the narrative which you did not expect?

2. When you look back, were there hints that something like this would happen?

3. Who do you blame or feel sorry for when bad things happen in your text?

4. How has the writer manipulated your feelings to make you feel more sorry for some characters rather than others?

George Eliot

Silas Marner by George Eliot (1861)

This morning he had been told by some of his neighbours that it was New Year's Eve, and that he must sit up and hear the old year rung out and the new rung in, because that was good luck, and might bring his money back again. This was only a friendly Raveloe-way of jesting with the half-crazy oddities of a miser, but it had perhaps helped to throw Silas into a more than usually excited state. Since the on-coming of twilight he had opened his door again and again, though only to shut it immediately at seeing all distance veiled by the falling snow. But the last time he opened it the snow had ceased, and the clouds were parting here and there. He stood and listened, and gazed for a long while—there was really something on the road coming towards him then, but he caught no sign of it; and the stillness and the wide trackless snow seemed to narrow his solitude, and touched his yearning with the chill of despair. He went in again, and put his right hand on the latch of the door to close it—but he did not close it: he was arrested, as he had been already since his loss, by the invisible wand of catalepsy, and stood like a graven image, with wide but sightless eyes, holding open his door, powerless to resist either the good or the evil that might enter there.

When Marner's sensibility returned, he continued the action which had been arrested, and closed his door, unaware of the chasm in his consciousness, unaware of any intermediate change, except that the light had grown dim, and that he was chilled and faint. He thought he had been too long standing at the door and looking out. Turning towards the hearth, where the two logs had fallen apart, and sent forth only a red uncertain glimmer, he seated himself on his fireside chair, and was stooping to push his logs together, when, to his blurred vision, it seemed as if there were gold on the floor in front of the hearth. Gold!—his own gold—brought back to him as mysteriously as it had been taken away! He felt his heart begin to beat violently, and for a few moments he was unable to stretch out his hand and grasp the restored treasure. The heap of gold seemed to glow and get larger beneath his agitated gaze. He leaned forward at last, and stretched forth his hand; but instead of the hard coin with the familiar resisting outline, his fingers encountered soft warm curls. In utter amazement, Silas fell on his knees and bent his head low to examine the marvel: it was a sleeping child—a round, fair thing, with soft yellow rings all over its head. Could this be his little sister come back to him in a dream—his little sister whom he had carried about in his arms for a year before she died, when he was a small boy without shoes or stockings? That was the first thought that darted across Silas's blank wonderment. *Was* it a dream? He rose to his feet again, pushed his logs together, and, throwing on some dried leaves and sticks, raised a flame; but the flame did not disperse the vision—it only lit up more distinctly the little round form of the child, and its shabby clothing. It was very much like his little sister. Silas sank into his chair powerless, under the double presence of an inexplicable surprise and a hurrying influx of memories. How and when had the child come in without his knowledge? He had never been beyond the door. But along with that question, and almost thrusting it away, there was a vision of the old home and the old streets leading to Lantern Yard—and within that vision another, of the thoughts which had been present with him in those far-off scenes. The thoughts were strange to him now, like old friendships impossible to revive; and yet he had a dreamy feeling that this child was somehow a message come to him from that far-off life: it stirred fibres that had never been moved in Raveloe—old quiverings of tenderness—old impressions of awe at the presentiment of some Power presiding over his life; for his imagination had not yet extricated itself from the sense of mystery in the child's sudden presence, and had formed no conjectures of ordinary natural means by which the event could have been brought about.

But there was a cry on the hearth: the child had awaked, and Marner stooped to lift it on his knee. It clung round his neck, and burst louder and louder into that mingling of inarticulate cries with "mammy" by which little children express the bewilderment of waking. Silas pressed it to him, and almost unconsciously uttered sounds of hushing tenderness, while he bethought himself that some of his porridge, which had got cool by the dying fire, would do to feed the child with if it were only warmed up a little.

 Check your understanding

1. How does Eliot make sure we share Silas's point of view and appreciate the exact moment when this incident happens?
2. Why is the New Year such an appropriate moment for this change in his life?
3. Why does he keep opening his door?
4. What is significant about the snow stopping and the clouds parting?
5. Which details bring out Silas's sense of his own solitude as he looks out of the door?
6. What has happened during the moments of Silas's 'catalepsy'?
7. How can Silas tell that some time has passed?
8. In what ways does the sleeping child seem to resemble his lost gold?
9. How is the child very different from the gold?
10. Who does it remind Silas of?
11. Why is he unsure what is dream and what is real?
12. Why does the child remind him of emotions which he has buried ever since he had to leave Lantern Yard?
13. Which words bring out a sense of mystery or the miraculous?
14. How does the last paragraph bring both Marner and the reader back to reality?

Pair and share

Explore through discussion the implications of language. We infer (or make inferences) when the writer has implied more than the surface meaning of the language. This is especially often the case in descriptive writing. Why do you think the writer set the scene in winter, surrounded by snow, on New Year's Eve?

Here the descriptions set not only the physical scene but also a certain emotional mood. George Eliot wants the reader to feel a sense of renewal and hope. She wants you to see that the arrival of the child will bring renewal and healing to Silas, in ways that accumulating money never could. Silas will need help to bring up the girl, Eppie, and that will involve him once again in the whole community of Raveloe, which, as he found in the Rainbow Inn, is surprisingly helpful and supportive. How do the following descriptions imply a special kind of atmosphere, and a hope which is almost miraculous? Where does choice of words imply some kind of magic, or the arrival of something special brought into Silas's winter world?

Quotation	Comment
he must sit up and hear the old year rung out and the new rung in	This image of the bells, change ringing to celebrate the new year, implies a change that might await Silas, which the Raveloe community wants him to enjoy
only a friendly Raveloe-way of jesting	They were only joking, but the irony is that a real change will occur
the snow had ceased, and the clouds were parting here and there	
the stillness and the wide trackless snow seemed to narrow his solitude	
the invisible wand of catalepsy	
stood like a graven image	
powerless to resist either the good or the evil that might enter	

Quotation	Comment
a red uncertain glimmer	
to his blurred vision, it seemed as if there were gold	
The heap of gold seemed to glow and get larger beneath his agitated gaze	

Your comments would reflect the idea that something very special is happening to Silas. We know that there is a rational explanation: Eppie is Godfrey Cass's child, abandoned by her dying mother Mollie; we know about what happened to Silas's gold too. The carelessness of the wealthy but dysfunctional Cass family lies behind the apparently mysterious events in Raveloe, which shows Eliot's clear social message about the true nature of community. However, for Silas everything is touched with the miraculous, and the event stirs up his memories of the religious community he used to belong to in Lantern Yard.

Before we look together at the last two paragraphs, it is important to work through the passage in sections, so that we see the writer's purpose in presenting Silas's limited and short-sighted viewpoint.

We see:

- Silas's excitement and hope that his gold will be miraculously returned

- his recovery from his cataleptic trance and discovery that the 'gold' is actually a child

- his dreams and visions that his life has been blessed by God

- the reality of the child and her needs, and how Silas begins to break out of his isolation and help her.

How does the writer's use of language make the discovery of the child both dramatic and revealing? This is clearly an emotional and exciting moment, but the language also encourages us to read symbolism into Silas's discovery. The writer uses a lot of contrast between coldness and warmth. Where do you find descriptions of coldness and cold colours? Where do these contrast with warmth? Where does Eliot contrast hardness and softness?

There are several key descriptions which need analytical comment. Discuss these together and work out your responses. You need to reflect not on the literal meaning, but the connotations of words. What is implied by calling the coins 'hard' and 'resisting'? In what ways is the child different?

Quotation	Comment
When Marner's sensibility returned, he continued the action which had been arrested	How does this suggest that Silas's actions are not under his control: as if he is being manipulated?
the chasm in his consciousness	What else has Silas not noticed, for many years?
to his blurred vision, it seemed as if there were gold	Think this time about the implications of Silas having a 'blurred' vision. What has made his vision of anything other than gold confused?
instead of the hard coin with the familiar resisting outline, his fingers encountered soft warm curls	What does this suggest about the difference between money and human love?
a round, fair thing, with soft yellow rings all over its head	How does the language present the child as an image of innocence and hope?
Silas fell on his knees and bent his head low to examine the marvel	What kind of miracle does Silas appear to be worshipping? What kind of implications does this have in the English winter, and in the Christmas season?

Silas himself, because of his upbringing and background, sees this as a miracle, or a present from God. The irony is that as readers we know the rational explanation and the more human and sordid circumstances which have led Eppie to be abandoned, albeit with very happy consequences.

The writer's choice of words (diction or lexis) is full of references to dreams or miracles. Highlight these and similar words in the second paragraph:

vision/mysteriously/treasure/amazement/marvel/ dream/inexplicable/message/awe/mystery/no … ordinary means

What other kinds of experience could this kind of language refer to? Silas at one point thinks he has seen a vision of his lost sister returned to life from the dead, and at another he sees the religious community of faith which he used to be a part of and feels the stirrings of the kind of religious experience he used to believe in when at Lantern Yard.

Not only does the diction suggest the miraculous, but the syntax, the length and structure of the sentences, also shows the transformation in Silas's mood. We have seen the importance of syntax in poetry; it is even more important in prose, where there is no regular beat to give the rhythm. The rhythm of sentences comes from their structure and gives you the emotions and excitement of the person whose viewpoint we share.

With your partner, mark out the sentence breaks in the second paragraph in one colour. Where are the sentences longer? Where do they get shorter? Where do you find that Silas asks himself a lot of questions? How long is the final sentence? Use another colour to highlight commas and dashes. Where do these pauses within sentences show Silas's agitation and excited, questioning emotions? What can you tell about his state of mind and heightened feelings from the language used to describe what he sees, or thinks he sees?

💡 Viewpoints

In Silas's dreams or visions, his past life seems to be literally flashing past him. The final sentence needs particular exploration:

The thoughts were strange to him now, like old friendships impossible to revive; and yet he had a dreamy feeling that this child was somehow a message come to him from that far-off life: it stirred fibres that had never been moved in Raveloe—old quiverings of tenderness—old impressions of awe at the presentiment of some Power presiding over his life; for his imagination had not yet extricated itself from the sense of mystery in the child's sudden presence, and had formed no conjectures of ordinary natural means by which the event could have been brought about.

It is a long and difficult sentence so it needs breaking down. Here Eliot uses semi-colons and colons to both split up and connect different parts of Silas's thoughts. Why is this a much more controlled form of punctuation than lots of commas? A colon precedes an explanation. How does Eliot explain Silas's idea that the child is a message to him from his past life? What is the emotional effect of the use of dashes and repetitions: ' – old quiverings of tenderness – old impressions of awe'? How do these descriptions combine physical and spiritual feelings?

Silas feels he is in the presence of a miracle, a gift from a higher Power. However, Eliot makes it clear that this is his point of view, and the narrator does not necessarily share it. Where do you find two 'negatives' in the final sentence? These 'nots and nos' suggest that Silas is feeling so positive that he can't think of any more rational explanation.

1. How does Eliot's description of the child's cry and of its needs bring the reader back down to earth?

2. How practical is Silas's response to the need to bring up the child?

3. How does this prevent the passage from being falsely sentimental or over emotional?

🔗 Language links

Revise the use of semi-colons and colons and examine the ways in which they can make your own use of language more effective. A colon precedes an explanation: it is therefore a useful way of showing that ideas are connected; semi-colons provide a pause as controlled as a full stop, while also making a clear link between this clause and the one preceding it.

💡 Viewpoints

You will have noticed that both the last two passages have hints of mystery or the supernatural, and confuse dream and reality in order to present events which are so surprising that they seem almost a miracle.

- Why do you think writers like to play with hints of the supernatural or mysterious?
- Do you believe in them?
- Or do you think the events in novels should have a rational explanation?
- Have you seen similar treatment of the supernatural in the text you are reading?

Debate these issues in class. Are stories more convincing and more powerful when more realistic? How far should we allow writers a touch of magic?

Form teams to argue for and against the motion that: *'Writers of fiction will interest us more if they stick to events we know are realistic.'*

You should have two prepared speeches on each side, a chairman to keep order, a floor debate with formal questions directed to the speakers and a summing-up by each side, answering points made by opponents and from the floor. Give the proposition the first and the last word. Then take a vote.

Remember that a good debating speech is based around arguments supported by examples and discussion of what they show (rather like a good literary essay!). It is not just a matter of demolishing the opposition's arguments, but also having good ones of your own.

There is no clear right or wrong side (the best speakers are likely to win the argument) – different readers have different tastes and writers often want both sides to be satisfied.

Writing techniques

To write about this passage, consider the writer's purpose and the reader's response. You should consider how Silas's character is communicated through his point of view, so that we understand what this moment means to him, but we should also consider our own response and viewpoint and how they are influenced by the kind of techniques which we have seen the writer use.

Look back at the passage of *Silas Marner*, perhaps informed by what you know of the novel.

1. How has George Eliot combined magic and **realism** in this powerful moment?

2. Has she managed to make it tender without making it too sentimental or unbelievable?

3. How has she made sure we understand the way Silas feels, and how important this moment is for him?

> **KEY TERM**
>
> **realism** = when a text closely corresponds to real-life events. Magic realism is when a text combines aspects of reality and fantasy.

Extend your learning

Choose the most dramatic moment from your own set text. The extract should be about a page of text. Analyse how the writing works in that extract by devising a series of 'Check your understanding' questions, then highlight a series of quotations, following them with comment on the effect of the writing. Think about the importance of that moment for the rest of the text. Share your ideas with a friend, and you are now ready to write. If you include ideas which move outside the extract and say what it reveals about a character or about other parts of the text, then you could use this extract for coursework.

How does the writer make this moment so dramatic and revealing?

Write an essay of 800–1,000 words in response.

8.8 Closure

Think ahead

A sense of the miraculous, or its opposite, the horrific, can help a prose text to achieve its closure. We tend to expect some form of justice, or appropriate ending for the characters. We have already seen that we have expectations of closure from the dramatic genres of comedy and tragedy, which can resurface in prose fiction. However, prose fiction can often also be open-ended ('resist closure') perhaps because the writer plans a sequel, or perhaps because he or she wants to leave the reader with a sense of mystery, be true to the messiness of real life (rather than the tidier endings of fiction) or leave the reader to make up their own minds about the ending.

Miss Prism, played by Margaret Rutherford

Do you feel that characters get the ending they appear to deserve? Consider these two quotations by two great comic dramatists, one of whom we have already met earlier in this book:

'The good ended happily, and the bad unhappily. That is what Fiction means.' – Miss Prism, *The Importance of Being Earnest*, Oscar Wilde (1854–1900)

'The bad end unhappily, the good unluckily. That is what tragedy means.' – Player King, *Rosencrantz and Guildenstern Are Dead*, Tom Stoppard (1937–)

1. Does your novel have the neatness of the kind of fiction Wilde's Miss Prism is talking about?

2. Or the kind of tragic justice Stoppard's Player King describes?

3. Which characters survive and what do you feel about the journey they have been on and what they have learnt?

4. Do you feel that characters get their 'just deserts' – in other words, the kind of ending they deserve?

5. What remains a mystery or uncertain at the end of your set text?

We looked at Stevenson's *The Strange Case of Dr Jekyll and Mr Hyde* in chapter 5. Utterson's narrative, and that of his friend Dr Lanyon, leave many questions unanswered and we need a third account of events, 'Henry Jekyll's Full Statement of the Case', in order to achieve full understanding of that character's double life and the price he has paid for it. We already know that Jekyll had found it increasingly difficult to control his transformation into the murderous Hyde, and that Hyde has been found dead, dressed in Jekyll's clothes. Lanyon's narrative told the story of seeing Hyde turn himself into Jekyll by taking a drug, suggesting that they really are the same person.

Throughout the chapter, we have explored the ways in which writers use viewpoint to present characters and their feelings. Here we see a character who is so divided he has become two people, the calm and respected Dr Jekyll and the 'Ape-like' and criminal Mr Hyde. Stevenson is suggesting that many of us may have a monstrous **alter ego**, waiting for the opportunity to break out. Here, at the end of the novel, Dr Jekyll confesses what has become of him.

> **KEY TERM**
>
> **alter ego** = double or alternative identity.

The Strange Case of Dr Jekyll and Mr Hyde by R.L. Stevenson (1886)

I was stepping leisurely across the court after breakfast, drinking the chill of the air with pleasure, when I was seized again with those indescribable sensations that heralded the change; and I had but the time to gain the shelter of my cabinet, before I was once again raging and freezing with the passions of Hyde. It took on this occasion a double dose to recall me to myself; and alas! six hours after, as I sat looking sadly in the fire, the pangs returned, and the drug had to be re-administered. In short, from that day forth it seemed only by a great effort as of gymnastics, and only under the immediate stimulation of the drug, that I was able to wear the countenance of Jekyll. At all hours of the day and night, I would be taken with the premonitory shudder; above all, if I slept, or even dozed for a moment in my chair, it was always as Hyde that I awakened. Under the strain of this continually impending doom and by the sleeplessness to which I now condemned myself, ay, even beyond what I had thought possible to man, I became, in my own person, a creature eaten up and emptied by fever, languidly weak both in body and mind, and solely occupied by one thought: the horror of my other self. But when I slept, or when the virtue of the medicine wore off, I would leap almost without transition (for the pangs of transformation grew daily less marked) into the possession of a fancy brimming with images of terror, a soul boiling with causeless hatreds, and a body that seemed not strong enough to contain the raging energies of life. The powers of Hyde seemed to have grown with the sickliness of Jekyll. And certainly the hate that now divided them was equal on each side. With Jekyll, it was a thing of vital instinct. He had now seen the full deformity of that creature that shared with him some of the phenomena of consciousness, and was co-heir with him to death: and beyond these links of community, which in themselves made the most poignant part of his distress, he thought of Hyde, for all his energy of life, as of something not only hellish but inorganic. This was the shocking thing; that the slime of the pit seemed to utter cries and voices; that the amorphous dust gesticulated and sinned; that what was dead, and had no shape, should usurp the offices of life. And this again, that that insurgent horror was knit to him closer than a wife, closer than an eye; lay caged in his flesh, where he heard it mutter and felt it struggle to be born; and at every hour of weakness, and in the confidence of slumber, prevailed against him, and deposed him out of life.

Check your understanding

This is a difficult passage, partly because it conveys difficult ideas, so we will pause and have a closer look.

1. Which words in the first sentence portray the calm Jekyll?

2. Which word shows the terror he feels at becoming Hyde?

3. Which details show that the drug is no longer working and it is becoming hard for him to hold onto this Jekyll identity and not involuntarily become Hyde?

4. What is the effect of this realization on Jekyll's health and happiness?

5. Which descriptions bring out the kind of emotions he feels as Hyde?

6. In what ways are Jeykll and Hyde still the same person, whatever the drug does to transform their appearance?

7. Which words show clearly the hatred and horror which Jekyll feels at the thought of Hyde?

Now read on and see how this passage develops. It examines what Hyde feels about Jekyll: remember that Jekyll is writing, so this shows the interesting ways in which he is both different from, and the same man as Hyde. Although they have different appearances and different emotions, they share the same consciousness. Hyde wants to take over Jekyll completely, and wants to stop playing a subordinate role.

The Strange Case of Dr Jekyll and Mr Hyde by R.L. Stevenson (1886)

The hatred of Hyde for Jekyll was of a different order. His terror of the gallows drove him continually to commit temporary suicide, and return to his subordinate station of a part instead of a person; but he loathed the necessity, he loathed the despondency into which Jekyll was now fallen, and he resented the dislike with which he was himself regarded. Hence the ape-like tricks that he would play me, scrawling in my own hand blasphemies on the pages of my books, burning the letters and destroying the portrait of my father; and indeed, had it not been for his fear of death, he would long ago have ruined himself in order to involve me in the ruin. But his love of me is wonderful; I go further: I, who sicken and freeze at the mere thought of him, when I recall the abjection and passion of this attachment, and when I know how he fears my power to cut him off by suicide, I find it in my heart to pity him.

It is useless, and the time awfully fails me, to prolong this description; no one has ever suffered such torments, let that suffice; and yet even to these, habit brought -- no, not alleviation -- but a certain callousness of soul, a certain acquiescence of despair; and my punishment might have gone on for years, but for the last calamity which has now fallen, and which has finally severed me from my own face and nature. My provision of the salt, which had never been renewed since the date of the first experiment, began to run low. I sent out for a fresh supply and mixed the draught; the ebullition followed, and the first change of colour, not the second; I drank it and it was without efficiency. You will learn from Poole how I have had London ransacked; it was in vain; and I am now persuaded that my first supply was impure, and that it was that unknown impurity which lent efficacy to the draught.

About a week has passed, and I am now finishing this statement under the influence of the last of the old powders. This, then, is the last time, short of a miracle, that Henry Jekyll can think his own thoughts or see his own face (now how sadly altered!) in the glass. Nor must I delay too long to bring my writing to an end; for if my narrative has hitherto escaped destruction, it has been by a combination of great prudence and great good luck. Should the throes of change take me in the act of writing it, Hyde will tear it in pieces; but if some time shall have elapsed after I have laid it by, his wonderful selfishness and circumscription to the moment will probably save it once again from the action of his ape-like spite. And indeed the doom that is closing on us both has already changed and crushed him. Half an hour from now, when I shall again and forever re-indue that hated personality, I know how I shall sit shuddering and weeping in my chair, or continue, with the most strained and fearstruck ecstasy of listening, to pace up and down this room (my last earthly refuge) and give ear to every sound of menace. Will Hyde die upon the scaffold? or will he find courage to release himself at the last moment? God knows; I am careless; this is my true hour of death, and what is to follow concerns another than myself. Here then, as I lay down the pen and proceed to seal up my confession, I bring the life of that unhappy Henry Jekyll to an end.

✏️ Check your understanding

1. What does Hyde hate about Jekyll?

2. How does he try to get his revenge on him?

3. Why is Hyde nevertheless afraid of going too far in his hatred of Jekyll?

4. Why does Jekyll feel 'pity' for Hyde?

5. Jekyll says that he has got used to the miseries of his double life: what is the problem which has brought on the final catastrophe?

6. What does he now think caused the formula in the drug he created to work?

7. What does the change in Jekyll's face and feelings show the reader about the success or failure of Jekyll's attempt to keep his own identity and that of Hyde completely separate?

8. Why will he now have to bring the experiment to an end though his own death?

9. Why is he worried if the manuscript will survive?

10. Hyde's dead body was found in Jekyll's clothes. What does this suggest about how closely linked the two identities really are?

💬 Pair and share

We have seen how the language that surrounded Silas Marner in the previous extract is full of implications of the miraculous. In his confession Jekyll surround himself with the language of tragedy. Look together at the text and highlight the terms which show his sense of fate or doom.

1. How often does Jekyll use the first-person pronoun ('I')? What does this suggest about how self-obsessed he is? Why is he now so isolated?

2. How often does Jekyll use the third-person pronoun ('he')? Who does this invariably refer to?

What does this suggest about his fear about the 'Other' (who is really a part of himself)?

3. Can you find the one moment when he refers to 'us'? Why is this so revealing?

Look back at the definitions of tragedy we explored in chapter 7. Is Jekyll a tragic figure, or is he entirely to blame for his own fate? With your partner's help, draw up reasons for and against sympathizing with Jekyll. We can call this the evaluation of a character. Of course, characters can have more than one side to them: that's especially true of Henry Jekyll!

Viewpoints

Looking back to *The Importance of Being Earnest*, you will have noticed how the 'double life', questions about whether your identity can be split and divided or whether you are a whole person (both body and soul) greatly troubled nineteenth-century writers.

1. Why do you think this was the case?

2. What would have been the influence of discoveries in science (e.g. evolution) and technology?

3. How might greater social mobility and the effect of urbanization have influenced these worries?

4. Notice that Hyde is referred to as 'Ape-like'. How might evolutionary theory and fear about other races have influenced these European obsessions with threats to the 'purity' of humanity?

5. Why might religious anxiety have been a factor?

6. Do these anxieties relate to declining belief in an after-life or the supernatural?

7. Do we have similar concerns today (e.g. over the creation of online 'avatars')?

Debate these questions with your classmates. Using the debate format we used earlier (on page 180), argue for or against the proposition:

Human beings only have one life, and need to make up their mind about how to live it.

 Look up the following terms in the glossary and revise their meanings: tragedy, revelation, irony, convention.

 See the following worksheets on the website:

Worksheet 6: Character evaluation

Worksheet 7: Character timeline

8.9 Reader response

Think ahead

We call the kind of ending we expect 'closure'. It gives a fate to the characters which they seem to deserve. Not all writers want their texts to have this kind of ending, where most of the loose ends are tied up. Increasingly in the later twentieth century and in more recent novels as well as plays, narratives are said to resist closure. Which is true of your set text? Did you feel happy and satisfied with the way your text ended? Or did you want something more? Either way, you can see that the text is written in a way which will stimulate 'personal response'.

Writers want their readers to respond to characters and situations, and want to work on your emotions. This is not just in order to sell more books: books often have a purpose which goes beyond the reader's engagement and entertainment. Why do you read books? How have they informed your understanding of the world and what you feel about it?

Harper Lee (1926–) wrote *To Kill a Mockingbird* at the beginning of the 1960s. Although it looks back to an earlier time, the time of her childhood in the American South before the Second World War, the themes of racism and injustice which it portrays so powerfully captured the mood of the time when the novel was published. It has since been studied in most American high schools and in secondary schools all over the world. Look up an online biography of Martin Luther King in order to appreciate the issues of racial segregation and discrimination which were current in the Southern states of America at this time.

How does your own set text achieve closure not only for individual characters, but also for the themes of the novel? How does it help the reader to reflect on their response to those themes?

In this scene from the 1962 film, Atticus Finch and Tom Robinson are seen in the courtroom

In the following passage, the narrative viewpoint is that of Scout, a young girl, as it has been throughout the novel. The life of her brother Jem has been saved by their neighbour, the mysterious Boo Radley. Boo has been confined to his house by his parents throughout the book up to this point, and the children have been afraid of him. Now Scout realizes that Boo was their friend and protector. This passage is part of the novel's epilogue (the part that comes after the main action is over). Scout realizes that her father, Atticus, was right, and that you can only understand another person if you are able to adopt their viewpoint. Scout is standing on Boo's front porch. As she looks back at the houses belonging to all her neighbours, she slips back in time. In her imagination, she sees things as Boo would, describing the events of the novel from his viewpoint (confined to his house) rather than hers. In the process, we see how she has grown up, and her view of the world has matured.

To Kill a Mockingbird by Harper Lee (1960)

Neighbours bring food with death and flowers with sickness and little things in between. Boo was our neighbour. He gave us two soap dolls, a broken watch and chain, a pair of good-luck pennies, and our lives. But neighbours give in return. We never put back into the tree what we took out of it: we had given him nothing, and it made me sad.

I turned to go home. Street lights winked down the street all the way to town. There were Miss Maudie's, Miss Stephanie's – there was our house, I could see the porch swing – Miss Rachel's house was beyond us, plainly visible. I could even see Mrs Dubose's.

I looked behind me. To the left of the brown door was a long shuttered window. I walked to it, stood in front of it, and turned around. In daylight, I thought, you could see to the post office corner.

Daylight…in my mind, the night faded. It was daytime and the neighbourhood was busy. Miss Stephanie Crawford crossed the street to tell the latest to Miss Rachel. Miss Maudie bent over her azaleas. It was summertime, and two children scampered down the sidewalk towards a man approaching in the distance. The man waved, and the children raced each other to him.

It was still summertime, and the children came closer. A boy trudged down the sidewalk dragging a fishing-pole behind him. A man stood waiting with his hands on his hips. Summertime, and his children played in the front yard with their friend, enacting a strange little drama of their own invention.

It was fall, and his children fought on the sidewalk in front of Mrs Dubose's. The boy helped his sister to her feet, and they made their way home. Fall, and his children trotted to and fro around the corner, the day's woes and triumphs on their faces. They stopped at an oak tree, delighted, puzzled, apprehensive.

Winter, and his children shivered at the front gate, silhouetted against a blazing house. Winter, and a man walked into the street, dropped his glasses, and shot a dog.

Summer and he watched his children's heart break. Autumn again, and Boo's children needed him.

Atticus was right. One time he said you never really know a man until you stand in his shoes and walk around in them. Just standing on the Radley porch was enough.

✎ Check your understanding

1. In the first paragraph, why does Scout feel sad about her relationship with Boo, now she realizes that he was the person who left presents in the tree?

2. In the second paragraph, why is Scout so interested in the view from Boo's house across to those of her neighbours, and across to her own house?

3. In the third paragraph, why does she now go back to stand outside Boo's shuttered window?

4. How can we tell that she now goes back in time, in her imagination?

5. Who do you think the children are, who she now looks at from Boo's point of view?

6. Why does Boo call them 'his' children?

7. Why might the children be 'puzzled' by what is left for them in the tree?

8. How does the whole passage support Atticus's claim that you can only understand another person if you can 'stand in his shoes'?

Pair and share

1. How have you come to understand the ways in which characters in the text you have studied think?

2. Decide on a character with whom you have empathized while reading your text. How did the writer encourage you to understand their point of view? Has it been through first-person narrative, the portrayal of their thoughts and feelings or through the things they have said?

3. Using your notes on characters, find quotations from the text to show ways in which you have come to understand characters very different from yourself.

4. Take different characters from your partner, and then share your notes and quotations. Do you agree about your experience of the novel or do you disagree?

5. It is possible to take very different views about characters, as we shall see in chapter 10. Which characters is it possible to see from more than one point of view?

6. How successful is the time shift in the extract here? How does the novel you have studied present the passing of time?

Draw up a timeline for a wall display, tracking the key events of the novel, and the key developments for the main character. Use this as a visual aid, to chart the progress of your novel, its characters and your understanding of them.

 Viewpoints

In this passage, we see that Scout has grown up, to add to what we have already seen is the fate of the other main characters. However, Harper Lee achieves closure not just for the characters of the text but also for her principal theme. Empathy is the ability to adopt the point of view of other people, or as Atticus puts it, standing in other people's shoes and walking around in them.

1. Why is empathy an important quality in combating prejudice and unfairness?

2. Why is empathy also an important quality in law and the administration of justice?

3. Why would empathy be a key characteristic of a writer?

4. How can empathy help the literature student to understand characters and their choices?

The passage makes it clear that Harper Lee writes with a purpose and that Scout has grown up. Indeed her voice and the techniques used to convey her thoughts are probably not now those of the young girl, but more like those of an older woman looking back, and finding words to describe the feelings of her younger self.

How does your text encourage you, as a reader, to look back over the events of the novel? Does the writing help you to make sense of what you have seen described? Does the novel still have something to say to readers today?

Extend your learning

Apply these ideas to the way in which the writer achieves, or resists, closure in your own text.

To what extent has the writing helped you to see the novel as a whole and to appreciate the writer's purpose in telling you this story?

- Base your answer on the close reading of a passage at or close to the end of the book.

- Use this to look back at events, characters and themes of the rest of the text.

- Consider both the writer's purpose and the reader's reaction at the end of the novel.

Looking back

In completing the class novel, or short stories, you have finished the biggest task on your Cambridge IGCSE Literature course. Well done! The last pages here have encouraged you to look back and reflect on what you have read. You will then need to re-read the text and revise it as you move closer to your exams, and later chapters will give you advice on how to revise prose. Looking back at this chapter, reflect both on the prose text you have read and what you have learnt.

Think about how your reading has extended your understanding of the following points.

1. The ways in which writers capture your attention
2. How writers use the conventions of different genres of prose (e.g. mystery, romance, science fiction, regional novel)
3. The importance of the setting in establishing the atmosphere of the text
4. Why the narrative voice and viewpoint are significant
5. How prose writers use allegory and symbolism
6. The importance of interesting and realistic characterization
7. The way writers use shock effects and mystery
8. How to explore time shifts during the course of a narrative
9. The extent to which novels reflect real-life events
10. The ways in which writers contrast the human and natural worlds
11. The function of irony and suspense, and how they create turning points and revelation in works of fiction
12. How writers create sympathetic and unsympathetic characters
13. The ways in which description takes the reader beyond surface meaning
14. The impact of revelation and closure on the reader's evaluation of character
15. How prose texts encourage different kinds of empathy from their readers

You can apply any of these ideas to the structure and expression of your own set text, either basing your answer around a single extract, or using several examples from different parts of the text to analyse ways in both which the text and the reader's understanding of it develop.

For further advice about preparing coursework essays, and revising your set texts, turn to chapter 10.

 Explore Worksheet 8, narrator checklist.

Studying poetry

Your Cambridge IGCSE poetry selection will either be a selection of texts from various different poets from different cultures and ages, or it will be a selection of the work of an individual poet. You will not need to compare poems in the exam. However, there may be a question which asks you about more than one poem, or which asks you to look at a theme or technique common to more than one poem, and to make a choice about which poem you write on.

You will need to read the poems very closely. Poems will need line-by-line annotation, with close attention to rhythm, imagery and the choice of words: you should work with a copy of each poem which you can mark up, as you were shown to do in chapter 4. For these reasons, you might choose to read the poems relatively late in your course, when you have developed good close reading skills.

All the questions on the exam paper will include a copy of the poems they refer to, and you should make the close study of individual poems the principal focus of your writing. When interpreting or evaluating a poem, what is distinctive and different is usually more interesting than what makes it similar to other poems you have read.

Above all, remember that structure, language and form should guide your response to poetry as much as their subject matter or narrative.

LEARNING POINTS

▶ To understand the ways in which poets use form and structure to shape their writing

▶ To explore the impact of the poet's choices of words (diction) and sentence structure (syntax)

▶ To appreciate in detail the ways in which **rhythm** shapes the music of poetry (tone)

▶ To respond in individual ways to poets' use of imagery to affect the reader's thoughts and feelings (mood).

KEY TERM

rhythm = the musical patterns of stress formed by the beat of a line of poetry.

9.1 Poetic voice

Think ahead

Thomas Hardy (1840–1928) was better known in his lifetime as a very successful novelist. He did not publish a poetry collection until 1898. However, just as Shakespeare may well have valued his poetry more highly than his drama, Hardy regarded his greatest achievements to be his verse, and this is a view increasingly shared by critics too.

Some of his finest poems were published after the death of his first wife, Emma Lavinia Gifford. Passionately in love when they married, they later became estranged and Hardy did not treat her well. He was taken by surprise, not just by her sudden death but also by the force of his feelings, in which guilt may have played a factor. He wrote a sequence of poems in which he is haunted by memories of Emma, and goes back to their 'old haunts', the places where they first fell in love, and which he had not revisited for many years. Gradually, by writing about it, Hardy is able to lay Emma's ghost to rest. Like many of his generation, Hardy was interested in the supernatural and in the possibility of life after death, but he was interested in science and he is sceptical and doubting when he writes about religion or spirits.

What else can you add to the notes above, from your own internet research about Hardy's life, his work, famous lines that he wrote, and critical opinions about his writing? In a group of four, construct a presentation, including illustrations or slides if you wish, in which you each take one of the following tasks or roles:

1. The biographer, presenting interesting aspects of his life: what made him an unusual and interesting man?

2. The literature professor exploring his famous works and a few well-known lines from them: what were his favourite themes?

3. The historian, presenting facts about Hardy's world: in what ways were his interests typical of people of his age?

4. The critic: use quotations to show what people said about Hardy's work, both in his own lifetime and since. Why has Hardy had a strong influence on other poets in the century since his death?

🔗 Language links

Activities like this can also form part of a Speaking and Listening assessment if you are studying Cambridge IGCSE First Language English. Make sure that you turn the presentation into an argument, by addressing an overall question, and that after the mini-presentation you debate the question as a group and reach an agreement. Your question could be:

What are the key factors which make Hardy such a well-known and significant poet?

Later in this unit, we will look at different ways of tackling either the selection or the set poet, in order to combine close reading with contextual understanding. However, here we will focus above all on form, structure and language.

Poetic form

When Hardy collected his poems about Emma, it was in a volume published in 1914 entitled *Satires of Circumstance*. Satire is a curious and ironic choice of title as we usually think of the form of satire as one involving mocking or ridicule. If Hardy is mocking anyone in these poems he is mocking himself, and perhaps the situation he found himself in. The usual term for a poem about mourning or loss is elegy. Elegies are very much a traditional form of poetry going back to the Ancient Greeks. It would be correct to call Hardy's *Satires* elegiac, as he is not only mourning the loss of his wife, but also their earlier selves and their love, and the main subject of the poems is probably the passing of time.

Look closely at the formal qualities of the poem which follows, paying careful attention to the following:

- stanza form
- rhyme
- rhythm
- sound patterns
- syntax

Then look more closely at word level, and broaden your thinking to consider the impact of the whole poem. The rhythms are especially interesting. See if you can mark up the stress patterns of the verse, as you learnt to do in chapter 4.

Put a stress mark over each vowel, either long (/) for a stressed syllable, which the beat falls on, or short (x) for a weak or unstressed syllable. Use the length of vowel sounds and the emphasis on individual words to guide you, and remember that poetry should not sound very different from the rhythms of standard speech.

Thomas Hardy

'The Voice' by Thomas Hardy (1912)

Woman much missed, how you call to me, call to me,
Saying that now you are not as you were
When you had changed from the one who was all to me,
But as at first, when our day was fair.

Can it be you that I hear? Let me view you, then,
Standing as when I drew near to the town
Where you would wait for me: yes, as I knew you then,
Even to the original air-blue gown!

Or is it only the breeze, in its listlessness
Travelling across the wet mead to me here,
You being ever dissolved to wan wistlessness,
Heard no more again far or near?

Thus I; faltering forward,
Leaves around me falling,
Wind oozing thin through the thorn from norward,
And the woman calling.

Thomas Hardy

mead = field, meadow
wistlessness = inattentiveness

norward = northern parts

✎ Check your understanding

Hardy is clearly speaking in his own voice, although we should always remember that a poet creates a character, even when he is speaking in the first person, about emotions he has probably felt. Remember that all poems are performances: for this reason we often call the voice of 'the poet' a **persona** (from the Greek for 'mask' – in other words, the kind of mask which an actor wears).

But who is he speaking to? This is always a good question to ask when reading a poem. He is addressing the dead Emma, whether as a ghost or something he can imagine hearing in the air. He imagines she is calling to him. Now answer the following questions:

1. How does the first stanza reveal that Hardy's wife has passed away?
2. Why does he use the present tense when he hears her calling?
3. How does she say that she has changed?
4. Why does that please Hardy?
5. How would he like to see her, as well as hear her?
6. What else could it be that is speaking to him?
7. If she isn't talking to him, what has become of her?
8. What time of year is it?
9. What does that suggest about Hardy's own life?
10. Which words suggest to you weakness or harshness?
11. The idea that she is calling him is repeated in the final line. What is the effect of this repetition?

Did you notice the alternation of masculine and feminine rhymes? Not only are the rhyme sounds different in the second and fourth lines (alternating rhyme) but the rhythms are also different. Lines one and three end with a weak (or unstressed) syllable – traditionally called a feminine rhyme – and lines two and four with a strong (stressed syllable) – traditionally called a masculine rhyme.

This is much clearer if you perform the poem by reading it out loud. You may need to mark up your copy of the poem first.

Pair and share

In pairs, read alternate lines out loud in order to hear the difference. One person should read out all the 'A' lines and the other all the 'B' lines.

```
 /  x    x    /      x   x   /  x   x   /  x   x
```
Woman much missed, how you call to me, call to me,   A
```
 /  x     x  /   x   x  /  x   x    /
```
Saying that now you are not as you were   B

What happens when you come to the last stanza?

Notice there are only FOUR strong beats in each line, so these are tetrameters.

The base rhythm is **dactylic** (strong/weak/weak), an unusual rhythm in English poetry, as it cuts across the normal, iambic, speech rhythm and creates a falling rhythm.

Why might this rhythm be appropriate for a poem about death and haunting?

When you read the final quatrain (four-line stanza), the rhythm switches, doesn't it? That is why the stanza is printed in a very different way.

It also becomes much harder to be sure where to place the strong stresses or even to be certain how many of them there are. The rhythm of the poem is breaking up, as if a signal has lost its strength, or the poet has lost his sense of direction. Why does this element of style suit the subject?

Which consonant sounds do you hear most frequently? Highlight all the 's' sounds, which we call **sibilance**. What is the effect of this repeated sound? What does the hissing, rustling sound remind you of?

Can you also hear a repeated vowel sound? This is set up by the first repetition and the first rhyme sounds. Highlight all the 'a' vowel sounds. Does this help you to hear the woman's call? Or the poet's own obsessiveness? Report back to your class on what you have found.

 Use a copy of the poem printed from the website to mark up stress patterns and highlight rhymes.

KEY TERMS

persona = The person who speaks in a poem – we often call this the poet, but that doesn't mean the poem is autobiographical.

dactylic = a running rhythm of STRONG weak weak / x x (rare in English poetry).

sibilance = lots of 's' sounds.

💡 Viewpoints

Having paid attention to the sound and structure of the poem, it is now time to pay more attention to its sense. As we have seen before, syntax helps you to make sense of poems.

Using a different colour, now highlight the poem's full stops, question marks and exclamation marks in order to see how it works through a series of statements and questions.

1. Why does Hardy ask whether he is really hearing Emma?

2. How would he like to see her?

3. What does he feel when she doesn't appear?

We see the poet himself very clearly in the final stanza:

> *...faltering forward*

Leaves around me falling

But we also hear the woman calling, just as at the start of the poem, although we are no more certain about whether she is really there, or just an aspect of his imagination.

The poem makes many references to time, and links this to nature. Hardy imagines Emma as she was *at first, when our day was fair*. Later, he is alone and autumn leaves are falling, *wind oozing thin through the thorn from norward*. As well as providing us with a haunting, elegiac music, Hardy is also creating a series of pictures, which give us images of their relationship. He shows how he used to look forward to seeing her, and how that contrasts with the wet, dismal, dying scene around him now. Contrast *the original air-blue gown* of Hardy's memory and the bare thorn of the final stanza.

You can apply this symbolism to the passing of time, the dying of love and the human life cycle. Hardy seems to be commenting on the transience of all human life, as well as mourning Emma's life and death. There is a powerful image of his own loneliness and lack of direction at the end of the poem. The last two stanzas have an image of dissolution and decay:

You being ever dissolved to wan wistlessness

Wind oozing thin through the thorn from norward

Why is the poem called 'The Voice'? Whose voice do you hear and how would you characterize that voice? You can answer these questions in more than one way, and thus shape your own informed personal response. Clearly Hardy leaves you to make up your own mind about whether there really is a ghost here or not.

Extend your learning

Compare some of Hardy's poems to those of Tennyson, Emily Brontë and other poets who began writing in the Victorian period. How do they address mourning in their poems?

Think ahead

Poets often seem 'much possessed by death'. This is not just because of personal circumstances, like those Hardy dramatizes in his elegies. Poets also want their work to be immortal, and to survive what Shakespeare describes in 'Sonnet 60' as 'the cruel hand of time'.

1. How might elegies celebrate life as well as death?

2. Which other elegies have you already read?

3. What kind of immortality might poetry celebrate?

4. How does rhythm help poets to express their feelings about life and death?

Emily Dickinson (1830–1886) was an American poet, who lived almost her entire life in seclusion in her family home in Amherst, Massachusetts. She shares the preoccupations of nineteenth-century English poets with the elegiac, and with religious faith and doubt, and her poetry also expresses private and personal emotions. Very few of her poems were published in her lifetime. However, she wrote prolifically and with a strong sense of audience. Her poems do not use conventional punctuation, and are full of symbolism, so are not to be read literally, or confined to a single meaning. You should be able to enjoy working out your own interpretations: like Hardy, she dramatizes herself and presents a poetic persona. Her poems are not necessarily autobiographical, but they share her personal concerns with the nature of life and death, and with the natural world. Read the poem out to yourself, or around the class. Can you pick up its regular rhythm?

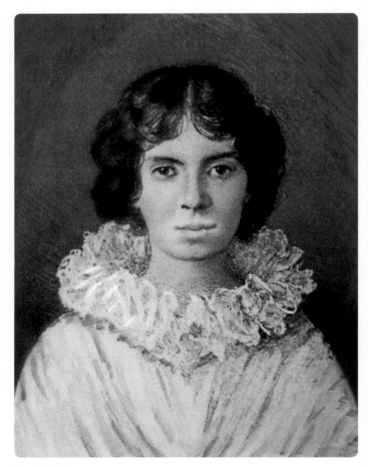

Emily Dickinson

'Because I Could Not Stop for Death' by Emily Dickinson (1862)

Because I could not stop for Death –
He kindly stopped for me –
The Carriage held but just Ourselves
And Immortality.

We slowly drove – He knew no haste
And I had put away
My labor and my leisure too,
For his Civility –

We passed the School, where Children strove
At Recess – in the Ring –
We passed the Fields of Gazing Grain –
We passed the Setting Sun –

Recess = break time at school

Or rather – He passed Us –
The Dews drew quivering and chill –
For only Gossamer, my Gown –
My Tippet – only Tulle –

A *tippet* is a scarf; *gossamer* and *tulle* are very light fabrics

We paused before a House that seemed
A Swelling of the Ground –
The Roof was scarcely visible –
The Cornice – in the Ground –

Cornice = ornamental moulding at the top of a building

Since then – 'tis Centuries – and yet
Feels shorter than the Day
I first surmised the Horses' Heads
Were toward Eternity –

✎ Check your understanding

1. Mark up the strong stresses on your own copy of the poem and note the regularity of the rhythm.

2. How does Dickinson use alternating rhythms and rhymes?

3. How does Dickinson, like Hardy, alternate feminine and masculine voices?

4. Who do you think are the feminine and masculine characters in this poem?

5. What is the effect of using so many capital letters?

6. What sort of character does Death have in this poem and what is surprising about this?

7. What does the poet abandon in order to ride with him?

8. What do they see on their journey?

9. Why does she feel cold?

10. What kind of house do they pause at in the penultimate stanza?

11. Where do they go next, and what is surprising about the final stanza?

12. Why is it important that the poem does not end with a full stop?

Pair and share

You should have been able to establish that the poet imagines that she is on a journey with Death, and that the other characters or sights in the poem may also be personifications or symbols. However, thanks to the rhythm of the poem, the tone is quite a bright one, very different from the bleaker sounds of mortality in Hardy's poem. What do you think the poem might mean?

With your partner, look at the poem's rhythms. Where do the strong stresses fall? Which are the masculine lines and rhythms? What is the effect of this degree of finality or closure?

What do you think is the effect of the punctuation? Hyphens link words and ideas, while dashes separate them. Which do you think Dickinson is using? Does this contradict the ways in which the rhythms of the poem suggest closure?

Having looked at the rhythms and patterns of the poem, it is now necessary to interpret its images. The poet is on a journey, and the stanzas show what she sees along the way in a series of pictures or images.

Imagery embraces personifications and metaphors, and can be characterized as the 'slide show' or pictures which we see while reading the poem. In discussion with your partner, try to visualize the images which follow, before interpreting them. Imagine you are in an art gallery, imagining why the artist has chosen these images and what they suggest to you. The first three are done for you to give you some guidance. Together, work out your own answers to the other images, using the questions provided as prompts.

Image	Interpretation
The Carriage held but just Ourselves And Immortality	The carriage might be the journey of life, while the personification of Immortality suggests that while the poet's body is mortal and hand-in-hand with death, perhaps an immortal soul is on the journey with them.
And I had put away My labor and my leisure too, For his Civility	Death is a gentleman, and the ride is a gentle one. The poet has given up both work and pleasure for him; it is almost as if they are married.
We passed the School, where Children strove At Recess – in the Ring –	Early in the journey they go past a school full of children, suggesting they are leaving childish things behind. The 'striving' suggests competition among the children. Perhaps the poet sees this as something childish which she has left behind, or something innocent which she has now grown out of.
We passed the Fields of Gazing Grain – We passed the Setting Sun	What do these symbolize? Why does the grain 'gaze'?
The Dews drew quivering and chill	The dew of evening is also alive: what does it represent?
For only Gossamer, my Gown – My Tippet – only Tulle	What kind of dress does she seem to be wearing? What point is she making by being ill-equipped for this journey?
The Roof was scarcely visible – The Cornice – in the Ground	The house is made up of a series of apparent contradictions? Is it really a house or a home? Why do they 'pause before it' instead of 'pass'? Where do they go next?
Since then – 'tis Centuries – and yet Feels shorter than the Day	What does this very abstract image suggest about the time frame of the journey? Does it take place in what we think of as 'real time'? If you imagined it in a series of pictures, what setting or time period would you give them?

the Horses' Heads Were toward Eternity	This is a difficult image to picture. What kind of horses are these and why are they hard to control? What might Eternity look like?

Did it help to visualize the words and what they might describe? If so find a series of images on the internet which might illustrate and support a reading of the poem. These can be projected to support a dramatic reading of the poem, as students read different stanzas aloud.

The imagery of poems allow them to be interpreted in the same way as we might interpret art. Like art these images can represent things in life-like ways, but are just as likely to be allegorical, metaphorical or abstract. Poems are like multi-media experiences: we see these poems, but they are also accompanied by music, in the form of rhythm.

The nature of the images make this journey by carriage alongside Death much more like a dream journey than anything real. How do dreams relate to real life and our real thoughts and feelings?

Put together an illustrated reading of the poem. One partner should concentrate on finding the images, and the other on a rhythmic reading of the poem's music. Do imagery and music match? Or is there a creative tension between them? Are those tensions resolved by the ending, or does the tone of the ending 'resist closure'? Discuss these questions as a class.

 ## Viewpoints

I first surmised the Horses' Heads

Were toward Eternity –

What kind of experience or discovery might the poem illustrate? What has 'the poet' discovered about her journey through life? Notice that she says she made this discovery long ago, but it seems like less than a day.

We know Dickinson chose to live a secluded life, never marrying or leaving the family home and devoting herself to poetry.

1. In what ways might the poem dramatize life choices?

2. Does the poem express pessimism about the inevitability of death and the brief nature of life?

3. Or does it celebrate immortality and suggest that death is nothing to be feared?

Find evidence for each interpretation above, by choosing quotations.

You will see that poems often have more than one meaning, and that they gain their meaning from the effect of the words on the individual reader.

Poems do not necessarily tell a literal story, or have a single theme. The poems in this chapter are much more complex, and even contradictory than those in chapter 4. For many of them, your own interpretation is as valid as someone else's, as long as you can support it with close attention to the language and images of the text.

Extend your learning

What would be Death's account of the ride described in the poem? Write a poem of your own using similar rhythmic patterns to portray the ride, seeing the journey from Death's point of view. What would the poet look like to him? Why has he chosen her?

9.3 Different cultures

Think ahead

We now move from Dickinson's small world of nineteenth-century Massachusetts, to the post-colonial era of the twentieth century. How have opportunities for women changed?

Find out what you can about the poet Sujata Bhatt (1956–), who has lived in India, the USA, the UK and Germany.

Start with the following webpage, where you can find information on her work:

A statute of a Hindu goddess

http://www.carcanet.co.uk/cgi-bin/indexer?owner_id=51

Here you will find an interview with her:

http://www.carcanet.co.uk/cgi-bin/scribe?showdoc=4;doctype=interview

In the poem which follows Bhatt compares the ancient classical gods with the gods of India. What do you understand by the term 'pantheism'? What difference might it make to believe that everything is sacred? What does that suggest about the place of human beings in the world?

'A Different History' by Sujata Bhatt (1988)

Great Pan is not dead;
he simply emigrated
         to India.
Here, the gods roam freely,
disguised as snakes or monkeys;
every tree is sacred
and it is a sin
to be rude to a book.
It is a sin to shove a book aside
               with your foot,
a sin to slam books down
         hard on a table,
a sin to toss one carelessly
         across a room.
You must learn how to turn the pages gently
without disturbing Sarasvati,
without offending the tree
from whose wood the paper was made.

         Which language
         has not been the oppressor's tongue?
         Which language

Pan = the Ancient Greek god of nature, part-man, part-goat; he was also very musical, playing 'pan-pipes', and was worshipped through music and dance.

Sarasvati = the Hindu goddess of the arts.

truly meant to murder someone?
And how does it happen
that after the torture,
after the soul has been cropped
with a long scythe swooping out
of the conqueror's face -
the unborn grandchildren
grow to love that strange language.

Sarasvati, the Hindu goddess of the arts

Check your understanding

Bhatt makes a number of complex points in this poem through a series of very striking images.

1. What does the word 'emigrated' suggest about different beliefs in different parts of the world?
2. Why do you think the poet chose to concentrate on the mischievous god Pan?
3. What is the effect of using the present tense?
4. How does the poet notice that the attitude to nature is different in India?
5. How is the attitude to books and the written word different?
6. What is the relationship between books, gods and the natural world?
7. Why does she move on to consider the relationship between language and oppression?
8. How might the history of colonization link language to murder and torture?
9. What seems to happen to the soul of people who are colonized?
10. What happens to the torturer's language for future generations?
11. Does this explain why Bhatt is writing in English here (some of her poems also use Gujarati, her mother tongue)?
12. Why does the poem not end with a question mark?

Pair and share

This poem does not have a regular rhythm. However, a strong rhythmic effect is created by the short lines, and by the writer's choice of line endings. Why are some lines long and others short? Why are some indented far from the margin? Where are we encouraged to pause? Why?

In pairs, use a copy printed from the website to mark up the poem, thinking about where the lines encourage us to read slowly, and where we are encouraged to read more quickly and make more links and connections between images or ideas. How would you read the poem aloud? What is the effect of giving each new sentence a new speaker? Divide the poem up between you and decide on the pace at which you will read it.

What is the effect of the repetition which gives the poem part of its structure? Explore the effect of:

1. the three references to 'a sin'

2. the two mentions of 'without'

3. the two questions

4. the two uses of the word 'after'

Why is the final sentence so long, and why does it eventually break free from all of these patterns?

Find images of Indian gods which combine the features of men and animals to illustrate a slide show accompanying this poem.

What does the poem remind you about books and how they are made? Research the process of making paper, and remember books are made out of what was a living thing. Can you find images to accompany this?

There are disturbing images of how language is abused and used for abuse in the second half of the poem. How has the language of colonizers been used to suppress native tongues and their speakers? What happens to the 'soul' if you are not allowed to express your thoughts and feelings in your native tongue? Why might writers nevertheless choose to write in English?

Find images which will support what the poem suggests to you about books and language, and how attitudes towards them have changed as a result of history

Now present a dramatic reading of the poem, in pairs or groups, illustrated by pictures.

 Viewpoints

In monotheistic religions, certain books are sacred because they are the revealed word of God. In pantheistic cultures, there is a different reason for seeing books as sacred. What is it?

Think about how the poet links the first and second halves of this poem. What do they have in common? How do they contrast? A key adjective like 'gently' can help you to contrast the mood and imagery of the two halves of the poem. Notice how ideas can be linked by their differences as well as their similarities.

Why does Bhatt call the poem 'A Different History'? In what ways does she help you to read history in a different way?

The images in the second half of the poem are disturbing and painful ones. They describe some languages conquering and other languages being oppressed. Language is used to 'crop' a people's soul and limit their ability to express themselves. Which languages do you know which are 'conqueror' languages, and which ones have been restricted? Is language change now a process which is less oppressive or restricting? How does knowledge of a world language help you to express yourself?

🔗 Language links

Debate the importance of being able to communicate in English. Has the dominance of English as a world language done more harm than good?

In poetry, as we have seen, different interpretations are possible, and a personal response is the best way to interpret a poem, grounded in exploration of language, structure and form. How has the music and the choice of words and images given this poem a particular tone? What mood does it communicate to you? Does it seem angry, full of wonder or quite reassuring? What does it suggest to you about violence and how it is overcome through respect?

Tone is how the writer fills the poem with expression, and mood is the emotional world of the poem. Note how tone and mood can help you to shape an interpretation.

9.4 Interpretation

Think ahead

Of course, poets do not need to dramatize versions of themselves, or present personal ideas in all of their poems. They can also tell stories or dramatize the stories of others. Poetry is usually lyrical, but it is often dramatic. Its reliance on images can also allow it to convey snapshots of things poets have seen, or people they have met. The words and images of poems can be like a webpage, or social network, communicating things the poet has seen, thought, or felt to others.

We live in a world of global travel. How many different countries have you and your classmates travelled to? Use a map of the world to pinpoint locations you and others know about. What stories can you tell about places you have seen? How has travel to different parts of the world made you aware of different histories and different cultures?

The English poet Carol Rumens (1944–) writes a weekly blog – Poem of the Week – for the online edition of *The Guardian* newspaper, which can be found at this link:

http://www.guardian.co.uk/books/series/poemoftheweek

In the poem which follows, Rumens describes something she saw on a visit to Morocco. It describes children at work weaving an Islamic carpet by hand on a frame-loom. What kind of images might this carpet have on it? What is the role of the carpet in Islamic worship? What images do we usually have of child labour? These children are at work in a madrasa, so their work forms part of their religious education.

Moroccan children working at a loom

Extend your learning

Look at ways in which both Dickinson and Bhatt are explaining why they write. For Dickinson, writing is a way of conveying an idea which goes on a journey beyond life and death towards immortality. For Bhatt, the written word is sacred, and alive: it embodies a respect for nature and for all life, even a history which is often an oppressive and violent word. For her, you cannot blame the language itself for its history and she encourages a gentle respect for the word.

Write an essay on the question below, which will conclude with an interpretation of each poem, but which grounds them in analysis of language and form. Look at how the question encourages you:

● to explore the writer's choices

● to analyse their effect on the reader

● to evaluate different responses and ways of interpreting the text.

How do Dickinson and Bhatt convey different ideas of the poet's need to express a personal vision of the world?

As this could be a coursework essay, write up to 1,200 words.

'Carpet-weavers, Morocco' by Carol Rumens (1994)

Their children are at the loom of another world.
Their braids are oiled and black, their dresses bright.
Their assorted heights would make a melodious chime.

They watch their flickering knots like television.
As the garden of Islam grows, the bench will be raised.
Then they will lace the dark-rose veins of the tree-tops.

The carpet will travel in the merchant's truck.
It will be spread by the servants of the mosque.
Deep and soft, it will give when heaped with prayer.

The children are hard at work in the school of days.
From their fingers the colours of all-that-will-be fly
And freeze into the frame of all-that-was.

Check your understanding

1. Why does the poet describe the creation of the carpet as making 'another world'?

2. What details make the children look well cared for and proud of their work?

3. What does the sight of their different heights remind her of?

4. Why does she suggest that the story they are weaving into the carpet is like television for them?

5. As the carpet gets bigger, what do they need to do to the children's working bench?

6. What kind of images are on the carpet?

7. Who will buy the carpet from the merchant?

8. Why will the carpet make a good surface for prayer?

9. What kind of 'school' do the children attend?

10. Why are the patterns they are making patterns of the future?

11. Why is the framework which surrounds the carpet a symbol for the past which surrounds the children?

12. What is the poet suggesting about the very traditional life which these children live?

Pair and share

It is a mistake to treat all poems in the same way and to have a template or checklist for analysis of poems. Some poems are very rhythmic, some are strongly visual and some are a combination of the two. Which is most important in this poem: its imagery or its music?

A focus on the visual suits this poem's colourful subject: highlight all the references to colour. Can you find references to the other senses? How do these accompany the strong visual appearance of the carpet?

There are sound effects in this poem: look for examples of alliteration. Discuss the ways in which the alliteration in the first, third and final stanzas support the sensuous qualities of sight, touch and movement. Why is there less alliteration in the second stanza: what does the poet concentrate on conveying here?

We have to imagine what the carpet looks like from the images we are given. What impression of the carpet do you gain from the following images?

Image	Your impression
'garden of Islam grows'	
'the dark-rose veins of the tree-tops'	
'the colours of all-that-will-be'	
'another world'	

How do the descriptions help you to picture the 'other world' which the carpet portrays? Why is it portrayed as a 'garden'? Think of the different connotations of the word garden.

For the children creating the carpet is like watching a television show, seeing a story unfold, or a school lesson about what to expect in future days. How do these metaphors work?

As the children are involved in activity, the poet uses a number of verbs to convey their actions. With your partner, highlight the verbs in your copy of the poem and discuss the following questions:

- Which words show the delicacy of their work and which words show their speed?

- What is the effect of the contrast between 'fly' in the second-last line and 'freeze' in the final line?

- What else do we apply the word 'freeze' to?

- Why does it fit well with the reference to the 'frame' which surrounds the carpet as it is being made?

- What makes this an especially effective last line?

A Moroccan carpet

Viewpoints

Is the poem really about the carpet, about the children, or about something else? You have choices when interpreting a poem. On the surface the poem gives a vivid, colourful, lively and sensuous image of a particular moment the poet has observed on her travels. That might be enough to make it a fine poem. However, perhaps we can go beyond surface meanings and explore the implications that could be less immediate.

To do this, we will need a different, less literal way of reading some of the descriptions. If you forget the literal image of the carpet-weaving for a moment, what connotations are suggested by the following images?

Image	Connotations
'at the loom of another world'	
'the garden of Islam grows'	
'it will give when heaped with prayer'	
'the school of days'	
'the colours of all-that-will-be'	
'the frame of all-that-was'	

Do you agree that these phrases suggest a different, more spiritual reading of the poem? Islamic Art replaces the representation of the human form with symbolism conveyed through geometrical and natural patterns. Can you see something similar happening in this poem?

How are the children transformed by the vision of what they are working on? How does their work and the 'school of days' determine their future? And what is the past, or tradition, which provides them with a framework?

The poet uses words to tell the story of the children's lives and their beliefs and destiny, just as the carpet is intended to tell stories about paradise and the after-life. How do the patterns and forms of the poem themselves show respect for the culture which is portrayed?

It is especially important to ensure that your different readings of a poem, both the literal, descriptive reading and the deeper, more symbolic interpretation, fit the final lines of a poem. You should have noticed that all the poems we have looked at in this chapter have especially memorable final lines. Think about the different ways you can interpret these final lines, and the ways in which they encourage you to evaluate the 'other world' portrayed:

From their fingers the colours of all-that-will-be fly
And freeze into the frame of all-that-was.

What is the effect of the enjambment between the lines? This 'run-on' between the lines makes connections, as well as showing the speed of the children's work. How do the hyphens also make 'connections'? In what ways might these point to a symbolic interpretation of the action of weaving? Do other patterns in the poem support this idea, such as the poet's use of alliteration, which you can also hear in these lines?

Consider how you might interpret the act of stopping the movement in a freeze-frame. How does the punctuation of the poem illustrate this idea? What has happened to the colours and activity of the children, and how does their future fit the patterns of the past?

Do you agree with this kind of reading of the poem? Sometimes students can be sceptical when discussing deeper meanings, and may think that the poet surely wouldn't have meant all this. Certainly we need to be careful about reading meanings which are not there. However, why might a poem not have words as carefully woven as the images in a carpet? Could the images have meanings the poet never intended? Once the work is complete, interpretation is the task of the reader. Like the people praying on the carpet in the mosque, they can ignore what the patterns suggest to them, or make as much meaning as they can, building associations with the words of the text.

Writing techniques

When exploring a poem beyond its surface meaning it is better not to be too definite. You will still be rewarded, even if the marker disagrees with your interpretation, especially if you use phrases like 'this could suggest…' or 'this might resemble…'.

Extend your learning

Write an essay of 800–1,000 words on the following question in order to explore the ways in which both the last two poems use the poet's craft to make interesting observations about cultural diversity and mutual respect.

How do both Bhatt and Rumens portray images derived from different religions and different cultures in order to show the reader how the world is changing?

Explore the ways in which different systems of belief and ways of life are conveyed, and how both poets use images of the past to illustrate visions of the future.

This is a good moment to apply your learning to other poems which you are studying. Look at the techniques we have explored so far, and list poems you have studied which illustrate them.

Poems addressed to particular people	
Poems with a very distinct rhythm or music	
Poems which use personification	
Poems which tell a story (narrative)	
Patterns of repetition within a poem	
Distinctive use of imagery or visual elements	
Poems which work at more than one level	
Memorable final lines	

9.5 Comparisons

Think ahead

You will notice that the poems you study in the anthologies do have thematic links, and these are explored in some of the questions set in exams, although you do not need to compare the poems. Exploring thematic links, as we did in chapter 4, can make the study of poems more coherent and enjoyable, and it can also allow you to look at poetry comparatively in your coursework, where you have more time to develop more complex arguments.

We will now look at two poems which address urban landscapes and the city. Poets tend to write about the natural world, which suits their habits of close observation, and a lot of poetry is hostile to cities and urbanization. Do you agree with this attitude? The two poems we are about to read explore cities in different ways. One is by the contemporary Singapore-born poet Boey Kim Cheng (1965–), the other is a sonnet by the English Romantic poet William Wordsworth (1770–1850).

1. What could twentieth-century Singapore and nineteenth-century London have in common?

2. How does urbanization affect the place where you live?

3. Do you see your future in the country or the city?

4. Why do poets often prefer to escape to the country?

The skyline of Singapore

'The Planners' by Boey Kim Cheng (1992)

They plan. They build. All spaces are gridded,
filled with permutations of possibilities.
The buildings are in alignment with the roads
which meet at desired points
linked by bridges all hang
in the grace of mathematics.
They build and will not stop.
Even the sea draws back
and the skies surrender.

They erase the flaws,
The blemishes of the past, knock off
useless blocks with dental dexterity.
All gaps are plugged
with gleaming gold.
The country wears perfect rows
of shining teeth.
Anaesthesia, amnesia, hypnosis.
They have the means.
They have it all so it will not hurt,
so history is new again.
The piling will not stop.
The drilling goes right through
the fossils of last century.

But my heart would not bleed
poetry. Not a single drop
to stain the blueprint
of our past's tomorrow.

All of these are ways of dulling consciousness of pain

piling = construction of concrete foundations

blueprint = architectural plan

✎ Check your understanding

1. The poet uses the third person in his first two stanzas. Who are 'they'?
2. What kind of city are they building?
3. Why has the city won a victory over the sea and the sky?
4. What is the extended metaphor which the poet uses throughout his second stanza?
5. Where does alliteration emphasize the work which is done in this stanza?
6. What are the 'teeth' which the country now wears?
7. What does the poet suggest has happened to history?
8. What kind of noises should we imagine while reading this stanza?
9. What is a blueprint, and why does it remain unstained?
10. What does the writer suggest will eventually happen to poetry in the world of the future?

Pair and share

Boey Kim Cheng's poem is one in which syntax plays an important role. Sentence structure gives the poem its shape, as the poet does not use rhyme. With your partner, use a copy of the poem to mark in all the punctuation. Would you call the poem fluent? Why do the poem's struggles for rhythm and connection suit the subject matter?

Where do you find longer sentences? What is the effect of these lines when taken together:

The buildings are in alignment with the roads
which meet at desired points
linked by bridges all hang
in the grace of mathematics.

Look at where the poet has placed the words 'linked' and 'hang'. Why has he left out the punctuation you expect? How does this mimic the way modern buildings, and especially skyscrapers, are constructed? What gives the mathematics of construction 'grace' in this image? In spite of his overall message, the poet seems to be suggesting that new cities do have a special kind of beauty. Where does he find it?

Find examples of where the sentences exactly fit the lengths of the lines. What is the particular effect of these lines? Why are they the most negative lines in the whole poem?

The poet uses the phrase 'Will not' several times, and 'will not stop' twice. Think about what this suggests about the way he imagines the future. What else adds a pessimistic note to the poem?

Where are the elements personified? What are they imagined as doing? Consider how this represents the triumph of technology and man-made construction.

Now let's explore that extended metaphor:

1. What do dentistry and city planning have in common?
2. What does the poet suggest about the triumph of artificial things over what is natural?
3. Why does the poet list different kinds of anaesthetic? What is his objection to wiping out pain?
4. How does dentistry make history new and erase flaws?
5. How does rebuilding a city do the same?
6. What is destroyed along the way?
7. How do both hide the pain?
8. What is the significance of destroying the 'fossils' of the past?

Most of us don't like going to the dentist. What kinds of emotion is the poet appealing to, and what does he suggest about the work of the planners?

What has happened to the history of a country which 'wears' a set of false teeth in the shape of its city skyscrapers? What does it suggest about ways in which the past is covered up, or about reasons for not trusting the way it smiles?

The juxtaposition of 'our past's tomorrow' could be considered to be ironic or paradoxical. Why? What future does he suggest there will be?

What is the tone of the final stanza? Is it bitter, sarcastic, mournful, ironic, elegiac?

Read the poem out loud in pairs, dividing it up between your two voices. Use the tone from the options above which you think fits the poem best and then see if your audience have correctly guessed the one you were thinking of.

 Viewpoints

Decide whether you agree with this pessimistic view of the future. Have technology and urbanization failed to make our lives happier? Does 'progress' simply erase the flaws of history and make all our cities appear to be the same?

Debate this question with your class. Has the poem influenced your own views?

Extend your learning

Search online for another of Cheng's poems called 'Report to Wordsworth', which combines allusions to a number of other Wordsworth poems. How does it share the dark vision of 'The Planners' and apply it to the way we treat the environment? How do other poems in your studies compare nature and the man-made world we choose to live in? What do they suggest we lose, when we uproot the past?

Think ahead

William Wordsworth (1770–1850) is perhaps the greatest of all the English Romantic poets. The English Romantics were poets writing at the end of the eighteenth century and the beginning of the nineteenth century. Some of them, such as Wordsworth and Coleridge (1772–1834), or Shelley (1792–1822) and Lord Byron (1788–1824), were close friends and shared ideas, but there were also tensions between the older Romantics and younger poets. Rivalries existed between them. Other writers, like William Blake (1757–1827) and John Clare (1793–1864), were outside these groups and worked alone. The label 'Romantic' is one that was only applied to these poets after most of them had died, so the grouping is a loose one. However, their ideas and style of writing became incredibly influential on later poets not just in Britain, but all over the world. You will sometimes come across the term 'post-Romantic'; we all are to some extent post-Romantics. Nineteenth-century novelists like the Brontë sisters and George Eliot were heavily influenced by these poets.

The Romantics wrote in the wake of the Industrial Revolution, and political Revolutions in America and Europe. They were influenced by the philosophy of Rousseau, and the rediscovery of earlier writers, such as Shakespeare. They re-asserted the importance of nature, and the education of the individual, and believed that art had to reflect ordinary human lives and passions more strongly. Their poetry presents highly individual visions of the world, but also appeals strongly to a sense of community. The poetry of places and their impact on the development of the individual mind is also important. Wordsworth's famous sonnet on London was written at a very important time in his life, when he was about to get married, and in the middle of the Napoleonic Wars. He was on his way to France with his sister Dorothy in 1802 as there was a brief peace between the two countries.

Initially excited by the French Revolution, Wordsworth returned to England as it became more violent, and turned to nature rather than political change for inspiration. The war had separated him from France, and he became increasingly patriotic. Like many of his poems, it was inspired by his sister's observations, recorded in her *Journal*, where she compared the man-made sights of the city to the beauties of nature.

'Upon Westminster Bridge' by William Wordsworth (1802)

Earth has not anything to show more fair:
Dull would he be of soul who could pass by
A sight so touching in its majesty:
This City now doth like a garment wear
The beauty of the morning; silent, bare,
Ships, towers, domes, theatre, and temples lie
Open unto the fields, and to the sky;
All bright and glittering in the smokeless air.
Never did sun more beautifully steep
In his first splendour, valley, rock, or hill;
Ne'er saw I, never felt, a calm so deep!
The river glideth at his own sweet will:
Dear God! the very houses seem asleep;
And all that mighty heart is lying still!

A painting of Westminster Bridge in London

✎ Check your understanding

1. How does the poet begin with personification?

2. Who are the only people who would pass such a sight without stopping to look?

3. How does the 'sight' affect more than one sense?

4. As the English monarchy had been fighting revolutionary France, why is Wordsworth's use of the word 'majesty' interesting?

5. If the City is a woman, how does the morning give her particular beauty?

6. What is the effect of the list in lines 5 and 6?

7. What is the effect of the enjambment between lines 6 and 7?

8. Which long vowel sound is stressed at the beginning of line 7, and what is the effect of this?

9. Why is the air smokeless and therefore the sight 'glittering'?

10. Why would this be unusual in the nineteenth century and show a rare harmony between man and nature?

11. How does Wordsworth compare the city and nature in lines 9 and 10?

12. Why is this sunrise even better than those he has observed surrounded by the natural world?

13. What is the impact on the poet in line 11, as he observes this sight?

14. Why do you think 'calm' had become important to Wordsworth, in the revolutionary times in which he lived?

15. In the last three lines, the examples of personification treat the city as if it were alive: what kind of life is it living at this moment?

16. Why do you think that Wordsworth preferred the city while it was asleep?

KEY TERMS

sonnet = a 14-line poem, often following a set pattern of rhymes.

octave = eight-line section of verse, especially in a sonnet.

sestet = six-line section of verse, especially in a sonnet.

volta = the turning point, usually after line 8 of a sonnet.

Viewpoints

You have seen that Wordsworth compares the city to nature in order to bring them together, rather than contrast them. However, as this only happens in the morning, when the city is asleep, there is still an implicit contrast.

1. To what extent is Wordsworth really glorifying the city?

2. Do you think this poem was written by a man who liked cities?

3. London was the capital of a mighty empire at the time. Can you find references to political power in this poem?

4. Which words call up images of peace and calm, and why might Wordsworth want to recommend similar calm to his readers?

5. What do cities represent in your own culture today?

6. How do they represent the values and hopes of your own society?

7. Do you share Wordsworth's optimism or Cheng's pessimism?

Debate urbanization and the modern city with your classmates. Can we, and should we, control the growth and spread of cities?

Extend your learning

Compare the importance   you are studying. of setting in the poems

1. How do the poets you are reading convey a sense of place, whether in the natural or man-made world?

2. What do places symbolize or represent to them?

3. How do the poets you are studying use form?

4. Are sonnet or stanza form important to them?

5. How does form give structure and expression to their writing?

6. How can you link poems in your set selection by theme?

7. How do the poems show contrasts in attitude or mood towards that theme?

8. How have poets used different forms and styles to express similar themes?

Draw up one table which links poems by theme and subject, and another which brings out differences in style and form. For example, formal structure/free verse, and imagery/sound patterns.

9.6 Studying the set poem

Set poems may be chosen from an anthology, or you may study a selection of poems from one poet.

When you study an individual poet, you have a better opportunity to relate the poems to their historical and biographical contexts, as we have just done with Wordsworth. You can look more closely at the poet's individual choices of subject, form, theme and expression in each poem, because you know that poet and his or her body of work better, and so you can see both what makes an individual poem different and explore links to the poet's preoccupations and style.

The next poem, for example, is another elegy, and we have already seen that this is a form Hardy often employs. However, this time he is writing not about personal loss, but about a young soldier who has died in a colonial war in Southern Africa (which had only just begun). In those days, soldiers' bodies were not sent back to their home countries, and unless they were officers, their graves were unmarked.

Writing techniques

Read each poem you study on its own: you will need extensive notes for revision. However, you will become sensitive to similarities of theme and expression, and develop the ability to interpret that poet's work. Essay questions will offer you opportunities to say what is characteristic about aspects of style or tone in the poem you are asked to focus on.

A South African veldt

'Drummer Hodge' by Thomas Hardy (1899)

They throw in Drummer Hodge, to rest
Uncoffined – just as found:
His landmark is a kopje-crest
That breaks the veldt around:
And foreign constellations west
Each night above his mound.

kopje = (Afrikaans) a small hill
veldt = (Afrikaans) plain

Young Hodge the drummer never knew –
Fresh from his Wessex home –

Wessex = the term for the South-Western counties of England where Hardy set most of his novels, stories and verse

The meaning of the broad Karoo,
The bush, the dusty loam,
And why uprose to nightly view
Strange stars amid the gloam.

the broad Karoo = a large desert region of South Africa

gloam = (rare) the period of twilight just after sunset

Yet portion of that unknown plain
Will Hodge for ever be;
His homely Northern breast and brain
Grow to some Southern tree,
And strange-eyed constellations reign
His stars eternally.

Check your understanding

This poem is striking for its simple structure and its unusual choice of words. Use these questions to help you to appreciate the effect of both of these:

1. How many rhymes does Hardy use in each stanza?

2. How does the rhythm alternate? Count the number of stresses in each line.

3. How does this maintain the simplicity of the poem?

4. Why is this simplicity better suited to the subject than the more complicated forms of 'The Voice' (page 193)?

5. Why does Hardy choose such a simple, monosyllabic name as 'Hodge'?

6. What is the effect of Hardy's choice of the verb 'thrown' in the first line?

7. Why does the unusual compound adjective 'uncoffined' make you pause to think in the second line?

8. Why does Hardy use Afrikaans words in the first stanza?

9. Even the stars are 'foreign' as this is a southern hemisphere sky: why does Hardy use 'west' as a verb?

10. How does Hardy repeat this reference to the stars in the second and third stanzas?

11. What kind of eternity do those stars represent?

12. 'Uprose' and 'gloam' are rare words: what kind of light and effect does Hardy want to describe here?

13. How does Hardy describe Hodge's transformation into part of this beautiful but strange landscape?

14. What is the effect of the choice of the adjective 'homely' in this context?

15. Where do you think the strong stresses fall in the final line?

16. Why are the stars now 'his'?

 Pair and share

You have seen how the poem depends on its contrasts between the 'homely' boy drummer (most drummers were teenagers) and the strange landscape where he ended up. Think about how the poem illustrates the following subjects which we know Hardy was preoccupied with:

1. death and what kind of afterlife human beings might have

2. time and its passing

3. fate and its strange twists and turns

4. tragedy and consolation

5. the importance of home

6. regions and people at the margins, rather than the centre of things

7. the relationship between man and nature

8. the contrast between our human concerns and eternity

Find and share other poems and works by Hardy which you can compare with this poem (including others in this book).

This elegy is striking for its simplicity and the way in which it is a poem about an imaginary individual but might easily stand for universal experience. A sensitive reading of the poem needs to bring out the individuality of its names and places and the patterns and rhythms which give it simplicity and inevitability.

Read the poem out aloud, sharing alternate lines between you and your partner. How does this help to bring out the effect of alternating longer and shorter lines as well as different rhymes? Why does this structure fit the mood and purpose of the poem so well?

Remember that the form of the elegy is meant to express mourning and loss but also consolation. The whole poem could be described as a search for meaning in Hodge's death. Where does Hardy seem to find this meaning?

Contrast the first two lines and the last two lines. Why is their tone so different? How do they help to create a very different mood for the first and third stanzas?

Viewpoints

We have looked at other poems about young men going off to fight in foreign lands in chapter 4. Look back at those poems.

1. What is different about Hardy's attitude to war and to his subject?

2. Why do you think he chooses not to express an opinion on the rights and wrongs of war?

3. Why do you think he chose to write about a particular, named young man?

4. Hardy employs tact when dealing with the reasons for the war and who to blame for Hodge's death. Why is his tact so sensitive and well-judged?

Looking back, we view these wars in South Africa very differently from the way they would have been seen at the time. What is it about Hardy's way of writing poetry which ensures that it still has meaning long after different histories and ways of looking at the world have changed our ideas?

Consider:

How much attention do we really need to pay to history and biography when reading poetry?

Look back at the poems we have explored in this book so far. History can help us to understand why poems were written, but why do we still read them?

Discuss the question above with your teacher and classmates, and then look back at your set poems and consider the ways in which they have been crafted. Does the meaning of the poem change over time? Is meaning purely what the writer intended, or do readers make their own meaning out of a text?

There is a superb lesson on this poem in Alan Bennett's play *The History Boys*. We have already seen how the playwright presented Mr Irwin's unusual teaching in chapter 5. Here, a rival teacher, Mr Hector, asks a student if he has any thoughts after a reading of Drummer Hodge.

Mr Hector's students, in 2006 film version of *The History Boys*

'The History Boys' by Alan Bennett (2004)

POSNER: I wondered, sir, if this "Portion of that unknown plain/ Will Hodge for ever be" is like Rupert Brooke, sir, "There's some corner of a foreign field…" "In that rich earth a richer dust concealed…"

HECTOR: It is. It is. It's the same thought…though Hardy's is better, I think…more…more, well down to earth. Quite literally, yes, down to earth.

Anything about his name?

POSNER: Hodge?

HECTOR: Mmm – the important thing is that he has a name. Say Hardy is writing about the Zulu Wars or later the Boer War possibly, these were the first campaigns when soldiers…or common soldiers…were commemorated, the names of the dead recorded and inscribed on war

> Posner is quoting from Rupert Brooke's famous poem 'The Soldier' (1915)

memorials. Before this, soldiers…private soldiers anyway, were all unknown soldiers, and so far from being revered there was a firm in the nineteenth century, in Yorkshire of course, which swept up their bones from the battlefields of Europe in order to grind them into fertilizer.

So, thrown into a common grave though he may be, he is still Hodge the drummer. Lost boy though he is on the other side of the world, he still has a name.

POSNER: How old was he?

HECTOR: If he's a drummer he would be a young soldier, younger than you probably.

POSNER: No. Hardy.

HECTOR: Oh, how old was Hardy? When he wrote this, about sixty. My age, I suppose.

Saddish life, though not unappreciated.

'Uncoffined' is a typical Hardy usage.

A compound adjective, formed by putting 'un-' in front of the noun. Or verb, of course.

Un-kissed. Un-rejoicing. Un-confessed. Un-embraced. It's a turn of phrase he has bequeathed to Larkin, who liked Hardy, apparently.

He does the same.

Unspent. Unfingermarked.

And with both of them it brings a sense of not sharing, of being out of it.

Whether because of diffidence or shyness, but a holding back. Not being in the swim. Can you see that?

POSNER: Yes, sir. I felt that a bit.

HECTOR: The best moments in reading are when you come across something – a thought, a feeling, a way of looking at things – which you had thought special and particular to you. Now here it is, set down by someone else, a person you have never met, someone who is long dead. And it is as if a hand had come out and taken yours.

Philip Larkin (1922–1985) was a fine English poet of the twentieth century

Think ahead

The two poems we have looked at by Thomas Hardy were both written at the very end of the nineteenth century. At the time, the British Empire was at its greatest height but its future was perhaps less certain, although no one could predict how quickly the world would change. Hardy was nearly sixty and his future was even less certain: he had achieved some fame and fortune, but he had written his last novel, and his marriage no longer brought him happiness. At the time he would have had no idea that his finest poems were yet to be written, he would achieve critical as well as popular acclaim, and that he would be an important influence on later generations of poets. Instead the prospect of a new year and a new century seemed threatening to him.

1. Why is the change of the years in northern hemisphere countries a dark time in several ways?

2. Why do people often make 'resolutions' or want to change aspects of their life or behaviour when a new year begins?

3. Find other poems on the theme of New Year. What do they have in common?

4. The most famous poem of them all is by Tennyson: 'Ring out, wild bells'. Look this up. Its tone is very different to that of Hardy. This poem is part of *In Memoriam A. H. H.*, a collection of 133 elegies which Tennyson wrote after the death of his best friend, Arthur Hallam who died in 1833.

Thomas Hardy

'The Darkling Thrush' by Thomas Hardy (1900)

I leant upon a coppice gate
When Frost was spectre-grey,
And Winter's dregs made desolate
The weakening eye of day.
The tangled bine-stems scored the sky
Like strings of broken lyres,
And all mankind that haunted nigh
Had sought their household fires.

The land's sharp features seemed to be
The Century's corpse outleant,
His crypt the cloudy canopy,
The wind his death-lament.
The ancient pulse of germ and birth
Was shrunken hard and dry,
And every spirit upon earth
Seemed fervourless as I.

At once a voice arose among
The bleak twigs overhead
In a full-hearted evensong
Of joy illimited:
An aged thrush, frail, gaunt and small,
In blast-beruffled plume
Had chosen thus to fling his soul
Upon the growing gloom.

So little cause for carolings
Of such ecstatic sound
Was written on terrestrial things
Afar or nigh around,
That I could think there trembled through
His happy good-night air
Some blessed Hope,
Whereof he knew
And I was unaware.

coppice = patch of wood

dregs = last remains, left overs

bine-stems = bare branches of woodbine

evensong = sung evening prayer in English churches

thrush = a small (but loud) English songbird

caroling = singing of winter songs of celebration

✎ Check your understanding

1. What does the word 'darkling' mean? Which other poets have used this word? (You can look this up in the Oxford English Dictionary).

2. What does the image of the poet leaning on the gate suggest? Why doesn't he go through it?

3. When Frost and Winter are personified, which details make them sound hostile?

4. How is the setting sun described, and why does this suit the mood of this stanza?

5. Lyres were once used to accompany poetry, as we have seen. What does the simile suggest about a comparison between the bare, scratchy trees and Hardy's own broken lyrical poetry?

6. Which words suggest ghosts or haunting?

7. How does the image of Hardy holding back from the household fires fit the image he often gives of himself in his poems?

8. When the old Century is personified, what has he become?

9. How does the landscape seem to fit the idea of the century's graveyard?

10. Why are the poet's spirits low, as well as those of the natural world?

11. At what point in the poem does the poet first hear the thrush?

12. What happens to the line endings at this point?

13. What are the physical characteristics of the thrush?

14. Why might the thrush and its song easily be a metaphor for Hardy and his poetry?

15. Which words suggest something other-worldly about the bird's song?

16. To what extent do you think Hardy shares the 'Hope' expressed in the bird's song?

💬 Pair and share

The questions in the previous box are already encouraging you to read the poem less literally and to interpret its metaphors. With a partner, now explore its form and language. On your own copy, mark up the patterns of rhyme and rhythm.

1. In what ways are the rhymes similar to 'Drummer Hodge' and in what ways are they different?

2. How do the rhythms fit into an alternating pattern?

3. Why do these patterns suit the poem's subject matter and mood?

4. Again, Hardy delights in unusual language. Following Mr Hector's hint, explore the meaning of these compound adjectives:

   a. spectre-grey
   b. outleant
   c. fervourless
   d. full-hearted
   e. illimited
   f. blast-beruffled

5. How do the words of the first two stanzas contrast with those of the second two stanzas?

6. Find as many contrasting pairs of gloom and joy as you can.

7. Are there still gloomy words in the second half of the poem? What does this suggest and why?

8. What do the words 'frail', 'gaunt' and 'trembled' suggest about the thrush's song? How do they contrast with words like 'full-hearted', 'ecstatic' and 'fling'?

9. Where does Hardy seem to find his idea of hope at the end of the poem?

Extend your learning

There is an interpretation of this poem in Carol Rumens' poetry blog:

http://www.guardian.co.uk/books/booksblog/2009/dec/28/poem-of-the-week-the-darkling-thrush-thomas-hardy

To what extent have you found Hardy to be a Romantic poet?

Writing techniques

When you have finished studying your set poet, you should have a strong sense of his or her preoccupations and interests, and of how the poems are related to the time when they were written. You should also have a sense of your poet's characteristic language and style, and of how much individual poems represent that style. This will allow you to notice interesting echoes and comparisons when writing about the poem you have chosen to explore in the exam, and to construct an argument which shows your overall understanding of the poet's work.

Viewpoints

We have seen how the nineteenth century was a period of British power, but also how writers often expressed doubts and anxiety. How does this poem express Hardy's concerns about the new century?

Hardy's concerns were also personal and biographical. Compare this poem with 'The Voice'. In what ways do both communicate a lack of confidence or faith? How do both poems invoke both the natural and the supernatural?

Hardy was equally concerned to find a new poetic language. Although the forms he uses here are formal, where can you find originality in his language and expression?

9.7 Longer poems

Think ahead

Finally in this chapter we will look at ways of tackling the longer poems which you may study as part of your course. Many older poems were much longer than the poems we have studied in these sections; even today verse is still used to tell much longer stories. A brilliant modern example is *Golden Gate* by Vikram Seth, a novel in verse.

As we have seen, poems were used in the past to tell epic stories about heroes. Tennyson was very familiar both with British epic stories of the Arthurian legends, and with Greek Homeric epics and his poems often retell aspects of these mythic stories. That is especially the case with the dramatic monologue 'Ulysses'.

1. Revise your understanding of the dramatic monologue. How does the form allow the poet to express feelings very different from his own?

2. In which poems did Homer's hero Ulysses (also called Odysseus) appear?

3. What qualities was he famous for?

4. Why might these qualities make him frustrated as the ruler of a small rocky island?

5. Why was Tennyson especially interested in death and the possibility of an after-life in 1833?

Read the poem carefully twice. Look at how Ulysses's thoughts wander and change. Then divide the poem into sections, according to the different emotions it expresses.

'Ulysses' by Alfred Lord Tennyson (1833)

It little profits that an idle king,
By this still hearth, among these barren crags,
Matched with an agèd wife, I mete and dole
Unequal laws unto a savage race,
That hoard, and sleep, and feed, and know not me.   5

I cannot rest from travel: I will drink
Life to the lees: all times I have enjoyed
Greatly, have suffered greatly, both with those
That loved me, and alone; on shore, and when
Through scudding drifts the rainy Hyades   10
Vexed the dim sea: I am become a name;
For always roaming with a hungry heart
Much have I seen and known; cities of men
And manners, climates, councils, governments,
Myself not least, but honoured of them all;   15
And drunk delight of battle with my peers,
Far on the ringing plains of windy Troy.
I am a part of all that I have met;
Yet all experience is an arch wherethrough
Gleams that untravelled world, whose margin fades   20
For ever and for ever when I move.
How dull it is to pause, to make an end,
To rust unburnished, not to shine in use!
As though to breathe were life. Life piled on life
Were all too little, and of one to me   25
Little remains: but every hour is saved
From that eternal silence, something more,
A bringer of new things; and vile it were
For some three suns to store and hoard myself,
And this grey spirit yearning in desire   30
To follow knowledge like a sinking star,
Beyond the utmost bound of human thought.

Ulysses is referring to himself here, as king of the small island of Ithaca

mete and dole = create and hand out

lees = the dregs at the bottom of a wine glass

Hyades = in Greek mythology these were the nymphs (in the form of stars) who brought rain

Ulysses is remembering his feats in the Trojan War

unburnished = unpolished (Ulysses is thinking of his sword)

This my son, mine own Telemachus,
To whom I leave the sceptre and the isle—

Well-loved of me, discerning to fulfil   35
This labour, by slow prudence to make mild
A rugged people, and through soft degrees
Subdue them to the useful and the good.
Most blameless is he, centred in the sphere
Of common duties, decent not to fail   40
In offices of tenderness, and pay
Meet adoration to my household gods,
When I am gone. He works his work, I mine.

There lies the port; the vessel puffs her sail:
There gloom the dark broad seas. My mariners,   45
Souls that have toiled, and wrought, and thought
              with me—
That ever with a frolic welcome took
The thunder and the sunshine, and opposed
Free hearts, free foreheads—you and I are old;
Old age hath yet his honour and his toil;   50
Death closes all: but something ere the end,
Some work of noble note, may yet be done,
Not unbecoming men that strove with Gods.
The lights begin to twinkle from the rocks:
The long day wanes: the slow moon climbs: the deep   55
Moans round with many voices. Come, my friends,
'Tis not too late to seek a newer world.
Push off, and sitting well in order smite
The sounding furrows; for my purpose holds
To sail beyond the sunset, and the baths   60
Of all the western stars, until I die.
It may be that the gulfs will wash us down:
It may be we shall touch the Happy Isles,

And see the great Achilles, whom we knew.
Though much is taken, much abides; and though   65
We are not now that strength which in old days
Moved earth and heaven; that which we are, we are;
One equal temper of heroic hearts,
Made weak by time and fate, but strong in will
To strive, to seek, to find, and not to yield.   70

Telemachus is the son of Ulysses. In the *Odyssey*, he is a teenager and a skilful diplomat, less of a fighter than his father.

discerning = able to make good judgments

gloom is used as a verb by Tennyson here

frolic = joyful, happy (used as an adjective here)

not unbecoming = not unsuitable for
the long day wanes = the long day (of Ulysses's life) comes to an end

smite/The sounding furrows = Ulysses is imagining his men taking up the oars of a longboat and rowing out to sea

Happy Isles = Ulysses is thinking of the islands where the dead live

the hero Achilles died young after having achieved fame in the Siege of Troy

Check your understanding

It is always a good idea to get an overview of the whole poem first, when interpreting or writing about it. Begin by asking yourself about who is speaking and capture the character of the speaker. Then ask yourself who the speaker is speaking to? Is there an audience for the poem? In this case, as with many dramatic monologues, there is. However, it isn't clear who Ulysses is talking to until about two thirds of the way through the poem.

On the whole poem

1. How old is Ulysses now?

2. Why is he restless and irritable?

3. Why does he compare the past with the present?

4. How does his mood seem to change during the course of the poem?

5. Which form does Tennyson choose for Ulysses' dramatic monologue? (Clue: it is the same verse form used by Shakespeare in his plays)

6. Who should we imagine he is addressing these words to?

7. What does he want to persuade his audience to do?

8. Would you want to follow him?

Next, explore the poem in sequence and observe the progression of thoughts and feelings. How does Ulysses convert restlessness into heroic purpose? How does he move from his present situation through thoughts about the past into a vision of the future? Use the questions which follow to write notes and to re-read and discuss the poem section by section. The questions build on the skills and analytical language you have learnt in this chapter, so you should be able to answer them without too much help.

On lines 1–5: the restless old king

1. How does the choice of adjectives reveal Ulysses' restlessness with his kingship, his wife Penelope and his people?

2. According to legend, he spent 10 years fighting at Troy and then 10 years travelling home, held up by the gods and by various adventures. He had to fight to win back his kingdom and his wife. Why should he not be happy to stay at home now?

3. Why do the lives of his people seem unattractive to him?

4. Why does he think his mariners would understand these feelings and be a sympathetic audience?

On lines 6–17: his heroic past

1. How do these lines show that Ulysses will never settle for a quiet life at home?

2. Why do you think Tennyson uses the first person pronoun ('I') so often in these lines? What is he suggesting about the hero's character?

3. What does Ulysses mean by 'I am become a name'?

4. How does enjambment in these lines complement and convey the sense of movement as Ulysses describes his past voyages?

5. What did Ulysses enjoy about the experience of sailing with his crew?

6. He seems to believe he gained both intellectually and emotionally from his travels. Where do we see this belief?

7. What is the effect of the list in line 14?

8. What do you think he means in line 15 by saying that he came to know himself?

9. What is the significance of the word 'honoured' in the same line?

10. Why do both of these ideas contrast very strongly with the feelings he expresses about his role and his people on the island of Ithaca?

11. How does the poet use alliteration in line 16 and the choice of adjectives in line 17 to capture Ulysses' heroic response to fighting in the Trojan War?

12. How would you characterize Ulysses' attitude to life in this section?

On lines 18–32: his philosophy

1. What does he mean when he says he is a 'part of all that I have met'? How has his heroic story become his identity?

2. Ulysses says that all experiences are just a glimpse of an 'untravelled world'. Tennyson, like Hardy, is

using an unusual compound adjective. What kind of unusual idea is this expressing?

3. Ulysses describes this other world as a horizon that keeps moving as he keeps moving. Why would a sailor choose this metaphor?

4. How does he use contrast to make other approaches to life seem unattractive?

5. What does he mean by saying 'little remains' of one life now?

6. He imagines two different ways of spending his last 'three suns': what are they?

On lines 33–43: his son

1. Ulysses plans to pass his powers to Telemachus. Why is he happy to do this?
Which adjectives does he use to describe Telemachus and his work?

2. Why are these very different words from the ones you would use to describe Ulysses?

3. How do Telemachus' 'offices of tenderness' contrast with Ulysses' attitude to Penelope?

4. Is Ulysses paying Telemachus sincere compliments, or do you think he is slightly patronizing when he refers to 'household gods' and 'he works his work'?

On lines 44-70: the final voyage

1. How do the verbs at the beginning of this section give you a sense of urgency and immediacy?

2. Why has Ulysses waited until this moment before addressing the mariners directly?

3. How does Ulysses appeal persuasively to his mariners through the way he describes the things they have done together?

4. What is the intended effect of choosing adjectives like 'frolic' and 'free'?

5. Do you think his mariners were really free?

6. Why does he think they need to prove themselves again before they die?

7. What is the effect of describing the sunset? How does Ulysses use this as a beautiful metaphor?

8. How does Ulysses use imagery derived from the natural world in order to overcome fear of death?

9. What is the effect of addressing the mariners directly as his 'friends' in line 56?

10. How many other persuasive devices can you find in this section?

11. How does this idea of a 'newer world' fit the philosophy Ulysses set out earlier in the poem?

12. In lines 58 to 61, how do the sounds of the words recreate the sounds of a sea journey?

13. Why does he want to sail to the west?

14. How do his lines juxtapose different ideas about death?

15. How does he contradict the arguments of those who would object to this final voyage?

16. How do repetition, rhythm and Tennyson's mastery of the iambic pentameter allow the final line to triumph over the weakness made by time and fate?

In an exam, you would look at a section of a long poem. Similarly, it is better in coursework to focus on a part of the poem. Which section would you choose to concentrate on and why?

💬 Pair and share

We will look at the ending and the persuasive language of this poem. The final lines of this poem are very famous indeed: they are on the memorial to Captain Scott and the Polar Expedition in Antartica, and were used to promote the London Olympics of 2012. Do you agree with this attitude to life?

There are two very different ways of reading this poem, depending on whether you think Tennyson approves of the attitude of his heroic speaker, or dramatizes an attitude that is egotistical, destructive and slightly mad. Is this persuasive rhetoric encouraging a heroic attitude towards old age and death, or is it an argument for a suicide mission?

To help you to make your own minds up, imagine you are two very different members of the audience for this poem.

- One of you can play the role of a mariner inspired by your captain and his glorious memories of the past. Collect the lines which have inspired you and explain why you agree with them and want to follow your leader.

- The other can play the role of Penelope or Telemachus. Which lines in the whole poem do you find offensive or patronizing? Which ones prove how difficult Ulysses is to live with? Which lines suggest madness and danger? Collect the evidence that Ulysses has become insane and delusional. How would this affect your response to the last 25 lines?

Now conduct a role play of the discussion between your characters.

1. Should Ulysses be allowed to make this voyage?

2. Or should his mariners be persuaded not to listen to his speech?

3. Is it time he retired from leadership altogether?

Create a performance which you can share with your class.

The final lines of Tennyson's poem were inscribed on a wall in the athlete's village at the 2012 Olympic Games in London.

Viewpoints

Have you now made up your mind about whether Tennyson shares Ulysses' attitudes? You should consider the weight of evidence: which side gets the last and strongest word?

1. How beautiful do you find Ulysses' philosophy of life and the strange vision of his final journey?

2. Do you agree with him that the 'safety first' attitude of Telemachus and the patient work of government is 'dull'?

3. Do you think Tennyson wants us to follow Ulysses, or is this heroic attitude to life something of the past?

For Tennyson himself, writing very soon after he heard the news of the death of his great friend Hallam, this poem was about attitudes to death. Ulysses will carry on fighting and searching, even though he knows it will end in death. Tennyson said two things about this poem:

> '…it gave my feeling about the need of going forward and braving the struggle of life perhaps more simply than anything in *In Memoriam.*'

and

'There is more of myself in Ulysses, which was written under the sense of loss and that all had gone by, but that still life must be fought out to the end. It was more written with the feeling of his loss upon me than many poems in *In Memoriam.*'

You can see that for Tennyson, writing about this poem much later in his life, it demonstrates an attitude to life and loss very different from the elegiac poems we have explored earlier in this chapter. However, should we trust what the poet says about his poem many years later, when he has his reputation to protect? Could the poem reveal anxieties which the poet later wanted to hide? As we have seen, poems belong to their readers as well as to their writers.

Discuss and debate your mood as you respond to the tone of the poem. Could you read it out in a way which makes Ulysses mad and delusional? Or will the rhetoric of heroism always win in the end? Is this poem an elegy for a heroic attitude to the world? Or is it a satire on the futility of heroism?

 Language links

Debate the following question:

Do we need heroes and role models in the modern world, or are they are thing of the past?'

Write a persuasive essay, using evidence and arguments to present the case for a person of your choice as a hero or role model.

Hold a 'balloon debate' in which each of you (a team of six would work well) imagines you are a character

from today's world, from history or from literature. You could even use the writers of your set texts! You are in a hot air balloon which is sinking. Make a speech to persuade your audience that you should stay in the balloon. The audience will take a vote to decide on who will have to jump out. You can continue the process of debate and persuasion until only one person is left!

Extend your learning

1. Compare this poem with Tennyson's **dramatic monologue** 'Tithonus' (written in 1859) which expresses a very different attitude to life and death.

2. Compare attitudes to death in this poem and in lyrics from *In Memoriam* (1850).

3. Compare this poem to Tennyson's late lyric 'Crossing the Bar'. Tennyson wanted this poem to be the last one in any collection of his verse. How similar are its emotions to those he gave Ulysses in the poem he wrote when still a young man?

KEY TERM

dramatic monologue = when a poet dramatizes the emotions of a character, as if writing the speech from a play, for example, Tennyson's *Ulysses*.

Looking back

This chapter has demonstrated models of how to study poetry from different periods and in different styles. The emphasis has been on close reading, but also on relating poems to their historical and cultural contexts and exploring ways to link and compare different poems within the set selections in order to make your study more interesting and to help you to construct longer coursework essays.

Review your learning by testing yourself with the following questions:

1. What is satire?
2. What do you understand by elegy and the elegiac?
3. What is alternating rhyme?
4. What is the persona a poet uses in poetry?
5. What do you understand by the term dramatic monologue?
6. Why are dramatic monologues often in blank verse?
7. Why are so many poems in the present tense?
8. What is the name for a four-line stanza?
9. What are the different parts which make up a sonnet?
10. What is the name for lots of 's' sounds?
11. Which techniques do we group together and call imagery?
12. What do you understand by a poem's syntax?
13. How does punctuation affect the ways in which you read poems?
14. Which word do we use to express the poet's choice of words?
15. Why are the words of a poem especially charged with connotations?
16. Which subjects were especially attractive to nineteenth-century poets?
17. Which beliefs and interests did the Romantic poets share?
18. What is the role of tone and mood in shaping your interpretation of a poem?
19. How much is the interpretation of a poem controlled by the writer's choices and how much by a reader's response?
20. Why are the last lines of a poem worth especially close attention?

You will find more advice on how to read and analyse poetry in chapter 11, which focuses on unseen analysis.

Last words

Ulysses' final words emphasize that his journey goes on. The voyage you began when you started your Cambridge IGCSE English Literature course also continues: as we have seen, plays, novels and poems continue to fascinate and provoke long after they were written, because debate about their meaning continues.

The emphasis of this book has been the development of your own reading skills by encouraging you to ask the right questions. Your writing skills have developed as you have learnt how to answer questions, and show that you are meeting the aims of the course.

As exams get closer, you will want more specific guidance on writing essays and preparing and revising for examination.

The chapters to support this are on the accompanying website so that you can more easily find and use the sections most relevant to your own course. These are extension units, aimed at taking your skills to a higher level. Your teachers can print out or display on a whiteboard the sections of these chapters relevant to your own studies and work on them with you.

They are chapter 10 (guidance for extended essays, especially for Component 5 – Coursework), chapter 11 (an extension unit for students studying Component 4 – unseen texts) and chapter 12 (a revision unit, giving examples of how to responds to different types of exam question).

Index